Defining the Victorian Nation

Class, Race, Gender and the British Reform Act of 1867

Defining the Victorian Nation offers a fresh perspective on one of the most significant pieces of legislation in nineteenth-century Britain. Catherine Hall, Keith McClelland and Jane Rendall demonstrate that the Second Reform Act of 1867 was marked not only by extensive controversy about the extension of the vote, but also by new concepts of masculinity and the masculine voter, the beginnings of the movement for women's suffrage, and a parallel debate about the meanings and forms of national belonging. The chapters in this book draw on recent developments in cultural, social and gender history, broadening the study of nineteenth-century British political history and integrating questions of nation and empire. Fascinating illustrations illuminate the argument, and a detailed chronology, biographical notes and selected bibliography offer further support to the student reader. Students and scholars in history, women's studies, cultural studies and postcolonial studies will find this book invaluable.

CATHERINE HALL is Professor of Modern British Social and Cultural History at University College London. She is the author of *White, Male and Middle Class: Explorations in Feminism and History* (1992) and (with Leonore Davidoff) *Family Fortunes: Men and Women of the English Middle Class 1780–1850* (1987).

KEITH McCLELLAND is Senior Lecturer in Social History at Middlesex University, London. He co-edited *E. P. Thompson: Critical Perspectives* (1990) and is the co-editor of the journal *Gender & History*.

JANE RENDALL is Senior Lecturer and co-director of the Centre for Eighteenth-Century Studies at the University of York. Her publications include *The Origins of Modern Feminism: Women in Britain, France, and the United States, 1780–1860* (1985), *Equal or Different: Women's Politics 1800–1914* (1987) and *Women in an Industrializing Society: England 1780–1880* (1990).

Frontispiece (overleaf) 'A Leap in the Dark'. *Punch*, 3 August 1867. As the Second Reform Bill goes through its final stages, Disraeli carries Britannia towards an unknown future.

D0061126

PUNCH, OR THE LONDON CHARIVARI.—August 3, 1867.

A LEAP IN THE DARK.

Defining the Victorian nation

Class, Race, Gender and the British Reform Act of 1867

Catherine Hall, Keith McClelland and Jane Rendall

A455830

PUBLISHED BY THE PRESS SYNDICATE OF THE UNIVERSITY OF CAMBRIDGE
The Pitt Building, Trumpington Street, Cambridge CB2 1RP, United Kingdom

CAMBRIDGE UNIVERSITY PRESS
The Edinburgh Building, Cambridge CB2 2RU, UK http://www.cup.cam.ac.uk
40 West 20th Street, New York, NY 10011-4211, USA http://www.cup.org
10 Stamford Road, Oakleigh, Melbourne 3166, Australia

© Catherine Hall, Keith McClelland and Jane Rendall 2000

This book is in copyright. Subject to statutory exception and to the provisions of relevant collective licensing agreements, no reproduction of any part may take place without the written permission of Cambridge University Press.

First published 2000

Printed in the United Kingdom at the University Press, Cambridge

Typeset in Plantin 10/12 pt in QuarkXPress™ [SE]

A catalogue record for this book is available from the British Library

JN
955
H35
2000

ISBN 0 521 57218 5 hardback
ISBN 0 521 57653 9 paperback

OLSON LIBRARY
NORTHERN MICHIGAN UNIVERSITY
MARQUETTE, MICHIGAN 49855

Contents

Illustrations

Plates

Figures

Preface

The idea of doing this book together arose originally from conversations we were having about our individual projects, each of which was concerned with aspects of the politics of 1867. We should say that each of the individual essays builds upon foundations laid in much earlier and shorter versions of the arguments: Catherine Hall, 'Rethinking Imperial Histories: The Reform Act of 1867', *New Left Review* 208 (1994), 3–29; Keith McClelland, 'Rational and Respectable Men: Gender, the Working Class, and Citizenship in Britain, 1850–1867', in Laura Frader and Sonya O. Rose (eds.), *Gender and Class in Modern Europe* (Ithaca, N.Y., and London: Cornell University Press, 1996), pp. 280–93; Jane Rendall, 'Citizenship, Culture and Civilization: The Languages of British Suffragists, 1866–1874', in Caroline Daley and Melanie Nolan (eds.), *Suffrage and Beyond: International Feminist Perspectives* (New York University Press, 1994), pp. 127–50.

In this volume we have chosen to preserve the individuality of each project while engaging in the collective work which is here represented in the introductory essay. But our early essays have been extended and transformed through the many discussions we have had over the past few years. Their final form owes a great deal to those talks. We would like to record here how enjoyable these meetings have been. We started talking about the issues here because we were friends and we are delighted to say that friendship has been strengthened by the work. Keith McClelland and Jane Rendall would also like to thank Catherine Hall for the hospitality which so aided our collaboration.

In the course of the work we have talked to many audiences, of very different kinds, in many places. We would particularly like to thank the students we have taught in various universities for how much they have taught us, not least those at Essex, Middlesex and York. We also have individual thanks to record: Catherine Hall would particularly like to thank Gail Lewis; Keith McClelland has learned a great deal from Bill Greenslade, Sonya Rose, Laura Frader, Eleni Varikas, John Hope Mason and, not least, Chris Robinson; Jane Rendall thanks Heloise Brown,

Joanna de Groot, Angela John, Simon Morgan, Helen Plant, Ted Royle and Allen Warren for all kinds of scholarly and friendly assistance, Adam Middleton for constant and unfailing encouragement, and the British Academy for its financial support for research for this book.

Jane Rendall must also thank the Mistress of Girton College Cambridge for the use of the Parkes and Davies Papers. We are also grateful to the British Library and the University of London Library for permission to use material in their possession; to the staff of the J. B. Morrell Library, University of York, and the Local Studies Unit, Manchester Central Library; and to the National Trust for the cover illustration. Thomas Woolner's sculpture of 'Civilization' stands in Wallington, Northumberland, a National Trust property. We are especially grateful to Pamela Wallhead of the National Trust, Wallington, for her assistance and to Paul Barlow for information on the sculpture.

Woolner's 'Civilization' (also known as 'The Lord's Prayer' and 'Mother and Child') was completed in November 1866. It was commissioned by Pauline Trevelyan and Sir Walter Calverley Trevelyan for Wallington.[1] Thomas Woolner wrote of his work that 'The idea of the group was to embody the civilization of England.' The figure of the mother teaching her boy to say the Lord's Prayer is contrasted with scenes of cannibalism and murder from ancient British life, in a contrast identified as that between primitive habits and the ideals of a modern life. The pedestal displays a mother feeding her child with raw flesh on the point of his father's sword. Woolner wrote of his choice to depict 'civilization' as a woman teaching, 'because the position of women in society always marks the degree to which the civilization of the nation has reached'.[2] This study of a defining moment in the political history of Britain is here illustrated through the imagination of an artist who draws upon gendered concepts of the modern and of the primitive to portray English civilisation.

CATHERINE HALL
KEITH McCLELLAND
JANE RENDALL
March 1999

[1] See Raleigh Trevelyan, 'Thomas Woolner: Pre-Raphaelite Sculptor. The Beginnings of Success', *Apollo* 107 (1978), 200–5; Paul Barlow, 'Grotesque Obscenities: Thomas Woolner's *Civilization* and Its Discontents', in Colin Trodd, Barlow and David Amigoni (eds.), *Victorian Culture and the Idea of the Grotesque* (Aldershot: Ashgate Press, 1999), pp. 97–118.

[2] MS, 'Mr Woolners [*sic*] description of his sculpture at Wallington', Wallington, Northumberland.

Chronology

1865	February	Inaugural meeting of the Reform League
	May	Surrender of last Confederate Army; end of US Civil War
	July	General election; John Stuart Mill is elected for Westminster
	October	Death of Lord Palmerston; Lord John Russell forms administration with W. E. Gladstone as leader of the House of Commons
		Black rebellion at Morant Bay, Jamaica; martial law is declared by Governor Edward John Eyre, who represses the rebellion brutally
	November	The news of Morant Bay reaches Britain; the government is pressed to establish an inquiry
		Kensington Society discusses 'Is the extension of the parliamentary suffrage to women desirable and if so under what conditions?'
	December	Formation of Jamaica Committee
1866	January	Royal Commission on Jamaica meets
	February	New Parliament meets; Lord Russell becomes prime minister; Habeas Corpus Act suspended in Ireland
	March	Jamaica Act makes the island a crown colony
		Reform Bill introduced by William Gladstone
	May	Redistribution Bill introduced
	June	John Stuart Mill presents women's suffrage petition to House of Commons
		The Reform Bills are defeated following revolt of the 'Cave of Adullam'; Russell resigns
		Report of the Royal Commission on Jamaica

	July	Lord Derby forms Conservative administration with Benjamin Disraeli as leader of the House of Commons
		Reform demonstration in Hyde Park; attack on the railings
		Parliamentary debate on the findings of the Royal Commission
	August	Parliament prorogued; extensive public agitation in most major cities of England and Scotland over reform
		Eyre returns to England
	September	Eyre burnt in effigy at Clerkenwell Green
	October	Formation of the Provisional Committee, 'Extension of the Suffrage to Women Society'
1867	February	Failure of a Fenian rising in Ireland and attempt to seize arms at Chester Castle
		Conservative Reform Bill presented to House of Commons
	March	British North America Act establishes Dominion of Canada
		Attempt to prosecute Governor Eyre
		Women's suffrage petition with 3,559 signatures presented to Commons by H. A. Bruce
	April	Manchester women's suffrage petition with 3,161 signatures presented by John Stuart Mill
	May	Reform League demonstration in Hyde Park in the face of government ban; Home Secretary Spencer Walpole resigns; Hodgkinson's amendment to the Reform Bill abolishing the distinction between personal payment of rates and compounding (paying the rates together with the rent to landlord) accepted by Disraeli
		John Stuart Mill's amendment to delete 'man' and substitute 'person' is defeated
	June	Murphy riot in Birmingham
		Dissolution of first London women's suffrage committee
	July	Third reading of the Reform Bill
		London National Society for Women's Suffrage formed

	August	The Reform Act receives royal assent Thomas Carlyle's 'Shooting Niagara' published
	September	Rescue of Fenian prisoners in Manchester; prison guard killed
	November	Execution of 'Manchester Martyrs' By-election in Manchester; Lily Maxwell votes
	December	Second attempt to engineer rescue of Fenian prisoners from Clerkenwell; twelve killed in explosion
1868	June	Reform Bills for Scotland and Ireland carried Murphy Riots Further attempts to prosecute Governor Eyre
	February	Resignation of Lord Derby; Benjamin Disraeli forms his first administration
	May–September	Concerted action to request overseers to place qualified women on the franchise; campaigns in registration courts
	November	Dismissal of women's cases in Court of Common Pleas Liberal victory in general election; thirteen women vote in Manchester
	December	Resignation of Disraeli; formation of Gladstone's first ministry
1869	April	Introduction of second Married Women's Property Bill by Russell Gurney; fails in Lords
	May	Women ratepayers to vote on same terms as men, Municipal Corporations (Franchise) Act
	July	Disestablishment of Irish church
1870	May	Jacob Bright's Women's Suffrage Bill passes second reading by thirty-three votes (4 May) Gladstone's first speech on women's suffrage in opposition Bill defeated (12 May) on going into committee by 126 votes
	August	Amended Married Women's Property Bill passed Western Australia granted representative government

Abbreviations

ASE	Amalgamated Society of Engineers
CC	Cowen Collection, Tyne and Wear County Record Office, Newcastle upon Tyne
CW	Mill, John Stuart, *Collected Works of John Stuart Mill*, gen. ed. J. M. Robson, 33 vols., University of Toronto Press, 1962–91
EWR	*Englishwoman's Review*
FAC	Foreign Affairs Committee
FCD	Davies Papers, Girton College, Cambridge
MCL	Manchester Central Library
ME	*Manchester Examiner and Times*
MNSWS	Manchester National Society for Women's Suffrage
MT	Mill–Taylor Papers, British Library of Political and Economic Science, London School of Economics
NCA	National Charter Association
NRL	Northern Reform League
NRU	Northern Reform Union
PP	Parliamentary Papers
PPG	Parkes Papers, Girton College, Cambridge

1 Introduction

Catherine Hall, Keith McClelland and Jane Rendall

Historians and the Reform Act of 1867

The events of 1865–8

> The Truth is that a vote is not a Right but a Trust. All the Nation cannot by possibility be brought together to vote and therefore a Selected few are appointed by law to perform this Function for the Rest. (Memorandum from Lord Palmerston to his secretary, 15 May 1864[1])

> The nation is now in power. (*Newcastle Daily Chronicle*, 7 November 1868[2])

The third Viscount Palmerston first entered the House of Commons in 1807, long before the first Reform Act of 1832. As Liberal prime minister from 1859 to 1865, he viewed claims for a wider franchise with suspicion. His idea of the vote was that it was a 'trust', both a privilege and a responsibility, to be exercised by those who had a propertied stake in the country, on behalf of all others. He resisted any widening of the electorate beyond the limited one established in 1832, which had enfranchised only 'a Selected few', in England and Wales just under one-sixth of adult men in 1861.

Lord Palmerston died in October 1865. Three years later, by 1868, when the radical *Newcastle Daily Chronicle* claimed that 'the nation is now in power', the electorate had radically changed. In those three years the qualifications for the franchise and, by implication, for the citizenship of the nation had been widely explored, in political debate inside and outside the House of Commons. In such debates, and through the terms of the Reform Acts of 1867/8, the privileges of citizenship were extended far beyond the 'Select few' defended by Palmerston. Yet at the same time both the House of Commons, and those whom the *Newcastle Daily*

1 Broadlands Papers, HMC, PM/A/16, cited in Jasper Ridley, *Lord Palmerston* (London: Constable, 1970), p. 565.

2 'The Progress of Society', *Newcastle Daily Chronicle*, 7 November 1868, p. 2, cited in Eugenio Biagini, *Liberty, Retrenchment and Reform: Popular Liberalism in the Age of Gladstone, 1860–1880* (Cambridge University Press, 1992), p. 312.

Chronicle represented, drew their own boundaries for the British nation, boundaries which we explore in the chapters that follow.

Many textbooks have summarised the events of those three years. What follows in this section briefly draws upon such familiar narratives. In the new and much more urbanised social and economic climate of the 1850s and 1860s, the movement for a wider franchise gathered strength. The Reform Acts of 1832 had introduced a uniform franchise in the boroughs of England, Scotland and Wales, favouring the pre-industrial middling sort, including shopkeepers and skilled artisans as well as the professional and manufacturing middle classes. They had also extended the qualifications for voting in the counties of England and Wales beyond the limit of the old 40s freehold to better-off tenants, and introduced a new and uniform county franchise to Scotland. Though the Irish Act of 1832 made relatively little difference to Ireland, voting qualifications there were transformed by the Irish Franchise Act of 1850, which allowed county and borough voters to qualify as occupiers of premises rated for the Poor Law at £12 and £8 respectively. As figure 1 shows, county voters were in the majority in the electorate for the United Kingdom in 1866, though significantly so only in Wales and Ireland.[3]

By 1865, an increasing number of politicians from both the Conservative and the Liberal parties tended to favour an extension of the franchise which recognised the claims of the skilled manual workers of the towns and cities. Yet Lord Palmerston was reluctant to introduce any measure of parliamentary reform which would open the way for broader debates, and an expansion of the political nation. In July 1865 a general election returned his Liberal government with a slightly increased majority. Four months later, his death transformed the political scene and created new possibilities for the reform of Parliament.[4]

The new Liberal prime minister, Lord Russell, had been a key figure in the introduction of earlier Reform Bills, in 1852, 1854 and 1860. The Conservative leaders, the Earl of Derby and Benjamin Disraeli, in their

[3] The population in 1861 was:

England	18,834,000
Ireland	5,800,000
Scotland	3,062,000
Wales	1,121,000
United Kingdom	28,817,000

(Figures from Eric Evans, *The Forging of the Modern State: Early Industrial Britain, 1783–1870* (2nd edn, London: Longman, 1996), p. 427.)

[4] For full and detailed discussion of the narrative of events, on which this summary account draws, see: F. B. Smith, *The Making of the Second Reform Bill* (Cambridge University Press, 1966); Maurice Cowling, *1867: Disraeli, Gladstone and Revolution* (Cambridge University Press, 1967). For brief, more recent accounts, see, for instance, Evans, *Forging of the Modern State*, ch. 40; K. T. Hoppen, *The Mid-Victorian Generation, 1846–1886* (Oxford: Clarendon Press, 1998), chs. 7–8.

Figure 1. *The electorate of the United Kingdom, 1866*

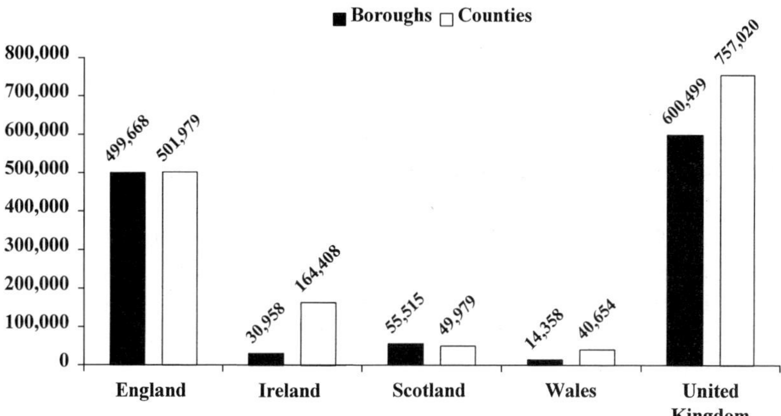

Source: R. Dudley Baxter, *The Results of the General Election* (London, 1869), p. 17, cited in F. B. Smith, *The Making of the Second Reform Bill* (Cambridge University Press, 1966), p. 236.

brief ministry of 1858–9, had also proposed a modest measure of enfranchisement.[5] Outside the House of Commons, initiatives had been taken even before the general election of 1865, in the formation in Manchester in 1864 of the Reform Union, which appealed to middle-class opinion, and in the founding in February 1865 of the Reform League, which spoke for the skilled working class. Both the Reform Union and the Reform League had been influenced by W. E. Gladstone's opinion, given in the House of Commons in May 1864, that 'every man who is not presumably incapacitated by some consideration of personal unfitness or of political danger is morally entitled to come within the pale of the constitution'.[6] Gladstone became Chancellor of the Exchequer in Russell's government. On 12 March 1866 he introduced a Reform Bill which proposed to add to existing qualifications the relatively high rental qualifications of £14 in the counties and £7 in the boroughs. These relatively limited proposals were opposed by a powerful group of backbench Liberals, sometimes referred to as the 'Cave of Adullam', led by Robert Lowe.[7] The Adullamite attack,

[5] See the appendices, pp. 239–40, for full details of these and subsequent proposals for reform. [6] *Hansard*, 3rd ser., vol. 185, cols. 324–5, 11 May 1864.

[7] This group was labelled by John Bright the 'Cave of Adullam' with reference to the verses in the Bible, I Samuel 22: 1–2, which described the 'Cave Adullam' where 'everyone that was in distress and every one that was discontented, gathered': *Hansard*, 3rd ser., vol. 182, col. 219, 13 March 1866.

supported by the Conservatives, brought down the Liberal government on 28 June 1866.

The Reform League responded to this defeat by further meetings and demonstrations. An attempt by the police to prevent the League holding a national demonstration in Hyde Park in July 1866 brought about what were to become, notoriously, the 'Hyde Park riots', in which part of the crowd broke down the railings and a few fought the police. Though these riots were not as violent as many electoral conflicts in Britain, they came to symbolise the threatening power of the working men's movement to Liberal and Conservative politicians alike. Their awareness of its potential led them to the view that the reform question had to be settled. Yet many historians would nevertheless argue that it was the parliamentary battle, rather than such external pressures, which determined the precise timing and shaped the provisions of the Reform Acts.

Derby and Disraeli believed that a limited measure of parliamentary reform would secure their government, and set limits on the electorate for the future. In February 1867 a Conservative Reform Bill was introduced, though its terms were hotly contested. One calculation suggests that there were ten significant changes in the terms of the bill between 9 February and 2 March. Disraeli had initially proposed a measure of household franchise, combined with a system of plural voting similar to that used for parish elections, and a further system of 'fancy franchises'.[8] He was prepared if necessary, however, to fall back on the terms of the Liberal bill, with a £6 rental qualification in the boroughs and £14 in the counties. The majority of Conservative backbenchers were in favour of the household franchise, though they were also committed to safeguards against too wide an enfranchisement, such as a three-year residential qualification, and the personal payment of rates. The latter was a very significant limitation since it excluded all lodgers who 'compounded' for their rates.[9]

The Conservative bill placed before the House of Commons on 18 March 1867 had by then provoked three Conservative Cabinet ministers to resign. It appeared to embody household suffrage in the boroughs, protected by the principle that only those who paid their rates in person

[8] Under the Sturges Bourne Act of 1818, which regulated voting in parish vestries, inhabitants rated at less than £50 had one vote, with those rated at more than £50 having one vote for every additional £25 up to a maximum of six votes. The same principle was embedded in the Poor Law Amendment Acts of 1834 and 1844: Brian Keith-Lucas, *The English Local Government Franchise: A Short History* (Oxford: Basil Blackwell, 1952), pp. 226–9. The Reform Bills of 1852, 1854 and 1859 had incorporated provisions for votes for those with a variety of educational or financial qualifications, known as 'fancy franchises'. These are listed in appendix C, pp. 239–40. Disraeli's original proposals combined these two principles.

[9] 'Compounding' was a widespread and convenient practice by which lodgers included payment for rates within the rent paid to a landlord.

might qualify. In the important division of 12 April, a group of Liberals – some ex-Adullamites, some convinced reformers and radicals – had supported the Conservatives, in what was known as the Tearoom Revolt. As a result the government won a victory of 310 votes to 289. But in future divisions, as Disraeli strove to maintain his majority, with some Liberal support, he allowed the all-important safeguards to slip away. Plans for plural voting were soon discarded. The residence requirement was reduced from three years to one. Lodgers 'of £10 annual value' were allowed to vote. And most significantly of all, on 17 May a motion from Grosvenor Hodgkinson abolished the practice of 'compounding' rates altogether. All male occupiers were in future to pay their rates personally, and therefore theoretically could qualify for a vote. Disraeli had no option but to accept the abolition of these safeguards, although he was still not prepared seriously to consider the enfranchisement of women. He did not accept John Stuart Mill's amendment to the bill of 20 May calling for the word 'person' to be substituted for 'man'.

The Reform Act for England and Wales, which passed into law in June 1867, gave the vote in the boroughs to all ratepaying adult male occupiers and lodgers in lodgings worth at least £10 a year, and resident for at least twelve months. In the other clauses of the act Disraeli made fewer concessions, with more modest extensions of the county franchise, and twenty-five of the fifty-two seats redistributed going to English counties.

This legislation for England and Wales was followed by the Reform Act for Scotland, introduced in May 1867 and finally passed in June 1868, with the same qualifications as the English bill, except that there was no lodger franchise because there lodgers were legally tenants. The delay was caused by a battle over the redistribution of seven seats gained for Scotland. The Irish bill, though expected in the late spring of 1867, was postponed indefinitely in June 1867, probably because of the opposition of influential Irish supporters of the Conservative leadership to further extension of the franchise. A year later, in June 1868, the Irish Reform Act reduced the borough qualification from £8 to £4, and maintained the county franchise at £12. There was no redistribution of seats.[10]

The Reform Acts did not ensure for Disraeli that security of tenure which he had hoped for after he succeeded Lord Derby as prime minister in February 1868. Gladstone's commitment to Irish affairs, and especially to the disestablishment of the Church of Ireland, won him a series of favourable votes in the House of Commons. He fought the general election at the end of 1868 on the issue of disestablishment, which had a

[10] F. B. Smith, *Making of the Second Reform Bill*, pp. 225–8. See the appendices for a summary of Reform Bills and Acts.

Figure 2. *Percentage of adult males over twenty-one enfranchised, 1861 and 1871*

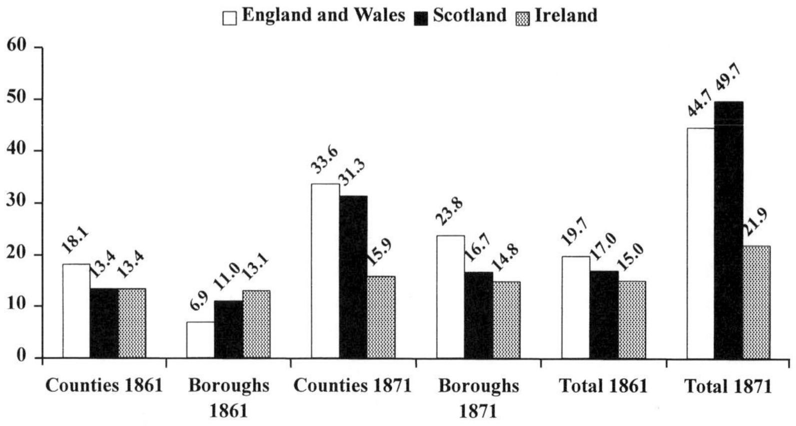

Source: K. Theodore Hoppen, 'The Franchise and Electoral Politics in England and Ireland, 1832–1885', *History* 70 (1985), 210, 215.

broad appeal to liberal, radical and nonconformist voters. Many aspects of the older system, such as the continuing importance of the smaller boroughs, remained unchanged. And the complexities of voter registration meant that the full impact of the Reform Acts was not experienced in the election of 1868. The Liberal party won a clear victory and Gladstone was able to embark upon the reforming programme of his first ministry.

Nevertheless, K. T. Hoppen has suggested that by 1871 the changes brought about by the Reform Acts, and their significance for the different parts of the United Kingdom, can be measured, as indicated in figure 2. Where the number of borough voters in England and Wales had more than doubled, county voters had increased by slightly less than half. The impact in Scotland was broadly similar, though the Irish Reform Act had relatively little effect.

The sketchy account given above does not, however, necessarily help us to understand what the *Newcastle Daily Chronicle* meant by the claim that 'The nation is now in power.' Recent historical work already offers wider interpretations, which pay far greater attention to the nature of extra-parliamentary activity, and to the social and cultural context of political life. In the 1990s the expansion of women's and gender history, attention to national identity and citizenship, and perspectives arising from the legacy of empire have all prompted new questions about nineteenth-century British politics.

The essays brought together in this volume have arisen from such concerns, and in this introduction we attempt to map out such new approaches. At the same time, we remain convinced that, for a full understanding of the events of 1865–8, recent and not-so-recent work in the field of 'high politics', work to which we are greatly indebted, must be fully recognised. So too must its relationship to a parallel strand of historiography, which since the 1960s has stressed the social and economic foundations of political life. In the following two sections, we examine these two approaches to nineteenth-century political history and, more specifically, to the events of 1865–8.

High politics and the Reform Act

The dominant interpretations of 1867, such as those by F. B. Smith and Maurice Cowling, all tend to stress the political origins of the Reform Acts and to see them as largely a consequence of events and processes 'internal' to high politics and the parliamentary domain. In particular, Smith's study, *The Making of the Second Reform Bill*, is indispensable both for an understanding of the political processes involved and for the details it provides of the complex technicalities involved in the drafting of the legislation. External events, such as the pressures from the organised working class through the Reform League, have a place in such interpretations but of an essentially secondary kind. So the organisation of the narratives comes to be structured largely by how key individuals, especially Gladstone and Disraeli, respond to events and put into effect particular political interests. As Cowling put it, there may have been a context of public agitation, but the 'centre of explanation' lay in Parliament itself, for 'parliament . . . was not *afraid* of public agitation: nor was its action determined by it'.[11]

There are, of course, variations within the historical arguments about the political origins of reform. Interpretations of Gladstone's conduct tend to be shaped by the weight given to two main elements. The first lies in Gladstone's commitment to questions of moral principle and duty, and his 'conversion' by 1864 to the cause of enfranchising at least a section of the respectable working class, and the second in Liberal calculations of political expediency.[12] Some historians, like Jonathan Parry, argue that to see Gladstone and the Liberals as appreciating the 'good moral sense of the respectable artisans' or perceiving an identity of interests between middle- and working-class Liberals is simply 'romantic'. The Reform Act was an accident but it was also a matter of hard-headed political calculation concerning the possible effects of the act on the Liberals' electoral

[11] F. B. Smith, *Making of the Second Reform Bill*; Cowling, *1867*, p. 3.

[12] Evans, *Forging of the Modern State*, p. 360, is representative of much of the conventional wisdom on Gladstone in this respect.

position in the constituencies, the possible impact of artisan votes on public expenditure, and the need to design a bill which would establish a clear identity to the parliamentary party.[13]

Disraeli and the Conservatives have similarly been seen as generally guided by such political calculations. In particular, they were driven firstly by the possibility of overturning the Liberals and Whigs – who had been overwhelmingly dominant in politics for twenty years – and, secondly, by the necessity of defending the counties, the core base of Tory politics, against urban encroachment. There are exceptions to this. Gertrude Himmelfarb has argued that, in pursuing reform, Disraeli was animated by the belief that the Tories were the national party and that there was a natural identity of interests between the aristocracy and the working class. Disraeli's enacting of a Reform Bill more radical than anything the Liberals had proposed is here not seen as an accident or the result of parliamentary tactics, as the majority of historians argue, so much as a more or less self-conscious enactment of a political strategy of building a Conservative nation, a 'Tory democracy'.[14] And some recent work on the history of Conservatism is tending, once again, to stress the importance within Disraelian Conservatism of the themes of the nation, the importance of empire, and the enduring importance within Disraeli's own thought of the romanticism of 'young England'.[15] But the conventional wisdom tends to eschew explanations of Conservative positions on reform except in terms of political tactics and calculation. Disraeli emerges as 'the man who rode the race, who took the time, who kept the time, and who did the trick', as they said at the Conservative Carlton Club on 12 April 1867.[16]

Thus the narrative is pursued through the parliamentary goings-on of 1866–7: the defeat of the Russell–Gladstone bill of 1866, the revolt of the Cave of Adullam led by Lowe, the manoeuvres of Disraeli, and the acceptance of Hodgkinson's amendment and of household suffrage. The result is that the origins of the Reform Act of 1867 are seen as largely contingent

13 Jonathan Parry, *The Rise and Fall of Liberal Government in Victorian Britain* (New Haven and London: Yale University Press, 1993), pp. 207–17.

14 Gertrude Himmelfarb, 'Politics and Ideology: The Reform Act of 1867', in Himmelfarb, *Victorian Minds: Essays on Nineteenth-Century Intellectuals* (London: Weidenfeld and Nicolson, 1968), pp. 333–92 (first published as 'The Politics of Democracy: The English Reform Act of 1867', *Journal of British Studies* 6 (1966), 97–138); see also F. B. Smith, 'The "Dependence of Licence upon Faith": Miss Gertrude Himmelfarb on the Second Reform Act', *Journal of British Studies* 7 (1967), 96–9, and Himmelfarb's reply, 100–4.

15 See among others, Paul Smith, *Disraeli: A Brief Life* (Cambridge University Press, 1996), p. 13. See, for instance, Hoppen, *Mid-Victorian Generation*, pp. 237–53.

16 W. F. Monypenny and G. E. Buckle, *The Life of Benjamin Disraeli, Earl of Beaconsfield*, 6 vols. (London: John Murray, 1910–20), vol. IV, p. 533, cited in Hoppen, *Mid-Victorian Generation*, p. 251.

upon the immediate political situation, its particular form a result of 'accident', its consequences unintended. As Parry has put it: here was 'the most unintentional revolution in the history of British politics'.[17]

Yet if the immediate origins of the act of 1867 have not been significantly reinterpreted, the history of nineteenth-century British politics, and thus the broader political context of 1867, have been. Indeed, there has been a considerable revival of political history in recent years. If the focus of much innovative historical work in the 1960s–80s was in social history, the focus of attention of many younger scholars in more recent years has shifted back to the political. Much of this work has built upon not only the rapid expansion and methodological innovations of social history but also upon the prior impact of political sociology upon the subject. As Jon Lawrence and Miles Taylor have suggested in a recent survey, electoral sociology of the kind pioneered in both the United States and Britain from the 1950s had a considerable impact upon the development of historical studies, largely in the field of electoral behaviour.[18] They emphasise the particular importance of four historians, H. J. Hanham, D. C. Moore, John Vincent and T. J. Nossiter.[19] To these one might add the work of Norman Gash.[20]

These historians differed considerably among themselves. Gash's studies of Parliament and the electorate in the 1830s and 1840s were pioneering in their detailed analyses of political structures after the 1832 Reform Act, and emphasised the essentially conservative character of both the Reform Act and its repercussions. Hanham's work was concerned with the impact of the Reform Act of 1867 on party organisation in the 1870s and 1880s. Moore attempted to demonstrate the limited

[17] Parry, *Rise and Fall of Liberal Government*, p. 216.

[18] Jon Lawrence and Miles Taylor, 'Introduction: Electoral Sociology and the Historians', in Lawrence and Taylor (eds.), *Party, State and Society: Electoral Behaviour in Britain Since 1820* (Aldershot: Scolar Press, 1997), pp. 1–26.

[19] H. J. Hanham, *Elections and Party Management: Politics in the Time of Disraeli and Gladstone* (London: Longmans Green, 1959); T. J. Nossiter, *Influence, Opinion and Political Idioms in Reformed England: Case Studies from the North East 1832–1874* (Brighton: Harvester Press, 1975); D. C. Moore, *The Politics of Deference* (Brighton: Harvester Press, 1976); John Vincent, *The Formation of the British Liberal Party 1857–1868* (1966; 2nd edn, Harmondsworth: Penguin, 1972), and his *Pollbooks: How Victorians Voted* (Cambridge University Press, 1968). Local political studies include: R. W. Davis, *Political Change and Continuity 1760–1885: A Buckinghamshire Study* (Newton Abbot: David and Charles, 1972); R. J. Olney, *Lincolnshire Politics, 1832–1885* (Oxford University Press, 1973); Patrick Joyce, *Work, Society and Politics: The Culture of the Factory in Later Victorian England* (Brighton: Harvester Press, 1980); John Garrard, *Leadership and Power in Victorian Industrial Towns, 1830–1880* (Manchester University Press, 1983).

[20] Norman Gash, *Politics in the Age of Peel: A Study in the Technique of Parliamentary Representation 1830–1850* (London: Longmans Green, 1953; 2nd edn, Hassocks: Harvester, 1977); Gash, *Reaction and Reconstruction in English Politics, 1832–1852* (Oxford: Clarendon Press, 1965).

impact of the 1832 Reform Act upon electoral politics and the persistence of 'deference' and aristocratic political authority within Victorian politics. Vincent's work on the Liberal party and on pollbooks stressed the 'pre-industrial' character of the electorate and the absence of class conflict – at least in the 'modern' sense – in political behaviour. Nossiter was concerned with the social basis of voting behaviour and the testing of alternative determinants of voting: 'influence', 'the market' and 'individualism'.

Whatever the differences between these historians, evident not only in their empirical concerns but also in their theoretical assumptions, the cumulative effect of their work suggests two main points of relevance here.[21] First, these studies placed a considerable stress on the persistent importance until about 1880 of a 'traditional' politics in which local, aristocratic and religious influences remained paramount as against the importance of class in the subsequent era.[22] Secondly, such work and the emphasis on the 'traditional' or 'conservative' character of politics and political change has been complemented by a great deal of work across the range of political history and, indeed, much recent social history. If there is a single theme that predominates, it is the persistence of aristocratic politics, evident, it is argued, not only in the limited consequences of formal electoral changes as in 1832 and 1867/8, but also in the revaluation of the character of political groups and parties.[23] For example, recent studies of the Whigs and Liberalism have stressed the capacity of Whiggery to adapt to changing circumstances, the continuities between the Whigs of the 1830s and 1840s and the subsequent Liberal party, and also, partly consequentially, the continuing dominance of 'aristocratic government'.[24]

This stress ties in with recent developments in social history. There is currently in train an effective reinterpretation of the social history of modern Britain, not only in method (to which we return below, in our discussion of the cultural history of nineteenth-century politics), but also in content. While the results of this are by no means settled, among the dominating themes that have emerged are those which emphasise the relatively slow, evolutionary and in many respects conservative development

[21] See Lawrence and Taylor, 'Introduction', for an interesting analysis of the relationship of this work to the development and assumptions of political sociology. [22] *Ibid.*, p. 11.

[23] A good brief introduction to the 1832 act, and to historians' changing views of it, is Eric J. Evans, *The Great Reform Act of 1832* (2nd edn, London: Routledge, 1994).

[24] See among others: Richard Brent, *Liberal Anglican Politics: Whiggery, Religion and Reform 1830–1841* (Oxford: Clarendon Press, 1987); Peter Mandler, *Aristocratic Government in the Age of Reform: Whigs and Liberals 1830–1852* (Oxford: Clarendon Press, 1990); Ian Newbould, *Whiggery and Reform, 1830–1841: The Politics of Government* (Basingstoke: Macmillan, 1990); Parry, *Rise and Fall of Liberal Government.*

of society and politics since the eighteenth century. The slow pace of industrialisation and the growth of 'gentlemanly capitalism', the persistent importance of the landed aristocracy in political and social institutions and cultural forms, the relative stability of British society as compared with societies elsewhere in Europe (and also the United States) and the absence of sharp discontinuities are all themes which have been prominent in the work of many social historians.

This focus entails a rejection of many of the dominant interpretations of the social history of the 1960s and 1970s, which still have very considerable influence in schools and universities and among general readers. At the centre of such work was the transforming character of the industrial revolution, effecting massive changes in society and culture as much as in economic structures.[25] Those stressing the significance of such social changes were generally agreed that there was an effective 'break' in British society and politics around 1848, as class relations came to stabilise around the hegemony of the urban, commercial and industrial middle class.

Much work in political history effectively rejects such interpretations, as do studies of the history of radicalism and the construction of the Liberal party in the 1850s–70s. Much of this work has been profoundly shaped by the work of John Vincent and of H. C. G. Matthew. John Vincent's *Formation of the British Liberal Party 1857–1868* has been immensely influential. This was partly because the book was located within a historical sociology of politics in which the formation of the party was seen as a binding together of elements of different social classes (elements of the working and middle classes and the Whig aristocracy), and political and religious factions and pressure groups (bourgeois or working-class radicals like John Bright or the Reform League, nonconformist organisations like the temperance United Kingdom Alliance, and so on). The context of this formation, and the subject of other work by Vincent, was an electoral structure which was essentially 'pre-industrial'.[26] In analysing this social formation Vincent departed from political histories which focused simply on the creation of a parliamentary vehicle of liberalism from 1859 onwards and the role of key individuals (Palmerston, Russell, Gladstone) in the transition from Whiggery to liberalism. But if the sociological basis of the party was subject to close examination and was of major importance in Vincent's account, the essential *explanation* of the formation of the Liberal party relied less upon the social or sociological than on the role of

[25] Such works range, for instance, from E. J. Hobsbawm's *Industry and Empire* (Harmondsworth: Penguin, 1969), the single most influential Marxist interpretation of British society as a whole since industrialisation, to Harold Perkin's *Origins of Modern English Society 1780–1880* (London: Routledge and Kegan Paul, 1969).

[26] Vincent, *Pollbooks*.

'charismatic leadership'. Here it was Gladstone who was central to this analysis, and who held the potentially rather fragile alliance of Liberalism together. At the same time, while Vincent suggested that what was created was a community of sentiment of liberalism, liberal ideas received rather less attention than they had done in earlier work, for Vincent did not see liberalism as the creation of a coherent ideology so much as a confluence of interests.

Matthew's analysis of Gladstone is crucial to an understanding of the development of liberalism.[27] He places Gladstone, and Gladstonian liberalism, firmly in relation to the Pitt–Peel tradition of Conservatism in the service of government, whilst recognising the departure of Gladstone from this tradition in his 'politicization of the chancellorship' as Matthew calls it.[28] Matthew's account focuses in particular on the political economy of Gladstone as Chancellor of the Exchequer, both in the general sense of examining Gladstone's conception of the economic functions of the state and in the more particular sense of his taxation policies. For Matthew, Gladstonian fiscal strategy, exercised in particular through his budgets of 1852 and 1860, was central to what he calls 'the social contract of the mid-Victorian state'. Gladstone was quite successful in redressing the balance between indirect taxation (which weighed disproportionately on the working class) and direct taxation (mainly income tax). One of the reasons, and by no means the least important, why working-class radicals came to look increasingly favourably upon Gladstone was the lessening of the burden of indirect taxation. At the same time the middle classes benefited from a more palatable income tax and the incentive to save which Gladstone, 'with spectacular political finesse', incorporated into his 1853 budget.[29]

This emphasis upon the fiscal question and its political implications is an important extension of our understanding of liberalism, because it helps put into place one of the precise mechanisms which allowed the formation of popular liberalism, and the coming together of differing political and economic groups into the Liberal party as described by Vincent. The arguments of Vincent and Matthew have both been heavily used in the recent work on radicalism from historians such as Eugenio Biagini. And much new work on the cultural history of politics shares an emphasis

[27] H. C. G. Matthew, *Gladstone 1809–1874* (Oxford: Clarendon Press, 1986); see esp. ch. 5, which incorporates material from Matthew's important and influential article, 'Disraeli, Gladstone and the Politics of Mid-Victorian Budgets', *Historical Journal* 22 (1979), 615–43.

[28] Matthew, *Gladstone*, pp. 112–20. Matthew's work meshes in with the effective revaluation of Peel, above all by Boyd Hilton, as the 'progenitor of Gladstonian liberalism': Hilton, 'Peel: A Reappraisal', *Historical Journal* 22 (1979), 585–614 (quote, 614).

[29] Matthew, *Gladstone*, p. 122.

on the relatively conservative character of the post-1832 electorate and political system and, more specifically, on the continuities between pre-1848 radicalism, particularly Chartism, and mid-Victorian popular liberalism.[30] Such themes are partly directed against Marxist interpretations, but are also influenced by the stress upon aristocratic and patrician government and politics. Hence it is argued that radicalism continues to have as its central focus for criticism the ill-reformed political system of Old Corruption and its political and cultural legacy.

Empirically, then, 1867 is placed in these accounts less as the product of a *class*-oriented radicalism than as the consequence of the persistence of a language and politics that was aristocratic, patrician and exclusive of the people. Such reinterpretation of radicalism poses the evolution of politics itself as the essential explanatory mechanism, in a variety of ways. Miles Taylor places rather less emphasis upon political languages and discourses than on government and its functions, including the strengthened role of the executive since 1832 and the changing scope for action of 'independent' MPs. That is, politics is seen primarily as a set of institutions that determine what is politically possible, inside and outside the House of Commons.[31] On the other hand Eugenio Biagini emphasises the 'languages' of radicalism and the continuities of the discourse with pre-1848 radicalism.[32] Such work is innovative in that it breaks down the concept of liberalism as a political monolith and takes seriously the world of politics itself, rather than seeing it as merely reflecting or being the expression of other formations, above all, social and economic class relations. These concerns have been central to new approaches to the cultural history of politics, discussed below (pp. 20–9).

However, to understand the impact of such work fully, it is important also to examine interpretations of nineteenth-century society and politics which have their roots in Marxist approaches, for Marxism has been the oppositional spectre haunting a great deal of work in social and political history.

Marxist explanations

Much nineteenth-century British social and political history has been dominated by the concept of class formation, with class providing the

30 The argument has also been extended to reinterpret late nineteenth-century labour and socialist politics: see, for example, the essays in Eugenio F. Biagini and Alastair J. Reid (eds.), *Currents of Radicalism: Popular Radicalism, Organised Labour and Party Politics in Britain, 1850–1914* (Cambridge University Press, 1991).

31 Miles Taylor, *The Decline of British Radicalism 1847–1860* (Oxford: Clarendon Press, 1995).

32 Biagini, *Liberty, Retrenchment and Reform.*

'master category' of political narratives. Such narratives can be found in periods of class conflict and disruption, as in the history of the Chartist movement in the 1830s and 1840s, or in the exploration of the temporarily stable politics of class coexistence, as in the 1850s and 1860s. The legacy of the work of Karl Marx, which took its shape from the British experiences of industrialisation, has here been immensely powerful. Both Marx and his intellectual and political collaborator, Friedrich Engels, were, of course, themselves close observers of the events of the British reform crisis of 1865–8.[33]

Marxism, both as a body of theoretical work and in its applications by historians, does not constitute a single stream of thought but has contained many currents, some of which have been, from time to time, strongly opposed to each other. But all have, by definition, a common point of theoretical origin in the writings of either Marx or Engels.[34] Most critically for our purposes both Marx and Engels thought that political institutions and conflicts – and indeed the history of British politics – were determined by social and economic developments.

In his 'Preface' to *A Contribution to the Critique of Political Economy* (1859)[35] Marx argued that at the base of any social formation (or 'society' in the usual phrase) lay what he referred to as the economic structure or 'real foundation' composed of two elements, the relations of production, or property relations between groups such as capitalists and wage-labourers, and the material forces of production, or means of production.[36] The 'real foundation' was held by Marx to 'determine' two other levels of the

[33] Chimen Abramsky and Henry Collins, *Karl Marx and the British Labour Movement: Years of the First International* (Basingstoke: Macmillan, 1965).

[34] Useful introductions to Marx for historians include Iain Hampsher-Monk, *A History of Modern Political Thought: Major Political Thinkers from Hobbes to Marx* (Oxford: Blackwell, 1992), ch. 10; Anthony Giddens, *Capitalism and Modern Social Theory* (Cambridge University Press, 1971), pt I; Philip Abrams, *Historical Sociology* (Shepton Mallet: Open Books, 1982), ch. 3; E. J. Hobsbawm, 'Marx and History', *New Left Review* 143 (1984), 39–50, repr. in Hobsbawm, *On History* (London: Weidenfeld and Nicolson, 1997), pp. 157–70, and his 'Karl Marx's Contribution to Historiography', in Robin Blackburn (ed.), *Ideology in Social Science* (Glasgow: Fontana, 1972), pp. 265–83; S. H. Rigby, *Marxism and History: A Critical Introduction* (Manchester University Press, 1987). T. B. Bottomore (ed.), *A Dictionary of Marxist Thought* (2nd edn, Oxford: Blackwell, 1991), is an extremely helpful work of reference.

[35] References here are to the edition edited with an introduction by Maurice Dobb, (London: Lawrence and Wishart, 1971).

[36] These include raw materials, technologies, technical and scientific knowledge used in production, and labour itself, which occupied a unique position within Marx's schema of being both a force of production and a constituent part of the relations of production. Most – but not all – commentators would agree that, for Marx, the relations of production have dominance over the forces of production. But see, for example, G. A. Cohen, *Karl Marx's Theory of History: A Defence* (Oxford: Clarendon Press, 1978), for a powerful and influential, though contentious, view that Marx attributed explanatory primacy to the productive forces.

social formation, the legal and political superstructure and 'definite forms' of social consciousness. By the superstructure Marx meant not only the government executive but also the other institutions of the state such as the bureaucratic machinery (state servants and the like), law and legal institutions, and the military and other policing forces; it was essentially produced by the foundation. Although Marx did not include forms of social consciousness within the superstructure in the terms outlined in the 1859 Preface, he evidently regarded such forms as being, like legal and political institutions, essentially secondary to the 'real foundation': 'consciousness must be explained from the contradictions of material life'.[37]

But what produced change in history? Marx located the dynamics of change not in politics or in cultural or ideological change but in the foundation itself. At particular moments, it was the conflict between the forces and relations of production that produced an era of 'social revolution', by which he meant not so much particular events like the French revolution of 1789–99 as longer-term changes such as those occurring in early modern western Europe. His rich empirical narratives, such as those on the French revolution of 1848, provide the most detailed workings through of the abstractions he formulated in other writing.[38]

However, the problem of what Marx meant by 'determination' remains a controversial and difficult one. In arguing that the economic structure 'determines' the superstructure or forms of social consciousness, what did he mean? At times he appears to refer to something like a homology, or 'close fit', between the different levels of social formation, as when he writes that forms of social consciousness 'correspond with' *or* are determined by the social relations of production. The term 'correspond with' suggests a match between the relations of production and ideological forms. It could be said, for instance, that there was a correspondence between the development of an industrial and commercial middle class and the growth of political economy as a body of doctrine. This does not, however, offer an explanation of that relationship. The notion of determination, by contrast, does offer such an explanation, in suggesting that forms of consciousness or political superstructure are dependent on certain kinds of economic and social relationships. This problem has produced some of the most inventive and stimulating developments in Marxism after Marx.

37 'Preface', *Contribution* (1859), p. 21.

38 Karl Marx, *The Class Struggles in France: 1848–1850* (1850), and *The Eighteenth Brumaire of Louis Bonaparte* (1852), both available in, among other places, *Karl Marx: Political Writings, vol. II, Surveys from Exile*, ed. David Fernbach (Harmondsworth: Penguin, 1973), pp. 13–142 and 143–249 respectively. For a very helpful discussion of these texts see, among others, Gwyn Williams, '18 Brumaire: Karl Marx and Defeat', in Betty Matthews (ed.), *Marx: 100 Years on* (London: Lawrence and Wishart, 1983), pp. 11–37.

Few Marxist historians have been prepared, at least in recent decades, to countenance an account of determination that simply takes changes in the social relations of production as a sufficient explanation of the ideological, cultural or political spheres. And, whatever the differences between them, what they all have in common is the rejection of the notion that determination entails unavoidable compulsion. The general tendency has been to allow that 'determination' includes both the notion that there are pressures of circumstances (or structures) on groups or individuals which limit and shape what they can be and do, and the notion that those groups and individuals can, in varying degrees, be agents of change. In Marx's phrase: 'Men make their own history, but not of their own free will; not under circumstances they themselves have chosen but under the given and inherited circumstances with which they are directly confronted.'[39] However, the weight to be given to each of the terms here – circumstances and 'making history', or structure and agency – has been a source of intense controversy.[40] Furthermore, all would argue that different levels within the whole social formation each have their own specific characteristics and particular effects. For example, the domain of the political – the state and other political institutions – has its own structures, rules and personnel but clearly has effects, of historically variable kinds, on the other levels of the social order.[41]

There is nothing uniquely Marxist about the notion that there are differentiated levels within a society. What makes Marxism distinctive in this regard is the recourse to the 'economic base' as ultimately determinant. And it is here that the concept of class is of central importance to understanding Marxist historiography. One may define two main axes in the definition of class within Marxist historiography, indicated by a celebrated passage by Marx himself in the course of his discussion of the French peasantry of 1848:

> In so far as millions of families live under economic conditions of existence that separate their mode of life, their interests and their cultural formation from those of the other classes and bring them into conflict with those classes, they form a class. In so far as these small peasant proprietors are merely connected on a local basis, and the identity of their interests fails to produce a feeling of community, national links, or a political organization, they do not form a class.[42]

[39] Marx, *Eighteenth Brumaire*, p. 146.

[40] The issues discussed here can be indicated only briefly, and are helpfully discussed in Raymond Williams, *Marxism and Literature* (Oxford University Press, 1977), pp. 83–9. The problem of structure and agency has been central not only to Marxism but also to social theory more generally. See, for example, Abrams, *Historical Sociology*.

[41] For a succinct statement of the problem, see, for example, Frederic Jameson, 'The Brick and the Balloon: Architecture, Idealism and Land Speculation', *New Left Review* 228 (1998), 27.

[42] Marx, *Eighteenth Brumaire*, p. 239.

The first emphasis here, upon the purely objective economic situation of a class, tends to produce explanations of the struggle between classes – central to Marxist analyses of actual historical developments, as in Marx's account of France in 1848–52 – as being formed primarily by economic interests given in the relations of production. Political developments and conflicts are then explained as reflecting, or being primarily and overwhelmingly determined by, those interests.

The second emphasis, on the formation of class consciousness and modes of class association, has been much more evident among Marxist historians in Britain. The most important and influential attempt to explore the actual historical formation of a class and the ways in which 'a feeling of community, national links, or a political organization' developed has been E. P. Thompson's *The Making of the English Working Class*.[43] His account abandoned explanations of class and of class struggle in terms simply of the economic formation of class and the expression, in politics, of its interests. Instead, he located the formation of class in terms of the elaboration of class as a whole way of life. He rejected a notion of base and superstructure in favour of a dialectic, or interchange, between social being and social consciousness in which experience mediated between the two terms. How English workers responded to the industrial revolution and the social and economic transformations it wrought was not simply a consequence of the economic events and experiences affecting them. Rather, those changes were 'handled' through the cultural resources both already available and newly created by working people.[44]

Thompson's work emerged out of a period, particularly in the late 1950s and early 1960s, of great richness in the production of British Marxist and related thought.[45] This body of work opened up the study of culture – the formation of identities and their embodiment in particular institutions and forms of social organisation, especially those of class – in wholly new ways. Thompson's book in particular offered an empirically rich and detailed account of the social, cultural and political life of the English working class. At the same time he proposed a powerful and influential argument about what happened in the period 1790–1832: that

43 First published London: Victor Gollancz, 1963; 3rd edn with a new preface, London: Gollancz, 1980. For discussions of Thompson's work, including *The Making of the English Working Class*, see among others, Perry Anderson, *Arguments Within English Marxism* (London: Verso, 1980); H. J. Kaye and Keith McClelland (eds.), *E. P. Thompson: Critical Perspectives* (Cambridge: Polity Press, 1990). Bryan D. Palmer, *E. P. Thompson: Objections and Oppositions* (London: Verso, 1994), is useful but tends to the hagiographic.

44 E. P. Thompson, *Making of the English Working Class*, p. 11.

45 See among others Dennis L. Dworkin, *Cultural Marxism in Postwar Britain* (Durham, N.C.: Duke University Press, 1997).

a class was formed and formed itself as a group conscious of its own identity as a class and antagonistic to other classes, and that class relations were the most important shaping force in British political and social life thereafter.

Yet if Thompson wished, as a matter of theory, to reject a model of determination by the economic, and to replace it with a model of apparent parity between social being and social consciousness, in practice the account he gave of the formation of the English working class was constantly pulled back to explanations of cultural and political formation in which social being had a privileged place over consciousness.[46] If Thompson ascribed a key role in the creation of working-class consciousness to the formation of particular movements, institutional forms and popular intellectuals, the languages and ideas deployed by them found a constant point of reference in the social experiences of the working class.[47] Later critics of Thompson, especially Gareth Stedman Jones, were to take off from this point.[48]

Thompson offered a compelling account of class formation in the industrial revolution and a non-reductionist way of thinking about that history. But historians of a later period were faced by a different set of problems. If the working class was 'made' by 1832 and in the Chartist years of 1838–48, the struggles of those years seemed largely to dissolve after 1848. Between then and the 1870s the working class appeared to have entered a new phase of internal divisions, cultural fragmentation and a relative acceptance of the boundaries and limits of the social, economic and political framework of 'mid-Victorian' Britain.[49]

What focused this discussion within Marxist historiography was the notion that there emerged a 'labour aristocracy', a stratum of workers who were in E. J. Hobsbawm's definition 'better paid, better treated and generally regarded as more "respectable" and politically moderate than the mass of the proletariat'. Hobsbawm's work on the subject has been the fundamental starting point for all subsequent discussions and critiques of the phenomenon.[50] He argued that from the 1840s differences

[46] For the difficulties in Thompson's account of experience, consciousness and determination, see among others William H. Sewell jun., 'How Classes Are Made: Critical Reflections on E. P. Thompson's Theory of Working-Class Formation', in Kaye and McClelland, *E. P. Thompson*, pp. 50–77.

[47] See, for example, the discussion of William Cobbett and the role of his *Weekly Political Register*, in E. P. Thompson, *Making of the English Working Class*, pp. 820–37, or, more generally, ch. 16, 'Class Consciousness'.

[48] See the following section, pp. 22–4, for discussion of this.

[49] This mid-century transition is not a theme confined to Marxist interpretations. See, for instance, W. L. Burn, *The Age of Equipoise* (London: George Allen and Unwin, 1964); Perkin, *Origins of Modern English Society*; Evans, *Forging of the Modern State*.

[50] E. J. Hobsbawm, 'The Labour Aristocracy in Nineteenth-Century Britain', in Hobsbawm, *Labouring Men* (London: Weidenfeld and Nicolson, 1964), p. 272.

of income, status and attitudes within the working class, already evident before then, were accentuated as the labour aristocracy became more sharply differentiated economically from the rest of the working class and socially more homogeneous and visible. There was a growing differential between those earning the highest and most regular wages and those below them. Underlying this was a structural recomposition of the working class, with the growth of a higher-paid male labour force in industries like engineering and shipbuilding.[51]

The concept of the labour aristocracy and the suggestion that its existence could explain the nature of popular and working-class politics in the 1850s–70s (to say nothing of the period 1870–1914) engendered much discussion.[52] Subsequent work among labour historians broadly sympathetic to Hobsbawm's analysis developed the account in two major directions. Particularly important here was the work of Royden Harrison, whose important collection of essays, *Before the Socialists* (1965), was the most detailed study of political conflict between 1850 and 1870 from this perspective. Harrison argued that the emergence of a labour aristocracy was reflected in the politics of the Reform League: 'the story of working-class politics in the third quarter of the nineteenth century is largely about the activities and aspirations of this stratum'.[53]

It underlay the emergence of 'Lib–Labism' or the alliance between the Labour leadership and the Liberal party. For Harrison, writing in 1965 and again in his second edition of 1994, the politics of class were central to both the form and the timing of the Second Reform Act.[54] Later, Robert Q. Gray and Geoffrey Crossick extended the cultural analysis of the labour aristocracy and its 'styles of life' in order to argue that the stratum had a distinctive existence not only as an economic group but also as a cultural one. Here, and particularly in Gray's work, the influence not only of E. P. Thompson but also of Antonio Gramsci, the Italian Marxist theorist of 'hegemony' and 'civil society', was strongly felt in an analysis which, ultimately, sought to explain not only the formation of a

Hobsbawm has revisited the notion on several subsequent occasions. See esp. 'Debating the Labour Aristocracy', 'The Aristocracy of Labour Reconsidered' and 'Artisans and Labour Aristocrats', in his *Worlds of Labour* (London: Weidenfeld and Nicolson, 1984), pp. 214–26, 227–51, and 252–72, and for a summary treatment, *The Age of Capital 1848–1875* (London: Weidenfeld and Nicolson, 1975), pp. 223–9.

51 For further discussion of this point, see Keith McClelland's chapter below (ch. 2).

52 For introductions to this debate, see Mike Savage and Andrew Miles, *The Remaking of the British Working Class* (London: Routledge, 1994), esp. chs. 2–3; Robert Q. Gray, *The Aristocracy of Labour in Nineteenth-Century Britain* (Basingstoke: Macmillan, 1981), which, though dated in some respects, remains of considerable value.

53 Royden Harrison, *Before the Socialists: Studies in Labour and Politics 1861–1881* (London: Routledge and Kegan Paul, 1965; 2nd edn, Aldershot, Gregg Revivals, 1994), p. 5.

54 Royden Harrison's 'Introduction to the Second Edition', in his *Before the Socialists* (1994), offers a detailed survey of the debates surrounding his earlier work, with his response to them.

particular stratum within the working class but the 'stabilisation' of the whole social and political order in the period between 1848 and 1880.[55] Although the notion of the labour aristocracy has had some currency among non-Marxist historians, critical discussion of the labour aristocracy in the literature on popular politics has identified this as primarily a category of Marxist historiography.[56] There are very significant differences of emphasis in the works of the historians discussed here in the weighting they would give to 'economic determination', but all wish to foreground questions of class in the analysis of politics.

New approaches to political history

In the 1980s and 1990s, both intellectual and political developments have taken historians into new paths. These paths offer alternatives to empirical studies of political conflict and to narratives of class relations. They suggest the possibility of different historical methodologies and identify a far broader political culture within which such histories may be located. They indicate that different perspectives, from the margins as well as the centre of the United Kingdom and the British Empire, may shift our understanding of even the most familiar events. This section traces the development of these new approaches and their relevance to the essays which follow.

Towards a cultural history of nineteenth-century politics

Some historians have turned attention from questions of political interest and socio-economic structures to a focus on the language, ideas and discourses of politics. In the 1990s, the shift has come to be referred to as 'the linguistic turn'. It reflects the response of historians to the postmodernist and post-structuralist theories most closely associated in this context with

[55] Robert Q. Gray, *The Labour Aristocracy in Victorian Edinburgh* (Oxford: Clarendon Press, 1976), and his 'Bourgeois Hegemony in Victorian Britain', in Jon Bloomfield (ed.), *Class, Hegemony and Party* (London: Lawrence and Wishart, 1977), pp. 73–93; Geoffrey Crossick, *An Artisan Elite in Victorian Society: Kentish London 1840–1880* (London: Croom Helm, 1978). See also John Foster's 'Leninist' analysis in *Class Struggle and the Industrial Revolution* (London: Weidenfeld and Nicolson, 1974); Neville Kirk, *The Growth of Working-Class Reformism in Mid-Victorian England* (London: Croom Helm, 1985). For Gramsci's influence in British historical and cultural studies, see, among others, Geoff Eley, 'Reading Gramsci in English: Observations on the Reception of Antonio Gramsci in the English-Speaking World, 1957–1982', *European History Quarterly* 14 (1984), 441–78.

[56] For the former, particularly germane to this book, see F. B. Smith, *Making of the Second Reform Bill*, ch. 1, 'The Emergence of the Labour Aristocracy'. For the latter, see e.g. Eugenio F. Biagini and Alastair J. Reid, 'Currents of Radicalism, 1850–1914', in Biagini and Reid, *Currents of Radicalism*, pp. 3–4.

the work of Michel Foucault and Jacques Derrida and to postmodern ways of thinking about the world. It is not possible to examine such movements here closely, though there are a number of useful guides now available.[57] Postmodernism, broadly, has offered a critique of those assumptions considered essential to modernity, assumptions about the certainty of all forms of rational and empirical knowledge. For historians, this has meant discarding evolutionary versions of the past, whether liberal or Marxist, which took for granted progress towards the desirable or at least the modern and advanced capitalist societies of the West. And the post-structuralism of Derrida, Foucault and many others has suggested to historians that they too need to think harder about the ways in which historical evidence is understood, and histories written.

This term 'post-structuralism' has first to be related to the work of the early twentieth-century linguistic philosopher Ferdinand de Saussure, whose work was based on the rigorous analysis of the structures of language. He suggested that linguists should study languages in their 'synchronic' state, that is, at a single, given point of time. This was to be contrasted to the 'diachronic' study of a language through time. He also differentiated between language systems and individual speech. Within language systems, words were not simply easily identifiable names, corresponding to objects. They were rather 'signs', which comprised both the obvious sound and expression, and also the 'signifier', the concept of what was implied. To Saussure there was no absolute or necessary connection between sound and expression, and meaning. Meaning could depend on convention or custom or practice.

Only in the 1960s and 1970s did 'structuralism' come to achieve a commanding position in French literary theory. Post-structuralists built upon such work to challenge the idea of the autonomous and rational individual, the self who might seek and achieve objective knowledge. Jacques Derrida's idea of 'deconstruction' suggested that language and its codes shaped the 'real world', since there was no necessary relationship between a word and its signifier. Texts could have multiple meanings, meanings shaped by those 'other' and opposite meanings implicitly available.

[57] Paul Rabinow (ed.), *The Foucault Reader: An Introduction to Foucault's Thought* (Harmondsworth: Penguin, 1984); Michael Lane (ed.), *Structuralism: A Reader* (London: Cape, 1970); A. Easthope, *British Post-Structuralism Since 1968* (2nd edn, London: Routledge, 1991); Keith Jenkins, *Re-thinking History* (London: Routledge, 1991); Patricia O'Brien, 'Michel Foucault's History of Culture', in Lynn Hunt (ed.), *The New Cultural History* (Berkeley: University of California Press, 1989), pp. 25–46; Penelope Corfield, 'Introduction: Historians and Language', in Corfield (ed.), *Language, History and Class* (Oxford: Basil Blackwell, 1991), pp. 1–29; Joyce Appleby, Lynn Hunt and Margaret Jacob, *Telling the Truth About History* (New York: W. W. Norton, 1994), ch. 6.

Michel Foucault focused on the centrality of 'discourse', which as Jeffrey Weeks suggests may be defined as: 'at its simplest a linguistic unity or group of statements which constitutes and delimits a specific area of concern, governed by its own rules of formation with its own modes of distinguishing truth from falsity'.[58] These rules shaped not only the discourse to be found in written texts, but also the discursive practices of human behaviour and institutions. Foucault was concerned to trace the emergence of forms of knowledge, constituted by discourses, which became modern disciplines such as economics or philology. And he was also deeply engaged in the connections between knowledge and different forms of power, writing of the ways in which nineteenth-century institutions – hospitals, asylums, schools – categorised, named and controlled normality and deviance, health and disease, heterosexuality and homosexuality.

Foucault himself was not interested in the history of what is conventionally known as political behaviour. Yet an attraction of these approaches for political historians was that they permitted the questioning of certainties about individual and social identities, whether of the working-class man or middle-class woman. The individual was no longer a stable subject, easily located through recognisable criteria, for instance in terms of socio-economic position or status. Individual subject-positions were, rather, constantly shifting as individual men and women identified and responded to different collectivities, shaped through terms such as 'humanity', 'the people', 'women' or 'the nation'.

Our concern here is to consider the impact of post-structuralist thinking on the historiography of mid-Victorian politics. The work of Gareth Stedman Jones on the language and politics of Chartism was pioneering in its questioning of the social character of that movement. His article on 'The Language of Chartism', first published in 1982, called for a close examination of Chartist political vocabulary as having its own autonomy, shaping the strategies and resistances of the movement.[59] Stedman Jones, like others, could and did draw upon new work in the history of ideas, work which allowed a closer and more discriminating understanding of the political rhetoric of the period, though it was not itself post-structuralist.[60]

[58] Jeffrey Weeks, 'Foucault for Historians', *History Workshop Journal* 14 (1982), 111.

[59] Originally published in James Epstein and Dorothy Thompson (eds.), *The Chartist Experience: Studies in Working-Class Radicalism and Culture, 1830–1860* (Basingstoke: Macmillan, 1982), pp. 3–58; an expanded version appeared as 'Rethinking Chartism', in Stedman Jones, *Languages of Class: Studies in English Working-Class History 1832–1982* (Cambridge University Press, 1983), pp. 90–178.

[60] Major works included in this discussion are: Stefan Collini, Donald Winch and John Burrow, *That Noble Science of Politics: A Study in Nineteenth-Century Intellectual History*

Such work was to expand our knowledge of the 'liberal culture' of Victorian Britain. In the 1990s, a group of theoretically engaged historians took up the challenge of constructing a cultural history of British politics, with especial reference to the middle to later nineteenth century. Their work is essential to that broader understanding of the Reform Act of 1867 which is our aim. Patrick Joyce, James Vernon and others have drawn extensively upon new theoretical approaches with their roots in post-structuralism.[61] They have embarked upon a fundamental questioning of older narratives of evolution towards democracy and of class conflict, identifying rather the unifying discourses of 'people' and 'nation'.

In 1982 Gareth Stedman Jones suggested that any study of the ideology of Chartism had to pay attention to the language of the movement, and the form of that language. His argument was based on the continuities of radical politics, which in this reading continued to be dominated by a political analysis that perceived the oppression of the working classes as ultimately due to their exclusion from political representation. The inheritance of the 'free-born Englishman' and of the constitutionalism of the past had dominated radical politics in the years before 1832. The major target for the Chartist movement remained an idle and parasitic ruling class, which monopolised the power of the state and the ownership of land, and distorted economic development. The vocabulary of class conflict was here identified as far less significant than the argument for an end to the monopoly of land and power within the state. Chartism responded to the innovations of state power, and especially to the extensive Whig legislation of the 1830s, on local government, the Poor Law, education and factory reform. To Stedman Jones, Chartism did not simply reflect economic and social changes in a rapidly industrialising society. Its perspective and vocabulary provided an autonomous 'political language' through which such changes might be apprehended and which might itself shape working-class responses and interventions. These arguments were to be deeply controversial, but are also very relevant to the

(Cambridge University Press, 1983); John Burrow, *Whigs and Liberals: Continuity and Change in English Political Thought* (Oxford: Clarendon Press, 1988), and Burrow, *A Liberal Descent: Victorian Historians and the English Past* (Cambridge University Press, 1981); Stefan Collini, *Public Moralists: Political Thought and Intellectual Life in Britain, 1850–1930* (Oxford: Clarendon Press, 1991).

61 The relevant works discussed here are: Patrick Joyce, *Visions of the People: Industrial England and the Question of Class, 1848–1914* (Cambridge University Press, 1991), and Joyce, *Democratic Subjects: The Self and the Social in Nineteenth-Century England* (Cambridge University Press, 1994); James Vernon, *Politics and the People: A Study in English Political Culture c. 1815–1867* (Cambridge University Press, 1993), and Vernon (ed.), *Re-reading the Constitution: New Narratives in the Political History of England's Long Nineteenth Century* (Cambridge University Press, 1996).

complex relationship between Chartism, radicalism and liberalism by the 1860s.[62]

Equally relevant is the work of intellectual historians who from the 1980s began to offer a much fuller analysis of the 'political languages' of the intellectuals and opinion shapers of nineteenth-century Britain. John Burrow, Donald Winch and Stefan Collini cut across disciplinary boundaries to place nineteenth-century political thinking and the shaping of the discipline of political science itself in a much broader intellectual context. They have indicated that thinking about the 'political' cannot be separated from other emergent disciplines such as English literature, political economy, anthropology and the developing social sciences. Though these writers would not place themselves within the context of the 'linguistic turn', Stefan Collini suggested the significance of the recovery of 'shared linguistic and cultural resources' and of the ways in which such shared resources complemented the individual 'public voices' of men like John Stuart Mill through 'a fabric or texture of arguments, assumptions, values, ideas, associations, and so on'.[63]

Burrow, in particular, has written of the problems of conceiving nineteenth-century political ideas primarily in terms of a liberal individualism closely linked to political economy, in that 'correspondence' between ideas and socio-economic change referred to above in the discussion of Marxist approaches. He has argued that it makes much more sense to consider some of the continuities between political thinking in the eighteenth and the middle of the nineteenth century, in the continued importance of such concepts as 'civil society', 'progress' and 'civilisation'. The four-stage theory of history, shaped in the Enlightenment, which assumed that all societies would ultimately go through the same stages of development, defined in material terms, from the nomadic to the

[62] Responses and discussion in the 1980s included: John Foster, 'The Declassing of Language', *New Left Review* 150 (1985), 29–46; G. Claeys, 'Language, Class and Historical Consciousness in Nineteenth-Century Britain', *Economy and Society* 14 (1985), 239–63; James Epstein, 'Rethinking the Categories of Working-Class History', *Labour/Le Travail* 18 (1986), 195–208; R. Gray, 'Deconstructing the English Working Class', *Social History* 11 (1986), 363–74; J. E. Cronin, 'Language, Politics and the Critique of Social History', *Journal of Social History* 20 (1986–7), 177–84; Neville Kirk, 'In Defence of Class: A Critique of Recent Revisionist Writing on the Nineteenth-Century Working Class', *International Review of Social History* 32 (1987), 2–47; Dorothy Thompson, 'The Language of Class', *Bulletin of the Society for the Study of Labour History* 52 (1987), 54–6; Joan Wallach Scott, 'On Language, Gender and Working-Class History', in her *Gender and the Politics of History* (New York: Columbia University Press, 1988), pp. 53–67; John Belchem, 'Radical Language and Ideology in Early Nineteenth-Century England: The Challenge of the Platform', *Albion* 20 (1988), 247–59.

[63] Collini, *Public Moralists*, pp. 3–4; John Burrow has also written of political theories 'as vocabularies we inhabit, with their various claims, opportunities and constraints [rather] than as doctrines to which we subscribe': Burrow, *Whigs and Liberals*, p. 5.

pastoral, the agricultural to the commercial, remained a powerful way of conceptualising other, non-British cultures and peoples in the nineteenth century. Such a notion of 'progress' was also one in which institutions and governments were inextricably linked to the 'social' relations, the 'civil society' of any people.

He has also suggested that the concerns of eighteenth-century civic humanism, which drew upon the classical notion of the citizen as fully participant in the government and defence of the republic for the common good, were in many ways rewritten for the new arenas of the nineteenth century. The Victorian language of 'character' implied the power of individuals to shape their own lives, and to exercise 'self-restraint, perseverance, strenuous effort, courage in the face of adversity'.[64] Those attributes might be related to the world of work, or family, but might also be displayed in a more public context, in the voluntary associations, the periodicals and the political campaigns, as well as the political parties and the House of Commons. And in such public service it was not the pursuit of an individualistic self-interest, but a sense of duty and strenuous effort and an altruistic disregard of private interests which were most valued.

In *That Noble Science of Politics*, Burrow, Winch and Collini considered the relationship between the changing functions of history and Victorian politics. The commonplace assumption of a broadly progressive future might be seen to leave little space for direct political action. The lessons of history, however, did suggest some role for those able to reconcile the inherited institutions of the past with the direction of change. In *Essays on Reform* (1867), an important collection of essays produced by university liberals, Albert Rutson wrote of the first French revolution: 'the violent convulsion of 1789–93 was itself the result of prolonged neglect to accommodate institutions to an altered state of opinion and an altered distribution of social forces'.[65] These essays were deeply shaped by the authors' historical knowledge and references, references of immediate relevance, it seemed to the authors, to the situation of 1867. What is also relevant is the way in which dominant figures within an academic history that celebrated the unique emergence of free English institutions had by the 1860s acquired a strongly Germanist and Anglo-Saxon outlook. William Stubbs, E. A. Freeman and J. A. Froude were all in these years to take their place within the universities. For instance, when Stubbs, appointed to the Regius Chair of History at Oxford in 1866, gave his first series of lectures there in 1867, he spoke of the German origin of English institutions:

[64] Collini, *Public Moralists*, p. 100.
[65] Collini, Winch and Burrow, *That Noble Science of Politics*, p. 191.

OLSON LIBRARY
NORTHERN MICHIGAN UNIVERSITY
MARQUETTE, MICHIGAN 49855

> The blood that is in our veins comes from German ancestors. Our language, diversified as it is, is at the bottom a German language; our institutions have grown into what they are from the common basis of the institutions of Germany.[66]

At the same time there were alternative possibilities to such an English historicism, opening up through the excitements offered by 'the comparative method', whether in history, law, philology or, increasingly, such new fields as 'anthropology' or 'sociology'.[67] Such a method was inspired notably by the work of a figure such as Sir Henry Maine, author of *Ancient Law* (1861), whose experiences in India, and study of early Indian and Teutonic legal codes and comparative approach, allowed him to formulate a new definition of the very concept 'civilisation', which he understood to describe the common stock of 'Aryan' or 'Indo-European institutions, including those of law, property and the family. These contexts, though apparently distant from the political conflicts of the 1860s, provided a series of shared reference points for all members of the political classes who read or contributed to the major periodicals of the day. Such approaches were among the 'cultural resources' of the opinion makers, though their individual political loyalties could differ widely.

In the 1990s Patrick Joyce, James Vernon and a number of other scholars have addressed the 'political languages' of Britain in the middle to late nineteenth century, and have suggested a creative rethinking of the familiar landmarks, and narratives, of the period. Both Joyce and Vernon have suggested the need to interpret a political culture far broader than that of formal local and national institutions. They have used the customs of the factory, the language of the ballad and the music hall, the growth of dialect literature and the school history textbook.

Patrick Joyce's study *Visions of the People* explored, in particular, the language not of class but of populism. The concept of 'the people' was one which helped to draw together the older vocabulary of popular radicalism with the language of liberalism. It had a universalistic and unifying appeal, and it could be linked with an appropriation of the idea of progress, identified with the advance of democratic politics. Class might be transcended in the interest of unity and progress. Even within the world of work, of employers and trade unions, relationships could be understood in terms of moral and religious obligations as well as through those of the market-place. The older notion of the trade still helped to shape the relations of the factory. The cotton spinners of Ashton-under-Lyne were to describe their mission in the 1850s as 'not

[66] William Stubbs, *Lectures on Early English History*, ed. Arthur Hassall (London, 1906), pp. 3–4.
[67] Collini, Winch and Burrow, *That Noble Science of Politics*, p. 209.

to live for ourselves alone, but to make mankind happy and comfortable'.[68] The everyday lives of communities and workplaces were infused by customary practices and local loyalties, interwoven with a sense of a historic past, sometimes an idealised notion of a 'golden age'. A deeply entrenched Protestantism had its own canon of texts, which might still include John Bunyan's *Pilgrim's Progress* and Foxe's *Book of Martyrs*. School history textbooks in place even before 1870 might reinforce a popular version of English history, in which the revolution of 1688 foreshadowed the steady history of eighteenth- and nineteenth-century progress.[69]

Such work has challenged past and present evolutionary versions of nineteenth-century British politics. James Vernon has suggested that the growth of the more formal political sphere and institutions such as political parties had the effect by 1867 of making English politics less rather than more democratic, privileging formal political communications and limiting oral and visual forms of expression. To Joyce and Vernon it is the narrative of the English [*sic*] constitution, which remains at the centre of this political culture:

> If we imagine the discourse of popular constitutionalism as the master-narrative of nineteenth-century English politics, we are able to examine not only its different appropriations by competing political groups seeking to inform the constitution with their own interpretation of the nation's past and its future destiny, but the shared tropes and forms of these competing narratives. Central to this struggle to interpret the constitution were the competing definitions of the category of the virtuous people, and their role in the battle to include or exclude various groups from the political nation.[70]

Unlike Stedman Jones, Joyce and Vernon do pay specific attention to the 'tropes and forms' of these political languages, and in particular to the conventions of melodrama. The simple tale of the lost utopia or 'golden age' and its restoration, in a world whose moral purpose was to be restored, could appeal to the imaginations even of those excluded from this nation, like women, or the dependent.[71]

Yet the meanings of the constitution were shifting, especially in the agitation leading up to the Second Reform Act. In tracing such shifts, Joyce noted the ways in which the narrative of the constitution could be fused with that of moral improvement and progress. Such a version of constitutionalism could span the divisions between working men's movements,

[68] 'To the Self-Acting Minders of the Hurst District', Cassidy MSS, Tameside Public Library, Stalybridge, cited in Joyce, *Visions of the People*, p. 109.

[69] Joyce, *Visions of the People*, p. 190.

[70] Vernon, *Politics and the People*, p. 328.

[71] Joyce, *Democratic Subjects*, pp. 192–204.

advanced radical and liberal politics, in bringing new power to the respectable, and improving, working man. Joyce suggests that, in his powerful speeches in Manchester and Glasgow in 1866, John Bright appealed not to a class, but to the nation: 'Let us try the nation.' He represented the reform agitation as one which might restore to the people their vanished Eden of the past.[72]

The strength of such approaches to nineteenth-century British political history lies in the way in which they enable us to understand the constant remaking of identities through rhetorics of belonging and exclusion, through local cultures and constitutional narratives. They also offer us ways of exploring the complexities of individual political subjectivities.

Eugenio Biagini's massive study of popular liberalism between 1860 and 1880, richly detailed though less theoretically ambitious, takes as its starting point 'the language of popular liberalism'.[73] Biagini also comes to emphasise the continuities between Chartism and popular liberalism and the 'community' aspects of the latter. He points to the similarities between the ceremonial rituals of Chartism on the one hand and Reform League demonstrations throughout the country in 1866–7.[74] He suggested that nineteenth-century radicals of the 1860s and 1870s before and after 1867 still drew on a language not dissimilar from that of the seventeenth-century Levellers. Even in the campaigns of the early 1870s, 'as in 1864–7, the appeal to the "ancient constitution" singled out the core of the workers' conception of democracy: they wanted the franchise for all "free-born" Englishmen, rather than for all Englishmen'.[75] The 'manhood' entitled to the franchise was the adult and socially useful man, not the pauper, the criminal or the lunatic.

Such approaches have pioneered new views of radical and liberal politics in nineteenth-century Britain, though mainly with reference to England. They remain extremely controversial. There have been regular and continuing debates in this area in the journal *Social History* and elsewhere.[76] Yet at the same time, Joyce, Vernon and others have identified the limits of their work. Their interpretations have uniformly stressed the masculinity of definitions of citizenship in the 1860s. Though women could play a part in the informal politics of the crowd, in the rituals of the hustings and in the processions in which they had a ceremonial role,

[72] *Ibid.*, p. 200. [73] Biagini, *Liberty, Retrenchment and Reform*. [74] *Ibid.*, pp. 261–3.
[75] *Ibid.*, p. 286.
[76] The debates around the 'linguistic turn' and postmodernism in social and political history can be pursued through Keith Jenkins (ed.), *The Postmodern History Reader* (London and New York: Routledge, 1997), esp. pt IV, which reprints in part or in full many of the relevant articles from *Social History*, *Past & Present* and *History and Theory*.

wherever politics took a more formal shape such modes of public life were masculinised. The gendering of political life is, however, rarely placed at the centre of historical concerns.

Moreover, though much interest has been shown in the shaping of identities rooted in narratives of the nation's past, in unifying concepts of 'community', 'region' and assumptions of a shared 'progress', relatively little attention has been given to those who were implicitly or directly excluded by such terms. Histories of the continuities between radicalism and popular liberalism, and of the making of Victorian liberal culture, have been written without reference to a broader canvas familiar to nineteenth-century men and women. The works described above have focused primarily on England without reference to other constituent parts of the United Kingdom and their cultural differences. In particular, the significance of the relations between Britain and Ireland, and the presence of growing Irish communities in Britain, for the making of British political identities remains to be explored. So too does the presence of other marginal communities, like the Jews. And the 1850s and 1860s saw major changes in the relations between the United Kingdom and different parts of the British Empire: Jamaica, Canada, Australia, India. The new confidence in the British 'nation' expressed throughout the reform agitation was based on political identities shaped partly through the making of those relationships, partly through the power of new languages, of unity and of differentiation, of nation, race and civilisation.

Women, gender and the history of politics

> In my young days it was considered rude to talk politics to the ladies. To introduce [the topic] at a dinner party was a hint for us to retire and leave the gentlemen to such conversation and their bottle. But the excitement that prevailed all over the country at the prospect of the Reform Bill of 1832 broke down these distinctions, while the new, and, as it seemed to us, splendid idea of 'a hustings at the Cross of Edinburgh' drove its inhabitants, both male and female, half frantic with delight.[77]

Margaret Mylne, writing from the vantage point of 1870, suggests to us some of the tensions which existed for women, between their formal exclusion from a political world assumed to be masculine, and the many

[77] Margaret Mylne, *Woman and Her Social Position: An Article Reprinted from the Westminster Review, No. LXVIII, 1841* (London: C. Green and Son, 1872), pp. iii–iv, quoted in Helen Blackburn, *Women's Suffrage: A Record of the Women's Suffrage Movement in the British Isles, with Biographical Sketches of Miss Becker* (London and Oxford, 1902), p. 14.

possibilities for political awareness and informal involvement. In our focus on the Reform Act of 1867 we hope to explore and historicise such tensions within a political history from which women have been almost entirely absent, and within which the gendering of politics has received very little attention. Much writing on women's history in Britain and North America since the 1970s has focused upon the language of 'separate spheres', of the two worlds of women and of men, separating the active and public role of men from the domestically oriented lives of women. The vocabulary of 'separate spheres' pervaded nineteenth-century prescriptive literature addressed to women. Its strength was apparent to those who challenged it. Bessie Rayner Parkes, writing in 1855, asked:

> the question which the age demands
> 'What is a woman's right and fitting sphere?'[78]

As a way of charting the limitations and oppressiveness of women's lives, this contrast between the spheres of women and of men, between public and private worlds, had many attractions to women's historians. It was a formulation which appeared to be a particular characteristic of Western capitalist societies, from the seventeenth century onwards; women seemed invisible in the representations of the political economies and modernising states of the nineteenth-century West. Women's historians, from the 1970s onwards, traced the history of this exclusion, of confinement and oppression for women. They began the recovery and positive revaluing of the history of women's private worlds, whether those of the letter-writing circles of nineteenth-century New England, or the family-oriented lives of the women of the British upper middle classes. 'Women's culture' could be linked to the study of the symbolic forms and representations found in the new cultural history.[79]

The political theorist Carole Pateman suggested, in an early essay in 1983, that the dichotomy between public and private worlds was central to the feminist struggle, 'ultimately what the feminist movement is about'.[80] And many historians of feminism have equally found that dichotomy important to their analysis of the languages and practices of nineteenth-

[78] Bessie Rayner Parkes, *Summer Sketches and Other Poems* (1855), repr. in *Poems* (London, 1855), pp. 164–5.

[79] See, for instance, Nancy Cott, *The Bonds of Womanhood: Woman's Sphere in New England, 1780–1835* (New Haven: Yale University Press, 1977); Pat Jalland, *Women, Marriage and Politics 1860–1914* (Oxford University Press, 1986); Cécile Dauphin et al., 'Women's Culture and Women's Power: Issues in French Women's History', in Karen Offen, Ruth Roach Pierson and Jane Rendall (eds.), *Writing Women's History: International Perspectives* (Bloomington: Indiana University Press, 1991), pp. 107–34.

[80] Carole Pateman, 'Feminist Critiques of the Public/Private Dichotomy', in Pateman, *The Disorder of Women: Democracy, Feminism and Political Theory* (Cambridge: Polity Press,

century feminists. They have identified a contrast between women who put their case on the basis of the 'different' qualities of women and men, rooted in women's orientation to private life, and those who claimed 'equality' with men, in the language of natural rights and individualism.[81] Histories of feminism have benefited from a greater understanding of women's relationships in circles of friendship, domesticity and philanthropy, and have shown how that could provide one route towards the staking of claims for an extended role in public life, bringing women's unique attributes and qualities into a wider arena. From the 1820s women campaigners in the anti-slavery movement and in the Anti-Corn Law League used the language of 'woman's mission'.[82] Others took their ground on the assertion of the 'natural rights' of women to participate in the public world on equal terms, as Harriet Taylor Mill was to do.[83]

The strength of this pattern of dichotomous thinking within women's history has in many ways been strengthened by engagement with definitions of the 'public sphere' introduced by Jürgen Habermas. In his major work, *The Structural Transformation of the Public Sphere*, Habermas distinguished the bourgeois public sphere both from the institutions of the state and from those of the market-place. He found that public sphere in the political associations and voluntary societies, in the periodicals and the press, and in the formation of a public opinion beyond the state, which emerged in western Europe, and especially Britain, from the eighteenth century onwards.[84] One response to this came from Joan Landes, writing on the French revolution. She argued that the creation of the bourgeois public sphere in the new democratic republic was from its inception intrinsically masculinist.[85] Alternatively, in work on the

1989), p. 119. The essay was first published in S. I. Benn and G. G. Gaus (eds.), *Public and Private in Social Life* (London: Croom Helm, 1983), pp. 281–306.

81 Karen Offen, 'Defining Feminism: A Comparative Historical Approach', *Signs* 14 (1988), 119–57, and subsequent debate in *Signs* 15 (1989), 196–209; Jane Rendall (ed.), *Equal or Different: Women's Politics 1800–1914* (Oxford: Basil Blackwell, 1987).

82 F. K. Prochaska, *Women and Philanthropy in Nineteenth-Century England* (Oxford: Clarendon Press, 1980), 'Introduction'; Alex Tyrrell, '"Woman's Mission" and Pressure Group Politics in Britain, 1825–1860', *Bulletin of the John Rylands Library* 63 (1980), 194–230.

83 Harriet Taylor Mill, 'Enfranchisement of Women', *Westminster Review* 55 (July 1851), 289–311.

84 Jürgen Habermas, *The Structural Transformation of the Public Sphere: An Inquiry into a Category of Bourgeois Society*, trans. Thomas Burger with Frederick Lawrence and intro. Thomas McCarthy (1962 in German; Cambridge, Mass.: MIT Press, 1989). For a variety of responses, see Craig Calhoun (ed.), *Habermas and the Public Sphere* (Cambridge, Mass.: MIT Press, 1992).

85 Joan Landes, *Women and the Public Sphere in the Age of the French Revolution* (Ithaca, N.Y.: Cornell University Press, 1988). Feminist theorists and historians have also criticised Habermas on a number of counts. See the essays in Joanna Meehan (ed.), *Feminists Read Habermas: Gendering the Subject of Discourse* (New York and London: Routledge, 1995).

eighteenth-century Enlightenment, and on the politics of nineteenth-century US cities, Margaret Jacob and Mary Ryan have both argued that such a public sphere permitted women a small but increasing share in participating in and shaping public opinion, whether in the enlightened masonic lodge, or in the ceremonial parade characteristic of city politics.[86]

Leonore Davidoff and Catherine Hall addressed these themes in *Family Fortunes* (1987).[87] In this work they traced the interaction of class and gender, in the shaping of the 'ideologies, institutions and practices' of the English middle classes from 1780 to 1850. They placed the shaping of gender differences, of historically specific forms of masculinity and femininity, at the heart of the processes of class formation. The language of separate spheres, embedded in nineteenth-century evangelicalism, was a powerful ideological construction through which the middle classes understood and shaped class and gender difference. It was posed in opposition to the gender practices of a still politically dominant aristocracy and gentry. It shaped a specific form of masculinity as well as prescribing the sphere of women.

Yet at the same time Davidoff and Hall also suggested that such an ideology and rhetoric should not blind us to the interpenetration of public and private worlds, through the centrality of the family and the sexual division of labour to capitalist enterprise. Using the ideas of Habermas, they also traced the formation of the sphere of public opinion in early nineteenth-century English provincial life, illustrating both the scope of men's voluntary activity, and the varying and inconsistent ways in which a minority of women might participate, whether, for instance, in attending public lectures, as those of the Birmingham Philosophical Institution, or occasionally in some local public office as an overseer or surveyor of highways. They might equally, however, be banned from such activities or their attendance might become a source of local conflict. *Family Fortunes* placed gender relations at the heart of social and political change, and investigated the construction of masculinity as well as femininity.[88] The attention given to the language of separate spheres attracted considerable controversy, in comments which did not always acknowledge the extent to which the authors had traced the interpenetration of men's and women's worlds.

In the North American context, historians were already questioning

[86] Mary Ryan, *Women in Public: Between Banners and Ballots 1825–1880* (Baltimore and London: Johns Hopkins University Press, 1990); Margaret Jacob, 'The Mental Landscape of the Public Sphere: A European Perspective', *Eighteenth-Century Studies* 28 (1994), 95–113.

[87] Leonore Davidoff and Catherine Hall, *Family Fortunes: Men and Women of the English Middle Class 1780–1850* (London: Hutchinson, 1987).

[88] *Ibid.*, ch. 10, '"Improving Times": Men, Women and the Public Sphere'.

the usefulness of this framework, suggesting that 'separate spheres' needed to be recognised as a metaphorical device, a powerful trope, by which women and men made sense of their experience and helped to structure it. Such a generalising term about 'women' rested on a class-specific language. In assuming a unity of interests based on gender differences, it ignored alternative loyalties and identities, which could be those of religious denominations, class or ethnicity.[89]

Joyce Thomas and Amanda Vickery questioned what they saw as a 'grand narrative' of gender relations in Britain which identified a particular and harsher version of the public/private dichotomy with modernisation and the growth of capitalism. Examining the arguments of *Family Fortunes* in more detail, Vickery suggested that the changing structure of gender relations within the gentry and their relationship to the middling classes needed to be addressed.[90] And Linda Colley, in examining women's involvement in patriotic activities during the Napoleonic Wars, suggested that a renewed emphasis on separate spheres could potentially reflect an increasing rather than diminishing participation by women in public life.[91]

The new approaches encouraged by post-structuralism both encouraged the study of gender, and cast doubt on the usefulness of dichotomous forms of explanation. The influential work of Joan Scott on gender as an analytic category called for the disruption of fixed oppositions, such as those between public and private worlds, and for analysis of the constantly changing nature of such rhetoric, always historically specific. Scott pointed also to the need to ask some very fundamental questions about the gendered nature of historical practice: 'How does gender give meaning to the organisation and perception of historical knowledge?'[92] In

89 Linda Kerber, 'Separate Spheres, Female Worlds, Woman's Place: The Rhetoric of Women's History', *Journal of American History* 75 (1988), 9–39; Nancy Hewitt, *Women's Activism and Social Change: Rochester, New York 1822–1872* (Ithaca, N.Y., and London: Cornell University Press, 1984); and Hewitt, 'Beyond the Search for Sisterhood: American Women's History in the 1980s', *Social History* 10 (1985), 299–321.

90 Joyce Thomas, 'Women and Capitalism: Oppression or Emancipation? A Review Article', *Comparative Studies in Society and History* 30 (1988), 534–49; Amanda Vickery, 'Historiographical Review: Golden Age to Separate Spheres? A Review of the Categories and Chronology of English Women's History', *Historical Journal* 36 (1993), 383–414. See also Jane Lewis, 'Separate Spheres: Threat or Promise?', *Journal of British Studies* 30 (1991), 105–15. A recent and balanced discussion can be found in Hannah Barker and Elaine Chalus, 'Introduction', in Barker and Chalus (eds.), *Gender in Eighteenth-Century England: Roles, Representations and Responsibilities* (London: Addison-Wesley Longman, 1997), pp. 1–28.

91 Linda Colley, *Britons: Forging the Nation 1707–1837* (New Haven: Yale University Press, 1992), p. 281.

92 Scott, 'Gender: A Useful Category of Historical Analysis', in Scott, *Gender and the Politics of History*, p. 31.

much historical writing, gender, or 'the social creation of ideas about women and men', has appeared to be relevant primarily to areas involving relations between the sexes, or women alone. As she points out, gender has seemed irrelevant to historians working on the history of war, diplomacy or high politics. Scott, seeking to redress this perpetuation of 'separate spheres' within the discipline, suggests that refusing such an opposition may in fact help us to understand the connections between gender and power relations. If we assume that gender differences are not fixed or essential, but constantly changing, then the different ways in which relationships of power may be conceived through gender become more visible. In this book one of our major concerns in understanding the complexities of the Reform Act of 1867 lies with the recovery of a political history – however different – for women, and with the essentially gendered nature of politics in nineteenth-century Britain.

Challenges to the opposition of public and private worlds have been further mounted through understanding how many different meanings these terms may bear. So the difference between what is public and what is private may refer to the contrast between the state and the market, or to that between the political community more broadly conceived and the world of private interest or 'civil society'. Or it may contrast the private and intimate world of the family with that of different forms of sociability. Or, if the private is taken as starting point, as feminist theorists have done, the family may be contrasted with the 'public', a residual but gendered category incorporating the market, civil society and the state.[93]

Denise Riley has taken up the need for precision in the use of such oppositional categories. In her work, the ambiguity of the very category 'women' meant that it had always to be explained through its specific meaning in a particular historical moment and location. She has argued that, because the differences between women and men were increasingly imbued by the end of the eighteenth century with the authority of Nature, legitimised by biology, women increasingly were identified not with the family or the household alone, nor with the political community, but within 'a newly conceived space . . . the nineteenth-century "social" . . . a blurred ground between the old public and private'. Women might be placed within this social framework within their families as both the agents of a progressive philanthropy and its subjects, working-class women, the most intimate details of whose domestic lives might be explored. Riley suggests that a consequence of this lay in 'the dislocation of the political', and the defining of women as sociological, rather than

[93] Jeff Weintraub, 'The Theory and Politics of the Public/Private Distinction', in Weintraub and Krishan Kumar (eds.), *Public and Private in Theory and Practice* (University of Chicago Press, 1997), pp. 1–42.

political entities.[94] The concept of 'the social' as a framework for action was indeed relevant to many middle-class women, and men, who attended the meetings of the Social Science Association, an important meeting place for social reformers in Britain throughout the 1860s. But in the absence of a more detailed understanding of women's political history in this period, it seems premature to assume its dislocation; the interaction of the discourses of politics and 'the social' will be explored below (pp. 116–17, 167–8).

There are already some signs of new moves towards a political history for women, one that is less constrained by a gendered paradigm. For instance, Sarah Richardson has noted how women from landed backgrounds continued to act as borough patrons in Yorkshire into the 1830s.[95] More work has been done on the participation of women in the ceremonial events, and the riots, of nineteenth-century elections in both England and Ireland.[96] Yet there is considerable scope for more research. At the level of local government, too, there still remains much research to be done. Before the Municipal Corporations Act of 1835, single or widowed women might exercise the municipal franchise, depending on local custom, and apparently in some boroughs did so. After that act, which excluded them from the franchise in all named boroughs, they could still vote in unincorporated towns. We do not know how extensively they did so, or how far they participated in elections or stood for minor offices at the parish level.[97]

[94] Denise Riley, *'Am I That Name?': Feminism and the Category of Women in History* (Basingstoke: Macmillan, 1989), pp. 49–51.

[95] Sarah Richardson, 'The Role of Women in Electoral Politics in Yorkshire During the 1830s', *Northern History* 32 (1996), 133–51; see also Cat Euler, 'Moving Between Worlds: Gender, Politics, Class and Sexuality in the Diaries of Anne Lister of Shibden Hall, 1830–1840', DPhil. thesis, University of York (1995); Elaine Chalus, '"That Epidemical Madness": Women and Electoral Politics in the Late Eighteenth Century', in Barker and Chalus, *Gender in Eighteenth-Century England*, pp. 151–78; Karl von den Steinen, 'The Discovery of Women in Eighteenth-Century Political Life', in Barbara Kanner (ed.), *The Women of England from Anglo-Saxon Times to the Present* (London: Mansell, 1980), pp. 229–58.

[96] Vernon, *Politics and the People*, pp. 92, 116; K. Theodore Hoppen, *Elections, Politics and Society in Ireland 1832–1885* (Oxford: Clarendon Press, 1984), p. 406.

[97] For England and Wales, two important eighteenth-century cases determined that ratepaying women might stand for and elect to the post of sexton, and that women who were substantial householders might act as overseers of the poor, if there were no local customs to the contrary (see below, pp. 142–3). J. C. Hobhouse's act of 1831, enabling though not imposing a more democratic form of parish government, explicitly provided for female ratepayers to participate. Women were not explicitly either permitted or prevented from acting as Poor Law guardians after 1834, though it appears that none did before 1875. See Catherine S. Williams, 'The Public Law and Women's Rights: The Nineteenth-Century Experience', *Cambrian Law Review* 23 (1992), 80–103; Keith-Lucas, *English Local Government Franchise*, pp. 164–5.

Those historians who have attempted a cultural history of nineteenth-century politics, who have in many ways pioneered a broader and gendered approach to the subject, tend to see the move towards democracy, the rhetoric of radicalism and the constitutional narrative as shaping an entirely masculine political community.[98] Anna Clark has written of the extent to which the masculinity of citizenship was both rewritten and strengthened in the course of the nineteenth century.[99] Our discussion of the politics of the Reform Act suggests that gender cannot be taken as an absolutely defining category in relation to the complexities of citizenship. We have as yet a very limited understanding of the continuities and power of customary local practice. And we need to differentiate much more carefully between the ways in which women were potentially enabled at different moments to participate in political activity, broadly defined – just as we should remember that the male electorate after 1867 remained limited (to 33 per cent of adult males in 1871), inherited many archaic local characteristics, varied across the constituent parts of the United Kingdom, and was dependent for registration largely on the intermittent zeal of local party workers.[100]

A broader perspective on what constitutes political activity might enable a more effectively gendered understanding. For instance, literary scholars like Nancy Armstrong have pointed to the political role of the woman novelist and writer in nineteenth-century Britain.[101] One historian of feminism who has taken a perspective which encompasses both the political and the literary is Kathryn Gleadle, who has examined the commitment of radical Unitarians 'to employ literature as a social and political instrument'.[102] Such a theme is entirely relevant to the cultural history of politics in the 1860s. So, for instance, even before she became one of the first Irish suffragists, Anne Isabella Robertson had already made political interventions, both in the debate about women's employment, and in the politics of landownership and religion in Ireland, in publishing her novels *Myself and My Relatives* (1863) and *The Story of Nelly Dillon* (1866).[103]

98 Vernon, 'Notes Towards an Introduction', in Vernon, *Re-reading the Constitution*, pp. 17–18, and his *Politics and the People*, pp. 327–8 and *passim*; Joyce, *Democratic Subjects*, pp. 196–7.

99 Anna Clark, 'Gender, Class, and the Nation: Franchise Reform in England, 1832–1928', in Vernon, *Re-reading the Constitution*, pp. 230–53.

100 K. Theodore Hoppen, 'The Franchise and Electoral Politics in England and Ireland 1832–1885', *History* 70 (1985), 202–17.

101 Nancy Armstrong, *Desire and Domestic Fiction: A Political History of the Novel* (New York: Oxford University Press, 1987).

102 Kathryn Gleadle, *The Early Feminists: Radical Unitarians and the Emergence of the Women's Rights Movement, 1831–1851* (Basingstoke: Macmillan, 1995), p. 55.

103 Anne I. Robertson, *Myself and My Relatives: A Story of Home Life* (London, 1863); Anne Robertson, *The Story of Nelly Dillon*, 2 vols. (London, 1866).

It has been suggested above that the question of gender cannot be divorced from other identities, whether those of class, religion, ethnicity or nationality. Working men shaped their claim to enfranchisement around their sense of themselves as breadwinners, independent heads of household, excluding women as they excluded paupers. Advanced liberal men saw education rather than gender as the key criterion for enfranchisement. Class differences between women in mid-Victorian Britain have long been recognised, though not always, perhaps, with sufficient attention to their diversity, and how they are represented. The discussion of the women's suffrage movement later in this volume will incorporate married and single women whose backgrounds were those of the English aristocracy and gentry, the upper, professional and bohemian middle classes, clerical workers, small shopkeepers and tradeswomen, and, occasionally, the women of the labouring poor. Their political identities were shaped not only by gender but also by class. The progressive and philanthropic middle-class woman identified her role in relation to those working-class women who were the objects of her social mission. Class was not, however, the only category which related to gender; national identity, religious difference and ethnicity are all relevant here.

The essays in this volume seek to avoid oversimplified dichotomies, though they also assume that women, and constructions of femininity, are associated with subordination, weakness and forms of power and influence which are nowhere equal to those expected of men and masculinity. We attempt to locate women's politics and constructions of gender within the complicated relationships of gender and class, and gender, nationality and ethnicity. So the discussion of the women's suffrage movement below will range across the different parts of the United Kingdom, though it is inevitably dependent upon existing historiographies, and its narrative rests on a parliamentary and metropolitan story. It will include references to women from the Catholic community, in Ireland and in Great Britain, and from the small Jewish community. As far as is known, no black women appear in our narratives of events in Britain.

Nations, nationalisms, national identities

Nations, conventionally defined as 'a large number of people of mainly common descent, language, history etc., usually inhabiting territory bounded by defined limits and forming a society under one government',[104] have recently returned to the centre of British historical

[104] *Concise Oxford Dictionary.*

analysis. For the great nineteenth-century historians, for Lord Macaulay and William Stubbs, the nation was the central object of study, and defining the particularity of English nationhood, with its unwritten constitution at its heart, was central to their task.[105] For Victorian historians the nation and its institutions were seen as the collective subject of English history, even though by the 1860s and 1870s the 'comparative method' was inspiring new approaches. The Whig tradition with its focus on progress and liberty encapsulated the ethnocentrism of a particular national approach to history. For many historians the link between history and the nation was self-evident: the point of history, as Bagehot put it, was nation-building.[106]

After two world wars, however, such a focus seemed less convincing. In the 1960s class displaced nation from the centre of historical concerns. The social history that was so influential in both Britain and the United States was more concerned with class relations than with national belonging. It took the decline of Marxism, the end of the Cold War, the rise of new nations and nationalisms both in eastern and central Europe, and elsewhere, combined with the contradictory focus on the global and the supra-national, to concentrate anew the minds of social theorists and historians on the phenomenon of the nation. While nations were once thought of as eternal and universal, the critical writing of the 1980s and 1990s has focused on their historically specific, modern, and created or imagined characteristics.[107] The turn from social to cultural preoccupations has been as marked in this field as in others. Questions about the meaning of the nation, and of national identity and consciousness, have come to the fore, while political and economic questions have received less attention.

In 1983 Ernest Gellner's influential study *Nations and Nationalism* argued that 'having a nation is not an inherent attribute of humanity, but it has now come to appear as such'. Gellner insisted on the historical specificity of nations as modern forms, linked nationalism to industrial development and argued that one state had come to mean one culture. In

[105] Robert Colls, 'Englishness and the Political Culture', in Colls and Philip Dodd (eds.), *Englishness: Politics and Culture 1880–1920* (London: Croom Helm, 1986), pp. 29–61; James Vernon, 'Narrating the Constitution: The Discourse of "the Real" and the Fantasies of Nineteenth-Century Constitutional Historians', in Vernon, *Re-reading the Constitution*, pp. 204–29.

[106] Cited in E. J. Hobsbawm, *Nations and Nationalism Since 1760: Programme, Myth, Reality* (Cambridge University Press, 1990), p. 1.

[107] Raphael Samuel argues in 'Epical History: The Idea of Nation' that the idea of the nation is as old as the oldest written histories, but Anderson, Hobsbawm and Gellner all argue for the specificity of the modern form of the nation. See Samuel, *Island Stories: Unravelling Britain* (London: Verso, 1998), pp. 3–20.

this context nationalism, defined as 'primarily a political principle, which holds that the political and the national unit should be congruent' and that ethnic boundaries should not cut across political ones, became a powerful movement.[108] Those who did not have a nation wanted one, for nations were seen as providing significant benefits, as part of the route to modernity.

In the same year Benedict Anderson's *Imagined Communities* noted how nations appeared to be natural.[109] This was a book which aimed to move beyond the idea of the nation as an anomaly, an idea which had been influential amongst Marxists who saw nations as declining before the inevitable spread of internationalism, and to analyse nationalisms as cultural artefacts of a particular kind. It was Anderson's emphasis on the cultural, his critique of narrow histories of nationalism which focused on states and definitions of citizenship, that was to be so important in encouraging new ways of thinking about nations and national identities. Nations, he argued, emerged in specific historical contexts from the late eighteenth century. They were imagined political communities, imagined as both inherently limited and sovereign. They were imagined in the sense that members never knew most of their fellow members yet had a sense of community with them; imagined as limited in that other nations lay beyond, yet sovereign in their forms of political rule; as communities in that there was a deep 'comradeship' or indeed 'fraternity' between members and that men would die for their nation. Anderson argues that nationalism is more akin to religion than to an ideology, drawing on established cultural roots and powerful notions of connection and belonging. As religion declined, it became possible 'to think the nation', to conceive new kinds of community bound in different ways, and to think in new temporalities, shifting from a sense of time which had no firm distinction between past, present and future to one measured by the clock and the calendar.

The image, therefore, of British newspaper readers all, simultaneously, reading their newspapers over breakfast, knowing that their fellow Britons are engaged in the same pursuit, provides a powerful symbol of this imagined community.[110] Capitalist development was inextricably linked to nation formation in Anderson's account, for print culture was central to the process of giving people new ways to think about themselves and relate to each other, in making new ideas accessible and popular. And national languages were vital. As Tom Nairn put it in his reflections on *The Break-Up of Britain*: 'The new middle-class intelligentsia of

[108] Ernest Gellner, *Nations and Nationalism* (Oxford: Basil Blackwell, 1983), pp. 6, 1.

[109] Benedict Anderson, *Imagined Communities: Reflections on the Origin and Spread of Nationalism* (London: Verso, 1983).

[110] *Ibid.*, pp. 31–40.

nationalism had to invite the masses into history; and the invitation-card had to be written in a language they understood.'[111]

Anderson's influence has been as much in the questions he raised as in the answers he sketched out. His provocative query as to patriotism – why it is that people are ready to die for the nation? – is one that he can answer only partially, for there is in his work no theory of subjectivity, no explanation of the ways in which individual men and women internalise particular beliefs. This is not a question which we can address here, though historians who work with psychoanalytic theories of subjectivity or Foucauldian notions of the ways in which subjects are formed are tackling these issues.[112] Anderson's 'imagined community' is both inviting and bounded. In his crucial insight: 'Seen as both a historical fatality and as a community imagined through language the nation presents itself as simultaneously open and closed.' One may be invited into the imagined community and every language is always open to new speakers, listeners and readers; yet such communities also have limits.[113] This emphasis on inclusion and exclusion, on those who belong and those who do not, is one to which we shall return frequently in this volume. His argument that racism has its origins in class and not national ideologies, and that nations were made possible in and through print languages rather than notions of biological difference and kinship, is unconvincing. The links between race and nation are explored below. Similarly his gender-blindness left open the question as to the different ways in which men and women imagined the nation.

European and Western historians have been actively engaged in developing work on nations and nationalisms, in contributing to the analysis of nations as politically and culturally constructed in particular historical conjunctures, usually linked to the Enlightenment and the French and American revolutions.[114] E. J. Hobsbawm and Terence Ranger's *The Invention of Tradition* (1983) attempted to deconstruct apparently archaic national symbols and locate their invention in particular historical

[111] Tom Nairn, *The Break-Up of Britain* (London: Verso, 1977), p. 340.

[112] There is now a considerable literature on the uses of psychoanalysis in history writing. For examples, see Sally Alexander, *Becoming a Woman and Other Essays in Nineteenth- and Twentieth-Century Feminist History* (London: Virago, 1994); Lyndal Roper, *Oedipus and the Devil: Witchcraft, Sexuality and Religion in Early Modern Europe* (London: Routledge, 1994); Graham Dawson, *Soldier Heroes: British Adventure, Empire and the Imagining of Masculinities* (London: Routledge, 1994).

[113] Benedict Anderson, *Imagined Communities*, p. 133.

[114] There is of course a body of work from the new nations of the 'Third World' on nations and nationalisms, some of which is discussed in the next section. See particularly Partha Chatterjee, *Nationalist Thought and the Colonial World* (Minneapolis: University of Minnesota Press, 1993), and Chatterjee, *The Nation and Its Fragments: Colonial and Postcolonial Histories* (Princeton University Press, 1993).

moments. Hobsbawm's *Nations and Nationalisms Since 1780: Programme, Myth, Reality* (1990) says much in its title, which compares the mythic characteristics of nations to their 'reality', a distinction that post-structuralists would not, of course, accept. Hobsbawm followed Gellner in defining nationalism as 'a principle which holds that the political and national unit should be congruent'. He assumed that nations are neither primary nor unchanging, that the nation 'is a social entity only insofar as it relates to a certain kind of modern territorial state, the "nation-state"',[115] with the citizen state of the French revolution as the dominant model; and that it is nationalisms that make nations and states rather than vice versa.

A few eighteenth- and nineteenth-century historians have begun to consider British history in the light of such work on the nation and national identity. Linda Colley's influential *Britons*, the only full-length study of a particular period of national history which concentrates on the making of the nation, focuses on unity: the making of Britain. She suggests that between 1707 and 1837 it was the experience of war which was crucial to the forging of a new nation, uniting English, Scots, Welsh and Irish in the late eighteenth and early nineteenth centuries, welding them into a new entity, Britain, characterised by its commitment to Protestantism, its powerful anti-Catholicism and its long-term enmity to France.[116] Samuel argues that her 'originality is to seize on the Anglo-Scottish dialectic and use it to refurbish a unionist history'.[117] Yet Colley's work appears to many critics to overstress the degree of unity achieved even between Scotland, Wales and England, and to understress the nature of English hegemony. Furthermore her refusal to consider Ireland is a strange omission in a book concerned with the making of Britain. E. P. Thompson, meanwhile, focuses on the absence of class and critiques her account as a late contribution to Whig historiography, describing the making of a ruling class rather than a nation.[118] Colley sees the nation as redefined by the early 1830s: redefined by the inclusion of Catholics, through Catholic emancipation; by parliamentary reform, which resulted in very substantial changes and made the nation more uniformly British than it had previously been, and considerably more democratic than any other European country; and by the movement for anti-slavery, which offered a new source of self-respect to the nation in the aftermath of the loss of the American colonies.

115 Hobsbawm and Ranger (eds.), *The Invention of Tradition* (Cambridge University Press, 1983); Hobsbawm, *Nations and Nationalism*, pp. 9–10.

116 Colley, *Britons*. See also her 'Britishness and Otherness: An Argument', *Journal of British Studies* 31 (1992), 309–29.

117 Samuel, *Island Stories*, p. 28.

118 E. P. Thompson, 'The Making of a Ruling Class?', *Dissent* (Summer 1993), 377–82.

If Colley's account has no place for radicalism and is significant partly for its recognition of loyalty and conservative sentiment, Margot Finn comes to the question of nation from another perspective again. She is interested in the place of the nation in English radical politics in the middle of the nineteenth century, and is concerned to put debates about nation and internationalism back into the centre of the historical frame. Her aim is to examine 'the role played by radical, national, international and class identities in mediating liberal popular politics after Chartism'.[119] Her focus is on the intersection between class and nation, but the nation is England. While Colley's lens is on the monarchy as at the heart of the nation, Finn is concerned with that alternative tradition of patriotism, first located by Hugh Cunningham, which linked nation to radicalism. As Cunningham argued, patriotism could be articulated to left or right.[120]

Anderson's focus on national belonging necessarily raised questions for feminists as to the differentiated positions of men and women. Such questions had been discussed before; in 1978 Anna Davin wrote an influential essay on the connections between imperialism and motherhood.[121] In 1989 Nira Yuval-Davis and Floya Anthias edited *Woman–Nation–State*, a collection of essays which focused on the particularities of women's relation to nation in a number of different societies. In theorising that relation Yuval-Davis and Anthias identified the different ways in which women participate in ethnic and national processes and in state practices. They do so as mothers, as biological reproducers of the members of ethnic collectivities. They are central to the ideological reproduction of the collectivity, and in the transmission of its culture, just as they also reproduce the boundaries between ethnic/national groups. They may also become the signifiers of ethnic/national differences, as visual and metaphorical symbols, as Britannia, or as Hibernia. Finally, they may be participants in national struggles as nationalists, as citizens, as soldiers and as feminists.[122] This categorisation of the different sites of women's engagement in the nation and national movements helps to delineate the range of research, both sociological and historical, which needs to be done if we are to grasp the complexity of women's relations to nations. In Yuval-Davis's recent account of *Gender and Nation*, she argues

119 Margot C. Finn, *After Chartism: Class and Nation in English Radical Politics, 1848–1874* (Cambridge University Press, 1993), p. 7.

120 Hugh Cunningham, 'The Language of Patriotism', in Raphael Samuel (ed.), *Patriotism: The Making and Unmaking of British National Identity*, 3 vols. (London: Routledge, 1989), vol. I, pp. 57–89.

121 Anna Davin, 'Imperialism and Motherhood', *History Workshop Journal* 5 (1978), 9–65.

122 Nira Yuval-Davis and Floya Anthias (eds.), *Woman–Nation–State* (Basingstoke: Macmillan, 1989), p. 7.

that the construction of nationhood involves specific notions of masculinity and femininity and that nationalist projects are constituted in relation to particular gender orders.[123]

Feminist historians have now been working in this area for some years, though mainstream historians of nationalisms continue to ignore their findings.[124] Nancy Leys Stepan has shown how issues around reproduction were part of ethnic and national strategies in the work of constructing new nations from the heterogeneous populations of post-colonial Brazil, Mexico and Argentina in the 1920s and 1930s.[125] In quite another context Marilyn Lake has written on the particular forms of masculinity that underpinned the Australian nation from its inception: an argument which has provoked a lively controversy.[126] Australia, with its vibrant tradition of feminist historical work, has produced the first gendered account of a national history: making the claim that nation-building has always been done by both women and men.[127]

Another fruitful arena for feminist historians has been the exploration of the complex relation between feminism and other emancipatory movements. While in some instances feminisms have been able to achieve gains for women through their involvement with national organisations, at other times they have been compelled to put aside questions of women's rights in the name of the larger struggle. In some instances the 'woman question' has been vital to the founding of new nations, as, for example, in Egypt.[128] Similarly, gender and sexuality played a crucial part in the national liberation and modernisation struggles in Iran, as Joanna de Groot has shown.[129] Clearly there is no necessary connection between feminism and nationalism, and indeed nationalisms have often been anti-feminist. An understanding of the relation between feminism

123 Nira Yuval-Davis, *Gender and Nation* (London: Sage, 1997).

124 For collections of some of this work, see the special issues of the following journals: 'Nationalisms and National Identities', *Feminist Review* 44 (1993); 'Thinking Through Ethnicities', *Feminist Review* 45 (1993); 'Gender, Nationalisms, and National Identities', *Gender & History* 5 (1994); 'Links Across Difference: Gender, Ethnicity and Nationalism', *Women's Studies International Forum* 18 (1995); 'Feminism and Nationalism', *Journal of Women's History* 7 (1995); and see also Andrew Parker, Mary Russo, Doris Sommer and Patricia Yaeger (eds.), *Nationalisms and Sexualities* (London and New York: Routledge, 1992).

125 Nancy Leys Stepan, *'The Hour of Eugenics': Race, Gender and Nation in Latin America* (Ithaca, N.Y.: Cornell University Press, 1991).

126 Marilyn Lake, 'Mission Impossible: How Men Gave Birth to the Australian Nation – Nationalism, Gender and Other Seminal Acts', *Gender & History* 4 (1992), 305–22.

127 Patricia Grimshaw, Marilyn Lake, Ann McGrath and Marian Quartly, *Creating a Nation: 1788 to 1990* (Melbourne: McPhee Gribble, 1994).

128 Margot Badran, *Feminists, Islam and Nation: Gender and the Making of Modern Egypt* (Princeton University Press, 1993).

129 Joanna de Groot, 'The Dialectics of Gender: Women, Men and Political Discourses in Iran c. 1890–1930', *Gender & History* 5 (1993), 256–68.

and nationalism depends on the historically specific conjunctures of political discourses, movements and peoples.

If feminist work has opened up many new debates, so has the proliferation of nationalisms. As early as 1975, J. G. A. Pocock suggested a new kind of British history, which recognised the shifting boundaries of the subject, from archipelago to empire.[130] The turn to new national histories, in recognition of the new nationalisms of the Scots and Welsh as well as the continuing history of Irish nationalism, has necessitated a recognition of the different nations which make up the United Kingdom. A number of historians have attempted to recognise their related but separate histories. Hugh Kearney argues for a move away from national histories and a turn to a 'Britannic' framework, one which focuses on territory rather than a nation or a people. Kearney discusses Hechter's model of 'internal colonialism', suggesting that England established a colonial relation with other parts of the British Isles from which it alone benefited. Kearney himself prefers to read the 'Britannic melting pot' as a complex of interacting cultures and struggles for supremacy. In the nineteenth century, nationalist movements made some headway, particularly in Ireland and Wales, and Scotland enjoyed a significant degree of civil and cultural autonomy. English hegemony has never been assured, and a complex pattern of conflict as well as integration has characterised the history of the British Isles. So in the 1990s it appears that there can be no simple or single national history, no one way of writing the 'new British history' or the 'history of the four nations'.[131]

The student who looks for an account of the events of 1865–8 as a part of the history of the four nations which made up the United Kingdom will find little, although K. T. Hoppen's work indicates some possibilities.[132] The different histories and institutions of those nations did of course

[130] J. G. A. Pocock, 'British History: A Plea for a New Subject', *Journal of Modern History* 47 (1975), 601–21; see also Pocock, 'The Limits and Divisions of British History: In Search of the Unknown Subject', *American Historical Review* 87 (1982), 311–36. For a recent review of the issue, see David Cannadine, 'British History as a "New Subject": Politics, Perspectives and Prospects', in Alexander Grant and Keith Stringer (eds.), *Uniting the Kingdom? The Making of British History* (London and New York: Routledge, 1995), pp. 12–30.

[131] Hugh Kearney, *The British Isles: A History of Four Nations* (Cambridge University Press, 1995), p. 1; Michael Hechter, *Internal Colonialism: The Celtic Fringe in British National Development, 1536–1966* (London: Routledge and Kegan Paul, 1975); David McCrone, *Understanding Scotland: The Sociology of a Stateless Nation* (London and New York: Routledge, 1992); Eric Evans, 'Englishness and Britishness: National Identities, c. 1790–c. 1870', and Keith Robbins, 'An Imperial and Multinational Polity: The Scene from the Centre, 1832–1922', both in Grant and Stringer, *Uniting the Kingdom*, pp. 223–43 and 244–54, respectively; Keith Robbins, *Great Britain: Identities, Institutions and the Idea of Britishness* (Harlow: Longman, 1998).

[132] Hoppen, 'Franchise and Electoral Politics'.

markedly inflect the character of such movements and the timetables of degrees of enfranchisement for women and men. The situation of Ireland and of the Irish community in Britain intersected with the political debates on reform and their aftermath throughout the 1860s and 1870s and, of course, beyond. Religious loyalties and identities determined the networks of reforming campaigns like the women's suffrage movement. Narratives of the Protestant constitution might frame women's perceptions of Irish enfranchisement as well as men's. Loyalty to a secularist politics might equally lead male liberals and radicals, and working men, to a deep distrust of Irish Catholicism. But there are no comparative discussions of women's suffrage campaigns in the constituent parts of the United Kingdom, although such journals as the *Women's Suffrage Journal* and the *Englishwoman's Review* (in spite of its title) did cover Scottish, Welsh and Irish, as well as English, meetings and issues.

The rediscovery of the four nations in part connects to the rediscovery of ethnicity. Ethnicity signifies cultural difference, the ways in which boundaries are drawn between peoples, marking those who are included and excluded, using such lines as religion, history and language.[133] While ethnicity was to do with culture, race was concerned with biology, the 'natural' differences marked by colour above all. Ethnicity as a term was invented by social scientists in the United States in an attempt to insist on the social nature of divisions between peoples, a refusal of the notion of fixed and innate biological difference and a move away from the 'scientific' racial theory of the nineteenth century. Yet so powerful were the associations of skin colour with hierarchies of power that the terminology of race has continued to be used despite the disproval by scientists of any theories of innate difference. Both terms, ethnicity and race, are used to denote the boundaries between 'them' and 'us'. Different ethnicities are frequently racialised, as in the example of the Irish in nineteenth-century England.

The great nineteenth-century social theorists expected ethnicity to become unimportant as nations and classes marked the route to modernity. Different ethnicities were expected to assimilate to the national identity. Italians, Poles, Germans, Irish, Jews, even 'negroes', in the terminology of the early to middle years of the twentieth century, would all abandon their distinctive cultures and embrace Americanness.[134] The

133 For a classic account of ethnicity, see Frederick Barth, *Ethnic Groups and Boundaries: The Social Organization of Cultural Difference* (London: Allen and Unwin, 1969); for a useful introduction to questions of both ethnicity and race, see John Solomos and Les Back, *Racism and Society* (Basingstoke: Macmillan, 1996).

134 For ways into discussion of these issues, see M. Omi and H. Winant, *Racial Formation in the United States from the 1960s to the 1980s* (New York: Routledge, 1989); Werner Sollors, *Beyond Ethnicity: Consent and Descent in American Culture* (Oxford University Press, 1986).

model was one nation, one people, one culture. For the United Kingdom, one nation, one dominant people, might have been a model closer to the truth, with the English occupying that hegemonic position. Yet, far from disappearing, ethnicities have become ever more significant in the late twentieth century, emphasising the distinctive and the different as globalisation, with its world market for commodities, has in other respects threatened to homogenise. As ethnic conflicts have exploded across the globe, most notably in Europe, Asia and Africa, historians, cultural critics and social scientists have had to address these issues anew.

Neither ethnicity nor race have fixed or essential meanings. Both are ways of constructing differences between peoples, markers of power which have to be understood discursively. The insights of post-structuralism have unhinged any assumptions as to the necessary meanings of class or gender, and have pointed attention to the ways in which such discourses are utilised to construct difference. The discourses of race and ethnicity operate in a similar way, and our question has to be: 'What meanings are produced when these discourses are used?'

Religious belonging was one of the most significant markers of ethnicity, and indeed of race, in the four nations in the nineteenth century. Britain was a religious society in the sense that Christian ideas and language were pervasive, structuring notions of morality, providing a vocabulary for the self and a political code. Christianity was a dynamic force in the middle of the nineteenth century, with evangelicalism (in both its Anglican and nonconformist varieties) and Catholicism as its most vigorous offshoots. Protestantism provided a form of connection for the four kingdoms and, at the same time, a set of divisions, both internally and with Catholicism. The Anglican church was the established church in England, Wales and Ireland, despite the fact that Irish Catholics outnumbered Protestants by four to one. In Scotland the established church was Presbyterian. As John Wolffe argues,

> at the middle of the nineteenth-century religion was taking a central role in the development and articulation of national consciousness in the British Isles. This applies equally whether we are concerned with the assertion of overarching 'British' identity; with the awareness of the Scots, Welsh and Irish of their own distinctiveness; or with the attitude of the whole towards continental Europe and the rest of the world.[135]

The language of national identity was intimately linked with the language of religion. But, as Keith Robbins notes, the diversity of religious

[135] John Wolffe, *God and Greater Britain: Religion and National Life in Britain and Ireland 1843–1945* (London: Routledge, 1994), pp. 31, 121.

convictions and institutions across the four nations was the most marked form of diversity in nineteenth-century Britain.[136] Irish Catholicism and Scottish Presbyterianism were intimately linked with nationalist sentiments, yet a generic form of Protestantism could link Scottish Presbyterians, Welsh dissenters and English Anglicans. While by no means everyone attended a place of worship, religious idioms were pervasive. Official forms of religion vied with unofficial and popular, hymns spoke of nation and empire as well as particular religious beliefs, civic occasions were redolent of a generalised Protestantism.

But there was also a narrower English identity available with a very particular set of associations. Anglo-Saxons were Protestants: England was a Protestant country and the chain of connection between the nation, the monarchy, the constitution and the Protestant church was a very strong one. From the time of the Reformation, as Christopher Hill argues, 'Protestantism and patriotism were closely linked.'[137] The great Catholic powers, Spain and France, were the traditional enemies of England (not of course of Scotland or Ireland), and English nationhood was formed through such mythic stories as those of the Armada and Guy Fawkes. Anti-Catholicism was a powerful cement, binding the nation together and excluding Irish Catholics in particular in that process. While Protestants and even agnostics could stand united in their refusal of Catholicism as a reactionary faith, they were deeply divided on many other issues and these divisions were of central importance to nineteenth-century politics.

Ideas of religious toleration and of greater laxity in theology gained ground through the century, and Jews as well as nonconformists organised to remove the barriers which prevented their full participation in civic and political life. The movement for disestablishment of the Anglican church marked a significant challenge to prevailing ideas of the relation between church and state. Meanwhile the links between nonconformity and the Liberal party meant that dissenting men found easier access to the political mainstream. The distinction between nonconformist and Anglican, new dissenter and old, were critical ones for nineteenth-century men and women, marking different beliefs and patterns of worship. But all were united by their Protestant ancestry and their antipathy to Rome. Englishness, even Britishness, was not confined to Anglicans but could reach out to include Baptists, Methodists, Presbyterians, Quakers and Unitarians;

136 Robbins, *Great Britain*, p. 237.
137 Christopher Hill, 'The English Revolution and Patriotism', repr. in Samuel, *Patriotism*, vol. I, p. 159.

in what ways it could include Jews or Irish Catholics was a matter of debate.

If one incentive for new work on nations came from the revival of nationalisms and their associated ethnicities as a global phenomenon, another came from the questions about national identity which the European Community and the presence of Afro-Caribbean and South Asian migrants in Britain presented, questions which emerged in a distinctive racial way. What did it mean to be English? Was it possible to be black and British? Would British sovereignty survive the challenge of the European Union? Enoch Powell's terrifying predictions of the 'swamping' of the white race focused a new attention on the relation between race and nation. While most British historiography denied the significance of race in the making of the nation, Paul Gilroy's *There Ain't No Black in the Union Jack* put race at the centre of the British cultural frame.[138] At the same time 'Englishness' became an object of study. A collection of essays with that title, edited in 1986 by Robert Colls and Philip Dodd, drew on Edward Said's *Orientalism*. They argued that much of the power of the dominant notion of Englishness in the late nineteenth and twentieth centuries lay in its ability both to represent itself to others and to represent those others to themselves.[139]

The Falklands War of the early 1980s and the widespread enthusiasm for it brought up very uncomfortable questions for historians on the left. Anxieties about the absence of any significant protest inspired a History Workshop, and subsequent three-volume publication on patriotism. 'Our aim', wrote Raphael Samuel, 'was deconstructive, to bring patriotism within the province of rational explanation and historical enquiry.' Against the supposed unity of the nation they drew attention to diversity and the constant redrawing of national belonging; their desire was for a more pluralist vision of politics.[140] The intentions were admirable, and the three volumes a great resource with their collection of classic and new pieces. But as Samuel himself acknowledged, they had little success in analysing their own sentiments and notions of tradition, and the attention to the diversity of Scots, Welsh and Irish was very strictly limited.

Since the 1970s many efforts have been made to write 'minorities and outsiders', as they are sometimes called, into British history and to recognise the extent to which there have always been significant 'others' within. The place of black people in Britain, the relation between Jews and

[138] London: Hutchinson, 1987.
[139] Philip Dodd, 'Englishness and the National Culture', pp. 1–28, and Colls, 'Englishness and the Political Culture', pp. 29–61, both in their edited volume, *Englishness*.
[140] Samuel, *Patriotism*, vol. I, 'Preface', pp. x, xi.

Englishmen, the place of the Irish in England and Scotland as well as in Ireland have all been subjects of study.[141] In the debate organised by History Workshop on 'History, the Nation and the Schools', part of the public discussion of the place of history in the national curriculum, Paul Gilroy argued that it was vital to move away from a consideration of national history to one of nationalism, to think about the effects of racism in relation to nationalism and nationalist historiographies of both the left and the right. 'We cannot plausibly enthrone the idea of national history while simultaneously seeking to take it, and all it symbolizes, apart.' He emphasised the productiveness of other models, of transnational rather than national accounts, of work such as that of Peter Linebaugh and Marcus Rediker, and of course one might add of Gilroy himself, which has focused on an Atlantic perspective, the connections across and between, the movements of people and ideas rather than on single national histories.[142]

National histories purport to tell the story of one people. Yet that notion of homogeneity can no longer be innocent, since there never is or has been only one united people. In this book, we do not attempt to tell 'a national history' but rather to show how a nation was defined at a particular moment. Homogeneity was a fiction, but a powerful one, with real political effects. The inclusion of some meant the exclusion of others, in a series of interconnected histories. We refer to the history of the four nations of Britain, although we are aware that, reliant on secondary sources as much of this must be, our attempt is in many ways speculative. But it is also an essential part of our argument that issues of race and ethnicity are central to the defining of nations. For as Edward Said and others have argued, in constructing aliens, minorities, outsiders and 'others', the West was also always centrally constructing itself.

The postcolonial critics

If new ideas about race, ethnicity and nation have been one source of rethinking British historiography, another closely interrelated strand has

141 See for example, Peter Fryer, *Staying Power: The History of Black People in Britain* (London: Pluto, 1984); David Feldman, *Englishmen and Jews: Social Relations and Political Culture 1840–1914* (New Haven: Yale University Press, 1994); Mary J. Hickman, *Religion, Class and Identity: The State, the Catholic Church and the Education of the Irish in Britain* (Aldershot: Avebury, 1995).

142 Paul Gilroy, 'Nationalism, History and Ethnic Absolutism', *History Workshop Journal* 30 (1990), 114–19; Peter Linebaugh, *The London Hanged: Crime and Civil Society in the Eighteenth Century* (Harmondsworth: Penguin, 1991); Marcus Rediker, *Between the Devil and the Deep Blue Sea* (Cambridge University Press, 1988): Paul Gilroy, *The Black Atlantic: Modernity and Double Consciousness* (London: Verso, 1993).

been the work of the 'postcolonial critics'. 'Postcolonial' is a difficult and contentious term. While it is widely recognised that the colonial system which dominated the nineteenth and early twentieth centuries has been dismantled, it is quite clear that neo-colonialism, informal economic domination by, for instance, the USA, continues to flourish. Is it, therefore, misleading to use the term postcolonial? The ending of the great empires of western Europe, however, marks a very distinct moment in world history, and the term postcolonial can be used descriptively, to signify the aftermath of those world systems built upon European 'discoveries' from the late fifteenth and sixteenth centuries.[143] This is not to suggest that all societies that were colonised were colonised in the same ways, nor that postcolonial societies are postcolonial in the same ways, but that the term draws attention to the systems of colonialism and the relations that operated between coloniser and colonised.

The new field of postcolonial studies is often seen as developing from the work of Edward Said. But long before Said, as he would be the first to recognise, intellectuals and political activists from the colonised world were engaged in the critique of Western social theory from a 'Third World' perspective. Some of their ideas have been central to rethinking national and imperial histories in the late twentieth century. C. L. R. James, Trinidadian writer and critic, who lived his life between Britain, the Caribbean and the United States, wrote his history of the Haitian revolution, *The Black Jacobins*, in 1938. That book, seriously neglected by white historians until very recently, tells the story of the successful slave revolution which took place in San Domingo in the wake of the French revolution. James argues that metropolitan politics were intimately interconnected with colonial politics and vice versa; that the French revolution was in part caused by the demands of the financial bourgeoisie whose fortunes were made by Caribbean slavery; and that the San Domingan revolution was inspired by the politics of Paris. In his account cause and effect linked so-called metropolis and periphery, challenging the assumptions that historical causality always runs from the metropolis to the colony, and that metropolitan domestic politics were unrelated to those of the colonies.[144] Furthermore, he argued that the crossing of national boundaries was quite as significant as that which took place inside those boundaries. As a Caribbean intellectual himself, living across

[143] Peter Hulme, 'Including America', *Ariel* 26 (1995), 117–23; Stuart Hall, 'When Was "the Post-Colonial"?: Thinking at the Limit', in Iain Chambers and Lidia Curti (eds.), *The Post-Colonial Question: Common Skies, Divided Horizons* (London: Routledge, 1996), pp. 242–60.

[144] C. L. R. James, *The Black Jacobins: Toussaint l'Ouverture and the San Domingo Revolution* (2nd edn, New York: Vintage, 1963).

borders, he was part of what Paul Gilroy later characterised as 'the Black Atlantic' – the movement of black peoples across Africa, Europe and North America which shaped black consciousness in the nineteenth and twentieth centuries.

Frantz Fanon also focused attention on the relation between Europe and the 'Third World', colonisers and colonised. Fanon, a Martiniquan who thought he was French until he arrived in France and understood that he was black and 'other', trained as a psychiatrist in Paris and then worked in Algeria and Tunisia, treating both torturers and victims of the war of liberation between Algeria and France. His passionate engagement with anti-colonial politics and his theorisation of colonialism and its effects have been profoundly influential. His first concern was with the colonised and the means for emancipation from the psychic as well as social and political oppression that they had suffered.[145] But he insisted on the impact of colonialism on the colonisers as well as the colonised. 'Europe', he argued, 'is literally the creation of the Third World.' The end of colonialism meant that Europe must reimagine itself.[146] This recognition of the degree to which colonialism made new subjects, both the officials and missionaries who ruled the colonial order and the servants and labourers whom they ruled, has been critical to the attempts to write new histories of empire, which recognised that the colonial order was as central to the metropolis as to the colonies, if in different ways. Taking colonialism as integral to Western modernity constructs a very different set of histories from the familiar narratives of progress.

Fanon, as Said notes, was also the first major theorist of anti-imperialism who offered a critique of nationalism, and one which extended to a grasp of the gendered implications of those politics.[147] As Anne McClintock points out, while Gellner's definition of nationhood rests on the male recognition of identity, men are of the same nation if and only if they recognise each other as being from the same nation, Fanon was able to move beyond the assumption that politics is about men to the intersection of gender and nationalism.[148] Sexuality was a formative element of anti-colonialism and nationalism, and shaped the struggles for liberation, as, for example, in the use made of the veil by militant women as a cover for their activities.

Since the mid-1980s postcolonial studies have flourished as a new

[145] Frantz Fanon, *Black Skin, White Masks* (London: Pluto, 1986), p. 10.

[146] Frantz Fanon, *The Wretched of the Earth* (Harmondsworth: Penguin, 1967), p. 81.

[147] Edward W. Said, *Culture and Imperialism* (London: Chatto and Windus, 1993), p. 330; Fanon, *Wretched of the Earth*, ch. 3, 'The Pitfalls of National Consciousness'.

[148] Anne McClintock, *Imperial Leather: Race, Gender and Sexuality in the Colonial Context* (London: Routledge, 1995), p. 353.

field of academic teaching and research. Said's *Orientalism* marked the cultural turn in relation to imperialism, for his critical argument was that 'European culture was able to manage – and even produce – the Orient politically, sociologically, militarily, ideologically, scientifically and imaginatively during the post-Enlightenment period.'[149] That management was a discursive production, through the discourse of Orientalism which made 'the Orient' into an object of knowledge and an object of power. Said argued that these forms of cultural power, organised through academic disciplines such as history, anthropology and philology, were as significant in the maintenance of colonial rule as the political, economic and military policies which had more frequently been attended to:

> These ideas explained the behaviour of Orientals; they supplied Orientals with a mentality, a genealogy, an atmosphere; most important, they allowed Europeans to deal with and even to see Orientals as a phenomenon possessing regular characteristics.

Said draws on Foucault's notion of discourse to examine the western European constructions of those who lived in the Middle East, and the ways in which Orientalist discourse became, in Foucault's terminology, a regime of truth. He linked this with Gramsci's notion of hegemony, or the winning of consent by the rulers for their rule. Truth resided in the power of writers and academics to tell tales of the Orient which claimed successfully to represent it. Those representations depended on a set of binary oppositions between Europeans and Orientals, which always worked to the detriment of the latter.[150] Yet the othering of Orientals also rested on fantasised notions of their sexuality which made them objects of Western desire. The work of Orientalist discourse, whether in museums, colonial offices, the academy or popular fiction, was to fix the binaries between West and East. This could only be done by constant discursive work, fixing and refixing the boundaries between Western rationality and Oriental irrationality, Western industry and Oriental laziness, Western self-control and the Oriental lack of it.

Said turned attention decisively to the cultural work of colonialism, of representing those who are ruled and thus legitimating that rule. At the same time he insisted, as Fanon had done, that Europeans were at one and the same time constituting themselves through difference. But as many have since noted, these attempts to fix the binaries are subject to constant instability. The unity of the West is as unattainable as the unity

[149] Edward W. Said, *Orientalism: Western Concepts of the Orient* (Harmondsworth: Penguin, 1985), p. 3. [150] *Ibid.*, pp. 41–2.

of the nation. Both are fictions, discursive constructions which attempt to suture the many differences and inequalities which coexist. As Homi Bhabha argues, national cultures are neither unified nor unitary, and the problem of the relation between outside and inside, the excluded and the included, is always to do with the process of hybridity, the ways in which new people are incorporated, new sites of meaning created.[151]

These arguments took place at the same time that, as we have seen above, feminists such as Joan Scott, again heavily influenced by Foucault, were arguing that gender was constructed through difference. In a related but different context some black feminist critics and historians have been working on the articulation between race and gender, and the ways in which relations of power are associated with, intersect and sometimes displace each other. Evelyn Brooks Higginbotham, in a particularly influential essay, argues that race often operates as a metalanguage, speaking for other hierarchies of difference, whether of gender or of class.[152] The attempts to think about these kinds of intersections have been especially significant for those feminists working in the postcolonial field. Anne McClintock's *Imperial Leather* is one such study, from a primarily literary perspective. It mounts 'a sustained quarrel with the project of imperialism, the cult of domesticity and the invention of industrial progress', and argues that race, gender and class came into existence 'in and through relation to each other'.[153]

Ann Laura Stoler's *Race and the Education of Desire* has argued convincingly that a re-examination of Foucault's thinking on race can provide new tools for an analysis of the 'colonial order of things', and explores the ways in which Foucault's insights into the construction of the bourgeois self can be utilised in a wider imperial context to reveal 'the work of racial thinking in the making of European bourgeois identity'. In mapping the features of what she defines as a 'colonial bourgeois order', she suggests that the Dutch, the British and the French 'each defined their unique civilities through a language of difference that drew on images of racial purity and sexual virtue'. Racial configurations were central to the processes of identifying marginal members of the body politic and constructing a politics of exclusion.[154] The focus here is on the making of the

151 Homi K. Bhabha (ed.), *Nation and Narration* (London: Routledge, 1990), 'Introduction'.

152 Evelyn Brooks Higginbotham, 'African-American Women's History and the Metalanguage of Race', *Signs* 17 (1992), 251–74.

153 McClintock, *Imperial Leather*, pp. 4–5.

154 Ann Laura Stoler, *Race and the Education of Desire: Foucault's History of Sexuality and the Colonial Order of Things* (Durham, N.C.: Duke University Press, 1995), pp. 5, 10. See also Frederick Cooper and Ann Laura Stoler (eds.), *Tensions of Empire: Colonial Cultures in a Bourgeois World* (Berkeley: University of California Press, 1997).

bourgeois world as the determining narrative, a focus which, despite all we know, is still hard to shift.

While Stoler draws heavily on Foucault, other feminists have been inspired by the critique which black feminists have made of white feminism to explore the nationalist and imperial context of British feminist movements.[155] Feminists from Mary Wollstonecraft onwards had drawn upon histories of 'civilisation' which had the progressive history of women and the family in the West at their centre, their idealised and domesticated role characterising the modern commercial societies of the West. Such progress was indicated through comparison with the harems and polygamy of an undifferentiated Orient, and the burdened and labouring women of 'savage' populations. It might be temporarily halted but was ultimately to be completed through full recognition and enfranchisement. By the 1860s British feminism was informed both by a consciousness of superior civilisation, and national identity, and by a mission to civilise. Such a movement, though in opposition to the dominant politics, could through its language and practices embody relations of power and subordination. As Mary Carpenter wrote on her return from India, in 1868, addressing her fellow British women on their civilising mission:

> Let them throw their hearts and souls into the work, and determine never to rest until they have raised their Eastern sisters to their own level; and then may the women of India at last attain a position honourable to themselves and to England, instead of, as is now so generally the case, filling one which can only be contemplated with feelings of shame and sorrow.[156]

Jane Rendall in her exploration of the politics of liberalism for the first generation of British suffragists demonstrates the extent to which such notions of civilisation and of progress framed their thinking.[157]

Catherine Hall and Mrinalini Sinha have recently written also of

[155] Clare Midgley, 'Anti-Slavery and Feminism in Nineteenth-Century Britain', *Gender & History* 3 (1993), 343–62, and her 'Anti-Slavery and the Roots of "Imperial Feminism"', in Midgley (ed.), *Gender and Imperialism* (Manchester University Press, 1998), pp. 161–79; Vron Ware, *Beyond the Pale: White Women, Racism and History* (London: Verso, 1992); Antoinette Burton, *Burdens of History: British Feminists, Indian Women, and Imperial Culture, 1865–1915* (Chapel Hill: University of North Carolina Press, 1994); Joyce Zonana, 'The Sultan and the Slave: Feminist Orientalism and the Structure of *Jane Eyre*', *Signs* 18 (1993), 592–617.

[156] Mary Carpenter, *Six Months in India* (1868), quoted in Ware, *Beyond the Pale*, p. 130.

[157] Jane Rendall, 'Citizenship, Culture and Civilisation: The Languages of British Suffragists 1866–1874', in Caroline Daley and Melanie Nolan (eds.), *Suffrage and Beyond: International Feminist Perspectives* (Auckland University Press, 1994), pp. 127–50.

'colonial masculinity'.[158] In the 'white brotherhood' of Britain, the United States and the white settler colonies, described by Catherine Hall, British men might find an arena within which there were new opportunities for Anglo-Saxon manliness to flourish. British manhood might carry many different meanings, from the strength and authority of the Anglo-Saxon race described by Carlyle, to the civilised manhood of John Stuart Mill, to the sternness of the missionary endeavour of the fictional St John Rivers in Charlotte Bronte's *Jane Eyre*. Yet all in some way were dependent on constructions that relied upon the 'others' of women, and the sometimes effeminised, sometimes savage, masculinities of different cultures and peoples.[159] Sinha's work focuses on the mutuality of the constitution of masculinities in specific metropolitan and colonial contexts. The 'manly Englishman' depended for his definition on the 'effeminate Bengali', whose 'effeminacy' was judged next to English 'manliness'.

As yet, however, the attempts to reconfigure British imperial or indeed domestic history in a way that is attentive to questions of race, ethnicity and nation and the insights of feminist, post-structuralist and postcolonial thinking have not been recognised in mainstream historical writing.[160] While many historians have turned to a rethinking of class, few give equivalent attention to questions of gender, race or ethnicity. Said remains a highly controversial figure, his lack of historical specificity providing an excuse for failure to take his arguments seriously.[161] While postcolonial criticism has had an enormous effect in literary studies, it remains on the margins of historical thinking. P. J.

158 Catherine Hall, 'Competing Masculinities: Thomas Carlyle, John Stuart Mill and the Case of Governor Eyre', in her *White, Male and Middle Class: Explorations in Feminism and History* (Cambridge: Polity Press, 1992), pp. 255–95; Catherine Hall, 'Imperial Man: Edward John Eyre in Australasia and the West Indies, 1833–1866', in Bill Schwarz (ed.), *The Expansion of England: Race, Ethnicity and Cultural History* (London: Routledge, 1996), pp. 130–70; Catherine Hall, 'Going a-Trolloping: Imperial Man Travels the Empire', in Midgley, *Gender and Imperialism*, pp. 180–99; M. Sinha, *Colonial Masculinity: The 'Manly Englishman' and the Effeminate Bengali in the Late Nineteenth Century* (Manchester University Press, 1995).

159 Catherine Hall, '"From Greenland's Icy Mountains . . . to Afric's Golden Sand": Ethnicity, Race and Nation in Mid-Nineteenth-Century England', *Gender & History* 5 (1993), 212–30.

160 For attempts to open up the debate, see Shula Marks, 'History, the Nation and Empire: Sniping from the Periphery', *History Workshop Journal* 29 (1990), 111–19; Antoinette Burton, 'Rules of Thumb: British History and "Imperial Culture" in Nineteenth- and Twentieth-Century Britain', *Women's History Review* 3 (1994), 483–500.

161 John MacKenzie, 'Occidentalism, Counterpoint and Counter-Polemic', *Journal of Historical Geography* 19 (1993), 339–44; MacKenzie, 'Edward Said and the Historians', *Nineteenth-Century Contexts* 185 (1994), 9–25; MacKenzie, *Orientalism: History, Theory and the Arts* (Manchester University Press, 1995).

Marshall, for example, the distinguished historian of India, has assessed the case that the imperial experience was a transforming one for Britain and finds it unconvincing. 'Imperial issues', he argues, 'were not often allowed to intrude on the inward-looking world of British domestic politics or even on the inward-looking world of British historiography.'[162] Martin Daunton and Rick Halpern, on the other hand, are more prepared to accept that 'what needs to be stressed, to a greater extent, is the way in which imperialism became a significant constitutive element in British identities'.[163]

In this volume we have drawn from the new forms of historical writing which we have discussed, together with older approaches. The nation was raced as well as classed, constituted through those 'others' within and without. Those 'others' included the Irish, white yet racialised, often described as 'a race apart', a term which was revealingly also used of sections of the working classes. They also included the peoples of Jamaica, black, white and 'coloured', who whilst living only in very small numbers in Britain were a part of the imagined empire of Great Britain, as were the settlers and indigenous peoples of Australia, Canada and New Zealand. In creating the colonised, as Fanon argued, Europe was also creating itself, and this insight, taken up and amplified by Said, has been central to our thinking. Furthermore, the colonies, as James demonstrated, were not simply peripheral to events in the metropolis: rather the two sets of histories were intimately connected and mutually constitutive.

Events both in Ireland and Jamaica had effects on the ways in which politics were thought in Britain. Fenian violence erupted both in Ireland and in England in 1867. The ethics of the bloody repression by Governor Eyre of the black rebellion at Morant Bay in Jamaica in 1865 were vigorously debated in Britain between 1865 and 1867. Eyre may have been born and died in England, but his masculinity was profoundly colonial, marked by his experience of the relation between coloniser and colonised, and his particular form of colonial masculinity was celebrated by Carlyle as quintessentially English.[164] He was part of the white imperial fraternity, the white version of the Black Atlantic, whose identities were formed by lives which crossed and recrossed the empire, as they took the metropolis to the colonies and the colonies to the metropolis, shaping both the domestic and the imperial.

162 P. J. Marshall, *Imperial Britain* (Creighton Lecture, University of London, 1994), p. 17.

163 Martin Daunton and Rick Halpern (eds.), *Empire and Others: British Encounters with Indigenous Peoples, 1600–1850* (London: UCL Press, 1998), p. 1.

164 Catherine Hall, 'Imperial Man'.

Citizenship and the nation

From the 1980s onwards a revived debate about the meaning of citizenship, both academic and political, focused attention not only on the significance of the legal and civil rights of individuals, but on political rights and their relationship to political participation. Such discussions have sought to clarify the relationship between the potentially politically active 'citizen' and the 'subject' with legally defined rights and obligations within the nation. These concerns have helped our study of the debates surrounding the Reform Acts of 1867/8, during which the language of citizenship was extensively employed. This section explores the legal ambiguities, and the limits, of British 'citizenship' in the 1860s, and, as a case study, the uses of the term by one man who figures in all the following chapters, John Stuart Mill.

The language of citizenship

On 11 December 1867 a letter to *The Times* by 'Historicus' posed the question 'Who is a British subject?' The writer was prompted to do so not in the aftermath of the debate on parliamentary reform, but in response to the situation of Irish Americans resident in the United States and active in the Irish Republican Brotherhood, theoretically unable to renounce their British citizenship and allegiance to the crown. The letter pointed out that by the common law of England [*sic*], confirmed by statute and by the authority of the eighteenth-century jurist William Blackstone, all those born in Britain, or of a British-born grandfather, owed 'indelible and indefeasible allegiance' to the British crown, which could not be renounced. The writer argued, and *The Times* in its editorial agreed, that there was an unanswerable case for change: 'If modern civilization means anything at all, it surely means that nations should be enabled in free and friendly debate to adjust the spirit of their laws to the necessities of modern society and the accommodation of existing claims.'[165] Both the newspaper and its correspondent saw modern nations, in opposition to an older feudal society, as requiring 'an international code of citizenship'. Yet the full implications of the passage from subject to citizen were not to be explored in the 1860s, and the term 'citizenship' remained a deeply ambiguous one.

In Britain in the middle of the nineteenth century, there were two broad traditions which informed thinking about citizenship: the 'classical' or 'republican' tradition deriving ultimately from the world of classical Greece and Rome, and the 'liberal tradition', the foundational

[165] *The Times*, 11 December 1867.

moment of which was the English revolution of the seventeenth century.[166] For the republican, the individual was both shaped by, and found fullest realisation in, the society in which he [*sic*] was born. The republic was the source of identity, belonging and meaning. The central value of the republican citizen was that of the *res publica* (the 'public thing' or commonwealth), the common good, the preservation and celebration of the *patria* (homeland). To be free meant not only not to be ruled by others but also to participate in the process of ruling, an activity that both protected freedom and was itself an exercise of freedom, in the practice of civic virtue. In this respect citizenship for the republican was, as well as a matter of legal and political status, formative of character.[167]

For the liberal, the individual was an autonomous being, having certain rights prior to the institution (or existence) of government. These rights were natural or human rights, meaning that they were potentially universal, the entitlement of all human beings, irrespective of social or political conditions or status. These rights were (almost all) formulated in terms of individual freedoms (of conscience, expression, privacy, property, justice, etc.). To be free meant to have the fullest opportunity to exercise these individual rights. Political rights (to vote, to stand for and hold public office) were secondary, in as much as the purpose of government was primarily to protect civil rights. In this respect citizenship for the liberal was (as well as a matter of legal and political status) instrumental, a means towards other goals.

In practice, these two traditions overlapped at many points. So, for example, campaigners for parliamentary reform in the 1860s in Britain were informed predominantly by the liberal tradition in their stress upon rights, though echoes of the tradition of civic republicanism can be found in an emphasis upon the duties of the citizen to the state. Such themes are explored at many points in the chapters which follow. Here however we begin to indicate the questions relevant to a fuller understanding of the notions of citizenship in play in Britain in the middle of the nineteenth century.

On what basis could a person enjoy rights and, specifically, the right to vote? Four frequently recurring criteria are relevant here: property; gender; nationality, which links to questions of race and ethnicity; and the nature of the 'free person'. These have frequently overlapped in theory and in practice. But each was invoked in the debates of 1867/8 and will be briefly considered here.

[166] Dawn Oliver and Derek Heater, *The Foundations of Citizenship* (London: Harvester Wheatsheaf, 1994), is a very useful introduction to the history, political theory and law of citizenship.

[167] John Hope Mason, 'Creativity in Action', in Iain Hampsher-Monk (ed.), *Defending Politics: Bernard Crick and Pluralism* (London: British Academic Press, 1993), p. 17.

Property as a prerequisite for the exercise of citizenship is one of the most familiar issues for the student of nineteenth-century British political and constitutional history in Britain, as indicated in the provisions of successive Reform Acts from 1832. But definitions of property were various. It could be argued that it consisted of the possession (or effective control) of such things as land or goods, though there were arguments too that the holding of shares, or an office, could qualify. It was also suggested by many from the Levellers in the English revolution to the radicals of the nineteenth century that property might also include 'property in the person'.

The issue of gender has typically been posed in terms of whether women can enjoy the same rights of citizenship as men (rather than the converse). The question of whether women and men had the same *capacities* to enjoy and exercise rights was frequently the subject of debate. Did women possess the same degree or capacity for *reason*, or for civic defence, as men? Were such identical capacities essential? These questions were frequently raised, from the European Enlightenment onwards, as in the work of Mary Wollstonecraft or in the debates in Spain and France on the rights, status and capacities of women.[168] By the 1860s they were familiar, yet still vehemently debated and opposed. In the United States after the Civil War, in the later 1860s, the antagonisms between women suffragists and black suffragists over the franchise raised the issue as to whose rights should have precedence in a particularly divisive way.[169]

Nationality is assumed to be a central criterion of citizenship in the modern world. Yet historically such assumptions are less relevant. The classical Athenians, for example, excluded resident immigrants as well as slaves and women from the polis, while the Romans of the fourth century BC were prepared to extend the rights of citizenship to those in territories which they conquered. Typically, citizenship in the modern West has been enmeshed with the question of birth, or the adoption of nationality,

168 Mary Wollstonecraft, *Vindication of the Rights of Woman* (1792), repr. in *The Works of Mary Wollstonecraft*, ed. Janet Todd and Marilyn Butler, 7 vols. (London: William Pickering, 1989), vol. V, pp. 79–266. The numerous discussions of Wollstonecraft include Cora Kaplan, 'Wild Nights: Pleasure/Sexuality/Feminism', in her *Sea-Changes: Essays on Culture and Feminism* (London: Verso, 1986), pp. 31–56, and Barbara Taylor, 'Religion, Radicalism, and Fantasy', *History Workshop Journal* 39 (1995), 102–12. For Spain and France, see among others Mónica Bolufer Peruga and Isabel Morant Deusa, 'On Women's Reason, Education and Love', *Gender & History* 10 (1998), 183–216.

169 Christine Stansell, 'White Feminists and Black Realities: The Politics of Authenticity', in Toni Morrison (ed.), *Race-ing Justice, Engendering Power: Essays on Anita Hill, Clarence Thomas and the Construction of Social Reality* (New York: Pantheon, 1992), pp. 251–68; Ellen Carol Dubois, *Feminism and Suffrage: The Emergence of an Independent Women's Movement in America, 1848–1969* (Ithaca, N.Y.: Cornell University Press, 1978).

and the extent to which the host nation-state is willing to grant legal status to a person. In practice, this has frequently become an extremely complex matter of law (both within particular nations or communities, such as the British Commonwealth, and in international courts). In nineteenth-century Britain and its empire there was no legal category 'citizen'. Here we encounter the critical distinction between the subject and the citizen. All living within the rule of a given state (which might include its own territory and also those conquered or subordinated areas subject to it) are subject to the laws, rule and force of the state; but only some are citizens in the sense of those who are thought to have rights within and relation to the state. The peoples of the British Isles and the British Empire were formally equal subjects of the British crown. Unlike France, for example, as Robin Cohen points out, it was not until the 1948 British Nationality Act that most UK inhabitants got citizenship, and then it was a passively received legal category rather than a status that had been won by revolutionary activity. It is only in the later twentieth century that increasingly narrow legal definitions have been created of the category 'British citizen', primarily with the intention of limiting the rights of entry of non-white peoples from the former empire. Since the British Nationality Act of 1981 came into effect, the longstanding principle of *jus soli*, that birthplace confers citizenship, has been breached and people born in Britain of non-British citizens do not automatically acquire British nationality and citizenship.[170]

In the nineteenth century Britain maintained free entry to all foreigners and prided itself on its rights of asylum, one of the famed 'English' liberties. The right to control entry and to deport 'aliens', those who did not belong and were not wanted, a key right of nations from the earliest times, had been established from 1066. The policing of the Channel was effected through the Cinque Ports, the five key control ports which gave rise to the notion of the 'passport'.[171] In the thirteenth century Jews and Flemings were deported amongst others, in the sixteenth and seventeenth centuries religious recusants of varying persuasions. From 1823, however, to the end of the century, as Bernard Porter shows, no refugee was expelled from Britain or prevented from coming. This policy of asylum was maintained by the absence of laws. In 1793 an Aliens Act had been passed in the context of the Napoleonic Wars and remained in force until 1826. In 1848 an act was put on the statute books for two years but

[170] Robin Cohen, *Frontiers of Identity: The British and the Others* (London: Longman, 1994), pp. 5, 18–19.

[171] T. W. E. Roche, *The Key in the Lock: A History of Immigration Control in England from 1066 to the Present Day* (London: John Murray, 1969), cited in Robin Cohen, *Frontiers of Identity*, pp. 37–40.

was never implemented: 'from 1826 until 1848, and again from 1850 to 1905, there was nothing on the statute book to enable the executive to prevent aliens from coming and staying in Britain as they liked'. As Lord Malmesbury put it in 1852 in a moment of English complacency:

> I can well conceive the pleasure and happiness of a refugee, hunted from his native land, on approaching the shores of England, and the joy with which he first catches sight of them; but they are not greater than the pleasure and happiness every Englishman feels in knowing that his country affords the refugee a home and safety.[172]

There were critics of this open door policy and considerable government discomfort at varying points but even *The Times*, no friend to wandering European revolutionaries, argued in 1858, during the debates on the Orsini affair, 'For better, for worse, we have long been wedded to liberty, and we take it with all its evils for the sake of its manifold blessings.'[173] These migrants never constituted a large number, though by the middle of the nineteenth century the presence of large numbers of Irish in England and Scotland was provoking considerable reaction. It was not until the arrival of large numbers of Jewish refugees from Russia and eastern Europe at the end of the century that a Royal Commission on Alien Immigration was established and the Alien Act of 1905 passed, which set up an immigration control bureau with the rights of expulsion. In the later twentieth century British governments have become increasingly concerned, as we have seen, to set clear limits on the definition of British citizenship: an exercise that has resulted in the construction of new categories with hierarchies of rights. All those who were once supposedly equal subjects of the British Empire have now been formally differentiated.[174]

If property, gender and nationality were all significant for an interpretation of the debates of 1867, so was the idea of freedom. The single most important historical issue in regard to whether a person is 'free' in some

[172] Cited in Bernard Porter, *The Refugee Question in Mid-Victorian Politics* (Cambridge University Press, 1979), pp. 1–3, 7.

[173] *Ibid.* In February 1858 Palmerston's government, pressured by the French state following the attempted assassination of Napoleon III by Felice Orsini, had introduced the Conspiracy to Murder Bill which sought to convert conspiracy to murder from a misdemeanour into a criminal offence. Most significantly the bill included within English law conspiracy to murder abroad, a clause aimed at the exiled community living in Jersey: see *ibid.*, ch. 6.

[174] There is a very considerable literature on post-war immigration legislation. For helpful ways in, see Robin Cohen, *Frontiers of Identity*; Kathleen Paul, *Whitewashing Britain: Race and Citizenship in the Postwar Era* (Ithaca, N.Y., and London: Cornell University Press, 1997); Gail Lewis, 'Citizenship', in Gordon Hughes (ed.), *Imagining Welfare Futures* (London: Routledge in association with the Open University, 1998), pp. 103–50.

sense has been the question of slavery, whether in the classical world of Greece and Rome, the British Empire before 1833, the Southern United States before the Civil War or elsewhere. But 'freedom' has also meant other states of being as well, such as whether or not a person is 'independent' in the sense of being free of such obligations or subordination to others as renders them unfit – or thought to be unfit – to make judgements of their own in the polity. This, for example, was a view widely held of 'servants' in seventeenth-century England. As a criterion it has been near-universal in relation to children,[175] frequently used in relation to women and to the very poor, and sometimes to those thought to be without sufficient education or other social 'qualification'. It could also be applied to those thought to be 'insane'.

Citizens have generally however not only been distinguished by possessing legal and political rights of some kind and to some degree but have also been expected to exercise duties. Indeed, many have effectively argued that there is a 'trade-off' between the two: citizens may get rights (such as the vote) but in exchange she or he is expected to obey the law and pay taxes and may be required to fulfil other obligations such as military service. To take an example particularly germane to the essays in this book, John Stuart Mill argued that those granted citizenship had a duty to participate in public life and to show a commitment to the affairs of the community.[176]

In the final section of this introduction we consider Mill's contribution to the language of citizenship in the 1860s.

John Stuart Mill and the question of citizenship

> *Question: What are the disadvantages we labour under in not having a vote, and the advantages we should possess in having one? (Oh.)*
>
> *Mr Mill*: The gentleman who had asked that question had asked him in effect to make a speech which would last the rest of the evening. The difference would be this – the man would be a citizen – (*loud cheers*) – and he would feel that he was a citizen . . . It seemed to him that the interests of citizenship – an equal right to be heard – to have a share in influencing the affairs of the country – to be consulted, to be spoken to, and to have agreements and considerations turning upon politics addressed to one – tended to elevate and educate the self-respect of the man, and to strengthen his feelings of regard for his fellow men. (*Cheers.*) These made all the difference between a selfish man and a patriot.

[175] The *age* at which a person is thought to become an adult and capable of exercising rights has, of course, been historically variable.

[176] For more on Mill, see below and pp. 123–4, 129–39, 164–7, 174–5, 188–91 and 226–9.

> (*Hear, hear.*) To give people an interest in politics and in the management of their own affairs was the grand cultivator of mankind. (*Cheers.*) That was one of the reasons why he wanted women to have votes; they needed cultivation as well as men. He could not conceive that a country was what it ought to be without an extension of a share of political right to all. (*Cheers.*) Those left without it seemed a sort of pariahs [*sic*].[177]

In early July 1865 John Stuart Mill, political philosopher and economist, journalist and civil servant, accepted an invitation from the Radical committee in Westminster to offer himself to that constituency as a candidate for election to the House of Commons. He responded with energy to those who challenged him in a series of unusual electoral meetings. But the questioner who asked him to name the advantages of citizenship touched on a theme which was at the heart of his own work, just as it was to pervade the debates about reform. To Mill, citizenship was about self-improvement, not self-interest or natural right, a self-improvement which was undertaken in a patriotic spirit, a kind of cultivation which should be open to women as well as to men. Mill's hearers probably assumed that his advocacy of 'a share of political right to all' implied a commitment to democracy. Yet both in his published writings and in his parliamentary speeches, Mill was to be much more cautious than in his electoral addresses. For the ability to achieve the appropriate level of cultivation could not be found at all levels of society, or in all societies. Beyond the literate and the educated, and outside the civilised West, there remained many still in the state of 'pariahs'. That metaphor, originally a Tamil term applied to those of low or no caste in southern India, and extended to stand for social outcasts more generally, would have been especially familiar to Mill, a civil servant at the India Office for his working life.

Stefan Collini has christened Mill an outstanding 'public moralist', for his energetic commitment to maintain, improve and diffuse the moral values of his society, through his books, journalism and political activism, and, especially, between 1865 and 1868, his membership of the House of Commons.[178] Mill's *Principles of Political Economy* and *On Liberty* were immensely influential works, circulating widely among self-educated working men as among the Victorian intelligentsia.[179] His advocacy of women's suffrage and presentation of the cause in the House of Commons was a key factor, and some would argue the most important

177 Election speech reported in the *Daily Telegraph*, 8 July 1868, reprinted in *Collected Works of John Stuart Mill* [hereafter *CW*], gen. ed. J. M. Robson, 33 vols. (University of Toronto Press, 1962–91), vol. XXVIII, *Public and Parliamentary Speeches*, ed. J. M. Robson and Bruce Kinzer (1988), p. 39.

178 Collini, *Public Moralists*, ch. 4.

179 The *Principles* was first published in 1848, *On Liberty* in 1859.

factor, in the degree of success achieved. The publication of the *Subjection of Women* in 1869 was greeted with enormous enthusiasm and interest among those committed to the cause. Mill had been a fierce antagonist of slavery and an active supporter of the North in the American Civil War. He was the central public figure in the Jamaica Committee, set up in 1866 to campaign for the prosecution of Governor Edward Eyre for his responsibility for the massacre of 439 black and 'coloured' men and women at Morant Bay, Jamaica. In 1868 he was to make an influential intervention also in the debate about the future of Ireland, through his pamphlet *England and Ireland* (1868).

In this final section of the introduction, we consider the major elements in the view of citizenship that Mill put before the electors of Westminster in 1865. Especially relevant are his views of the freedom of the individual for men and for women, his attitude towards democracy and his concept of 'civilisation'.[180] Such views shaped his criteria for citizenship, criteria which were not the same as those of Disraeli or the Reform League, but which also had considerable influence. Mill too sought to expand the political nation beyond its existing boundaries, yet also to draw certain limits.

Mill's views of the freedom of the individual drew upon both the utilitarian legacy of his early years, and later and more eclectic influences. Born in 1806, Mill grew up in the utilitarian atmosphere shaped by his father, James Mill, a man educated for the Scots Presbyterian ministry, who having lost his Christian faith became the disciple and onetime secretary of Jeremy Bentham. In his *Autobiography* (1873), John Mill famously recorded the rigid and ambitious education which his father provided for him from a very early age. He was rapidly introduced to the classics, history and political economy, though to very little imaginative literature. Benthamite utilitarianism was based on the psychological theory that all individuals desire pleasure and avoid pain. Bentham's advice to legislators was to use their power to design the working of their society so as to maximise the total amount of pleasure or, in other words, 'the greatest happiness of the greatest possible number'.[181]

James Mill was not merely a populariser of Bentham, but shifted the emphasis of utilitarianism in certain important ways. He was interested especially in what was known as the psychology of associationism, or how

[180] For general introductions to Mill's life and works, see M. St John Packe, *The Life of John Stuart Mill* (Basingstoke: Macmillan, 1954); J. M. Robson, *The Improvement of Mankind: The Social and Political Thought of John Stuart Mill* (University of Toronto Press, 1968); Alan Ryan, *J. S. Mill* (London: Routledge, 1974); William Thomas, *Mill* (Oxford University Press, 1985); William Stafford, *John Stuart Mill* (Basingstoke: Macmillan, 1998).

[181] For brief guides to Bentham's thinking, see John Dinwiddy, *Bentham* (Oxford University Press, 1989); D. Manning, *The Mind of Jeremy Bentham* (London: Longmans, 1968); Ross Harrison, *Bentham* (London: Routledge and Kegan Paul, 1983).

circumstances and the right kind of association of habits and ideas shaped character. He emphasised character, intelligence and duty much more than self-interest or the psychology of pleasure. His vision was of a society whose educational system might eventually encourage all individuals to place the public benefit first, but which might first have to depend on the moral example of that class most susceptible to enlightenment, the 'middle rank'.[182]

From the early 1820s Mill was a part of group of young men known as the Philosophic Radicals, who drew upon the ideas of Bentham and James Mill, and hoped to diffuse them in the *Westminster Review*, founded in 1824. However, in his *Autobiography* John Mill tells us of his 'conversion' from utilitarianism in 1826. It was a crisis induced by the apparent barrenness and lack of emotion in utilitarian philosophy and psychology. Over the next ten years, Mill was to broaden his interests and activities in ways which remained important to his thinking in the 1860s. From Samuel Taylor Coleridge, and from Thomas Carlyle, he took a new interest in the world of the imagination, in literature and poetry, and he began to doubt whether enlightened self-interest could provide the basis for a progressive future society which would be not only more rational but more moral. In 1830 Mill met Harriet Taylor, a young married woman, almost certainly through William Johnson Fox, the Unitarian minister of the South Place Chapel. Fox, and Harriet Taylor, introduced him to Unitarian circles with a wide range of educational and literary, as well as political, interests, circles which were already reflecting on the situation of women. His political activities were expanding too, as he supported a group of Philosophic Radicals in the House of Commons through his editing first of the *London Review* and then the *London and Westminster Review*.[183]

By 1840, when the Philosophic Radical initiative was clearly in decline, he began to devote himself to his ambition to construct a coherent science of politics. Mill believed that the methods of natural science could be applied to social scientific subjects, and his *System of Logic* (1843) was devoted to such questions of philosophy and methodology. But because of his own lack of progress on this, in the early 1840s he began with his *Principles of Political Economy* (1848), which owed much to the classical economist David Ricardo. While Mill was strongly committed to the principles of laissez-faire in the economy, he was nevertheless reluctant to endorse a philosophy of unrestrained economic growth. In the seven

182 J. Hamburger, *James Mill and the Art of Revolution* (New Haven and London: Yale University Press, 1963); Robert A. Fenn, *James Mill's Political Thought* (New York and London: Garland, 1987).

183 For discussions of Mill's career in these years, see esp.: Joseph Hamburger, *Intellectuals in Politics: John Stuart Mill and the Philosophic Radicals* (New Haven and London: Yale University Press, 1965); William Thomas, *The Philosophic Radicals: Nine Studies in Theory and Practice 1817–1841* (Oxford: Clarendon Press, 1979), ch. 4.

editions of the *Principles* published during Mill's lifetime, he was to shift his attitude towards socialism. In particular, in the third edition of 1852 he gave socialism – here utopian socialists like Robert Owen and Saint-Simon – a sympathetic review the tone of which is often attributed to Harriet Taylor. His chapter 'On the Probable Futurity of the Labouring Classes' suggested the role of future producer co-operatives, which though competitive would be autonomous and self-governing, offering individual working men their chance to participate in the direction of future progress.[184]

This stress on individual self-development provided one key to Mill's concept of citizenship. For Mill, the individual was not only a rational but a 'progressive being'. His *On Liberty* (1859) explored the conditions under which such human progress might be fostered, and celebrated the freedom of the individual, in relation to the power of the state.[185] The only reason for restraining the actions of the individual should be self-defence, individual or collective. The disapproval of public opinion, even if in a great majority, could not justify any limitations on individual freedom. What Mill wanted to do was to defend individuality, even eccentricity, as part of his vision of the individual's self-fulfilment and growth; and there is no doubt that this was a personal vision, of the highly cultivated, intelligent and morally aware individual. Citizenship was an essential element in that self-fulfilment.

In occasional published and unpublished writing before the 1860s, Mill had begun to look at the impact of the social and legal disabilities of women, both on their own education and character and on society as a whole. *The Subjection of Women*, published in 1869 but largely completed by 1860, should be seen in this context.[186] Women, disempowered by exclusion from such possibilities for self-development, could not therefore achieve their full potential. *The Subjection of Women* was attributed by Mill almost entirely to the influence of Harriet Taylor Mill, and drew, if cautiously, on her earlier published work.

For Mill the oppressive disabilities suffered by women were the remnants of an older past, paralleled only in more backward societies of the

[184] See Mill, *Principles of Political Economy, with Some of Their Applications to Social Philosophy* (London, 1848), repr. in *CW*, vols. II–III, ed. J. M. Robson (1965), and esp. J. M. Robson, 'Textual Introduction', vol. II, pp. lxv–lxxxvii, and vol. III, appendix G, pp. 1026–37.

[185] Modern discussions, besides the above, include C. L. Ten, *Mill on Liberty* (Oxford: Clarendon Press, 1980); John Gray, *Mill on Liberty: A Defence* (London: Routledge and Kegan Paul, 1983). A useful anthology on its reception is Andrew Pyle (ed.), *Liberty: Contemporary Responses to John Stuart Mill* (Bristol: Thoemmes Press, 1994). For critical, and more controversial, views, see Gertrude Himmelfarb, *On Liberty and Liberalism. The Case of John Stuart Mill* (New York: Alfred Knopf, 1974), and Maurice Cowling, *Mill and Liberalism* (Cambridge University Press, 1963).

[186] For Mill's earlier work, see *Essays on Equality, Law and Education*, ed. J. M. Robson, *CW*, vol. XXI (1984); Ann P. Robson and John M. Robson (eds.), *Sexual Equality: Writings by*

present. Marriage in a more advanced society, freed from an oppressive male power and the burdens of custom and prejudice, could, in this account, be an ennobling and fulfilling partnership as was that of Mill and Taylor themselves. Their relationship seemed, however, to many contemporaries and later historians, one of common intellectual pursuits and interests, though curiously passionless. And there were other themes on which Mill's writing seemed distanced from experience. His championing of the equal political and social rights of women did not extend to any understanding of the links between marriage and the sexual division of labour. He called for women to be educated equally with men to play their part in present and future societies. Yet, while fully defending women's right and need to take on the duties of citizenship in the political community, he assumed that most married women would see their future not in the world of employment but within the home.

Citizenship, for Mill, was not dependent on the introduction of democracy. Alexis de Tocqueville's work on *Democracy in America* had appealed to him because de Tocqueville had confronted what Mill also perceived as the dangers of democracy, and suggested how such dangers might be met.[187] In his *Considerations on Representative Government* (1861), Mill discussed how, within a more advanced society, the evils of democracy could be avoided.[188] For Mill was no democrat; like de Tocqueville he was closely aware of the threatening tyranny of a majority which would be lacking in the kind of education and moral cultivation he sought. His remedies were relatively simple. He told the electors of Westminster in 1865 that he would impose an educational test for the franchise, would allow only taxpayers to vote and would disqualify paupers and bankrupts.[189] He was interested in plural voting for the highly qualified. And he was sympathetic to the proposals made by Thomas Hare for a form of proportional representation which would ensure representation of minority opinions, and of individuals without charismatic or demagogic attractions.

John Stuart Mill, Harriet Taylor Mill, and Helen Taylor (University of Toronto Press, 1994). Mill's views are discussed in: Julia Annas, 'Mill and the Subjection of Women', *Philosophy* 52 (1977), 179–94; Susan Mendus, 'The Marriage of True Minds: The Ideal of Marriage in the Philosophy of John Stuart Mill', in Mendus and Jane Rendall (eds.), *Sexuality and Subordination: Interdisciplinary Studies of Gender in the Nineteenth Century* (London: Routledge, 1989), pp. 171–91; Gail Tulloch, *Mill and Sexual Equality* (Boulder: University of Colorado Press, 1989). For the reception of *The Subjection of Women*, see below, pp. 154, 164–5, and Andrew Pyle (ed.), *'The Subjection of Women': Contemporary Responses to John Stuart Mill* (Bath: Thoemmes Press, 1995).

[187] See esp. Iris W. Mueller, *John Stuart Mill and French Thought* (Urbana: University of Illinois Press, 1956); R. K. P. Pankhurst, *The Saint-Simonians, Mill, and Carlyle* (London: Sidgwick and Jackson, 1957).

[188] See: J. H. Burns, 'John Stuart Mill and Democracy, 1829–1861', in J. B. Schneewind (ed.), *Mill: A Collection of Critical Essays* (Basingstoke: Macmillan, 1969), pp. 280–328; Dennis Thompson, *John Stuart Mill and Representative Government* (Princeton University Press, 1976).

[189] Mill, *Public and Parliamentary Speeches*, pp. 30–1, 37, 43.

He says very clearly, however, in this work that differences of sex were 'as entirely irrelevant to political rights as difference in height or in the colour of the hair'.[190] Mill was not in favour of the secret ballot, because he thought it counter to a primary function of the franchise, 'opening his heart to an exalted patriotism and the obligation of public duty'.[191] Public duty required public demonstration. Local government was among the institutions which could foster the kind of public spirit required.

Such a representative government was to Mill integrally associated with patriotism and with a nation's identity. He wrote: 'it is in general a necessary condition of free institutions that the boundaries of governments should coincide in the main with those of nationalities'.[192] Yet this was clearly not always the case, either within contemporary Europe or within the United Kingdom. And once Mill looked beyond Europe, his ideal of citizenship would give place to more immediately utilitarian imperatives. For another constant theme in Mill's philosophy lay in his approach to that concept of 'civilisation', which alone had the potential for the development of individual character within the structures of representative government.

That concept owed something to his father's influence. James Mill had worked from 1806, the year of his son's birth, to 1817 on his major *History of British India* (1817). John Mill helped to correct the proofs. The *History* was in many ways a product of a historical framework drawn from those writers and teachers of the Scottish Enlightenment who had moulded James Mill's early years.[193] They assumed a common and progressive history applicable to all human societies, through stages of economic development, which were indicators not only of economic progress, but of the social, cultural and political state of any society. And such progress, though an assumed part of historical development, could be delayed or accelerated, by accident, by climate or, sometimes, by intervention. James Mill firmly ranked Muslim and Hindu at a low level on a staged hierarchy of progress; nevertheless, drawing in a different spirit upon utilitarian objectives rather than upon assumptions of progress, he suggested that both would best be served by the intervention of a utilitarian legislator.

John Mill was an Examiner in the East India Office from 1823 to 1858. In 1826 one of his earliest published reviews showed his familiarity with Scottish writers such as John Millar.[194] In 1836 in his essay on 'Civilization', he conventionally elaborated the criteria for that term:

190 Mill, *Considerations on Representative Government* (London, 1861), repr. in *CW*, vol. XIX, *Essays on Politics and Society*, ed. J. M. Robson (1977), p. 479.
191 *Ibid.*, p. 489.
192 *Ibid.*, p. 548.
193 J. H. Burns, 'The Light of Reason: Philosophical History in the Two Mills', in John M. Robson and Michael Laine (eds.), *James and John Stuart Mill/Papers of the Centenary Conference* (University of Toronto Press, 1976), pp. 3–20.
194 See below, pp. 123–4.

> Wherever there has 'arisen' sufficient knowledge of the arts of life, and sufficient security of property and person, to render the progressive increase of wealth and population possible, the community becomes and continues progressive in all the elements which we have just enumerated. These elements exist in modern Europe, and especially in Great Britain, in a more eminent degree, and in a state of more rapid progression, than at any other place or time.[195]

Although in that essay he expressed his anxieties about the progress towards democracy and the consequent dangers of mediocrity, he nevertheless expressed his sense of the immense contrast between 'civilised' societies and those still in 'a rude state'. In 1865 he wrote of his father as having thrown 'the light of reason on Hindoo society'.[196] There is much to suggest that, although Mill hoped for a much more sophisticated and philosophically grounded approach to 'the science of society', his political framework was still fundamentally moulded by Enlightenment assumptions of progress.

For Mill there were certain conditions under which representative government was not applicable. It might be imposed, or not be valued. It would be inappropriate where a nation was not sufficiently advanced to benefit from it, if its people had failed to acquire habits of obedience, or on the contrary had accustomed themselves to despotism. Where such peoples were mixed, Mill wrote that a minority population, especially one which was less advanced, could be beneficially reconciled and ultimately blended with its neighbour, who might be 'both the most numerous and the most improved'. Mill's thoughts here were first, perfunctorily, of Bretons and Alsatians in France, but more seriously of England and Ireland. Mill noted past centuries of British misgovernment in Ireland. He had already, in his *Principles of Political Economy*, indicted British landlords, and called, though inconsistently, for attention to the need for security of tenure for tenant farmers there. Yet he suggested in 1861 that in the middle of the nineteenth century all serious grievances were being redressed so generally that there was now little to prevent the Irish nation from understanding the immense benefits of the union, and association with their wealthy, civilised and free neighbours.[197]

By the early 1860s Mill was closely watching developments in the United States. For Mill, slavery, an absolute form of inequality and a corruption of power, had characterised the earliest and least advanced societies. He found extensive sympathy for the South in Britain, and sought to

[195] Mill, 'Civilization: Signs of the Times', *London and Westminster Review* 3 and 25 (April 1836), 1–28, repr. in *CW*, vol. XVIII, *Essays on Politics and Society*, ed. J. M. Robson (1977), pp. 117–48.

[196] Mill, *August Comte and Positivism* (London, 1865), repr. in *CW*, vol. X, *Essays on Ethics, Religion and Society*, ed. J. M. Robson (1969), p. 320, quoted in Burns, 'Light of Reason', p. 5.

[197] Mill, *August Comte and Positivism*, pp. 364–5.

educate public opinion. In the work of his Irish friend John Elliot Cairnes, *The Slave Power* (1862), he found arguments which he too advanced, on the insatiable and aggressive nature of Southern expansion. Mill hoped to see the total defeat of the Southern states and their incorporation in the North, as the only way forward to a future representative government for the United States as a whole.

Mill's liberalism must be placed in the light of his commitment to a progressive history and future, towards the continuing improvement of self and society. Such a liberalism had its limits. Just as democracy might not be the most appropriate means to an end in an advanced society, so in a similarly utilitarian spirit, liberty and representative government might in other societies be inappropriate:

> a ruler full of the spirit of improvement is warranted in the use of any expedients that will attain an end, perhaps otherwise unattainable . . . Liberty, as a principle, has no application to any state of things anterior to the time when mankind have become capable of being improved by free and equal discussion.[198]

The citizenship which Mill advocated so strongly to the electors of Westminster was not to be extended to the colonial subjects of the United Kingdom, though nowhere does Mill exclude the future possibilities of the spirit of improvement.

It was to be as a member of Parliament, endorsed by his constituents, that Mill placed himself at the heart of the battle over the conduct of Governor Eyre, and became the major spokesman for women's suffrage in the House of Commons, both identified as among his 'crotchets'. His words were heard with great respect on the extension of the franchise and on the condition of Ireland, as over the next three years he became a distinctive and surprisingly adept parliamentarian. Mill helped to shape that politics of advanced liberalism which characterised the 1860s, though, as we illustrate below, his own position was always complex, and his alliances never straightforward. The chapters that follow focus more upon those forces in British politics that were favourable to reform, and especially upon the many varieties of liberalism, radical-liberalism and the politics of labour, in urban rather than rural contexts. Though Mill's politics are often viewed as marginal to the Reform Act, in these chapters his construction of the citizenship of the nation will be one constant point of reference.

198 Mill, *On Liberty* (London, 1859), repr. in *CW*, vol. XVIII, *Essays on Politics and Society*, ed. J. M. Robson (1977), p. 224; John Gibbins, 'J. S. Mill, Liberalism, and Progress', in Richard Bellamy (ed.), *Victorian Liberalism: Nineteenth-Century Political Thought and Practice* (London and New York: Routledge, 1990), pp. 91–109.

2 'England's greatness, the working man'

Keith McClelland

When a substantial section of the working class was given the vote by the Reform Acts of 1867 (in England and Wales) and 1868 (in Scotland), it was of course some *men* who got the vote.[1] But the fact that these were men – and what meanings were attached to this – is one of cultural and political signification, not merely a fact of biology. If the Reform Acts were in part the result of a changing relationship of the working class to the state and of the perceptions of the status of the working class within the society, a consequence of the acts was to legitimate the working-class citizen in new ways. But who was being brought within the pale of the constitution was a particular kind of man whose definition – the social, political and moral qualities he was thought to carry, his perceived relationship to processes of government and politics – was crucial to the redefinition of what the political nation was and might become. This was not only a matter of political argument in the narrow sense of parliamentary debates and extra-parliamentary political discourses. It was central to the debates about culture in and after 1867, evident across the range of intellectual argument and controversy, from Arnold's *Culture and Anarchy* or Carlyle's essays on the

[1] It is not known how many working-class men got the vote under the acts. But it is clear (a) that the proportion of working-class voters newly enfranchised varied a great deal over the boroughs (where the new working-class voters were) and (b) that as a whole the working class remained markedly under-represented. Many of the most important discussions of the size of the working-class vote focus on the era after the 1884–5 Reform Acts and concern the importance of the franchise factor to the growth of the Labour party after 1906. But the literature also throws a retrospective light on the period 1868–84. Relevant discussions include H. J. Hanham, *Elections and Party Management: Politics in the Time of Disraeli and Gladstone* (London: Longmans Green, 1959); Neal Blewett, 'The Franchise in the United Kingdom, 1885–1918', *Past & Present* 32 (1965), 27–56; Ross McKibbin, Colin Matthew and John Kay, 'The Franchise Factor in the Rise of the Labour Party', *English Historical Review* 91 (1976), repr. in McKibbin, *Ideologies of Class: Social Relations in Britain 1880–1950* (Oxford: Clarendon Press, 1990), pp. 66–100; John Davis, 'Slums and the Vote', *Historical Research* 64 (1991), 375–88; John Davis and Duncan Tanner, 'The Borough Franchise After 1867', *Historical Research* 69 (1996), 306–27.

Plate 1 'The mob pulling down the railings in Park Lane'. *Illustrated London News*, 4 August 1866 (University of London Library).

political right to Positivists like Frederic Harrison or E. S. Beesly and liberals like John Morley.[2]

The axial figure within the controversies of 1866–7 about who was to be enfranchised was the 'respectable working man': could he be trusted if he were to be given the vote? How was he to be differentiated from the 'rough' or 'unrespectable'? His opponents saw him as surrounded by a mass of the coarse and ignorant by whom he might always be subsumed. Those who proclaimed his fitness for and right to the vote saw him as capable of separating himself from the rough and as the bearer of a manly virtue. One may glimpse these contrasts in the responses to one of the great demonstrations held by the main organisation of the working-class movement for parliamentary reform, the Reform League, which it held in Hyde Park, London, on Monday, 23 July 1866.

[2] For Arnold and Carlyle, see Catherine Hall's chapter in this volume, pp. 179–233; for the Positivist and liberal intellectuals, see among others Christopher Kent, *Brains and Numbers: Elitism, Comtism, and Democracy in Mid-Victorian England* (University of Toronto Press, 1978); Christopher Harvie, *The Lights of Liberalism: University Liberals and the Challenge of Democracy 1860–1886* (London: Allen Lane, 1976).

Plate 2 'Scene of destruction near the Marble Arch'. *Illustrated London News*, 4 August 1866 (University of London Library).

Since June a Conservative government had been in office following the defeat of the Russell–Gladstone Reform Bill. Faced by the prospect of the demonstration, the home secretary, Spencer Walpole, responding to fears emanating from politicians and 'the classes' that 'mob rule' would threaten the order and tranquillity of the nation, and acting in concert with Sir Richard Mayne, chief of the Metropolitan Police, banned it from the park.

Despite their strong opposition to the ban, the Reform League's leaders, notably Edmond Beales, its president, had with a certain timidity taken the official demonstration to Trafalgar Square. But the mass of demonstrators, inspired in part by the 'left' of the Reform League whose leaders included the former Chartist Benjamin Lucraft and the editor of the *Bee-Hive* and trade unionist, George Potter, went instead to Hyde Park, where they were met by a police cordon. Under the pressure of the crowd the railings were broken down and the crowd established

Plate 3 'The broken railings at Hyde Park Corner'. *Illustrated London News*, 4 August 1866 (University of London Library).

possession of what was seen as a place that was the 'property of the nation' and thus should be available for the people.[3] Over the course of the next three days there was 'intermittent skirmishing' between demonstrators and police.[4]

How important these events, the further demonstrations of May 1867 and in general the pressures for reform from the organised working class were in determining the timing and form of the Reform Act has been much debated.[5] But for the moment it is the terms in which the

[3] Beales asserted this in his exchange of correspondence on the question of the right to use Hyde Park with Sir Richard Mayne: the correspondence of 18 and 19 July 1866 was published in the *Bee-Hive*, 21 July 1866, and is repr. in John Breuilly, Gottfried Niedhart and Antony Taylor (eds.), *The Era of the Reform League: English Labour and Radical Politics 1857–1872. Documents Selected by Gustav Mayer* (Mannheim: Palatium Verlag im J. & J. Verlag, 1995), pp. 176–8 (quote, p. 177).

[4] Royden Harrison, *Before the Socialists: Studies in Labour and Politics 1861–1881* (London: Routledge and Kegan Paul, 1965), p. 82.

[5] The classic account emphasising their importance is Royden Harrison, *Before the Socialists*, ch. 3, 'The Tenth April of Spencer Walpole: The Problem of Revolution in

Plate 4 'Manhood Suffrage'. *Punch*, 15 December 1866. For critics of reform like Robert Lowe, the inevitable outcome of allowing respectable working men to vote would be that the 'unrespectable' would also exert their influence.

demonstration and its participants were constructed that I want to focus on. This can be seen in two contrasting accounts of the events, one from *The Times*, the other from the *Bee-Hive*, one of the most important organs of organised working-class opinion.[6] What was posed in the contrasting descriptions about the character of those attending the demonstration is apparently familiar: there is claim and counter-claim about whether this was a *respectable* working class.

On the one hand *The Times*, with its familiar contempt for working people, allows that there may have been a few 'decent' people attending – even some of the middle class; but, in essence, this was a 'mob':

> the multitude brought together was not of that decent and respectable character which the promoters of these gatherings would lead the public to expect. The processions did, indeed, contain a certain number of decent mechanics, and some persons who, from their dress and appearance, seemed to belong to the middle class; but these were almost lost in a surrounding and interpenetrating mass of the coarsest mob. The great majority of the people in the crowded streets were the usual slouching, shambling man-boys who constitute the mass of the ordinary London multitude.[7]

On the other hand, the report in the *Bee-Hive* showed a certain hesitancy in its defence of the crowd. It displayed a desire to distance itself from the 'unrespectable' or 'rough' elements while at the same time being anxious to show that it was respectable and rational men who had asserted their constitutional right of meeting. It admitted that there were some of the 'roughs' present but, it was argued, there were bound to be:

> the bringing together large masses of the people, however good the object, also brings together a large body of thieves, roughs, and other disorderly characters, and therefore there is danger. But does not this objection equally apply to the opening of Parliament by Her Majesty, to a review in the park, or to any other of our monarchical or national festivities?[8]

But, the *Bee-Hive* thought, the numbers present, the orderly character of the demonstration and Walpole's subsequent and rapid admittance of the

footnote 5 (*cont.*)
Relation to Reform, 1865–1867'. By contrast the bulk of works of political history play down the significance of extra-parliamentary pressure in determining the shape of the act. For further comments on this, see the introduction to this volume, pp. 7–9.

[6] For the *Bee-Hive*, see Stephen Coltham, 'George Potter, the Junta and the *Bee-Hive*', *International Review of Social History* 9 (1964), 390–432, and 10 (1965), 23–65; Stephen Coltham, 'The *Bee-Hive* Newspaper: Its Origins and Early Struggles', in Asa Briggs and John Saville (eds.), *Essays in Labour History* (Basingstoke: Macmillan, 1960), pp. 174–204.

[7] *The Times*, 24 July 1866 (leader comment).

[8] *Bee-Hive*, 28 July 1866; cf. the leader comment in the liberal *Daily Telegraph*, 24 July 1866: 'there were fewer "roughs" amongst its ranks than are to be met with in the wake of every Lord Mayor's show'.

right to demonstrate in the park conceded to the Reform League a great moral victory. Indeed, the League felt entirely vindicated two days after the 'invasion' of the park on the Monday, when it held its peaceful demonstration in the park on Wednesday the 25th. The Reform League effectively policed the event: 'the greatest order and good humour prevailed amongst the people, and any tendency on the part of unthinking lads, or disorderly boys, to create a disturbance, was promptly checked by the mass of working men present'.[9]

What is striking in these accounts is the way in which the characterisation of the demonstrators is pivoted on the kind of masculinity on show. In the depiction of *The Times* the predominant element in the crowd of 'man-boys' – who 'slouch' – were not 'proper' men: they were 'coarse'. Against this the terms in which the *Bee-Hive* asserted the moral worth of the demonstration was that such 'lads' and 'boys' were held in check by working *men*.

In asserting this, and the wider claim for the vote itself, the *Bee-Hive* and the Reform League were affirming something that has long been acknowledged: the working men represented by the League were seeking entry to the political nation as respectable and sober citizens.

What the terms of the claim to citizenship were and how they came to be defined and mobilised is the subject of this chapter. As we have emphasised in the introduction, questions of citizenship always entail issues of exclusion and inclusion, of drawing boundaries around 'legitimate' citizens and *against* those who are not. Citizenship in the Britain of the 1860s was about political rights: but *how* citizenship came to be defined was a question of social and cultural identities, their formation and articulation in movements and ideas. *The Times* might define the moral qualities of the people in one way; the *Bee-Hive* in another. How the issue was constructed and resolved was crucial to the redefinition of the political nation in 1866–8.

This chapter will consider, in particular, two broad areas: first, the building of a political movement for reform and the kinds of claims for citizenship made within it, and, secondly, some of the ways in which the pivotal figure of the respectable working man was situated in the structures and cultures of work and the economy and the bearing this had on the plane of the political.

From Chartism to the Reform League

Between 1838 and 1848 the Chartist movement, the great working-class movement for the vote, flourished as the largest and most important

[9] *Bee-Hive*, 28 July 1866.

political movement of working people in nineteenth-century Britain.[10] But by 1848 it was clearly finished as a mass movement, and following its decline political activity among the working class was weak and fragmented.[11] Chartism itself was by no means dead. It continued to have strength in London, in the West Riding of Yorkshire, on Tyneside and in pockets elsewhere, and to sustain the central preoccupation with manhood or universal suffrage.[12] At the same time Chartists did not confine themselves to advocating the People's Charter, although they would certainly seize every opportunity to do so. Rather, Chartism in its moment of decline was a passage through which many continuing or ex-Chartists were to move into a network of overlapping activities.[13] In its time of greatest strength, between 1838 and 1842, Chartism had always

[10] For brief and good introductions to Chartism, see Clive Behagg, *Labour and Reform: Working-Class Movements 1815–1914* (London: Hodder and Stoughton, 1991), ch. 3, or Edward Royle, *Chartism* (3rd edn, London: Addison-Wesley Longman, 1996). The fullest account is Dorothy Thompson, *The Chartists: Popular Politics in the Industrial Revolution* (London: Maurice Temple Smith, 1984).

[11] Some historians would place the decline earlier. The best-known statement of this case is Gareth Stedman Jones, 'Rethinking Chartism', ch. 3 in his *Languages of Class: Studies in English Working-Class History 1832–1982* (Cambridge University Press, 1983), esp. pp. 163–78. For the alternative view, which insists on the importance of 1848, see esp. John Saville, *1848: The British State and the Chartist Movement* (Cambridge University Press, 1987), which also offers a critique of Stedman Jones's position.

[12] For the West Riding, see Kate Tiller, 'Late Chartism: Halifax, 1847–1858', in James Epstein and Dorothy Thompson (eds.), *The Chartist Experience. Studies in Working-Class Radicalism and Culture, 1830–1860* (Basingstoke: Macmillan, 1982), pp. 311–44; for Tyneside there is some material in Nigel Todd, *The Militant Democracy: Joseph Cowen and Victorian Radicalism* (Whitley Bay: Bewick Press, 1991). See also Breuilly et al., *Era of the Reform League*, p. 16. For the most important single figure in late Chartism, see John Saville, *Ernest Jones: Chartist* (London: Lawrence and Wishart, 1952). There is a need for a thorough history of late Chartism.

[13] One may see this in particular individuals. For example, John Emerson's biography reads like a microcosm of at least one trajectory that radicalism could take in the first three-quarters of the nineteenth century. Born on Tyneside in 1782, he worked first as a metal moulder and then as a waterman on the Tyne, and involved himself in the 'affairs of the trade', that is, trade unionism. Becoming an active radical in 1808, Emerson corresponded with some of the most prominent and influential radicals of the day – Major Cartwright (whom he always claimed to follow), William Cobbett, T. J. Wooler of the *Black Dwarf*. Emerson was a council member of the Northern Political Union in the reform agitation of 1830–2 and by 1838–9 was a leading Chartist in his home village of Winlanton. He then went on in the 1850s and early 1860s to be take part in the important local internationalist campaigns, particularly in support of Italian nationalism – speaking at a meeting 'To Garibaldi, from the Friends of Italian Freedom on Tyneside' in 1859 and again at a meeting in his support in 1862 – and in the renewed movement for the vote. He became a council member of the Northern Reform Union, the chief organisation working for parliamentary reform in the north-east in 1857–62. Still active towards the end of his life (he died in 1868), at the age of eighty-four he joined the NRU's successor organisation, the Northern Reform League and took part in the demonstrations of 1866–7. Throughout his life he was also a dedicated autodidact. See esp. his obituary in *Newcastle Weekly Chronicle*, 11 July 1868, and also: *Newcastle Daily Chronicle*, 17 March 1859, 14 September 1859, 20 September 1862, 26 March 1864; *Newcastle Weekly Chronicle*, 26 January 1867; W. Bourn, *History of the Parish of Ryton* (Carlisle, 1896), pp. 125–6.

been an umbrella movement, sheltering and interlocking with other concerns and movements, from temperance to education, from trade unionism to women's rights. And this persisted in the regrouping of the 1850s.

Chartists were involved in campaigns and organisations such as republicanism, secularism or the demonstrations in 1855 over Sunday trading and against the sabbatarians, on social and economic issues such as in the demonstrations against unemployment in London and elsewhere in 1857–8, or in a range of other issues including temperance and sanitary reform, or education and the provision of public libraries.[14] They might also move into local and parliamentary elections. In Sheffield, to take the best-known local example, Isaac Ironside became a prominent local councillor,[15] while in Tower Hamlets, east London, there was campaigning in support of the parliamentary candidacies of William Newton, of the Amalgamated Society of Engineers, in 1852 and George Jacob Holyoake, secularist, rationalist and free-thinker, co-operator and journalist, in 1857.[16]

In a network of clubs and institutions Chartists and other working-class radicals and political activists would meet to argue the case for this or that good cause. In London they might gather at the John Street Institution in Clerkenwell, the Eclectic Institute in Denmark Street, Soho or at the South Place Ethical Society.[17] Outside London there were similar venues. In Newcastle, for instance, Joseph Barlow's bookshop in the centre of the city was a continuing 'centre of active public life':

> It combined the features of a news agency, publishing house, debating society, and club. All manner of men were to be met with there – teetotallers, anti-teetotallers, Chartists, Urquhartites, and Conservatives; professors of the most orthodox and most heterodox creeds, and men entertaining the most diverse views on social organisation.
>
> Whenever there was a man in the district identified with progressive or reform movements he was certain to find his way to Mr Barlow's, and learn there how the cause he was advocating, or opposing, was advancing.

[14] On these and related movements there is much material in, among others, Margot C. Finn, *After Chartism: Class and Nation in English Radical Politics, 1848–1874* (Cambridge University Press, 1993), ch. 3; Iorwerth Prothero, *Radical Artisans in England and France* (Cambridge University Press, 1997); Edward Royle, *Victorian Infidels: The Origins of the British Secularist Movement 1791–1866* (Manchester University Press, 1974).

[15] See John Salt, 'Isaac Ironside', in Joyce Bellamy and John Saville (eds.), *Dictionary of Labour Biography*, vol. II (Basingstoke: Macmillan, 1974), pp. 201–7; John Salt, 'Local Manifestations of the Urquhartite Movement', *International Review of Social History* 13 (1968), 350–65; Gregory Claeys, 'Mazzini, Kossuth, and British Radicalism, 1848–1854', *Journal of British Studies* 28 (1989), 225–61.

[16] F. E. Gillespie, *Labor and Politics in England 1850–1867* (1927; repr. London: Frank Cass, 1966), pp. 101–3, 126–7.

[17] Finn, *After Chartism*, pp. 134–5 and generally ch. 3; Stan Shipley, *Club Life and Socialism in Mid-Victorian London* (Oxford: History Workshop Pamphlets, 5, 1972).

Here men might hear the views of W. J. Linton on republicanism, Thomas Cooper on questions of religion and the state church or Lloyd Garrison on slavery in the United States.[18]

But the most important campaigns in the 1850s, other than explicitly for the vote itself, were on international questions. Throughout the decade there was a vibrant current of sustained support for the causes of European nationalism and the victims of oppressive regimes, at least in Europe and North America. Working- and middle-class radicals – the latter including individuals like the Unitarian and member of the Courtauld family, P. A. Taylor, Joseph Cowen jun. the north-eastern industrialist and entrepreneur and newspaper publisher, James Stansfeld, the liberal champion of (among many other things) birth control, and activist women like Jesse White Mario or the Ashurst sisters – were energetic and generous in their enthusiasm. They welcomed Hungarian nationalists like Kossuth in 1851, the Polish exiles of 1853–4 and, above all, championed the cause of Italian nationalism in its Mazzinian and Garibaldian varieties. For some the key institutional means of mobilising international support were the Foreign Affairs Committees, established during the Crimean War, intensely hostile to Palmerstonian belligerence and including a curious admixture of David Urquhart and his followers, Chartists, republicans, radical and 'extreme' liberals and even the occasional Tory.[19]

One may see instances of the support such people gave to international causes in the cases of the Jersey exiles and the 'Orsini affair'. In the former, in 1855 radical internationalists sought to defend French political émigrés, including the socialist Félix Pyat and the writer Victor Hugo, against their expulsion from Jersey by the British government. In this instance they failed, facing the determination of the government and the relative indifference of public opinion. More significant were the rather more successful campaigns of the 'Orsini affair'. Palmerston had bowed

[18] Obituary of Barlow, *Newcastle Daily Chronicle*, 16 October 1886. The paper thought Barlow of sufficient importance that it devoted a leader column to him as well as an obituary.

[19] For the FACs, see among others Olive Anderson, *A Liberal State at War* (Basingstoke: Macmillan, 1967), pp. 83–4, 143–52; Richard Shannon, 'David Urquhart and the Foreign Affairs Committee', in Patricia Hollis (ed.), *Pressure from Without* (London: Edward Arnold, 1974), pp. 239–61; Miles Taylor, 'The Old Radicalism and the New: David Urquhart and the Politics of Opposition, 1832–1867', in Eugenio F. Biagini and Alastair J. Reid (eds.), *Currents of Radicalism: Popular Radicalism, Organised Labour and Party Politics in Britain, 1850–1914* (Cambridge University Press, 1991), pp. 23–43. For some of the local flavour of the FACs, see among others R. G. Gammage, *History of the Chartist Movement, 1837–1854* (1894 edn; repr. London: Merlin Press, 1969), p. 189; Brian Harrison and Patricia Hollis (eds.), *Robert Lowery: Radical and Chartist* (London: Europa, 1979), pp. 162–4, 167–70.

to pressure from the French state consequent upon the attempted assassination of Louis Napoleon by Felice Orsini and had introduced a bill to convert conspiracy to murder into a criminal offence; to try Simon Bernard, a French exile accused of manufacturing bombs for Orsini; and to prosecute Edward Truelove and Stanislaus Tchorzewski for printing and distributing W. E. Adams's pamphlet, *Tyrannicide: Is It Justifiable?*, which sought to absolve Orsini of any moral guilt in the face of the oppression of the contemptible French emperor. The sustained campaign against the government on these related issues was notable for the widespread condemnation of its actions but also as being a genuinely cross-class movement, drawing in not only many working-class radicals but also from across the spectrum of middle-class radicalism. On each of the elements the government was defeated: in Parliament over the Conspiracy to Murder Bill; in the courts over Bernard; and by withdrawing from the prosecution of Truelove in the face of public and hostility.[20]

Internationalism, Chartism and other popular radical activities in the 1850s played a crucial role in the bridge between the Chartism of 1838–48 and the movement for reform in the 1860s. They sustained organisation; they linked both the older concerns – particularly with the vote itself – with newer emphases; and they were the ground on which a reshaping of popular politics was taking place. But if we look back to the great era of Chartism or forward to the reform agitation of 1865–7, what is striking is less the persistence of activity, and more the weaknesses of that politics in the 1850s.

Chartists and others advocating parliamentary reform faced major problems in the 1850s. In the first place Chartism itself was institutionally divided. Its organisation was sustained most importantly through the National Charter Association, led by Ernest Jones from its foundation in 1850[21] until its final conference in 1858. But already in the wake of 1848 the movement had seen the fissiparous formation of a number of rival organisations, among them William Lovett's People's League, the People's Charter Union and Bronterre O'Brien's National Reform League.[22] One consequence was characteristic of minority political movements in crisis – the tendency to stricter controls being exercised

[20] W. E. Adams, *Tyrannicide: Is It Justifiable?* (8 pp., London, 1858); for Adams's own account of this affair, see his *Memoirs of a Social Atom* (1903; repr. with intro. by John Saville, New York: Augustus M. Kelley, 1968), chs. 36–7. See also his later *Bonaparte's Challenge to Tyrannicides by the Author of 'Tyrannicide: Is It Justifiable?'* (1867; 'A Suppressed Pamphlet'; copy in British Library). For the Orsini affair, see esp. Bernard Porter, *The Refugee Question in Mid-Victorian Politics* (Cambridge University Press, 1979), ch. 6; Finn, *After Chartism*, pp. 180–7.

[21] When it succeeded the National Charter and Social Reform Association.

[22] Gillespie, *Labor and Politics*, pp. 67–71.

from their centre. Even Ernest Jones was not immune to this, attempting to impose an increasingly centralised domination of the NCA by 1856.[23]

Further, between 1848 and 1858 Chartism was split by two major issues. First were the questions of political economy and the wider objectives of the movement. Jones and others like George Julian Harney saw the future in terms of the creation of a socialist movement in which the question of political rights and power could only be seen as a means to the wider objective of social reconstruction. But against them stood those, and not least trade unions, who wished to continue to restrict the purposes of Chartism to the demand for the vote alone, and who were at best suspicious, at worst hostile to 'socialistic' meddling.[24] The second question was the necessarily related one of strategy and tactics. Should the movement ally with middle-class radicals in campaigning for parliamentary reform? The issue had always had a presence within Chartism before 1848: afterwards it became central. In April 1851 there had already been a severe split when the Manchester Chartists opposed the 'socialism' of the NCA and joined the predominantly middle-class Parliamentary and Financial Reform Association.[25] And of course the hostility of many Chartists to joining with the middle class was severely tested by the practical alliances forming around international questions.

Chartism and related movements faced not only their own internal problems but also the relative indifference of its intended constituency, the working class, to its activities. Many Chartist meetings were held but the numbers involved were small. Many former Chartists had probably withdrawn from politics altogether, moved into other organisations and concerns or perhaps above all – although how can we tell? – into the relatively private world of the home and its immediate orbit.[26] Some will have simply grown too old to be involved. But, whatever the reasons, there is a pervasive feel of defeat in much working-class radicalism in the 1850s, which might incline those involved to pessimism and a certain despair.

[23] Breuilly et al., *Era of the Reform League*, p. 16; J. T. Ward, *Chartism* (London: Batsford, 1973), pp. 232–4.

[24] See esp. John Belchem, 'Chartism and the Trades, 1848–1850', *English Historical Review* 98 (1983), 558–87, for the hostility of trade unionism to 'socialist' developments within late Chartism.

[25] See Gillespie, *Labor and Politics*, pp. 89–90, esp. p. 89 n. 4; *Northern Star*, 25 January, 1 and 8 February 1851; *The Council of the Manchester Chartist Association to the Democratic Reformers of Great Britain* (1851; pamphlet in Lovett Collection, Goldsmith's Library, University of London).

[26] Note, for instance, Thomas Cooper's later and much-quoted lament (in 1872) of the abandonment of the cause of political justice by 'well-dressed working men' in favour of talk of their shares in co-ops and building societies and a concern, scarcely less contemptible in Cooper's eyes, with walking their whippets: see his *Life of Thomas Cooper* (London, 1873), p. 393.

One Chartist, Thomas Thompson, a sailcloth weaver of North Shields, gravitating from the movement into the Northern Reform Union's campaign for parliamentary reform in 1859, wrote of what he saw as the sheer difficulty of rousing the people from their apathy (even though the NRU was to rouse the people more than any other in the area had done since the earliest days of Chartism). Attempting to gather signatures he wrote to the organisation's secretary, Richard Bagnall Reed, that 'i feell it my duty to inform you that i am far from getting on to my own satisfaction or i am afraid yours either, you may go into fifty houses and not get a single signature in this town with a Floating population'.[27] He had 'proposed out door meetings to call public attention to the matter to give a little stimulus but no encouragement is given'. It was, he wrote, 'like driving snails to Jerusalem'.[28]

The cause of parliamentary reform was also operating in politically unpropitious circumstances. The Reform Bills of the 1850s received little enthusiasm or support.[29] Moreover, radicals of all persuasions faced the dominance of governments which were prepared to go to war in the pursuit of 'British interests' – pursued incompetently but more or less successfully in the Crimea in 1854–6, with savage brutality in India in 1857 or with imperious and imperialist arrogance in Persia in 1856–7 and in China between 1856 and 1860.[30] At the same time the decade was witnessing the recasting of Liberal politics into its more organisationally and ideologically coherent shape of Palmerstonian and Gladstonian liberalism, drawing together into a bloc of political sentiment and alliance, high Whig landowners and Peelite Tories, nonconformist businessmen, radicals of various kinds – be they 'radical reformers', independent liberals or Manchester School advocates[31] – and 'gentlemen of liberal views', a bloc in part articulated by the growth of an enlarged metropolitan and provincial press. If the foreign policies of Palmerstonian liberalism were essentially imperialist and inclined to belligerence, what was being cast in these years was also the die of what came to be central to the party and the wider political culture of liberalism in the 1860s: an emphasis upon financial probity and retrenchment, upon modest degrees of institutional

[27] Thompson was referring to the seamen who predominated in the town.

[28] No addressee but probably to R. B. Reed; from North Shields, 10 January 1859 (Cowen Collection [hereafter CC], Tyne and Wear County Record Office), C387.

[29] See appendix C, pp. 239–40, for details of the proposals.

[30] In 1856–7 Britain went to war to force the Persians out of Afghanistan, in order to secure the Indian north-west frontier against both the Persians and the Russians; in the Second Anglo-Chinese War (1856–60), the British government attempted to force its trading 'rights' upon the Chinese.

[31] See Miles Taylor's very helpful discussion of the characteristics of these three sections of radicalism in his *Decline of British Radicalism 1847–1860* (Oxford: Clarendon Press, 1995), ch. 1 and *passim*.

reform in the state, upon the sustenance of free trade and, largely speaking, laissez-faire, and on building a politics which was presented as transcending class division in the name of creating a 'social contract' between all sections of the 'nation as a whole'. Here Gladstone's fiscal policies were of crucial importance, as Matthew has argued.[32]

If elements of this were crucial to the success of the campaign for parliamentary reform in 1867–8, working-class radicals in the 1850s largely encountered it as a set of problems and difficulties. Part of the problem here was the central one of making alliance with middle-class advocates of reform. Chartists may split over the issue; they like other radicals may also have to rethink the particular demands they were going to make. But the more fundamental problem was that before 1858 the varieties of middle-class radicals prepared to espouse parliamentary reform were not very interested in the fundamental element of working-class claims, namely an extension of the suffrage. Middle-class radicals, as individuals or in organisations like the Parliamentary and Financial Reform Association or the Administrative Reform Association, were essentially concerned with the question of redistribution, partly because of the realisation that 1832 had not secured the untrammelled advance of progressive forces against Old Corruption and the aristocratic state, partly in the name of enabling MPs to put restraints on state expenditure and the overbearing power of the executive within government.[33] Such problems were faced nationally; but they were also local, particularly where working-class radicals faced the presence of the radicalism of the electorally extremely significant 'shopocracy', 'characterized', as Theodore Hoppen has written, 'by a special kind of tight-fisted meanness' and organised through Ratepayers' Associations, tending to a militant Protestantism, and making their entry into local government to exercise tight controls over expenditure and, in some areas, in opposition to the prevailing Whig cliques who dominated local politics. Such men as these were usually hostile, at least in the 1850s, to Chartists and others demanding suffrage reform. For example, in Newcastle an alliance with local Ratepayers' Associations and others seemed to be on the cards in 1858–9; but any hopes of it were destroyed in the election of 1859. P. A. Taylor, the candidate put forward by the NRU, stood on a platform of manhood suffrage. But when he was beaten hope-

[32] See above, introduction, p. 12, for a brief statement of Matthew's views. For important reassessments of Palmerston's politics, compare Miles Taylor, *Decline of Radicalism*, esp. pp. 328–31, with E. D. Steele, *Palmerston and Liberalism* (Cambridge University Press, 1991), chs. 4–5. For liberalism, John Vincent, *The Formation of the British Liberal Party 1857–1868* (2nd edn, Harmondsworth: Penguin, 1972), remains fundamental as is H. C. G. Matthew, *Gladstone 1809–1874* (Oxford: Clarendon Press, 1986).

[33] Thomas Gallagher, 'The Second Reform Movement, 1848–1867', *Albion* 12 (1980), 147–63; Miles Taylor, *Decline of Radicalism*, pp. 163–4.

lessly into third place, Joseph Cowen attributed the defeat to 'the mere shopkeeping class'.[34]

In contrast to the difficulties of the 1850s the revived agitation for parliamentary reform of 1865–7 was a very different affair, operating in a significantly altered context. What crucially redefined the possibility of a new reform movement were a number of developments. The first was the involvement of the trade unions. Following the economic crisis of 1857–8, between 1858 and 1862 there had occurred a revival of class conflict within trades and industries and, with it, of trade unionism. Central was the struggle in the building trades (particularly in 1859–60) when building workers in London demanded the nine-hour day. The ensuing strike and lock-out initiated a new phase in trade union activity and organisation. Institutionally, the movement gave rise to the formation of the London Trades Council and brought together those key leaders of trade unionism whom the Webbs called the 'Junta', partly in the stimulus the struggle gave to the formation of trade unionism elsewhere, and partly in stimulating trade unions to move into a more political phase.[35] The central reason for this growing involvement of trade unions in politics was the legal restrictions imposed on trade unionism by the Master and Servant Law and the use of the common law of conspiracy against the unions. Many more unions were committing themselves to the necessity of action on the suffrage in order to secure the 'rights of labour'. These shifts were aided by the foundation of what was to become a key instrument of political and trade union radicalism in the 1860s, the *Bee-Hive* newspaper edited by George Potter.[36] The crystallisation of this political shift within the unions was the formation of the Manhood Suffrage and

[34] K. Theodore Hoppen, *The Mid-Victorian Generation, 1846–1886* (Oxford: Clarendon Press, 1998), pp. 48–9. For an excellent local study of the shopocracy (although including one or two errors of detail), see T. J. Nossiter, *Influence, Opinion and Political Idioms in Reformed England: Case Studies from the North East 1832–1874* (Brighton: Harvester Press, 1975), ch. 9. See also R. J. Morris, *Class, Sect and Party: The Making of the British Middle Class, Leeds 1820–1850* (Manchester University Press, 1990), pp. 133–7; M. J. Winstanley, *The Shopkeeper's World 1830–1914* (Manchester University Press, 1983), pp. 19–27. For Cowen's condemnation of 'the shopocracy', see *Northern Reform Record* 12 (July 1859).

[35] The period also saw the formation of Trades Councils elsewhere: see John Saville, 'Trades Councils and the Labour Movement to 1900', *Bulletin of the Society for the Study of Labour History* 14 (1967), 29–34; W. H. Fraser, *Trade Unions and Society: The Struggle for Acceptance 1850–1880* (London: George Allen and Unwin, 1974), pp. 42–9. For the Junta and critiques of the notion, see esp. G. D. H. Cole, 'Some Notes on British Trade Unions in the Third Quarter of the Nineteenth Century', *International Review of Social History* 2 (1937), repr. in E. M. Carus-Wilson (ed.), *Essays in Economic History*, 3 vols. (London: Edward Arnold, 1962), vol. III, pp. 202–21, and Royden Harrison, *Before the Socialists*, pp. 6–19. For the building dispute and its political significance, see F. M. Leventhal, *Respectable Radical: George Howell and Victorian Working-Class Politics* (London: Weidenfeld and Nicolson, 1971), pp. 25–32.

[36] See above, n. 6.

Vote By Ballot Association in the autumn of 1862. In turn this led to the formation of the Reform League by the unions and sympathetic reformers in 1865.[37]

The second major development was the concern with international questions and in particular with three issues – Polish independence, Italian nationalism and the Civil War in the United States.[38] The campaigns on these issues were important because they were a junction between working-class radicals and reformers and middle-class radical parliamentarians – above all John Bright – and a range of middle-class enthusiasts for international causes, like Edmond Beales who was to become the president of the Reform League, Joseph Cowen in the north-east or radical Unitarians like Peter Taylor. As indicated above, men like Cowen had been involved in the 1850s and had done much to sustain internationalism in the north-east and in Britain more generally. But what changed in the 1860s was the sheer number of working-class men, and sometimes women, who were drawn in.

Internationalism also carried within itself an ideology that, in stressing a radical 'patriotism', emphasised the cause of 'the people' against despotism and the aristocracy and undemocratic regimes. This may have led some, as in the responses to the US Civil War, to advocating the cause of the people against capitalist despots and in favour of the Southern plantation owners. But most radicals, both working- and middle-class, were firmly on the side of the North against slavery. As Royden Harrison has argued, 'the great majority of politically conscious workmen were pro-Federal and firmly resolved to oppose war', and the issue proved to be of major importance for the subsequent history of the British labour movement.[39]

Yet the paradox of internationalism was that it was firmly grounded in the nation. It sought – and this is a point to which I will return – not the dissolution of the nation (a largely twentieth-century idea) but the inter-

[37] An intermediate organisation was the Universal League for the Material Elevation of the Working Classes. For the events leading up to the formation of Reform League, see esp. Gillespie, *Labor and Politics*, pp. 203–12, and Leventhal, *George Howell*, ch. 3.

[38] For contrasting discussions of the importance of internationalism, see Royden Harrison, 'The British Labour Movement and the International in 1864', in Ralph Miliband and John Saville (eds.), *The Socialist Register 1964* (London: Merlin Press, 1964), pp. 293–308; Royden Harrison, *Before the Socialists*, esp. ch. 2, 'British Labour and American Slavery'; Finn, *After Chartism*; Breuilly et al., *Era of the Reform League*, esp. pp. 54–70.

[39] Royden Harrison, *Before the Socialists*, pp. 65, 68–9. The extent of popular support for the North has been questioned by, above all, Mary Ellison, *Support for Secession: Lancashire and the American Civil War* (University of Chicago Press, 1972). For an effective rebuttal of her views, see Philip S. Foner, *British Labor and the American Civil War* (New York and London: Holmes and Meier, 1981). Chapter 2 of Foner's book surveys the debate on the question. See also Eugenio F. Biagini, *Liberty, Retrenchment and Reform: Popular Liberalism in the Age of Gladstone, 1860–1880* (Cambridge University Press, 1992), pp. 69–83.

action of nations and of peoples in a harmonious whole and the entry of the people into their individual nation-states through attaining political rights. But, as Catherine Hall discusses (in chapter 4), there were distinct limitations on who might be drawn into this vision.

The political conditions for the emergence of a revived reform agitation were also changing. Three elements were of importance here: the question of an alliance between working- and middle-class radicals; events at the parliamentary level; and the role of John Bright in the revival and shaping of the reform movement.

To take the first: there was a clear shift among popular radical reformers to an acceptance of the need for an alliance with middle-class radicals (even though, as in the case of the north-east cited above, the full realisation of such an alliance was not always possible). Among the Chartists, the NCA under Jones was espousing the need for this by the autumn of 1857, confirmed by its conference in February 1858 when the Political Reform Union was established. At the same time many manhood suffrage associations were being formed in London and beyond and a renewed national movement was once again being built. For example, in the north-east, the Northern Reform Union was established in January 1858 (following the evident revival of a reform agitation from May 1857).[40] Elsewhere in the country meetings were held and associations established: for example, in the north-west in Manchester, Rochdale and Salford; in Yorkshire in Leeds and York; in the West Midlands in Birmingham and Dudley; in Scotland in Renfrew.[41]

At the parliamentary level there were two further attempts to introduce Reform Bills within the House of Commons – the Conservative measure of Derby and Disraeli introduced in 1859 and the Russell bill of 1860. When the Conservative party formed the government after the 1859 election they did so in the wake of the previous Liberal government's declared commitment to introducing, if not very enthusiastically, some measure of reform. But the bill Disraeli introduced was, as John Bright put it, a 'country gentleman's bill' designed essentially to shore up and strengthen the Conservative position in the counties. Disraeli explicitly rejected the idea of altering the level of the existing borough franchise, by declaring that if they lowered the qualification the result would be the predominance of 'household democracy'. But in the wake of the defeat of the Disraeli/Derby government at the subsequent election, Disraeli admitted

[40] *Northern Daily Express*, 13 May 1857; NRU Minute Book, CC, C6; *Northern Daily Express*, 12 January 1858; *Manchester Guardian*, 13 January 1858; *Morning Star* (London), 14 January 1858; see also *Jersey Independent*, 20 January 1858, for G. J. Harney's account of the foundation.

[41] Gillespie, *Labor and Politics*, pp. 160–7.

that the borough franchise would have to be lowered in order to admit a working-class constituency.[42] Following this the Liberals introduced but then withdrew their own modest proposals, essentially based upon the earlier bills of 1852 and 1854. Yet if this caused great disappointment to radical reformers in their manhood suffrage associations, these political events helped to put on the agenda once again the question of working-class votes, even if the subsequent five years of Liberal government and the sustained indifference of Palmerston to suffrage extension were to effectively prevent the issue from reaching the parliamentary stage.

Decisive for the formation of popular associations and the explosion of activity around the reform question was the public 'conversion' (as it is sometimes called) of John Bright to the cause of reform, which went beyond simply a concern with redistribution but raised the issue of a lowering of the franchise qualification. In October 1858 Bright announced his commitment at two meetings in Birmingham. He then went on a speaking tour to publicise his views. In fact Bright's reform proposals were extremely cautious. While he advocated both radical redistribution and the secret ballot – both measures part of the well-established stock of reform proposals among the radical middle class – he advocated no more than a £10 household suffrage in boroughs (and one in which the voter would be required to pay rates directly rather than being 'compounded'), the exclusion of lodgers and a £10 householder franchise in the counties. The proposal made him vulnerable to popular and working-class radical criticism. Ernest Jones, for instance, charged Bright with producing a franchise for the middle classes: Bright's borough proposal was, he said, 'household suffrage clogged with the ratebook; household suffrage dependent on the rate collector and the landlord – a suffrage for the middle classes, – and exclusion for the great masses of the people'. His exclusion of the lodger would place an undue emphasis upon the married man as against the single. And Jones also raised the issue of the possibilities of the vote for working men who did not live in boroughs but in the counties, who included not only agricultural labourers but, for example, many miners and other industrial workers. Bright's county franchise proposal, said Jones, was 'just as exclusive towards the working classes as a fifty-pound franchise itself'. What, argued Jones, should working men do? They should act as men and as members of the working class:

> Working men! brother Chartists! and honest reformers of all classes . . . Rush together in your meetings, and pass formal and emphatic resolutions, openly and formally repudiating the measure of Mr Bright, . . . and declaring yourselves for

[42] W. F. Monypenny and G. E. Buckle, *The Life of Benjamin Disraeli, Earl of Beaconsfield*, 6 vols. (London: John Murray, 1910–20), vol. IV, pp. 247–8.

registered manhood suffrage ... Repudiate the cotton-lord measure; act like men; and we yet will save the cause of freedom from their grasp.[43]

Jones was not alone in criticising Bright on these grounds. But it remains the case that Bright's intervention in the reform question was of major importance for the building of a popular movement. This was partly because he invested his commitment with a profound moral passion and style which appeared to speak both to and, in a sense, from his audiences, and to summon up the popular audience – of workers and others – as embodying a moral purity and energy which spoke as 'the nation', as has been argued by Patrick Joyce.[44] But what Joyce radically underestimates is that Bright's importance lay in the *content* as well as the style of his rhetoric. The decisive shift he made was not only to raise the issue of suffrage extension, albeit in a very limited mode, but also to link this to the question of taxation and working-class consumption. For Bright's position on reform demonstrated that those men without votes were suffering the excessive burdens of consumption taxes on tobacco and paper. Such men were, as a consequence, deserving of the vote as they were also deserving of what radical reformers had consistently argued for, and what working-class radicals also saw as central, the reform of taxation. In doing this Bright helped to ensure, as Miles Taylor has argued, that there reappeared the language of the 'industrious versus the idle, the common people versus the upper ten thousand' and that the question of parliamentary reform became more democratic. Henceforth, as he puts it, the debates about democracy would be centred on the franchise and the 'intelligent artisan'.[45]

Arguments for reform

But what were the arguments and claims being made by working men and popular radical organisations for reform?

The simple explicit demands of the Reform League were for manhood suffrage but limited by three qualifications: first, it should be restricted to men aged twenty-one and over; secondly, they should be registered as being in permanent residence of a dwelling for at least one year; and, thirdly, it would exclude those who were a 'burden' on society as criminals or as paupers.[46] In addition radicals added to the demand for the vote

[43] *Cabinet Newspaper*, 22 January 1859.
[44] Patrick Joyce, *Visions of the People: Industrial England and the Question of Class 1848–1914* (Cambridge University Press, 1991), pp. 47–9, and Joyce, *Democratic Subjects: The Self and the Social in Nineteenth-Century England* (Cambridge University Press, 1994), pt II.
[45] Miles Taylor, *Decline of Radicalism*, pp. 334, 335.
[46] Programme of the Reform League, cited in, for example, *Morning Star*, 13 March 1865.

by ballot and, usually, a more equitable distribution of seats, shorter parliaments and the payment of MPs. In themselves these demands constituted a narrowing of working-class franchise demands as compared with Chartism or, indeed, any of the movements for parliamentary reform between the Corresponding Societies of the 1790s and Chartism. The major shift was the exclusion of those who were not 'registered and residential'. But to understand the significance of that shift it is necessary to turn to the arguments and assumptions within which the demands were embedded, and to see not only the ways in which the Reform League and its ilk defined the potential working-class citizen as being a particular kind of worker – respectable and independent – but also the ways in which the questions of gender and differentiation within the working class were threaded through each other.

When Edmond Beales, president of the Reform League, delivered the organisation's inaugural address to a packed meeting in St Martin's Hall, London, in May 1865 he put forward arguments that were common among reformers and were to be repeated up and down the country during 1866–7 when the agitation was at its height. Typical of such speeches was the continued emphasis on the *right* of working men to the vote. One component of this was the claim that working men had a *constitutional* right to the suffrage. Against those who denounced the prospect of manhood suffrage as being 'contrary to the whole spirit and the system of our own constitution', Beales asserted that it was 'the present restricted and limited suffrage [which] is opposed to that spirit and system'.[47]

Yet what did reformers mean by the constitution? Comparisons were frequently made with the supposedly democratic constitutions of other countries. Indeed, said Beales, the absence of manhood suffrage in Britain was 'scarcely credible . . . some six hundred years after the establishment in this country of the representative system, nearly a hundred years after the establishment of manhood suffrage amongst American brethren . . . and, whilst the same suffrage is not only in full and most beneficial operation in our own colonies, but has been even employed for one of the most important of all political operations – the election of a sovereign in both France and Italy'.[48]

[47] Report of the meeting in *The Miner and Workman's Advocate, 20 May 1865*, in Breuilly et al., *Era of the Reform League*, pp. 139–44 (Beales's speech is on pp. 139–42).

[48] Beales in Breuilly et al., *Era of the Reform League*, p. 140. As Breuilly et al. point out (*ibid.*, p. 126 n. 4), Beales's references to the election of Louis Napoleon as president of the French Second Republic in December 1848 and the referenda held in some Italian states in 1860 on the question of fusion with the Piedmontese monarchy were rather inaccurate. One can add that his references to the colonies and to the United States in effect screened out the vast majority of the populations of those regions!

Characteristically, reformers also argued that there existed a historical constitution in which there had been manhood or universal suffrage and forms of democratic government. It was widely believed that there was a moment – the dating of which varied, from sometime during the Reformation, to prior to 1066 – when universal manhood suffrage had existed. It was, in essence, a continuation of the tradition of the Norman Yoke, continued in the 1850s and 1860s by the spate of research by Chartists and others which claimed to show that there had existed rights which had been stolen by feudalists, despots or Tom Paine's 'armed banditti'.[49] For example, Thomas Doubleday, co-author of (among many other works) a widely circulated *Handbook for Reformers*, claimed in 1867 that 'I am well convinced that manhood suffrage was the practice under the original English Constitution for more than two centuries.'[50]

The emphasis upon rights was usually couched in moral and ethical terms. Contrary to those intellectuals writing on the question of reform in the 1850 and 1860s, the argument from natural rights was often to be found in popular reform circles and certainly did not disappear after Chartism.[51] An important strand within reform thinking continued to insist that men were equal simply because they were men. And while a language of politics couched in religious terms was of diminishing importance in this period, for many the equality of men derived from God, was sanctioned by the Bible and Christianity, and transcended any differences of power or quality resulting from the possession of property. 'Britannicus', writing in the *Newcastle Weekly Chronicle*, cited the Leveller tract, *An Arrow Against All Tyrants and Tyranny* (1647), in support of the claim for the suffrage:

49 Tom Paine, *Common Sense* (1776), in *The Essential Thomas Paine*, intro. Sidney Hook (New York: New American Library, 1969), p. 34.

50 For the 'Norman Yoke', see Christopher Hill, 'The Norman Yoke', in his *Puritanism and Revolution* (repr., London: Panther, 1968), pp. 58–125; for the search for historic precedents in the 1850s, Olive Anderson, *A Liberal State at War*, pp. 139–43; Doubleday's view was in a letter to the *Newcastle Weekly Chronicle*, 2 February 1867, cited in Biagini, *Liberty, Retrenchment and Reform*, p. 266 n. 64. It summarised the views he had put forward with James Paul Cobbett in their *Hand-Book for Reformers* (London, Manchester and Newcastle upon Tyne, 1859). Although widely quoted in north-eastern reform circles from 1859, the book then seems to have disappeared: the only extant copy in Britain known to me is in the Mitchell Library, Glasgow.

51 Hoppen, *Mid-Victorian Generation*, p. 238. These works included Thomas Hare, *The Machinery of Representation* (2nd edn, London, 1857), and his *Election of Representatives, Parliamentary and Municipal: A Treatise* (1859), 3rd edn, with a preface, appendix, and other additions (London, 1865); Earl Grey, *Parliamentary Government Considered with Reference to a Reform of Parliament: An Essay* (1858; revised edn, London, 1864); John Stuart Mill, *Thoughts on Parliamentary Reform* (2nd edn, London, 1859), repr. in *Collected Works of John Stuart Mill* [hereafter *CW*], gen. ed. J. M. Robson, 33 vols. (University of Toronto Press, 1962–91), vol. XIX, *Essays on Politics and Society*, ed. J. M. Robson (1977), pp. 311–39; *Essays on Reform* (London, 1867); and *Questions for a Reformed Parliament* (London, 1867).

by natural birth all men are equally and alike born to like propriety, liberty and freedom, as we are delivered by God into the hands of Nature into this world, every one with a natural innate freedom and propriety . . . even so are we to live, everyone equally and alike to enjoy his birthright and privilege, even all whereof God by nature hath made him free.[52]

When Richard Reed, secretary of the Northern Reform Union (1857–62) and prominent in the Northern Reform League (1865–7), spoke to a meeting of miners in Swalwell in the north-east, he justified the claim to the vote in terms of Christianity, citing

several texts from the New Testament to prove that it advocated the equality of men in the sight of God, high and low, rich and poor. The philosophy of Christianity was that men should not be honoured because they possessed wealth, yet our legislature refused to allow a man to vote without he had a pecuniary or property qualification.[53]

The right of working men to the vote was also based on arguments about law, taxation and the defence of the nation. 'No taxation without representation' – and in particular the claim for a reduction of indirect taxation and cheap government – continued to be a major concern and slogan.[54] Moreover, to require men to agree to such conditions and obligations without being able to participate actively in the creation of such conditions and obligations was to produce not consent to government but, as W. E. Adams put it, 'mere passive obedience'.[55] Because men were taxed and subject to law and might be required to defend the country, it was illegitimate to deny them a place in the governance of the nation.

In articulating this concern, the reformers reached back deep into the radical tradition – to Hampden and those who protested against the arbitrary rule of Charles I in the 1620s, to the Levellers of the 1640s, to Major Cartwright in the 1770s and the popular radicals from the 1790s onwards. In important respects the demand for manhood suffrage continued to be informed by that tradition, and in particular by the legacy of the radical critique of Old Corruption, which had been paramount within it during 1790–1832 and, to a degree, Chartism. Some radicals maintained this into the 1850s and 1860s, with one of the most important sources of this being the mass-circulation *Reynolds's Newspaper*.[56]

[52] Cited in Biagini, *Liberty, Retrenchment and Reform*, p. 271.

[53] *Newcastle Daily Chronicle*, 12 October 1859.

[54] It was used, for example, as the motto of the *Northern Reform Record* (12 issues, July 1858 to July 1859), organ of the NRU, and subsequently appeared in Reform League publications.

[55] W. E. Adams, *An Argument for Complete Suffrage* (London, Manchester and Newcastle upon Tyne, 1860).

[56] For which see Virginia Berridge, 'Popular Sunday Papers and Mid-Victorian Society', in

Surveying the 'Prospects of the Democratic Cause' in 1850, G. W. M. Reynolds wrote that the institutions of England were perishing under the weight of their intrinsic rottenness, with its 'bloated' church establishment, its arrogant, greedy, ignorant and selfish hereditary aristocracy, its monopolising landowners and its ridiculous, pompous and ostentatious court.[57] What enabled the Old Corruption (or 'Old Iniquity' as Reynolds called it elsewhere[58]) of the landed and monied oligarchies to sustain their control was the system of taxation, and especially of indirect taxes. This, said the NRU in 1858,

> was the trunk of the tree of misgovernment, whence spring innumerable branches, the unwholesome fruits of which have poisoned the body-politic of England; have impoverished the blood, debilitated the limbs, degraded the features, and deprived . . . almost every natural function of what should be a free and healthy State.[59]

Yet if strands of the anti-Old Corruption argument persisted, what had shifted was both the context and content of the argument. The oppositional radicalism of the taxation argument – in which the control of taxation was the basis on which the state and ruling class inflicted injustices upon the industrious classes and the poor[60] – was undercut by its placement within mainstream, Gladstonian liberalism: it was no longer possible to argue that the state's hostility to the poor and the working class was based on exploitation through indirect taxation when the state began to reduce its burdens. And, as I have indicated earlier, John Bright's linking of tax to suffrage was central to making possible and building an alliance of working- and middle-class reformers. If these elements made possible a degree of homology between the claims of working-class reformers and the shifts in high liberal politics, it also had the effect of diluting and taking the sting out of the old radicalism. Yet what underpinned this was also – and I shall return to this later – the changing conception of the relationship between economy and polity in radical thought.

The moral argument for reform was also buttressed by continual evocation of the ways in which working men had demonstrated their fitness for the vote through the social and cultural associations. Such associations displayed 'character' – that key 'Victorian value' – in the sense used

George Boyce, James Curran and Pauline Wingate (eds.), *Newspaper History from the Seventeenth Century to the Present Day* (London: Methuen, 1978), pp. 247–64.

57 *Reynolds's Newspaper*, 5 May 1850. 58 *Ibid.*, 10 January 1858.

59 NRU, *To the People of Great Britain and Ireland* (4 pp.; issued 1 March 1858, Newcastle); copy in NRU Scrapbook 1 in CC; also reprinted in *Newcastle Daily Chronicle*, 12 March 1858. 60 For this argument, see esp. Stedman Jones, 'Rethinking Chartism'.

by those like Samuel Smiles when he wrote of 'human nature in its best form' or 'truthfulness, integrity and goodness . . . the essence of manly character'.[61] When Gladstone referred to the growth of institutions like savings banks and friendly societies as showing the trustworthiness and newly won stature of the working class he was in accord with the representations of those developments by working men and reforming organisations. Thus for instance Beales spoke of the

> wonderful advancement made of late years by the working classes in all the habits of prudence, temperance, and social and Christian life and virtue [and] the benefit, building, co-operative, temperance, and other societies, institutes, and exhibitions existing amongst them, involving the disposal of hundreds of thousands of pounds, and the exercise of large administrative power and great faculty of self-denial and self-control.[62]

These were the men who in their 'intelligence [and] respectability . . . were worthy of having a fair share in the representation of the country'.[63]

Yet if entry to the political nation was often justified in part on the ground of historical right, what working men would bring to the constitution would be *benefits* – moral purification of politics and a disinterestedness of purpose. Above all, this meant that if it was the working class (or classes) who were claiming the vote, their entry into the political nation would entail the end of class politics. Politics and the constitution as it existed meant that class rule prevailed. Restricting the suffrage to particular interests – land, commerce, the army or any other of the 'interests' frequently referred to – guaranteed that selfishness would prevail. On the contrary, if manhood suffrage were to be granted, then what would ensue would not be the rule of the working class but the unification of all classes in the interests of the nation as a whole. It was not the case, reformers frequently and categorically said, that an extension of the franchise would result in a subversion of the constitution or the establishment of a democracy of the poor which would 'swamp and substantially disenfranchise the other classes' and that the 'management of the affairs of this great empire [would be placed] in the hands of the working classes'.[64] Rather, the

[61] See Samuel Smiles, *Self-Help* (London, 1859), ch. 13, 'Character: The True Gentleman', and his *Character* (London, 1871), for representative statements of the nature of 'character'. And for the importance of character in Victorian culture, see Stefan Collini, *Public Moralists: Political Thought and Intellectual Life in Britain 1850–1930* (Oxford: Clarendon Press, 1991).

[62] Beales in Breuilly et al., *Era of the Reform League*, p. 140. For two reformers' detailed substantiation of such an argument, see the widely read J. M. Ludlow and Lloyd Jones, *The Progress of the Working Classes 1832–1867* (London, 1867); see also their essay of the same title in *Questions for a Reformed Parliament*, pp. 277–328.

[63] William Hunter, a chain maker at Armstrong's engine and ordnance works in Newcastle, at a Newcastle reform demonstration in January 1867: *Newcastle Weekly Chronicle*, 19 January 1867.

[64] Beales in Breuilly et al., *Era of the Reform League*, p. 141.

interests of all classes would be attended to, and this was a mark of a free country. As Beales put it at the inaugural meeting:

I verily believe that it is most unwise and most perilous to the best interests of England to perpetuate grossly unjust distinctions, and consequently dangerous animosities, amongst the different classes in the state, and that he is the truest and best friend of his country who seeks to put an end to these distinctions and animosities, and to weld all classes together by unity of interest into one harmonious whole. (*Applause.*) That harmony, that unity of interest which every patriot, every true statesman, every earnest Christian ought to long for can never exist whilst forty-nine-fiftieth of the working classes and thousands of other English men are excluded from that franchise.[65]

The language of reform which Beales and others used was, as these passages from his speech indicate, pervaded by a further element of the claim to the vote, namely the claim from *class*. Men referred continually to the working class, or working classes, as both being deprived of the vote and thus having a claim to it. If classes were socially distinct but not antagonistic to each other, it was nonetheless the case that men should have the vote because they were the foundations of the nation. J. B. Leno, speaking at the inaugural meeting of the Reform League, and announced as 'a working man', took a more forceful position on class than Beales had done:

It was not unfrequently said that the interests of the working classes were identical with the interests of those who filled a higher sphere in life. If that were so, in heaven's name, how was it that the working classes had not a voice in making the laws for the protection of those interests? The real truth was, those interests were not under all aspects identical.[66]

Labour, it continued to be argued, was the source of wealth and, it was often said, 'national greatness'. It was because men laboured to produce tangible things – ships, railways, coal – that they both constituted a distinctive interest within society and were deserving of the vote. Thus, for example, at a huge reform meeting in Newcastle in January 1867 Robert Warden, a brass founder at Stephenson's locomotive works, said that,

in their various occupations, the working classes had shown great energy, intelligence, and perseverance, which proved them to be worthy of being admitted to the franchise. (*Cheers.*) They were able to build leviathan ships to carry the commerce of the world across the mighty oceans; they were able to construct mighty iron warps to connect two distant continents together; but the opponents of Reform did not consider that those same artizans were able to choose their representatives in Parliament.[67]

[65] *Ibid.* [66] Leno in Breuilly et al., *Era of the Reform League*, p. 142.
[67] *Newcastle Weekly Chronicle*, 19 January 1867.

Yet if the basis of what the Reform League and other radical reformers wanted was framed in terms of a working class that should be included within the political nation franchise as of right, the counterpoints to this were the restrictions and exclusions they advocated. With the exception of that diminishing number of reformers prepared to sustain a belief in full manhood suffrage, all the reformers were by the 1860s framing their claims by exclusions.

Much has been made of the ways in which the registered and residential qualifications excluded the poor and the 'residuum',[68] and I will turn to this in a moment. But rather less has been said of the exclusion of women. Yet this too was central to the framing of the demands, not least in articulating an opposition between dependency and independence. At the same time, it has to be said that the question of women's suffrage was raised only infrequently before 1867, and when it was, particularly by feminist women, their arguments were generally refused or, at best, interpreted within a very narrow framework. For example, Caroline Ashurst Biggs, Frances Gill and Jeanette Nasham all wrote to the NRU in August 1858 asking whether the organisation would include women in the claim for the vote. They evidently received some sympathy but nothing else. As Frances Gill wrote to Richard Reed: his expressions of sympathy simply prove 'barren' for, 'until those who feel with us will venture out, the story of wrong & oppression will be infinitely repeated', not least because 'the conduct of Englishmen as a nation, to women has not been such as to inspire us with the confidence you seem to expect'.[69] Indeed, the NRU had at an early stage contemplated including women's suffrage within its demands but abandoned the possibility.[70] But even where there was more than mere sympathy for the idea of women's suffrage among reformers before 1867, the most 'advanced position' was, at best, that put by the *Bee-Hive* in 1866. As Biagini has observed, the *Bee-Hive* gave some space to questions of the emancipation of women, including enthusiastically to the publication of Mill's *Subjection of Women*. But in so far as votes for women were to be countenanced, this should be restricted to 'independent', unmarried women and widows, since married women were already 'virtually represented' by their husbands.[71] However, this was neither the only nor the most important way in which women were excluded from the purview of reformers: as I will

[68] E.g. Royden Harrison, *Before the Socialists*, pp. 117–18; although cf. Biagini, *Liberty, Retrenchment and Reform*, pp. 268–9, on this point.

[69] See letters from Caroline Ashurst Biggs (of Tunbridge, Kent), 4 and 12 August 1858, CC, C139 and 146; Frances Gill (Shrewsbury), August 1858, CC, C147 and C150; Jeanette Nasham (London), 23 August 1858, CC, C157.

[70] See *Morning Star*, 22 October 1858.

[71] Biagini, *Liberty, Retrenchment and Reform*, p. 308.

suggest, the deep structures of the reform movement in both its ideas and practice effectively restricted the claim to the vote to both men and a masculinised popular politics.

Restricting the vote by residence and rating qualifications was to exclude the mass of the poor and poorer sections of the working class. It may be true, as Biagini has suggested, that the 'pauper's exclusion' occurred only gradually',[72] but it became firmly embedded in the Reform League proposals. Adopting this position was to mark out a decisive break with Chartism and the earlier radical tradition and to render marginal those, like Ernest Jones, who had maintained a commitment to the inclusion of the poor. It had been an important dimension of the turn to the social in late Chartism that pauperism and poverty were the consequences of prevailing economic conditions. Those among the ranks of reformers who sought to exclude the poor generally did so on the criterion of dependency. For instance, at the London reform conference of January 1858 which sought to build a cross-class alliance, Passmore Edwards, veteran of the Anti-Corn Law League and prominent metropolitan middle-class radical, had argued for the exclusion of paupers because they were 'too dependent'. Ernest Jones had countered by asserting that within manhood suffrage he would 'even [include] the pauper. The man who was prevented by our system from getting work ought to have the vote in order to redress his own injuries.'[73]

But Jones's position was, by the 1860s, a minority one, for the argument about why paupers and the poor should be denied the vote had become deeply embedded in the idea that only those who were independent should be granted the suffrage. A classic statement of this was made by John Bright, although there is no reason to suppose that most working-class reformers would have disagreed with him. More than anyone at the time, Bright established a political connection between the claims to citizenship and the question of poverty when he famously defined the 'residuum', linking the right to the vote to the question of taxation:

> I believe that the solid and ancient basis of the suffrage is that all persons who are rated to some tax . . . should be admitted to the franchise. I am quite willing to admit there is one objection to that wide measure, which exists . . . in almost every franchise you can establish. At this moment, in all, or nearly all boroughs, as many of us know sometimes to our sorrow, there is a small class which it would be much better for themselves if they were not enfranchised, because they have no independence whatsoever, and it would be much better for the constituency also that they should be excluded, and there is no class so much interested in having that small

[72] *Ibid.*, p. 273. [73] Cited in Breuilly et al., *Era of the Reform League*, p. 27.

class excluded as the intelligent and honest working men. I call this class the residuum, which there is in almost every constituency, of almost helpless poverty and dependence.[74]

Excluding the 'residuum' was to create a boundary around a particular kind of respectable working-class man. And the model of who that man was was crucially shaped by a model of a domesticated working class. As José Harris has observed in her discussion of this passage, Bright's opposition to the residuum established a polarity between 'the regularly employed, rate-paying working man (possessed of a house, a wife, children, furniture, and the habit of obeying the law) [who] was the heir of the Anglo-Saxon freeman' and a residuum which was 'intemperate', 'profligate' and 'naturally incapable'.[75]

The model of the family was a persistent theme in the parliamentary discussion of household and manhood suffrage in 1866–7, although, as Jane Rendall shows (see chapter 3), one must observe the absence of discussion of the fact of large numbers of *female* heads of households. But an important criterion for the advocates of household suffrage was that the vote should be restricted, in effect, to those who were not only heads of households but also fathers. As Anna Clark has suggested, fatherhood was seen as an index of that crucial Victorian moral value, 'character',[76] and was a theme that ran through the liberal vision of what an upright, sober working-class man was.[77] It invested a primarily sociological and economic phenomenon, the head of the household, with a moral status which could be embedded in a political argument. As J. A. Roebuck, radical MP for Sheffield, put it in the reform debate of 12 April 1867: 'if a man has a settled house, in which he has lived with his family for a number of years, you have a man who has given hostages to the state, and you have in these circumstances a guarantee for that man's virtue'.[78] Where those in the Reform League differed from such a position was in their commitment to manhood suffrage rather than to household suffrage: a *man* should have the vote rather than simply those men who were heads of households. But where they shared this vision it was in espousing the virtues of domesticity and the demonstration that to be a father and husband with a dependent

[74] *Hansard*, 3rd ser., vol. 186, cols. 626–42, 26 March 1867; cited in José Harris, 'Between Civic Virtue and Social Darwinism: The Concept of the Residuum', in David Englander and Rosemary O'Day (eds.), *Retrieved Riches: Social Investigation in England 1840–1914* (Aldershot: Scolar Press, 1995), p. 74.

[75] Harris, 'Between Civic Virtue and Social Darwinism', pp. 74–5.

[76] For the idea of character, see esp. Collini, *Public Moralists*, ch. 5.

[77] Anna Clark, 'Gender, Class and the Nation: Franchise Reform in England, 1832–1928', in James Vernon (ed.), *Re-reading the Constitution: New Narratives in the Political History of England's Long Nineteenth Century* (Cambridge University Press, 1996), pp. 239–41.

[78] Quoted *ibid.*, p. 240.

wife and children was to show, in one important way, how the respectable working class had won its position of deserving the vote.

The emphasis upon fatherhood and the household head was also to exclude lodgers, be they single men living in the households of others or sharing rooms with another man. All the bills for reform, whether Liberal or Conservative, and the final act of 1867, included restricted provision for lodgers, essentially aimed at enfranchising only middle-class ones.[79] Where the Reform League were sharply differentiated from this was in their insistence on including lodgers. What was at issue here was the criterion of independent manliness. It was an independent man, whether or not he was a householder or lodger, who must have the vote. As Ernest Jones had put it when criticising John Bright's stance on reform in 1859, his exclusion of the lodger was to place an undue emphasis upon the married man as against the single: 'as though married men did not live in lodgings also, and as though the thoughtful, prudent man who does not rush into an early marriage was not as worthy of the vote as the youth who hurries blindly to the altar'.[80]

The play of independence and dependence within the discourse of reform takes one into the underlying cultural structures of radical thought. What was meant by independence? It was not to be a slave. The longstanding sympathy of working-class radicals and others for the cause of anti-slavery in the British Empire and the United States was commonly enunciated in terms of what was taken to be its antinomy: it was the 'virtue' of Englishness that England was the home of the 'free-born'. Yet the hostility to slavery was also to the 'slavery' of the factory and wage system, most powerfully articulated in the factory reform movements of the 1830s and 1840s which embraced 'Tory' and popular radicals in Lancashire and the West Riding of Yorkshire, and still to be heard in the 1850s and 1860s. Counterpoised to slavery was the freedom to sell his labour power in conditions of equity and justice: that a man should be able to maintain himself without recourse to charity or the state Poor Law; that he would have a degree of freedom in the regulation of his trade or job; and that collective organisation of the trade, in formal unions or otherwise, was desirable, if not always possible.[81] What was also becom-

[79] In practice the imprecision of the lodger franchise entailed considerable, confused and largely unintended political consequences for the nature of the electorate after 1868: admitted to the vote were some whom the 1867 act had been designed to exclude. See John Davis, 'Slums and the Vote'.

[80] *Cabinet Newspaper*, 22 January 1859; cited in Breuilly et al., *Era of the Reform League*, p. 41.

[81] On the importance of the trade union in this, note for instance the remark of Thomas Wright: 'trade unions do more than any other existing institution to secure the working men "the glorious privilege of being independent". Trade unionists are, generally speaking, the best respected and most self-respecting of working men' (Thomas Wright [The Journeyman Engineer], *Our New Masters* (London, 1873), p. 282).

ing much more visible in the discourse in the second half of the nineteenth century was the notion that the independence of a man rested on being able to maintain his family as well as himself. Contrary to the views of some recent historians of labour, who have generally ignored the fact, it is evident that the bargaining strategies of trade unions were increasingly informed by the notion that what had to be maintained were not only the trade and its customs, its wages and conditions of work, but also the family economy of the members of it.[82] Defending the trade meant claiming the 'family wage', sufficient to cover wife and children as well as the male worker.[83]

Much of the language of independence derived from the popular radical assimilation, over a long period, of the language and ideas of the tradition of 'civic humanism' or 'republicanism'.[84] In this tradition those who could become citizens were free male householders. Women, servants, slaves and wage-labourers were generally regarded as inferior. As Carole Pateman has argued, the supposed equality of men was structured upon an ability to control and dominate household dependants, and, in particular, women. This was the 'sexual contract' at the heart of the 'social contract'.[85]

Civic humanism and the republican tradition had developed as an oppositional ideology within early modern European political regimes. But its initial location was in relation to landownership. When it was absorbed and reformulated within the elaboration of a commercial- and industrial-based middle class in the eighteenth and early nineteenth centuries, central elements of the tradition became embedded in the culture of separate spheres. Virtue became attached, not least, to the cultivation of domesticity in which a man was independent and respectable by means of being able to maintain a dependent wife and children within

[82] Cf., e.g., E. F. Biagini, 'British Trade Unions and Popular Political Economy, 1860–1880', *Historical Journal* 30 (1987), 811–40.

[83] For the notions of the family wage and the male breadwinner, see among others Harold Benenson, 'Victorian Sexual Ideology and Marx's Theory of the Working Class', *International Labor and Working-Class History* 25 (1984), 1–23; Keith McClelland, 'Masculinity and the "Representative Artisan" in Britain, 1850–1880', in Michael Roper and John Tosh (eds.), *Manful Assertions: Masculinities in Britain Since 1800* (London: Routledge, 1991), pp. 74–91; Sonya O. Rose, *Limited Livelihoods: Gender and Class in Nineteenth-Century England* (London: Routledge, 1992), esp. pp. 55–9; Deborah Valenze, *The First Industrial Woman* (Oxford University Press, 1995), pp. 100–1.

[84] This discussion draws heavily upon Anna Clark, 'Manhood, Womanhood, and the Politics of Class in Britain, 1790–1845', in Laura Frader and Sonya Rose (eds.), *Gender and Class in Modern Europe* (Ithaca, N.Y., and London: Cornell University Press, 1996), pp. 263–79.

[85] See Carole Pateman, *The Sexual Contract* (Cambridge: Polity Press, 1988), and her *Disorder of Women: Democratic Feminism and Political Theory* (Stanford University Press, 1989), esp. p. 6.

the household. Middle-class men could claim the vote in 1832 as owners of capital who were heads of households.[86]

Important elements of this were assimilated by the popular and working-class radical tradition from Tom Paine onwards. But two crucial differences emerged in the ways in which elements of this complex culture were structuring the discourses of reform in that tradition. First, and this had been evident from 1790s, the basis of a popular claim for universal manhood suffrage became the notion that the property which working men possessed was property in their labour. This was the foundation of that defence of skill or labour more generally, to which I referred above. To be in possession of this property was to be free, to have possession of one's self and to have the potential to shape and dispose of one's labour and person. In other words, one could become, or so it was believed, an autonomous agent in the world. This was a particular instance of the disciplined individual.[87] If this was an individual subject to obligations and constraints, it was because he had chosen to accept those limits. As a worker he would meet the obligations he had to other workers in the way of maintaining the customs, habits and bargaining position of the trade, and also to the employer. If the employer had a duty and moral responsibility to treat the worker decently then the worker had the expectation that he would be a responsible and good employee.[88]

The second difference was a newer emphasis. In drawing the political boundaries against the poor and the 'rough' working class, the reformers of the 1860s no longer took property in labour as the simple basis of a masculine political identity. They overlaid the idea of property in labour with cultural distinctions which differentiated between forms of working-class masculinity – between a sober, respectable and independent manhood and those 'rough' men. The result was a narrower political definition of the putative citizen than any dominant strand of popular radicalism had been prepared to draw between 1790 and 1848.

How was this shift possible? In part it was the consequence of strategic shifts within popular politics. While elements of Chartism persisted, there was a decisive break with it not only in terms of political doctrine but also

86 See above all Leonore Davidoff and Catherine Hall, *Family Fortunes: Men and Women of the English Middle Class 1780–1850* (London: Hutchinson, 1987).

87 The notion derives partly from Michel Foucault. For an illuminating use of the notion, see Mary Poovey, *Making A Social Body: British Cultural Formation, 1830–1864* (University of Chicago Press, 1995), p. 20 and ch. 5.

88 For a characteristic example, see the evidence of Daniel Guile, secretary of the Friendly Society of Iron Founders, to the Royal Commission on Trade Unions and Other Organisations, 5th Report (Parliamentary Papers 1867–8 [3980–I] XXXIX), e.g. q. 8,745.

in methods, tactics and strategy. Making alliance with middle-class reformers had been canvassed at various points within Chartism but the mainstream of the movement rejected it in favour of the working class making their own history. Clearly this was no longer the case by the 1860s. If the Reform League was disappointed by the terms of the Gladstone bill of 1866, it was nonetheless anxious to support it and the Liberal party because it promised at the least an instalment of reform. It was no longer thought possible to hold out for the maximum programme of manhood suffrage at the cost of abandoning any halfway decent measure. However, an explanation of the changes in working-class politics that restricts itself to analysing shifts in political strategy is insufficient: it is necessary to situate political change in relation to social developments.

Social change and politics

As we have suggested in the introduction, a major theme of recent writing on the history of politics has been the abandonment of explanations of politics in terms of social and economic determinants in favour of those which stress political determinants, such as the structures of government or the languages and discourses of politics. Real gains in our understanding have accrued as a consequence; but there have also been considerable costs to the extent that it has sometimes led to the utter neglect of the relationship between social and economic change on the one hand, and politics on the other. Yet if one is to make sense of the discursive emergence of the 'respectable and independent' man and his positioning as a new political subject it is essential to take stock of some of the important social and economic changes which were reshaping the working class in the third quarter of the nineteenth century.

At the centre of those changes was the shifting composition of the working class consequent upon the consolidation of the industrial revolution in what Hobsbawm and others have called its 'second phase'.[89] Two aspects of this are of particular importance here. First, there was a significant differentiation in the sexual division of labour and paid employment as women workers became more concentrated in distinct types of jobs – notably in domestic service, textiles and the clothing trades – while men's jobs were increasingly separated from the household. This pattern was not universal across the economy, but these tendencies were greatly reinforced in the long boom of 1848–73, not least by the second

[89] See E. J. Hobsbawm, *Industry and Empire* (Harmondsworth: Penguin, 1969), ch. 6, or his *Age of Capital 1848–1875* (London: Weidenfeld and Nicolson, 1975), ch. 2.

major aspect of this phase of industrialisation, namely the shift of men into higher-paid occupations.[90] The most dramatic manifestation of this was the expansion of coal-mining and of the iron industries, engineering and iron shipbuilding. Where this happened, as in the north-east of England or in the industrial belt around Glasgow, the effects were to transform the social landscape into a recognisably 'modern' urban and industrial society and to create the kind of working class which increasingly dominated the world of labour until the middle of the twentieth century. At the same time, those industries and that working class were shaped by the continuing reliance upon the skilled manual worker whom machinery and organisational changes in production did not or could not displace.[91] For example, in shipbuilding the skilled men in the metal-working trades, mainly organised in the Boilermakers' Society, came to have pre-eminence, while in engineering the position of the new types of workers, especially the fitters and turners, who first emerged between 1820 and 1850, was consolidated and extended, and formed the core of the ASE.[92] Yet if such changes accentuated the divisions in many industries between the higher-paid and often more highly skilled, and those men on lower rates of pay and with less bargaining power in the labour market, what they also did was to broaden the gap between men's and women's skills and earnings, and the wider social and cultural community of a male-centred world of 'work' and a female-centred world of the local neighbourhood, the street and the home.

These developments have continued to be central to social explanations of working-class politics. Changes in the structure and composition of the working class have been an essential aspect of the explanation of a

[90] For discussion, see, among others, Hobsbawm's essays on the 'labour aristocracy', esp. 'Labour Aristocracy in Nineteenth-Century Britain', in his *Labouring Men* (London: Weidenfeld and Nicolson, 1964), pp. 272–315, and 'Debating the Labour Aristocracy', 'The Aristocracy of Labour Reconsidered' and 'Artisans and Labour Aristocrats', in his *Worlds of Labour* (London: Weidenfeld and Nicolson, 1984), pp. 214–26, 227–51, and 252–72; see also E. H. Hunt, *British Labour History 1815–1914* (London: Weidenfeld and Nicolson, 1981), esp. chs. 1 and 3, and his 'Industrialization and Regional Inequality: Wages in Britain, 1760–1914', *Journal of Economic History* 46 (1986), 935–66.

[91] A major assessment of this remains Raphael Samuel, 'The Workshop of the World: Steam Power and Hand Technology in Mid-Victorian Britain', *History Workshop Journal* 3 (1977), 6–72.

[92] For engineering, see Keith Burgess, *The Origins of British Industrial Relations* (London: Croom Helm, 1975), ch. 2, and Jonathan Zeitlin, 'Engineers and Compositors: A Comparison', in Royden Harrison and Zeitlin (eds.), *Divisions of Labour: Skilled Workers and Technological Change in Nineteenth-Century Britain* (Brighton: Harvester Press, 1985), pp. 185–250; for shipbuilding, see Keith McClelland and Alastair Reid, 'Wood, Iron and Steel: Technology, Labour and Trade Union Organisation in the Shipbuilding Industry, 1840–1914', pp. 151–84 in the same volume; and Sidney Pollard and Paul Robertson, *The British Shipbuilding Industry, 1870–1914* (Cambridge, Mass., and London: Harvard University Press, 1979).

radical politics which could find accommodation with liberalism, largely by way of the 'labour aristocracy' argument. That is, what happened in the period c. 1848–75 was, according to the argument, a strengthening of divisions within the working class between the 'upper strata of the working class, better paid, better treated and generally regarded as more "respectable" and politically moderate than the mass of the proletariat'.[93] The evolution of popular politics reflected this to the extent that it represented the interests, culture and outlook of such labour aristocrats.[94]

It is not necessary to wholly accept or wholly reject the notion of the labour aristocracy to recognise that the literature on it pointed to some fundamental developments within the working class. Not least of these is the evidence of changes in wages and the standard of living which points to a clear rising of standards for at least a significant section from around 1860, and probably an increasing differential between many skilled and lesser- and unskilled male workers.

Of course there are considerable unresolved problems about assessing living standards in the period which make analysis of the precise shape of change difficult and, perhaps, ultimately impossible. What we know about standards of living is extremely patchy. Notoriously, figures for real earnings that take account of periods of unemployment, short-time working or overtime and, on the other side, costs of consumption (primarily food and rent) are extremely hard to come by. This is to say nothing of the qualitative aspects of standards of living such as changes in the hours of labour and intensity of work. There *are* figures: and it certainly does seem plausible that at least some groups of the working class became better off; much qualitative evidence clearly suggests it.[95]

But the question of living standards and changes in real wages becomes more complex when we consider changes in the incomes not simply of particular trades and occupations but of households. After all, most working-class people lived in households of more than one person and most in families of one kind or other. The critical points are what were the incomes of households and how did these change over time? Here things become much more difficult because we know so little about the earnings of women and of children and young people, especially where people were earning part-time (either on a regular basis or for only certain parts

93 Hobsbawm, 'Labour Aristocracy in Nineteenth-Century Britain', p. 272.

94 For further remarks about this, see the introduction, pp. 18–20.

95 The best general introduction to the subject for this period remains Hunt, *British Labour History*, ch. 3. A useful general introduction which takes into account recent literature is Hoppen, *Mid-Victorian Generation*, pp. 72–90. That there had been real improvements in the standard of living of the working class was fundamental to the outlook of many working-class reformers and their allies of the time: e.g. Ludlow and Jones, *Progress of the Working Classes*.

of the year). The problem can be illustrated with a simple arithmetical example: if we take a household with only one (male) breadwinner, he may be earning a wage which puts him within the 'labour aristocracy' – say 30s (£1.50) a week. On the other hand there may be a household where a man is earning only 20s (£1.00) but where his wife earns 10s. The total household income for the two households is, of course, the same; but the one has been cast as 'labour aristocratic', the other as merely part of the unskilled or labourers. There may of course be persistent differences of status; and there may also be regional differences here. Thus the male workers of the north-east of England – miners, shipbuilders, engineers and the like – generally appear to have lived in households in which relatively few women worked for wages, at least on a discernible basis. On the other hand the proportion of married women working for wages in Lancashire was relatively high: by 1870 or so the north-east was high-pay area whereas male wages in Lancashire were perhaps generally a bit lower.[96]

At the same time, a major associated change in this period was the widespread sense of the permanence of urban, industrial and capitalist society, and yet its persistent insecurities. It came to be widely assumed within the working class that the future of waged workers and their families was very largely determined by the future of the economy – its continuing expansion through commerce and industry, preferably within a free-trade regime – and the extent to which workers could extract collective and individual gains from the system through trade unionism and collective bargaining, or through varieties of self-help. Symptomatic of this was the virtual disappearance from the 1840s onwards of aspirations to establish co-operative production, be they in the form of the ambitious schemes of the Owenites of 1833–4 or the more modest co-operatives of small groups of artisans.[97]

Yet the world of the working class was also one in which scarcity and insecurity were persistently dominant features of their lives. Chronic insecurity was a basic fact of life for all, even for the apparently best paid, and shaped the behaviour and attitudes of all, both as individuals and where they were able to operate collectively in trade unions, friendly societies or other institutions. All knew that gains in wages or favourable changes in the conditions of work might be merely temporary. As Robert Knight of

96 See E. H. Hunt, *Regional Wage Variations in Britain, 1850–1914* (Oxford: Clarendon Press, 1973), and his 'Industrialization and Regional Inequality', for regional variations.

97 In contrast to the persistence of such aspirations in much of continental western Europe, where rather different economic and political conditions prevailed: see for example the remarks of Hobsbawm on this in 'Debating the Labour Aristocracy', pp. 223–4, and 'Artisans and Labour Aristocrats', pp. 260–1.

the Boilermakers' Society put it, workers must 'make the best of the sunshine we now enjoy, for as certain as night will return, so surely will the clouds of depression again surround us with gloom, loss of work, and consequent suffering to ourselves and families'.[98]

Changes in the working class and the sense of both the permanence of industrialism and the insecurities of the system were crucial to the beliefs not only that the future of the economy was central to the future of men and women as workers, but also that the sphere of the economy itself was in some considerable measure a distinct one, governed largely by the laws of the market, and that the interests of workers were essentially dependent upon their position as economic beings: being working *class* was largely a matter of economics rather than politics.

This constellation of ideas was considerably reinforced in this period by cultural and ideological changes. Central here was the changing valuation of 'work' and its associated meanings. There was a widespread emphasis upon the moral bearings of work across the whole society. As Collini has suggested of the respectable Victorian middle-class man, 'work was the chief sphere in which moral worth was developed and displayed'.[99] And those who spoke for the working class frequently emphasised the virtues of work not only in making the wild deserts blossom but also in demonstrating the claims of working men to respect for their skill, intelligence and contribution to national well-being. The Boilermakers' Society could proclaim 'England's Greatness, the Working Man'[100] while John Burnett, leader of the Nine Hours' League in the north-east in 1871 and subsequently general secretary of the ASE, declared the engineers to

> have always been an intelligent body of men. At the present time a higher average of intelligence and education prevails amongst them than we find in the trades of any of the great productive trades of the country. Their work requires both skill and intelligence, and the best workmen are really scientific artisans, working under conditions which require the exercise of the very highest faculties of brain and hand.[101]

Yet the valuation of work depended crucially upon not only its role as a prime source of individual and collective identity for men[102] but also in

98 Boilermakers' Society, *Annual Report*, 1881, p. XIII. The argument in this and the preceding paragraph draws upon Keith McClelland, 'Time to Work, Time to Live: Some Aspects of Work and the Re-formation of Class in Britain, 1850–1880', in Patrick Joyce (ed.), *The Historical Meanings of Work* (Cambridge University Press, 1987), pp. 180–209.

99 Collini, *Public Moralists*, pp. 105–6.

100 Motto on a banner carried by the Boilermakers' Society (Tyne and Wear District) in a public demonstration, Newcastle upon Tyne, Whitsun 1865: *Newcastle Weekly Chronicle (Supplement)*, 10 June 1865.

101 [John Burnett], 'A Model Trade Society', *Newcastle Weekly Chronicle*, 3 July 1875.

102 For further elaboration, see McClelland, 'Time to Work, Time to Live', and 'Masculinity and the "Representative Artisan"'.

the increasingly sharp differentiation between the virtues of paid work for men and women. It had been widely assumed until about the 1830s that working-class women should work for wages and even that it might be desirable to do so. However, within the following decades there was an increased emphasis among working-class men, and perhaps among working-class women, that married women should not work for wages. To a degree this reflected the great pressures exerted upon the working class from within both the state and civil society to exclude or restrict women from certain kinds of work – the Mines Act of 1842 and the Factory Act of 1844 are the critical pieces of legislation – while it also reflected and was reinforced by male trade union advocacy of the family wage.[103]

At the same time what was lost in this period, as compared with the years from 1825 to 1848, was an alternative valuation of work in relation to the economy and society as a whole. In that earlier period there had been a flourishing popular-radical critique of the existing social order and its economic foundations. However, in the decades after 1848 there was an assimilation of many of the dominant ideas of orthodox political economy, at least to the extent that it was assumed that the market ultimately determined labour's rewards. This did not entail the complete acceptance of political economy, but it did reflect and affirm the hegemony of 'purely' economic calculation rather than customary-market and 'non-economic' valuations of labour by trade unionists and others. Trade union action and collective bargaining continued to have an important moral element: the establishment and enforcement by collective action of the rate for the job entailed notions of mutual aid as well as instrumental solidarity; and the typical claim for a 'fair day's wage for a fair day's work' carried ideas of reciprocal duty and justice in relations between employers and workers. However, moral considerations were increasingly subordinated to market ones. As the wage was believed to be ultimately determined by the 'laws' of supply and demand, collective bargaining would not be able to transcend these 'laws' but establish what the 'traffic would bear'. But it could do so only if – and this was a primary assumption – employers and workers were able to meet in the market as bargaining agents of equal capacity.[104]

[103] See esp. Anna Clark, 'The Rhetoric of Chartist Domesticity: Gender, Language, and Class in the 1830s and 1840s', *Journal of British Studies* 31 (1992), 62–88, and Sally Alexander, 'Women, Class and Sexual Difference in the 1830s and 1840s', *History Workshop Journal* 17 (1984), 125–49.

[104] A remarkable and forthright exposition of this view of bargaining can be found in *The Chain Makers' Journal*, nos. 1–20 (July 1858–December 1859), *passim*. Sidney Webb and Beatrice Webb, *Industrial Democracy* (London, 1898), remains essential to the analysis of the philosophy of trade unionism in the period: see esp. ch. 13, 'The Assumptions of Trade Unionism'. Of the modern discussions, E. J. Hobsbawm,

How did these developments in the social, economic and cultural context of work and workers shape the politics of the reformers?

In the first place, the popular movement for parliamentary reform of 1858–67 was a much more masculine affair than earlier campaigns had generally been. The fact that the claim for the vote was made by and for working men was rather less novel than the fact that the movements for it were ones in which scarcely any women participated. A number of historians have shown that there was a considerable participation of women in movements of popular protest and politics in Britain from eighteenth-century crowd actions over food to Chartism in the 1830s and 1840s. As the forms of popular politics and protest shifted from the 'pre-political' to the demonstrations, organisations and movements in favour of parliamentary reform in the earlier part of the nineteenth century, it is evident that the involvement of women in the creation of a working-class 'public sphere' was significant and continuing. Thus in the period 1815–20 one sees the formation of female radical societies; in the Owenite movement, the creation of the first currents of 'socialist-feminism'; and, in Chartism, at least in its earlier phases of 1838–42, a sustained commitment to the cause of political rights among many women. It is also of course evident that powerful countervailing forces existed, and were being strengthened, which threatened to push women out of the 'public sphere' or prevent them from transcending the boundaries between it and the 'private'. This was reflected in the characteristic demands of many women themselves: where they demanded the vote it was generally not for themselves but for their husbands, fathers and brothers in order that the conditions of their own lives and their families might be improved. Yet what is especially striking, as Dorothy Thompson and others have argued, is the extent and rapidity of women's virtual disappearance from the working-class public sphere after 1840–2.[105]

footnote 104 (*cont.*)
'Custom, Wages and Work-Load in Nineteenth-Century Industry', in his *Labouring Men*, pp. 344–70, is fundamental. Contrasting discussions of the extent to which trade unionists and others absorbed the doctrines of political economy can be found in R. V. Clements, 'British Trade Unions and Popular Political Economy, 1850–1875', *Economic History Review* 14 (1961–2), 93–104, Royden Harrison, *Before the Socialists*, pp. 16–18, and Biagini, 'British Trade Unions and Popular Political Economy'.

105 A general survey of women and popular politics is Jane Rendall, *The Origins of Modern Feminism: Women in Britain, France and the United States 1780–1860* (Basingstoke: Macmillan, 1985), ch. 7; for women and Chartism, see esp. Dorothy Thompson, 'Women in Nineteenth-Century Radical Politics: A Lost Dimension', in Ann Oakley and Juliet Mitchell (eds.), *The Rights and Wrongs of Women* (Harmondsworth: Penguin, 1976), pp. 112–38; Dorothy Thompson, *The Chartists*, esp. ch. 7; Dorothy Thompson, 'Women, Work and Politics in Nineteenth-Century England', in Jane Rendall (ed.), *Equal or Different: Women's Politics 1800–1914* (Oxford: Basil Blackwell, 1987), pp. 57–81; Jutta Schwarzkopf, *Women in the Chartist Movement* (Basingstoke: Macmillan, 1991).

The institutional base of the political movement from 1857 to 1858 was a variety of political associations and, by 1866–7, the trade unions above all. This partly reflected the transformation of the social landscape through the extension of large-scale industry, partly the increasing strength and visibility of trade unionism to the extent that it was the core of labour organisation, one built upon virtually exclusively male foundations.[106]

One may see the development at a local level by considering, for example, the Tyneside case. There the period from the mid-1860s to the early 1870s was marked by the emergence, on a new scale, of trade unionism, largely, though not exclusively, based in the most highly skilled and best-paid sections of the working class. In shipbuilding the Boilermakers' Society had established an unrivalled degree of organisation by the early 1870s. In engineering, trade unionism was less well established, but the fitters and turners who dominated the ASE were beginning to make the union a significant presence. In iron, formal organisation came with the establishment of the Ironworkers' Union in 1863 in which the puddlers predominated. Beyond these there was a general spread of both formal and informal unionism. On Tyneside it was being extended among not only the skilled trades, like the various societies of industrial blacksmiths or the ironfounders, but also among the semi- or unskilled, like smiths' strikers or the 4,000 labourers who were said to have been members of the short-lived Tyneside Labourers' Union in 1864. In the wider area of Northumberland and Durham, the most notable development was the re-establishment of continuous formal organisation among the miners: in Northumberland in 1862, in Durham between 1867 and 1869.

The extension of trade unionism was not the only significant change within the working class in the 1860s and beyond, although it was the most important one. There are clear signs of the extension and sustenance of a working-class public sphere across a range of working-class institutions and practices in these years, including the co-ops, friendly societies, working men's clubs and reading rooms, and working men's temperance organisations that flourished.[107] Moreover, there are signs

106 That this was so resulted from a complex interplay of working men's bargaining strategies, in some instances (such as cotton spinning) the deliberate exclusion of women from trade unionism, the strategies of employers and cultural constructions of male and female workers: for an excellent account stressing such considerations, see Sonya Rose, *Limited Livelihoods*.

107 On the notion of the public sphere, see the introduction to this book, pp. 30–7, and esp. Geoff Eley, 'Edward Thompson, Social History and Political Culture: The Making of a Working-Class Public, 1780–1850', in H. J. Kaye and Keith McClelland (eds.), *E. P. Thompson: Critical Perspectives* (Cambridge: Polity Press, 1990), pp. 12–49; Geoff Eley, 'Nations, Publics, and Political Cultures: Placing Habermas in the Nineteenth Century', in Craig Calhoun (ed.), *Habermas and the Public Sphere* (Cambridge, Mass.: MIT Press, 1992), pp. 289–339.

too that some working men and working-class organisations could be drawn into political agitations in ways that had not been fully realised in the 1850s. (It has to be said that this was not true of all: for instance the Newcastle branch of the Provincial Typographical Association would have no truck with politics, at least officially.) Perhaps most significant here were the demonstrations and activities mounted to support Garibaldi in 1864. Just as the FACs had been an important link, in the early 1850s, between radical organisations and ideas in the 1840s and the NRU, so too the Garibaldi demonstrations were important in connecting the politics of the 1850s to the revived reform agitation of the 1860s. And they showed more than the continuation of radical ideas, in their denunciations of foreign, oligarchical government; they also revealed the possibility of a much greater scale of activity. In part this reflected the determination of some working-class radicals to effect a juncture between political activity and trade organisations. They were able to galvanise into action representatives from a number of major Tyneside factories, including many of the key engineering and iron companies like Armstrong's, Hawthorn's, Stephenson's and Hawks, Crawshay's. In doing so they were able to give some form, through the Garibaldi Committee, to the widespread enthusiasm for the Italian patriots. For these people Garibaldi was not simply a romantic hero, fighting Italian tyrants, but one who stood for 'the people' against all corrupt and aristocratic rulers.[108]

The potential opened up by these events was confirmed when the NRL's agitation commenced in the autumn of 1866. In this phase of activity there is a more self-confident appraisal of possibilities than was evident among the NRU reformers. Where that organisation had confined itself very largely to collecting signatures for petitions and the organising of indoor public meetings, the NRL's main mode of agitation was the outdoor demonstration, for which the model was not only the great political demonstrations of earlier in the century or being held in London and other major cities in 1866–7, but also the small-scale, celebratory demonstration of the trades, a common feature of Tyneside working-class life.

[108] The support for Italian nationalism and Garibaldi had been evident since the 1850s and was perhaps stronger on Tyneside than anywhere else bar London. For example, Garibaldi received an enthusiastic welcome on Tyneside in March 1854: see, among others, E. R. Jones, *Life and Speeches of Joseph Cowen* (London, 1885), pp. 17–18, and W. Duncan, *Life of Joseph Cowen* (London and Newcastle upon Tyne, 1904), pp. 9–13; for working men's preparations for his visit to Tyneside in 1864, see esp. *Newcastle Weekly Chronicle*, 16 April 1864, which gives details of the factories sending representatives to the welcoming committee. In the event Garibaldi was prevented by the government from undertaking a provincial tour. A good brief analysis of the enthusiasm for Garibaldi in England is John A. Davis, 'Garibaldi and England', *History Today*, December 1982, 21–6.

In the meetings held to plan the greatest of the 1866–7 demonstrations, that of 28 January 1867, it was the trades- and factory-based representatives who predominated. Men from the shipbuilding, engineering and metal trades, from the building, glass, tailoring and other trades and industries, joined with those from individual associations within the NRL and from temperance groups, friendly societies and working men's clubs. There was little doubt in the minds of these men that they represented a large constituency: one meeting, by no means solely attended by delegates from all those trades which subsequently participated, claimed to represent over 11,000. Moreover, it was thought to be an *active* constituency in which the level of enthusiasm was higher than had been the case in the 1850s. For instance, a delegate from the North Eastern Railway Company's engineering workshops said that the 'employees in the shop were almost to a man in favour of the demonstration'. Such enthusiasm, and the expectations born of it, was confirmed by the demonstration itself: 60,000 were said to have turned out.[109]

The extent of political mobilisation among the trade unions and factories was not only evident in 1866–7 but also again in 1873 when there was a renewed campaign for parliamentary reform. Of course, by then the NRL was operating in a different situation. The Liberal government's ambivalent attitude to trade unionism, reflected in its legislation, had antagonised many working people; the expansion of trade unionism, especially in the 'explosion' of 1871–3, was sharpening the lines of class conflict; and, importantly in the north-east, the miners felt very aggrieved by the consequences of the anomalies of the 1867 Reform Act, which left many miners unable to qualify as county electors or get on to the borough registers. The miners' unions of Northumberland and Durham established an association to press for universal manhood suffrage and the assimilation of the borough and county franchises.[110] But while the miners were pre-eminent in the agitation, they were joined by representatives of Tyneside unions and industries. In the enormous demonstration of 12 April 1873, it was claimed that 200,000 turned out on the Newcastle Town Moor. The list of those on the speakers' platforms gives some indication of the degree to which this new political consciousness was spread over the trades and something of the weighting towards particular groups. The forty-five delegates included twenty-three miners,

[109] For the preparations, see e.g. the reports in *Newcastle Weekly Chronicle*, 15 December 1866 and 12 January 1867 (quote); for the demonstration of 28 January, see the extensive coverage in *Newcastle Weekly Chronicle*.

[110] See esp. W. H. Maehl, 'The Northeastern Miners' Struggle for the Franchise, 1872–1874', *International Review of Social History* 20 (1975), 198–219; Biagini, *Liberty, Retrenchment and Reform*, pp. 278–88.

eleven from the shipbuilding, engineering and metal trades, five from the building trades, five other tradesmen, and a bookseller and former Chartist, James Watson.[111]

The centrality of organisation, and especially trade union organisation to the building of a reform movement, is of course central not only to the local story, such as in the Tyneside case, but also nationally. From its foundation the Reform League's Council had sought to mobilise the trade unions. A combination of economic and political circumstances in 1866–7, acting on the ground already prepared by the earlier revival of a reform movement and the impact of the internationalist movements, made such a mobilisation possible on a new scale. The financial crisis and economic depression of 1866–7, marked by rising levels of unemployment and distress in areas like the East End of London and workers striking in defence of wage levels and working conditions (at least, where they were able to do so), stimulated renewed political activity among the trades.[112] At the same time the rejection of the Liberal Reform Bill in June 1866, the accession of a Conservative government and the responses to the Hyde Park demonstrations in July further galvanised the movement. From then onwards, faced by a Conservative government, the Reform League's base expanded rapidly, both in London and elsewhere in Britain. Growth occurred initially in Birmingham, where the local Trades Council took the lead, and the West Midlands, but also in the north-west, the north-east (especially the West Riding of Yorkshire) and Scotland. By late 1866 there were 67 London branches and 177 in the English provinces. By the summer of 1867, the figures were 113 and 409, with a further 12 branches in Wales and 64 in Scotland. By that point there were some 65,000 people with membership cards.[113]

While the trades were central to this growth, it would be a mistake to suppose that it was only the 'aristocratic' trades and trade unions that took part in the League's demonstrations. For example, in London, if the League branches were 'solidly artisan' there was also some support among the unskilled as well as from non-working-class elements like shopkeepers. At the same time there were, as always, considerable

[111] *Newcastle Weekly Chronicle (Supplement)*, 19 April 1873.

[112] For the East End, see Gareth Stedman Jones, *Outcast London: A Study of the Relationship Between Classes in Victorian Society* (Oxford: Clarendon Press, 1971), esp. pp. 241–2. A vivid contemporary description of the crisis and its effects is Karl Marx, *Capital: A Critique of Political Economy*, vol. I (1867), trans. Ben Fowkes (Harmondsworth: Penguin, 1976), pp. 822–5.

[113] For analysis of the membership of the Reform League, see A. D. Bell, 'The Reform League from Its Origins to the Reform Act of 1867', DPhil. thesis, University of Oxford (1961), esp. pp. 130, 176, 203–4, 211. A little over two-thirds of the 522 English branches in July 1867 were in the West Midlands, the north-west and Yorkshire, and London.

differences in status and conditions of the trades. 'Superior' trades like the boilermakers might be involved; but so too were vulnerable and poorly organised ones like the French polishers.[114]

At the same time, League activities among the trades might be inhibited by local political conditions or hostility among some local trade union leaders to political activity. Thus in Glasgow there were unionists who sought only household, rather than manhood, suffrage, while in Manchester the Trades Council was dominated by conservative working men: Manchester reformers had to establish an alternative, and successful, Trades Demonstration Committee to organise reform activities.[115]

Alongside the trades the League's organisational base also drew on disparate radical groups and popular associations to form an effective coalition for reform.[116] But because reform activities were operating on the terrain of the political they were, necessarily, structured by local political conditions as well as the determination of those such as the trades to win the vote. In the north-east the strong working-class movement allied with a powerful phalanx of radical middle- and lower-middle-class 'advanced liberals' sympathetic to the social and political claims of labour, the most notable of these figures being Joseph Cowen jun. Similarly, in Manchester the social basis of the reform movement in 1866–7 was the working class and the trades. However, outside Manchester in many smaller towns, where moderate Liberals held the balance of power between manhood suffragists and Conservatism, 'the Reform Leagues of the cotton areas generally relied on the shopkeeper–small tradesmen class as the main source of its strength, rather than upon Trade Unionism'.[117]

Yet what was brought to the movement was not only the mere fact of being male or of being dominated by male organisations, but particular definitions of the nature and scope of politics and of those who might be political subjects. The reform movement sought to mobilise and articulate a particular kind of constituency, but one which was always ambiguously categorised. Thus, for instance, while the movement clearly sought to represent itself as embodying the respectable and independent, it was bound to get caught up in the arguments of those who wrestled with the problem of where to draw the line between those who were 'fit' for the vote and those who were not. Indeed, the central issue in many ways of the parliamentary debates on reform was fought out over precisely this

114 *Ibid.*, p. 148; Finn, *After Chartism*, p. 246 and n. 54.

115 Fraser, *Trade Unions and Society*, pp. 130–2.

116 Prothero, *Radical Artisans*, pp. 224–7.

117 M. Dunsmore, 'The Northern Department of the Reform League: The Working Classes, the Reform League and the Reform Movement in Lancashire and Yorkshire', MA thesis, University of Sheffield (1962), ch. 3, and p. 127; see also Bell, 'Reform League', pp. 254, 262.

moral terrain.[118] Was it, as Robert Lowe contended, that the consequence of admitting *any* section of the working class would be to introduce dissolution and danger into the constitution? Enfranchising 'the artizan' he thought would bring 'venality . . ., drunkenness, and facility for being intimidated' associated with people who are 'impulsive, unreflecting, and violent'.[119] On the other hand, had the artisans displayed the necessary qualities in their 'self-help' institutions and the like to be trusted, as men like Gladstone believed? Yet if they had, where still was the line to be drawn? What characterised the arguments of those like Gladstone on this issue was that moral and social criteria for evaluating working-class fitness – i.e. were these men respectable? – were reduced to a crass economism: the economic status of a man would determine his moral possibilities.

For some popular radicals the solution to the problem was that the movement ought to draw working men together in ways that transcended economic and social, or indeed ethnic, differences, although not sexual ones. As James Birkett, an iron moulder, declared, the movement should not be restricted to, say, union men as against non-unionists, to the artisans rather than the labourers, or to Englishmen rather than Irish or Scots. On the contrary, 'they recognised men as men' and that was sufficient.[120] Yet, in practice, the ranks of the reformers were not able to always transcend differences, most clearly evident in relation to the question of Ireland. While many British radicals were sympathetic to Irish nationalism, the development of Fenianism in the 1860s and the upsurge of pro-Garibaldi sentiment exposed some of the limits of British popular radicalism. As Catherine Hall discusses in her chapter (pp. 204–20), there was widespread anti-Irish racism in the Britain of the 1860s, while the conflict between popular Protestantism and Catholicism was revealed in such events as the Garibaldi and Murphy riots. Men like Birkett might seek to build a universalist movement of men as men, but the Reform League itself became deeply divided over Fenianism. While there was an Irish Reform League established in 1866, the British Reform League leaders, Howell and Beales, self-consciously distanced themselves from Fenian activities and from those radicals like Ernest Jones who pleaded for the Manchester Martyrs; from 1868 onwards they allied themselves with Gladstonian policy on Ireland.[121]

[118] As is stressed by, e.g., Stefan Collini, 'Political Theory and the "Science of Society" in Victorian Britain', *Historical Journal* 23 (1980), 216–18, and Collini, *Public Moralists*, pp. 111–12.
[119] *Hansard*, 3rd ser., vol. 182, col. 150, 13 March 1866.
[120] *Newcastle Weekly Chronicle*, 19 January 1867.
[121] Breuilly et al., *Era of the Reform League*, pp. 254–5.

At the same time the universalist aspirations of seeing men as men evoked some of the older radical tradition that while working men should be admitted to the political nation as *citizens* they were excluded because they were a *class*. Indeed, a greater sense of class exclusion and antagonism was once again evident in the 1860s (and, after 1867, in the trade and political movements of the early 1870s) than had been the case between 1848 and 1864. Yet a limit upon the universalism of claiming the vote simply as working men was partly the formal boundary of the political claims. This was not the mobilisation of the poor, as Gertrude Himmelfarb has characterised Chartism,[122] but the mobilisation of those represented as a distinct type of working class.

However, what also buttressed this was a shifting understanding of the relative place of politics and economics in the social order. The dominant tendency in pre-1850 popular politics had been a conception of the political as the overdetermining element in the social order. A change in the nature of political representation would lead to the relieving of the economic and social burdens imposed by Old Corruption. Within that tradition the major dividing lines in society were defined as originating in the political system, essentially those between the represented and the unrepresented, between the oligarchy and the people. Who 'the people' were was defined initially in the early nineteenth century as the 'productive classes' and then, as a result of 1832, increasingly as the working class. A critical part of the definition of this political tradition was that which located the putative subject of politics as the *male* citizen, endowed with the necessary potentialities of reason.[123]

Of course, there were nuances in this tradition and tensions produced by the developing ideas and practices of trade unionism, Owenism and Chartism in the 1830s and 1840s. While aspects of these views certainly persisted after the collapse of Chartism in the late 1840s, a decisive shift occurred in that the political was no longer seen as the prime *determining* force but rather as an essentially *intrusive* one which ought to be separated from economic and social activities. The consequences of this were to strengthen what one might call – although it is an ugly phrase – the 'masculinisation' of popular politics. For if it was economic relationships that

[122] Gertrude Himmelfarb, *The Idea of Poverty: England in the Early Industrial Age* (London: Faber and Faber, 1984), ch. 9.

[123] For contrasting discussions of the pre-1850 Radical tradition, see among others Patricia Hollis, *The Pauper Press* (Oxford: Clarendon Press, 1970), chs. 6–8; Iorwerth Prothero, 'William Benbow and the Concept of the "General Strike"', *Past & Present* 63 (1974), 132–71; Stedman Jones, 'Rethinking Chartism'; Catherine Hall, 'The Tale of Samuel and Jemima: Gender and Working-Class Culture in Nineteenth-Century England', in Kaye and McClelland, *E. P. Thompson*, pp. 78–102; and the articles cited above in the introduction, n. 62.

determined the position and prospects of the working men *as* working men, it was desirable that the conditions be established under which masters and men could meet as 'free' and 'equal' agents within the economy and the market. In turn this entailed a certain narrowing of the scope of political action. Continuous participation in politics was seen as essential in order to defend and extend the interests of labour, individually and collectively, yet the prime purposes for which this was necessary were in order to defend or achieve largely instrumental gains, exemplified in the campaigns of the early 1870s to establish a secure legal place for trade unionism.

What this did was to fix the concerns of popular politics as very largely the concern of the *man at work*. Of course, this boundary did not hermetically seal off popular politics from wider concerns, but it was to take two kinds of movements – late nineteenth-century socialism and the development of a women's suffrage movement – to at least offer the possibility, if not the realisation, of moving the politics into a wider, less instrumental and less narrowly focused register.

I have suggested that the central agent of this popular politics was a man who represented himself in terms of his work, his independence and his respectability. Yet a much fuller account of working-class politics and the relationship of it to the wider patterns of political and social formation would need to extend the narrative to say something about how this figure came to be defined not only by some economic and social forces and by his own manner of self-presentation, but also by other agencies. Such investigation would need to examine the impulses from civil society that differentiated the sober, respectable and desirable male figure and his family from others and that situated him as a suitable object for social inclusion and even celebration. Of particular importance here were those initiatives concerned with 'rational recreations' and temperance. The virtues of the *sober* man to those of the drunkard were continually lauded, while the temperance movement persistently stressed the sexual exploitation and domestic sufferings of women and families at the hands of intemperate and unrespectable men.[124]

At the same time there were major changes within state social policies. Especially important here were changes in the Poor Law.[125] The post-

[124] The major study of the British temperance movement, which is full of insight into other moral crusades, is Brian Harrison, *Drink and the Victorians: The Temperance Question in England 1815–1872* (London: Faber and Faber, 1971).

[125] For the Poor Law, see Pat Thane, 'Women and the Poor Law in Victorian and Edwardian England', *History Workshop Journal* 6 (1978), 29–51; Michael E. Rose, 'The Disappearing Pauper: Victorian Attitudes to the Relief of the Poor', in E. M. Sigsworth (ed.), *In Search of Victorian Values: Aspects of Nineteenth-Century Thought and Society* (Manchester University Press, 1988), pp. 56–72, and his 'Crisis of Poor Relief in England 1860–1890', in W. J. Mommsen in collaboration with Wolfgang Mock (eds.),

1834 Poor Law not only in fact was especially concerned with women as recipients, but the intentions of its authors had been to punish the able-bodied man who did not or would not work. In this arena the state effected a decisive emphasis upon disciplining, as matter of state policy, the independent man who would be able to care for his family and who would rise up from the 'impoverished and dehumanized aggregate' of the pauperised to a 'state of free market (self-disciplined) agency'.[126] This emphasis persisted throughout the history of the Poor Law and it was perhaps no accident that, within a few years of admitting 'independent artisans' to the franchise in 1867, the state tightened up the law and made it even more punitive in 1871.[127]

These impulses were complemented in the regions of sanitary reform and 'environmental politics', where one also may see as a matter of policy the differentiation of the independent man at the head of the respectable family who needed to be separated out from the threat of 'degradation' and political danger within the unhealthy body – literal and metaphorical – of the city. In Edwin Chadwick's view, disease in the city would destroy the 'able-bodied' and virtuous men and leave a residuum who were, as he put it in 1845, 'always young, inexperienced, ignorant, credulous, passionate, violent, and proportionately dangerous, with a perpetual tendency to moral as well as physical deterioration'.[128]

Similarly, examination of the issue of prostitution and its regulation through the Contagious Diseases Acts of 1864–9 shows a crucial demarcation of prostitution as a 'problem' in ways similar to the shifts in social policy concerning the poor and the urban environment, but also the fixing of the female prostitute as the 'pollutant' figure whom the state must punish. Against her there was established, not least within the movement to repeal the acts, a binary opposition of the respectable working man, evident in the participation of such men in the campaign. He was seen, and saw himself, as the household head who was the protector of 'his' wife and daughters against sexual immorality and danger.[129]

The Emergence of the Welfare State in Britain and Germany (London: Croom Helm on behalf of the German Historical Institute, 1981), pp. 50–70.

126 Mary Poovey, 'Thomas Chalmers, Edwin Chadwick, and the Sublime Revolution in Nineteenth-Century Government', in her *Making a Social Body*, pp. 98–114, esp. p. 107.

127 Which has been called 'the most sustained attempt of the century to impose upon the working classes the Victorian values of providence, self-reliance, foresight, and self-discipline': Matthew, *Gladstone*, p. 170.

128 Cited in U. R. Q. Henriques, *Before the Welfare State* (London: Longman, 1979), p. 127. For two very helpful discussions of 'environmental politics', see Frank Mort, *Dangerous Sexualities: Medico-Moral Politics in England Since 1830* (London: Routledge and Kegan Paul, 1987), and Mary Poovey, 'Domesticity and Class Formation: Chadwick's 1842 *Sanitary Report*', in her *Making a Social Body*, pp. 115–31.

129 See, above all, Judith R. Walkowitz, *Prostitution and Victorian Society: Women, Class, and the State* (Cambridge University Press, 1980).

Yet if an examination of the wider social and cultural demarcation of the 'independent and respectable' working-class man would tell us much about how it became possible to regard him as a potential citizen, in the end the 'fixing' of this man as citizen rested upon specifically political conditions. Here it would become necessary to examine not only the origins of 1867, the major concern of this chapter, but also the subsequent assimilation of the politics of the working man – both as subject and object of politics – into the workings of politics after 1867. The 1868 election appeared to seal the relationship between working-class politics and liberalism, in part through the secret deals done between Howell of the Reform League and G. G. Glyn, the Liberal chief whip, which delivered financial assistance to the League in exchange for its help in electoral activities.[130] Yet it is clear that this became an unstable alliance and formation. In part this was because of the immediate difficulties of the Gladstone government of 1868–74, not least over the questions of trade union legislation and of education policies, in part because the Liberal party was both less quick and less successful in the long-term work of building the local community and constituency organisations to sustain working-class voters than the Conservatives proved to be. At the same time, the very forces and themes that had sustained the working-class claim to entry into the political nation were also those which opened labour to integration into the conservative nation if not necessarily Conservative politics. Although it was not translated into concrete and coherent policies, Disraelian conservatism, enunciated in the celebrated Manchester and Crystal Palace speeches of 1872 and pursued in the government of 1874–80, was the first politics to try to establish links between social policy, imperialism and the nation, and the working class. Outside Lancashire, working-class conservatism was to remain relatively weak in the later nineteenth century. However, what did not remain weak was the integration, to very considerable extent, of the working class into a politics in which the integrity of the nation and empire and of hierarchically organised relations of class, gender and race were of paramount importance to the politics of later nineteenth-century Britain.

[130] See Royden Harrison, *Before the Socialists*, ch. 4, 'The Reform League and the General Election of 1868'.

3 The citizenship of women and the Reform Act of 1867

Jane Rendall

> Dear Madam,
> I think that while a Reform Bill is under discussion and petitions are being presented to parliament from various classes – asking for representation or protesting against disfranchisement, it is very desirable that women who wish for political enfranchisement should say so.[1]

In the correspondence between Barbara Leigh Smith Bodichon and Helen Taylor in May 1866, it is clear that the introduction of a Reform Bill for England and Wales in 1866 inspired the first organised petition to Parliament for the enfranchisement of women. The long history of the struggle for the parliamentary vote for all adult women, from 1866 to 1928, has tended to obscure how closely the first stages of that movement were linked to the national debate about parliamentary reform. It has also obscured what were understood by contemporaries as early advances in the struggle.

Four years after this letter was written, on 4 May 1870, the Radical–Liberal MP for Manchester, Jacob Bright, introduced a Women's Disabilities Removal Bill which passed its second reading in the House of Commons by a majority of thirty-three votes. That result seemed to John Stuart Mill to represent 'enormous progress', as it did to Lydia Becker and the Manchester National Society for Women's Suffrage who viewed it as signalling 'a great advance in public opinion'.[2] The weight of continuing political opposition to women's suffrage should not of course be underestimated. But a historiography that assumes a movement progressing from small beginnings to final success may have distorted a rather different, not necessarily linear, and much more complex history. This essay seeks, first, simply to recover the relationship between

[1] Helen Taylor to Barbara Leigh Smith Bodichon, draft letter, 9 May 1866, Mill–Taylor Papers, London School of Economics [hereafter MT], vol. XII, ff. 105–6.

[2] Mill to Charles Kingsley, 9 July 1870, in *Collected Works of John Stuart Mill* [hereafter *CW*], gen. ed. J. M. Robson, 33 vols. (University of Toronto Press, 1962–91), vol. XVII, *The Later Letters of John Stuart Mill, 1849–1873*, ed. Francis Mineka and Dwight N. Lindley (1972), p. 1744; MNSWS, *Third Annual Report of the Executive Committee* (Manchester, 1870), p. 12.

early demands for women's suffrage, and the reform agitation and its aftermath, inside and outside the Houses of Parliament, between 1866 and 1870. In doing so it notes the differential histories that may be told for England and Wales, Scotland, and Ireland.[3]

Secondly, the debate around citizenship initiated by the Second Reform Bill also defined the boundaries of the imagined British nation. Chapter 2 considered the 'masculinisation' of popular politics and the emergence of the male voter not only as head of household but as breadwinner. In this essay, written from different sources and perspectives on the debates of the 1860s, that definition of citizenship may appear more fluid and less clear-cut, as some barriers to women's political activities were lifted, and as a few women came to play a part, if a very limited one, in both formal and informal political contexts. But perceptions of gender differences were clearly cut across by divisions of class, by the different political and religious 'national' experiences within the United Kingdom and by constructions of race. In 1869, three years after Helen Taylor's letter to Barbara Bodichon, Charles Kingsley, the defender of Governor Eyre, wrote with sympathy of the claim for suffrage made by 'refined and educated women', to defend themselves and 'their lowlier sisters' from the 'tyranny' of uneducated men.[4]

Citizenship for 'women' was variously defined by campaigners for and sympathisers with women's suffrage, both women and men, like Helen Taylor and Barbara Bodichon, Jacob Bright and Charles Kingsley. The argument could rest on 'all those attributes of reason and conscience which raise humanity above the brute', attributes shared by women and men.[5] But the claim for citizenship might also be constructed in terms which, though they might admit some women within

[3] The only detailed narrative remains that of Helen Blackburn, *Women's Suffrage: A Record of the Women's Suffrage Movement in the British Isles with Biographical Sketches of Miss Becker* (London and Oxford, 1902; repr. New York: Source Book Press, 1970); see also Sandra Holton, *Suffrage Days: Stories for the Women's Suffrage Movement* (London: Routledge, 1996). Recent studies of the early years include: Ann P. Robson, 'The Founding of the National Society for Women's Suffrage 1866–1867', *Canadian Journal of History* 8 (1973), 1–22; Barbara Caine, 'John Stuart Mill and the English Women's Movement', *Historical Studies* 18 (1978), 52–67, and her 'Feminism, Suffrage and the Nineteenth-Century English Women's Movement', *Women's Studies International Forum* 5 (1982), 537–50; Andrew Rosen, 'Emily Davies and the Women's Movement 1862–1867', *Journal of British Studies* 19 (1979), 101–21; Jane Rendall, 'Citizenship, Culture and Civilisation: The Languages of British Suffragists 1866–1874', in Caroline Daley and Melanie Nolan (eds.), *Suffrage and Beyond: International Feminist Perspectives* (Auckland University Press, 1994), pp. 127–50.

[4] Charles Kingsley, 'Women and Politics', *Macmillan's Magazine* 20 (1869), 557.

[5] Lydia Becker, 'The Political Disabilities of Women', *Westminster Review* 97 (o.s.), 41 (n.s.) (January 1872), 50–70.

the boundaries of the political nation, also depended for their force on excluding others, whether on the grounds of marital status, class, ethnicity or race. Gender was one of the most significant determinants of the boundaries of that political nation, but its operation cannot be understood in isolation.

In October 1865 the death of Lord Palmerston signalled the possibility of a renewal of interest in parliamentary reform, as Lord Russell, who was strongly committed to moderate reform, formed a new ministry. In November 1865 the Kensington Ladies Debating Society put on their agenda for discussion the question: 'Is the extension of the parliamentary suffrage to women desirable and if so under what conditions?'[6] Already in 1865 there were in London as in other major cities small groups of women and men interested in and committed to women's suffrage, ready to take up the opportunities presented by the reform crisis.

The background to the women's suffrage movement, 1790–1865

The argument that women should have a voice in the selection of their parliamentary representatives had been made – although only in passing – by Mary Wollstonecraft in her *Vindication of the Rights of Woman* (1792).[7] Few responded to that suggestion in the 1790s or in the conservative reaction which followed. Yet in the 1820s the cause of anti-slavery led many women to consider the political strategies best fitted for their cause: the female voluntary association, the economic boycott, the parliamentary petition.[8] And the reform crisis of 1830–2 prompted some consideration of women's claim to the franchise. The Tory landowner from Halifax, Anne Lister, regretted in her diary that women of property were unable to exercise the vote, though they might, as she herself did, strive to influence the electoral process. In August 1832 a petition to the House of Commons from Mary Smith of Stanmore asked for the vote for 'every unmarried woman having that pecuniary qualification whereby the other sex is entitled to the said franchise'. Matthew Davenport Hill, a radical Unitarian, endorsed women's suffrage in his election campaign in 1832 in Hull. But the Reform Act itself for the first time defined the voter as

6 Emily Davies, 'Family Chronicle', Davies Papers, Girton College, Cambridge [hereafter FCD], ff. 423–4; Rosen, 'Emily Davies and the Women's Movement', 107–9.

7 Mary Wollstonecraft, *Vindication of the Rights of Woman* (1792), repr. in *The Works of Mary Wollstonecraft*, ed. Janet Todd and Marilyn Butler, 7 vols. (London: William Pickering, 1989), vol. V, p. 217.

8 Clare Midgley, *Women Against Slavery: The British Campaigns, 1780–1870* (London and New York: Routledge, 1992), ch. 2.

'male'.[9] In the 1830s women became increasingly active in the petitioning campaigns of the anti-slavery movement, their involvement encouraged by the accession of Queen Victoria in 1837. The all-female petitions of 1833 and 1838 were the largest single petitions against slavery and apprenticeship.[10] And in 1848 in a parliamentary debate on the franchise, Benjamin Disraeli ironically signalled his own support for the principle of voting rights for women with property, referring to the claim for women's votes in the French revolution of that year.[11]

This early history indicated the legal difficulties of the claim. Single women and widows could own, lease or rent property, whether a country house or a cottage, on the same terms as men. But under English common law, a married woman's legal existence was subsumed into that of her husband, who assumed legal rights either as owner or as guardian of his wife's property at marriage. In such a situation the married woman could not legally qualify in a voting system dependent on the ownership of property, nor could she convincingly claim 'independence' as a head of household, so widely viewed as an essential attribute of citizenship. Even the law of equity, which allowed married women's property to be protected in a trust, did not give them the customary responsibilities of property.[12]

By the 1830s and 1840s, the case for female suffrage began to be heard more widely, and to be put in more radical terms. Within the 'utopian' and communitarian movement led by Robert Owen, a minority of male and female Owenites saw the rights of women, including enfranchisement and political activism, as central to their cause.[13] Within a Chartist movement primarily committed to universal manhood suffrage, a few followed their radical politics to a logical conclusion. So, in 1838, 'a working-woman of Glasgow' was to write as a 'Real Democrat' to the Chartist paper, the *Northern Star*, to suggest 'that it is the right of every woman to have a vote in the legislation of her country', a view she shared with male Chartist leaders like George Holyoake and

[9] Helen Blackburn, *Women's Suffrage*, p. 12; Cat Euler, 'Moving Between Worlds: Gender, Politics, Class and Sexuality in the Diaries of Anne Lister of Shibden Hall, 1830–1840', DPhil. thesis, University of York (1995), p. 240; *Journal of the House of Commons* 87 (1832), 551; Kathryn Gleadle, *The Early Feminists: Radical Unitarians and the Emergence of the Women's Rights Movement, 1831–1851* (Basingstoke: Macmillan, 1995), p. 71.

[10] Midgley, *Women Against Slavery*, pp. 65–7.

[11] *Hansard*, 3rd ser., vol. 99, col. 950, 20 June 1848.

[12] See Lee Holcombe, *Wives and Property: Reform of the Married Women's Property Law in Nineteenth-Century England* (Oxford: Martin Robertson, 1983), chs. 2–3; Mary Lyndon Shanley, *Feminism, Marriage and the Law in Victorian England, 1850–1895* (Princeton University Press, 1989).

[13] Barbara Taylor, *Eve and the New Jerusalem: Socialism and Feminism in the Nineteenth Century* (London: Virago, 1983), pp. 180–2.

Ernest Jones.[14] And, by 1851, the Sheffield Female Political Association could call in an address 'To the Women of England' for 'the entire enfranchisement of our sex'.[15]

From the dissenting denomination most associated with political radicalism, the Unitarians, came a small group, with interests in democratic and socialist movements, who consistently argued for women's suffrage, in their own periodicals, in Robert Owen's *New Moral World* and in the Chartist movement. The ideas at first associated with the progressive Unitarian minister and journalist, William Johnson Fox of South Place Chapel in Finsbury, were disseminated more widely. By the 1840s young lawyers like William Shaen and James Stansfeld, and Unitarians close to Owenism like Catherine and Goodwyn Barmby, had already clearly identified women's enfranchisement as an essential element in the political transformation which they hoped to see. In their Declaration of Electoral Reform of 1841 the Barmbys demanded universal adult suffrage. These members of the radical Unitarian intelligentsia were joined by individuals like the Quaker Anne Knight, and Scotswomen like Margaret Mylne and Marion Reid, who published pleas for enfranchisement in 1841 and 1843. And novelists like Mary Leman Grimstone and Geraldine Jewsbury alluded indirectly and subtly but still recognisably to the same cause in their fiction.[16]

Kathryn Gleadle has argued that in these years radical Unitarians developed a concept of women's oppression significantly different from that found within Chartism, and one which focused on the metaphor and symbol of slavery. Such a view was sited first of all within an Enlightenment historical heritage that traced the evolution of women's condition from the slavery of early savage societies to that of the modern commercial West.[17] John Stuart Mill's earliest published writing on the condition of women, in 1826, was located precisely within that heritage. Comparing the gallantry of an age of chivalry with 'the Asiatic kingdoms', he wrote of both as characterising 'that period in the progress of society

[14] *Northern Star*, 23 June 1838, quoted in Dorothy Thompson, 'Women in Nineteenth-Century Radical Politics: A Lost Dimension', in Ann Oakley and Juliet Mitchell (eds.), *The Rights and Wrongs of Women* (Harmondsworth: Penguin, 1976), p. 123.

[15] Gail Malmgreen, 'Anne Knight and the Radical Subculture', *Quaker History* 71 (1982), 100–13; Jutta Schwarzkopf, *Women in the Chartist Movement* (Basingstoke: Macmillan, 1991), pp. 250–1; *Northern Star*, 22 February 1851.

[16] Gleadle, *Early Feminists*, chs. 2–3; Margaret Mylne, *Woman and Her Social Position: An Article Reprinted from the Westminster Review, No. LXVIII, 1841* (London: C. Green and Son, 1872); Marion Reid, *A Plea for Woman* (1843; repr. Edinburgh: Polygon, 1988); Malmgreen, 'Anne Knight and the Radical Subculture'.

[17] Gleadle, *Early Feminists*, pp. 62–70; Jane Rendall, *The Origins of Modern Feminism: Women in Britain, France, and the United States, 1780–1860* (Basingstoke: Macmillan, 1985), pp. 21–32; Sylvana Tomaselli, 'The Enlightenment Debate on Women', *History Workshop Journal* 20 (1985), 101–25.

which may be termed the age of false refinement, and which is situated half way between savage and civilized life'. To Mill the seclusion of women in Asia and the exaggerated gallantry of feudal Europe were equally marks of 'the same low state of civilisation'.[18]

Radical Unitarians agreed with Mill that it was not, as the Chartists tended to suggest, the drudgery of hard labour for women which constituted slavery for women, but the effects of longstanding patriarchal oppression and its shaping of the submissive – or slavish – character of women. W. J. Fox, like Harriet Taylor and John Stuart Mill, wrote of the survival of brute force in the relations between men and women, though it had long disappeared from other social relationships.[19] For the radical Unitarians, as for Harriet Taylor and John Stuart Mill, only a progressive transformation including but not limited to political enfranchisement could finally eliminate the remnants of barbarism and savagery, and indeed the code of chivalry itself.

The metaphor of slavery was a powerful one, reinforced by the involvement of so many middle-class women, evangelical, Unitarian and Quaker, in the anti-slavery and abolitionist movements from the 1830s to the 1860s. The World Anti-Slavery Convention held in London in 1840 had raised the right of women abolitionists to participate; American supporters of William Lloyd Garrison claimed that right, though the British committee refused to accept female delegates. Some British women abolitionists were inspired by the example of the American women. Yet the more conservative British movement was divided, with many activists, especially those with committed evangelical views of the 'separate sphere' of women, expressing strong disapproval of the claim for women's rights. Only by the 1850s were those Unitarians and radical Quakers who united their commitment to abolitionism and women's rights able to assert their claim to a more equal role within the movement. Two of the strongest groups of the 1850s were the Bristol and Clifton Ladies Emancipation Society, led by Mary Estlin, and the Edinburgh Ladies Emancipation Society, led by Eliza Wigham.[20]

In 1851 Harriet Taylor Mill's article, published anonymously, on 'The Enfranchisement of Women' took as its occasion the Women's Rights

[18] Mill, 'Modern French Historical Works – Age of Chivalry', *Westminster Review* 6 (July 1826), repr. in *CW*, vol. XX, *Essays on French History and Historians*, ed. J. M. Robson (1985), pp. 46–8.

[19] W. J. Fox, 'On the Requisite Adjuncts, Social and Political, of National Education', in *Reports of Lectures Delivered at the Chapel in South Place, Finsbury* (1860), quoted in Gleadle, *Early Feminists*, p. 69.

[20] Midgley, *Women Against Slavery*, ch. 7, and her 'Anti-Slavery and Feminism in Nineteenth-Century Britain', *Gender & History* 5 (1993), 343–62; Kathryn Kish Sklar, '"Women Who Speak for an Entire Nation": American and British Women at the World Anti-Slavery Convention, London, 1840', in Jean Fagan Yellin and John C. Van Horne (eds.), *The Abolitionist Sisterhood: Women's Political Culture in Antebellum America* (Ithaca, N.Y.: Cornell University Press, 1994), pp. 301–34.

Convention held in Worcester, Massachusetts, in October 1850. But it noted the claim as one made by 'radicals and Chartists' in Britain and by 'democrats on the Continent'. She hoped that the petition of the Sheffield Reform Association of 1851 might prove the first step to be taken in Britain. In that article she called for the absolute equality of women and of men; and she also expressed her doubts of the 'sentimental priesthood' of philanthropic women. But her writing had no immediate effect in these years of retreat and political stability.[21]

The first stages of the women's movement in Britain were to take a rather different course, and from the mid-1850s to the mid-1860s the issue of women's suffrage was not foremost on the agenda. This period saw, rather, middle-class women coming together to forge their own pressure groups and create their own periodicals. In this they were less reliant on, though never completely at a distance from, male-led radical and reforming movements. In the mid-1850s two young Unitarian women, Bessie Rayner Parkes and Barbara Bodichon, from politically radical middle-class families, helped to initiate a petition for reform of the legal position of married women. They subsequently established the *English Woman's Journal* and, in Langham Place, a centre for women's activities. They drew in women from a variety of backgrounds, including the clergyman's daughter Emily Davies, the upper-class Jessie Boucherett, the Bohemian Matilda Hays. Their journal was at the forefront of attempts to secure a better standard of education for middle-class girls. It campaigned, with the Society for the Promotion of Employment for Women, for the opening of a wide variety of occupations to women. It promoted the idea of a 'sanitary mission' to be carried by middle-class women to the homes of the poor.[22] Yet at its launch in 1858, the editor Bessie Rayner Parkes declared her nervousness of contentious issues such as 'divorce & the suffrage', and her desire rather to rely on gradual changes in public opinion.[23] By 1864, the situation had changed to the extent that the *Journal* printed its own abstract, with selected extracts, of Harriet Taylor's article, which the then editor Emily Davies still viewed as a 'startling manifesto' with a bitterness of tone which she distrusted.[24]

[21] Harriet Taylor Mill, 'Enfranchisement of Women', *Westminster Review* 55 (July 1851), 289–311.

[22] Jane Rendall, '"A Moral Engine?": Feminism, Liberalism, and the *English Woman's Journal*', in Rendall (ed.), *Equal or Different: Women's Politics 1800–1914* (Oxford: Basil Blackwell, 1987), pp. 112–38; Barbara Caine, *Victorian Feminists* (Oxford University Press, 1992), ch. 2.

[23] Bessie Rayner Parkes to Barbara Bodichon, 5 January 1858, Parkes Papers, Girton College, Cambridge [hereafter PPG], vol. V, f. 86.

[24] *English Woman's Journal* [hereafter *EWJ*] 13 (July 1864), 289–96; Emily Davies to Barbara Bodichon, 3 December 1862 and 21 August 1866, Bodichon Papers, Girton College, Cambridge, B. 302 and 316.

It is easy to read the history of the women's movement in the decade before 1865 as one of a 'little band of faulty, stormy, clever warm hearted women', as Bessie Parkes saw it.[25] Yet it is clear that from the earliest stages the movement also had considerable masculine support. Not all supporters, women or men, came from radical or reforming backgrounds. The backgrounds of Emily Faithfull, the daughter of a country parson, and of Jessie Boucherett, from the Lincolnshire gentry, did not necessarily predispose them to the cause. The Conservative recorder of London, Russell Gurney, was to prove an important stalwart to the cause in the House of Commons. Yet, overall, the movement for women's enfranchisement drew most extensively upon different and overlapping networks of radical and liberal opinion. Support came partly from the more radical sections of the nonconformist and urban provincial leadership, united not only by the campaign against slavery, but also by the Anti-Corn Law League, by the common interests of nonconformity and by sympathy with a nationalist politics. The small but influential and very closely knit Quaker and Unitarian religious communities provided a disproportionate number of these activists, both women and men. There were familial dynasties: the extended Bright, McLaren, Priestman and Estlin connections which stretched across Manchester, Bristol and Edinburgh, the Taylors and Courtaulds of London and Essex, the Fords and Luptons of Leeds, the Davenport Hills of Bristol, the Rowntrees of York, the Wedgwoods of Etruria and the Cowens of Newcastle. Many of these dynasties included leading manufacturers and merchants in the northern and Midlands industrial towns, and the tenets of Manchester School political economy were a part of their world, though these were also for many in the process of moderation by a more paternalist vision. There were key ministers, like the Unitarians Henry Crosskey of Birmingham and Saul A. Steinthal in Manchester, and supportive newspaper editors like Alexander Ireland of the *Manchester Examiner and Times* and Richard Reed of the *Newcastle Daily Chronicle*.[26]

Yet other backgrounds too helped to shape the discourses of the women's movement in the specific circumstances of the 1860s. In these years, there were important bridges between provincial nonconformity,

[25] Bessie Rayner Parkes to Barbara Bodichon, 21 August [no year], PPG, vol. V, f. 158.

[26] For discussion of some of these networks, see: June Hannam, '"An Enlarged Sphere of Usefulness": The Bristol Women's Movement c. 1860–1914', in Madge Dresser and Philip Ollerenshaw (eds.), *The Making of Modern Bristol* (Tiverton: Radcliffe Press, 1996), pp. 184–209; Holton, *Suffrage Days*, chs. 1–3; Brian Harrison, 'A Genealogy of Reform in Modern Britain', in Christine Bolt and Seymour Drescher (eds.), *Anti-Slavery, Religion and Reform: Essays in Memory of Roger Anstey* (Folkestone: Dawson, 1980), pp. 118–48; Philippa Levine, *Feminist Lives in Victorian England: Private Roles and Public Commitment* (Oxford: Basil Blackwell, 1990), ch. 2.

academic liberalism and the intellectual world of London. The campaign to improve the education of women from the mid-1850s had brought as patrons Christian socialists like F. D. Maurice, Thomas Hughes and Charles Kingsley, and academic liberals like Henry Sidgwick and Charles Pearson. They shared a common interest in university extension movements as well as in higher education for women. In the Universities of Oxford and Cambridge, the campaign against the Tests Act (which restricted university posts to Anglicans) and support for the North in the American Civil War had already, by 1865, brought such liberals closer to a campaigning nonconformity. Many were to be supportive of the cause of women's suffrage.[27]

There were other points of contact. The first agitation for reform of the married women's property legislation in the 1850s had brought feminists into close contact with young reforming lawyers first in the Law Amendment Society and later in the important National Association for the Promotion of Social Science. Many women's groups affiliated themselves to that association, and prepared papers for its annual congresses, held in the major cities. It provided a major forum for discussion of the possibility of a new kind of 'social science', and helped to bring together reforming opinion.[28]

The question around which so much recent work on the political history of this period has focused has been the relationship between middle-class radicalism and a working-class politics of reform. Between the radical Unitarians of the 1840s, Chartists and Owenites, there had been a continuing exchange in relation to the position of women. In the 1850s, many retained their commitment to a radical politics, and in particular focused upon nationalist aspirations within Europe, for Hungary, Italy and Poland, and indeed in Ireland. As Margot Finn has suggested, the movements of support for nationalism arose within a 'middle-class radical culture centred on family life, private houses, Nonconformist chapels and liberal salons'.[29] Such centres included Joseph Cowen jun.'s Stella Hall in Newcastle, Peter and Clementia Taylor's Aubrey House in

[27] Christopher Harvie, *The Lights of Liberalism: University Liberals and the Challenge of Democracy, 1860–1886* (London: Allen Lane, 1976), p. 89. Harvie suggests, p. 304n, that the majority of academic liberals were not sympathetic to women's suffrage, but this is not borne out by the sources of the women's movement.

[28] Kathleen McCrone, 'The National Association for the Promotion of Social Science and the Advancement of Victorian Women', *Atlantis* 8 (1982), 44–66; Lawrence Goldman, 'The Social Science Association, 1857–1886: A Context for Mid-Victorian Liberalism', *English Historical Review* 101 (1986), 95–134; Eileen Janes Yeo, *The Contest for Social Science: Relations and Representations of Gender and Class* (London: Rivers Oram, 1996), ch. 6.

[29] Margot C. Finn, *After Chartism: Class and Nation in English Radical Politics, 1848–1874* (Cambridge University Press, 1993), p. 160.

London and the home of William Ashurst at Muswell Hill, all of whom entertained Mazzini, Kossuth and Louis Blanc, and had also been, since the 1840s, centres of support for women's rights and enfranchisement.[30]

In the early 1860s the relationship between middle-class radicals and working-class supporters was shifting, though it also varied greatly with locality. The fervour of support for Garibaldi which swept England in 1864 contributed to this, though it also divided secularists, Anglicans and nonconformists of all classes from Catholics in England and Ireland.[31] Former Chartists also came together with liberals in support for the North in the American Civil War. The membership list of the Union and Emancipation Society of the North of England founded in 1864 united John Stuart Mill with the Christian Socialist Thomas Hughes, the radical journalist W. E. Adams, and George Wilson and his political associates, representing Manchester Liberalism.[32] Though the founding of the National Reform Union in Manchester in 1864 was dominated by a Liberal politics inherited from the Anti-Corn Law League, it too incorporated radicals with a strong commitment to interventionism abroad, like Joseph Cowen jun.

When in February 1865 the Reform League was founded in London to promote manhood suffrage, its campaigns met increasing support from middle-class liberals including the Christian socialist Thomas Hughes, the radical employer Samuel Morley, the Unitarian Peter Taylor and academics such as John Elliot Cairnes, the friend of Mill.

But – though all these individuals supported women's suffrage in the debates of 1866–8 – the consequences of these networks and their 'radicalisation of liberal culture' for women's suffrage could be determined by local political conditions.[33] In London the Reform League maintained the initiative in working-class politics, with little evidence of direct support of or interest in women's suffrage. In Manchester, the continuing strength of middle-class radicalism tended to subsume working-class radicalism in a United Liberal alliance, which was to prove temporarily more sympathetic to women's suffrage.[34] What is clear remains the variety of

[30] *Ibid.*, pp. 166–7. [31] *Ibid.*, p. 204.

[32] *Ibid.*, pp. 217–25; a list of members of the Union and Emancipation Society is prefixed to W. E. Adams, *The Slaveholders' War: An Argument for the North and the Negro* (Manchester, 1863), p. 2; Eugenio Biagini, *Liberty, Retrenchment and Reform: Popular Liberalism in the Age of Gladstone, 1860–1880* (Cambridge University Press, 1992), pp. 70–6; Antony David Taylor, 'Modes of Political Expression and Working-Class Radicalism 1848–1874: The London and Manchester Examples', 2 vols., Ph.D thesis, University of Manchester (1992), vol. I, p. 357.

[33] Finn, *After Chartism*, pp. 236–8, 309.

[34] I owe this contrast to Antony Taylor, 'Modes of Political Expression', vol. I, ch. 6, and *passim*, though for the Manchester women's suffrage movement, 1866–8, see below, pp. 134–5, 139–49.

political beliefs and loyalties within radical–liberal politics, a variety which could also come to incorporate a commitment to women's suffrage.

The one individual to whom virtually all radicals and liberals looked with respect was John Stuart Mill, elected to the House of Commons in June 1865. Two years after the death of Harriet Taylor in 1858, Mill began to write *The Subjection of Women*, although it was not published until 1869. Nevertheless, his opinions on women's issues were widely known, from Taylor's essay and from his *Principles of Political Economy* (1848), and *Considerations on Representative Government* (1861).[35] Mill had placed the issue of women's suffrage firmly before the electors of Westminster, and women from the Langham Place circle campaigned for him.[36] Mill's own circle included his stepdaughter Helen Taylor, and a group of male liberals, academics and politicians, including Thomas Hare, Henry Fawcett and John Elliot Cairnes. Helen Taylor's attendance at the Kensington Ladies Debating Society, founded in May 1865, was to bring those women previously active at Langham Place into contact with Mill and with his circle, though the relationship was not to prove an easy one.[37]

The emergence of the women's suffrage movement in 1866–8 can be understood as part of the internal development of a 'woman-centred' movement, yet also in the context of a 'liberalism exuberant' from 1866.[38] The narrative that follows is a highly provisional one, awaiting much further research. It is rooted in the perspectives and some of the sources of the women's movement, but attempts to place that movement within the wider context of British political and cultural history. It also suggests that, in the complex process of claiming the franchise for 'women', activists defined the different kinds of ways in which women voters might be citizens of the British nation.

[35] For relevant discussions of Mill, see the introduction, pp. 62–70.

[36] Bruce L. Kinzer, Ann P. Robson and John M. Robson (eds.), *A Moralist in and out of Parliament: John Stuart Mill at Westminster, 1865–1868* (University of Toronto Press, 1992), pp. 113 and 270–1.

[37] On Helen Taylor, see Ann P. Robson, 'Mill's Second Prize in the Lottery of Life', in Michael Laine (ed.), *A Cultivated Mind: Essays on J. S. Mill Presented to John M. Robson* (University of Toronto Press, 1991), pp. 215–41.

[38] The best interpretation of the place of the women's suffrage movement within a 'woman-centred politics' is to be found in Levine, *Feminist Lives in Victorian England*, Preface and ch. 6. The phrase 'liberalism exuberant' is to be found in Jonathan Parry, *The Rise and Fall of Liberal Government in Victorian Britain* (New Haven and London: Yale University Press, 1993), ch. 10.

Women and the Reform Act of 1867

Women's suffrage and the passing of the Reform Act, July 1865–August 1867

The appearance of women in John Stuart Mill's successful election campaign in 1865, and the political climate of that year, signalled new possibilities. Mill had been returned to the House of Commons with other sympathetic members of the Victorian intelligentsia.[39] For a meeting of the Kensington Ladies Debating Society to be held on 21 November 1865 on women's suffrage, five women, including Barbara Bodichon and Helen Taylor, wrote papers. The idea of a committee to work towards the suffrage for women had clearly already arisen. As Emily Davies wrote on 10 November, 'some people are inclined to begin a subdued kind of agitation for the franchise'.[40]

In early 1866 Lord Russell's government was in the process of preparing a Liberal Reform Bill, their task complicated by the absence of any reliable survey of the electorate itself, and the desire to preserve adequate safeguards against the dangers of universal male suffrage. The problem was made more difficult by the complexities and local variations in the system of registration for the suffrage, which excluded householders, who 'compounded' for payment of their rates.[41] John Lambert, an official of the Poor Law Board, asked to make an estimate of the numbers of working men to be enfranchised by a £6 rating qualification, reported in March that an accurate calculation was impossible given the large numbers of tenants compounding, and of female occupiers in this category.[42] On 27 April 1866, in the heat of the exchanges between Gladstone and Disraeli, Disraeli suggested, probably with a customary opportunism, though he prided himself on his consistency, that the suffrage should not be confined to men, and that women of property, who might hold manorial and parish offices, might also possess the elective franchise.[43] He may have assumed, as others of his party did, that this was more likely to produce a conservative, even 'deferential' vote.

There is some evidence that Disraeli's words may have stimulated immediate action, though Emily Davies was later to deny this.[44] Two

39 F. B. Smith, *The Making of the Second Reform Bill* (Cambridge University Press, 1966), p. 54.

40 Emily Davies to Mr Tomkinson, 10 November 1865, FCD, f. 439.

41 For the details of franchise qualifications and the bill of 1866, see the introduction, pp. 3–4, and appendix C, pp. 239–40.

42 F. B. Smith, *Making of the Second Reform Bill*, p. 65.

43 *Hansard*, 3rd ser., vol. 183, col. 99, 27 April 1866.

44 As Emily Davies pointed out, Helen Blackburn, in *Women's Suffrage*, p. 53, confused two

months after the Liberal bill had been introduced by Lord Russell into the House of Commons, and ten days after Disraeli's words, on 9 May 1866, Barbara Bodichon sought the guidance of Helen Taylor and John Stuart Mill on the most suitable date for the presentation of a petition on the extension of the suffrage to women, in the months of the bill's discussion.

The drafting of the petition immediately raised a significant issue of principle in the situation of married women. Though women like Barbara Bodichon had been campaigning for the improvement of their legal position since 1854, the movement for women's suffrage had to consider its tactics. Helen Taylor wrote to Bodichon in May 1866, 'no idea is so universally accepted and acceptable in England as that taxation and representation ought to go together', and argued that people would listen to the case for single women and widows of property, if not to a more general argument against discrimination on grounds of sex. All women could ask for the franchise for those women who qualified, 'just as men who are not seven pound householders petition in favour of the present reform bill'.[45] The final petition modestly asked that the House 'consider the expediency of providing for all householders, without distinction of sex, who possess such property or rental qualification as your Honourable House may determine'.[46] That wording reflected not the desire to enfranchise only 'women of property' but the continuing discussion within the House of Commons as to the appropriate level of enfranchisement for all householders, including tenants. The wording of the petition did not deliberately exclude married women. Emily Davies reflected: 'I do not see that in *limiting* our claim, we necessarily pronounce upon the rights of people, outside that claim . . . We ask for what there is some remote chance of getting.'[47] The conflict between political expediency and principle continued to divide activists throughout these years.

Bodichon, Taylor, Emily Davies and Kensington Society activists circulated the petition, gaining 1,521 signatures, mainly through the energy of individual canvassers.[48] Though the Reform Bill under discussion

speeches by Disraeli, those of 20 July 1848 and 27 April 1866. The meeting between Barbara Bodichon, Jessie Boucherett and Emily Davies, which Blackburn describes as inspired by Disraeli's speech, apparently took place on 18 October, according to Davies (Davies, FCD, ff. 484–5).

45 Draft letter of Helen Taylor to Barbara Bodichon, 9 May 1866, MT, vol. XIII, ff. 107–10.

46 'Petition for Extension of the Electoral Franchise to All Householders, Without Distinction of Sex . . . (7 June 1866, No. 8501)', *Reports of the Select Committee of the House of Commons on Public Petitions, Session 1866*, appendix, p. 305.

47 Emily Davies to Helen Taylor, 6 August 1866, MT, vol. XIII, f. 183, quoted in Ann P. Robson, 'Founding of the National Society', 11.

48 Correspondence between Bodichon and Taylor, May 1866, MT, vol. XII, ff. 105–14. For a detailed analysis of the petition and its signatories, see Ann Dingsdale, '"Generous and

applied only to England and Wales, the petition referred to the principles of the 'British constitution' and included both Irish and Scottish names.[49] Mill presented the petition on 7 June, but, as was customary, did not speak to it, indicating his intention to place a motion before the Commons on the issue at a later date. It was reported straightforwardly in the press.

Russell's Liberal government fell on 26 June 1866; his successors, Derby and Disraeli, could form only a minority government. Mill, speaking on 17 July from the opposition benches, put a motion for a return of the potential number of voters who, fulfilling all other qualifications, were excluded only by sex, reflecting the anxious concerns of the Liberal ministry for more effective knowledge of those potentially to be enfranchised.[50] Mill spoke briefly and cautiously, and took the prudent step of reminding Conservatives that their leader had indeed endorsed the principle of enfranchising women with property. He now posed no threat to a Liberal bill, and the Conservatives did not wish to divide the House and risk defeat on such an issue. He was heard with respect and the motion was agreed. As Ann Robson has argued, in this session he had succeeded in getting women's suffrage on to the parliamentary agenda and had avoided undue ridicule.[51]

The next twelve months, between August 1866 and the passing of the Conservative Reform Bill, saw the organised emergence of a women's suffrage movement in Britain. It also saw the emergence of differences, of both personality and principle, among the women and men involved in rival provincial and metropolitan networks. Already from the summer of 1866 differences between the women active in the Kensington Society and in Langham Place and the circle around John Stuart Mill were becoming evident. The conservative Emily Davies had significant doubts about associating the movement too closely with Mill and his 'crotchets':

footnote 48 (*cont.*)
Lofty Sympathies": The Kensington Society, the 1866 Women's Suffrage Petition, and the Development of Mid-Victorian Feminism', DPhil. thesis, University of Greenwich (1995).

49 Mary Cullen, 'Anna Maria Haslam', in Mary Cullen and Maria Luddy (eds.), *Women, Power and Consciousness in Nineteenth-Century Ireland* (Dublin: Attic Press, 1995), p. 173; 'Petition for Extension of the Electoral Franchise', appendix, p. 305.

50 Mill, *Public and Parliamentary Speeches*, vol. XXVIII, *CW*, ed. J. M. Robson and Bruce Kinzer (1988), pp. 91–3.

51 Ann Robson, 'No Laughing Matter: John Stuart Mill's Establishment of Women's Suffrage as a Parliamentary Question', *Utilitas* 2 (1990), 88–101; Kinzer, Robson and Robson, *A Moralist in and out of Parliament*, ch. 4. The return of female householders was eagerly awaited though apparently never made: Emily Davies to Helen Taylor, 18 July and 26 November 1866, MT, vol. XIII, ff. 181 and 189.

The newspapers have got into a way of treating the question as an individual crotchet of Mr Mill's . . . If Mr Mill had made it his *first* concern, it would have been a different case. As it is, we get mixed up in the public mind with Jamaica & the Reform League, which does us no good.[52]

Davies was deeply unhappy about too close an identification with the politics of male working-class reform in the aftermath of the events in Hyde Park in July 1866. She also distrusted the increasingly militant commitment of John Stuart Mill and the Jamaica Committee to the prosecution of Governor Eyre for the massacre of Morant Bay.[53] To Davies, the politics of gender took priority over other Liberal commitments which she did not share.

Discussions continued in London on the formation of a committee on women's suffrage. Emily Davies and Barbara Bodichon thought that the most practical way forward was to demand the vote for single and widowed women who qualified, though Mill and Taylor were increasingly unprepared to accept any explicit exclusions. Taylor believed that a women-only committee should be set up, though Davies and Bodichon preferred a mixed general committee. Negotiations were complicated by Taylor's absence in Avignon, and Bodichon's in Algiers, though Taylor was kept constantly informed of developments.

On 20 October 1866 a committee of women active in the Kensington Society and Langham Place was formed for 'obtaining the abolition of the legal disabilities which at present unqualifies [*sic*] women for voting for members of Parliament'.[54] But Helen Taylor refused to join, and indicated to the committee and to other sympathisers that Mill would not give his support. The new committee, which by late November had eight women and five men as members, adopted for circulation a petition that explicitly called for 'granting the suffrage to unmarried women and widows on the same conditions on which it is, or may be, granted to men'.[55] By February the committee had adopted as its letterhead 'Enfranchisement of Unmarried Women and Widows possessing the necessary property qualification'. Its members included some supporters of Mill and Taylor, like Clementia Taylor and John Elliot Cairnes. Its affairs for the next nine months were troubled and unsatisfactory, with Davies as its reluctant leader. The majority of the committee were unsympathetic to political radicalism, and Helen Taylor and John Stuart Mill remained

[52] Emily Davies to Barbara Bodichon, 21 August 1866, Bodichon Papers, Girton College, B. 316. [53] See below, pp. 201–4.

[54] Rosen, 'Emily Davies and the Women's Movement', 114.

[55] Ann Robson, 'Founding of the National Society', 13–16; Helen Blackburn, *Women's Suffrage*, pp. 58–9.

critical and hostile.[56] Meanwhile, the need for greater publicity was evident to all in sympathy with the cause, and Bodichon, Taylor and other members tried to secure it through the major periodicals, through the *Englishwoman's Review*, and through the launching of the new petitioning campaign.[57]

In late 1866 and early 1867, the agitation for reform outside the Houses of Parliament became more demanding, and Disraeli's proposals were eagerly awaited. The national leadership of the divided London committee for women's suffrage was to be challenged from Manchester. A Manchester committee for women's suffrage, in which Elizabeth Wolstenholme was active, was already in existence in 1866, though its first recorded meeting was held in January 1867. At that meeting Wolstenholme came together with Max Kyllmann, a German friend of Mill, Saul Alfred Steinthal, a local Unitarian minister, and Jacob Bright, brother of John Bright, who took the chair. Lydia Becker of Manchester, who was to be the major force behind the women's suffrage movement nationally for the next few years, had already been in correspondence with Emily Davies in London about the plans for a further petitioning campaign. In February she was appointed secretary of the Manchester committee. The Manchester suffrage movement drew upon the same impetus, and activists, as the North of England Council for Promoting the Higher Education of Women, founded in autumn 1867, and the formation of the Married Women's Property Committee in April 1868.[58]

The Manchester committee also, however, drew on the energies for reform generated by the National Reform Union, founded in 1864, which had brought together northern middle-class liberals and radicals in the cause of reform. Becker wrote publicly to three local MPs, including the two Manchester moderate Liberal MPs, to ask for their support, on

[56] Davies to Lydia Becker, 28 February 1867, and Harriet Cook to Lydia Becker, 8 April 1867, M50/1/2/13 and 18, Manchester Central Library [hereafter MCL]; Ann Robson, 'Founding of the National Society', 11–22; and Rosen, 'Emily Davies and the Women's Movement', 111–21.

[57] Bodichon's publications included her *Objections to the Enfranchisement of Women Considered* (London, 1866), and *Reasons for the Enfranchisement of Women* (London, 1866), the latter repr. in Jane Lewis, *Before the Vote Was Won: Arguments for and Against Women's Suffrage 1864–1896* (London and New York: Routledge and Kegan Paul, 1987), pp. 38–46; Helen Taylor's includes 'The Ladies' Petition, Presented to the House of Commons by Mr J. Stuart Mill, June 7th 1866', *Westminster Review* 31 (n.s.) (January 1867), 63–79, subsequently published as *The Claims of Englishwomen to the Franchise Constitutionally Considered* (London, 1867), also repr. in Jane Lewis, *Before the Vote Was Won*, pp. 21–37.

[58] Shanley, *Feminism, Marriage and the Law*, pp. 52–3; Audrey Kelly, *Lydia Becker and the Cause* (Centre for North-West Regional Studies, University of Lancaster, 1992); Helen Blackburn, *Women's Suffrage*, pp. 58–60; Holton, *Suffrage Days*, pp. 20–2 and 254 n. 25; Davies to Becker, January–March 1867, M50/1/2/1–35, ff. 1–17, MCL.

the grounds of the self-reliance and industry shown by Manchester women in a variety of occupations. Thomas Bazley and Edward James of Manchester and John Cheetham of Salford gave support in principle, though were wary of diverting the issue from the immediate one of a Reform Bill.[59] The young Richard Marsden Pankhurst, a member of the Reform Union, attended his first women's suffrage committee meeting in February 1867. Other committee members included former Chartists like Ernest Jones and Edward Hoosen, the ex-Owenite, Robert Cooper, and the Liberal MP for Rochdale, Thomas Bayley Potter.[60] And in the pages of the Radical–Liberal *Manchester Examiner and Times*, committee member Mary Hume-Rothery called for universal adult suffrage.[61] Common ground could – for some – be found in the cause of women's suffrage.

In February 1867 Benjamin Disraeli presented the Conservative Reform Bill to the House of Commons, though that hastily prepared bill was to go through many changes before it became law. John Stuart Mill took care to follow the Liberal party line, and to avoid irritating Gladstone by intruding the question of women's suffrage at politically charged moments. In that spring, the energies of the Manchester committee and of Lydia Becker in particular were put into the canvassing of signatures for petitions. The plan was to present one national petition from women qualified as householders, and another open to all women and men to sign, besides other locally organised petitions.[62]

On 28 March a general petition with 3,559 signatures collected by the London committee was presented to the Commons by Henry Austin Bruce, South Wales industrialist and landowner, and on 5 April Mill presented one with 3,161 signatures from Manchester. A petition from 1,605 women qualified to vote was presented on 8 April by Russell Gurney, and a number of others followed, though at no stage did the size or scale of petitions reach very large numbers. Overall, Emily Davies was blamed by some members of the London committee for the lack of

59 *Manchester Examiner and Times* [hereafter *ME*], 9 March 1867.

60 List of members, 'Manchester Committee for the Enfranchisement of Women', n.d., and list of supporters headed 'Enfranchisement of Women', M/50/1/9/1 MCL (this early list of Manchester committee members can be dated by its commitment to prepare the two petitions presented in April 1867); on Jones, Hoosen and Cooper in these years, see Antony David Taylor, 'Ernest Jones: His Later Career and the Structure of Manchester Politics 1861–1869', MA thesis, University of Birmingham (1984), and his '"The Best Way to Get What He Wanted": Ernest Jones and the Boundaries of Liberalism in the Manchester Election of 1868', *Parliamentary History* 16 (1997), 185–204.

61 *ME*, 2 and 20 April 1867.

62 Ann Robson, 'No Laughing Matter'; correspondence between Davies and Becker, 3 January–30 March 1867, M50/1/2/1–17, MCL.

publicity given to the petitions and the distinguished list of signatories gained. Jessie Boucherett wrote to Helen Taylor to ask her to consider organising a second committee.[63]

The Conservative bill was originally a mixture of household suffrage with a series of safeguards which were gradually amended or discarded in the Commons, though it was still the case that there was little accurate information before the government as to the precise numbers of male voters to be enfranchised.[64] Most notably, on 17 May Grosvenor Hodgkinson's amendment abolishing the practice of compounding for rates was passed. Few understood the potential radicalism of this measure at the time. Its implied consequence for women householders was the abolition of what was to them a convenient method of incorporating the payment of rates into the rent, without any corresponding benefits and a potential extra cost.[65]

Mill was anxious for an appropriate moment to introduce his amendment to the Reform Bill on women's suffrage, and was fortunate to be able to introduce it to a relatively poorly attended House, early in the evening of 20 May. He moved that 'person' be substituted for 'man' in clause 4 of the Reform Bill, which dealt with the occupation qualification for voters in the counties. His speech was acknowledged even by his opponents to be a polished and powerful one. He limited himself to the concerns of women with property, acknowledging in passing the principles of the British constitution in favour of linking taxation and representation. He pointed out the absurdity of criticising women for not demanding the vote as men did, by implication for failing to hold mass meetings and demonstrations like those in Hyde Park. He spoke of 'a silent domestic revolution', of a transformation among the educated classes in the relationship between women and men which had to be acknowledged. But he also spoke of the fallacy of virtual representation, whether of farmer and labourer, or husband and wife, the latter suggested by the records of wife-beating and murder, by the legal treatment of married women and by the absence of educational provision for the daughters of the educated. Looking to the future, he did not rule out a far wider enfranchisement, though for the present he addressed himself only to qualified women.[66]

[63] Rosen, 'Emily Davies and the Women's Movement', 118–19; Boucherett to Taylor, 30 April 1867, MT, vol. XII, ff. 149–53.

[64] For the details of the bill, see the introduction, pp. 4–5 and appendix D, p. 242.

[65] F. B. Smith, *Making of the Second Reform Bill*, pp. 202–3; Brian Keith-Lucas, *The English Local Government Franchise: A Short History* (Oxford: Basil Blackwell, 1952), p. 73.

[66] Mill, *Speech of John Stuart Mill, MP on the Admission of Women to the Electoral Franchise: Spoken in the House of Commons, May 20th 1867* (London, 1867), repr. in Mill, *Public and Parliamentary Speeches*, pp. 151–62.

Plate 5 'The Ladies' Advocate'. *Punch*, 1 June 1867. On 20 May 1867, Mill's amendment to the Reform Bill, substituting 'person' for 'man', had been defeated in the House of Commons.

Mill's amendment attracted 73 votes (81 including pairs and tellers) against an opposition of 196, or 204. He was supported of course by his closest disciples in the Commons, Henry Fawcett and Viscount Amberley, and by a group of advanced Liberal and Radical MPs from the major industrial cities. The O'Donoghue, nephew of Daniel O'Connell, was a Reform League activist and supporter. Although the amendment was relevant of course only to England and Wales, thirteen supporters held Irish seats, including at least four active Home Rulers, perhaps through loyalty to Mill's commitment to Irish land reform. Only five members from Scottish seats supported the measure. The largest single group of voters, however, thirty-five, came from the backbenches of the Liberal party. Twelve Conservatives also voted in support, including William Gore-Langton, whose wife Lady Anna was an active supporter of the cause. Benjamin Disraeli apparently told Mill that, though in favour of female suffrage, he could not vote for the amendment 'on account of his colleagues, but that he was working for it within the Cabinet'.[67]

Although the degree of support for the amendment may appear limited, it surprised and pleased many, though the *Englishwoman's Review* had hoped for more.[68] The national and local press covered the debate seriously, with even those opposed, like *The Times*, giving it full coverage.[69]

In spite of the failure of the amendment, it was pointed out in subsequent debates that, in this area as in very many others, the bill had been drafted so hastily that the legal implications were unclear. As George Denman indicated on 29 May 1867, the bill already, technically, included women. Romilly's Act of 1850, which clarified the terms to be used in parliamentary legislation, had very specifically prescribed that the term 'man' should also incorporate women, and that 'male person' should be used in all legislation where the intention was gender-specific. That requirement was ignored, and the term 'man' was used almost throughout.[70] As early as March 1867, Emily Davies had scanned the clauses of the bill and noted this peculiarity, and the single exception of the educational clauses, which did refer to 'male persons'.[71]

[67] Becker to Stephen Heelis, 29 May 1868, ff. 198–9, Lydia Becker's Letter-Book, 1868, M50/1/3, MCL; for a more detailed discussion of parliamentary support, see Jane Rendall, '"The Real Father of the Whole Movement"?: John Stuart Mill, Liberal Politics, and the Movement for Women's Suffrage, 1865–1873', in Amanda Vickery (ed.), *Women, Power and Privilege* (Stanford University Press, 2000).

[68] *Englishwoman's Review* [*EWR*] 4 (July 1867), 199. The Conservative Jessie Boucherett had hoped for more from Disraeli.

[69] Ann Robson, 'No Laughing Matter', 100–1.

[70] *Hansard*, 3rd ser., vol. 187, cols. 833–5, 29 May 1867.

[71] Davies to Becker, 30 March 1867, M50/1/2/17, MCL.

The act which was passed into law in August 1867 was one which had been transformed, both by radical amendments and by concessions to the Conservative majority. But to MPs who sat for the larger urban constituencies, the act offered the prospect of a considerably expanded electorate, even a 'borough franchise revolution', though the scale of the revolution was in 1867 by no means clear-cut, given the complexities of rating legislation.[72] To those active within the women's suffrage movement, it presented a new point of departure and a different set of possibilities for the future.

By that point, however, the divisions within the original London committee had brought about its dissolution. Mill's fine speech on 20 May had strengthened the position of Helen Taylor, and on 17 June the first women's suffrage committee had resolved on dissolution. A new London committee was formed which excluded the former Langham Place activists, and suffered from Taylor's frequent absence with Mill in Avignon. This schism had a lasting effect on the movement, in that it left an executive subject to weak and often absent leadership, with many formerly active women channelling their energies elsewhere. It allowed the more dynamic though politically less radical Lydia Becker to play the major organisational role in the first years of the women's suffrage movement, a role which also allowed her to appeal to the Radical and Liberal networks of the major industrial cities.[73]

Votes for women and the general election of 1868, August 1867–December 1868

In spite of the failure of Mill's amendment, the appeal of the women's suffrage movement increased in the aftermath of the Reform Act, and a form of national organisation was soon adopted. In August 1867 the Manchester committee adopted its formal constitution, and in November of that year the informal Edinburgh committee became the Edinburgh National Society for Women's Suffrage, some months before the Scottish Reform Act was introduced in February 1868. The London, Manchester and Edinburgh societies agreed to form one union, though not one united by any formal structure. The union was to consist entirely in the adoption of the name National Society for Women's Suffrage, and the amalgamation of the names of all members into one consolidated list of supporters. The Bristol society was formed in January 1868, and the Birmingham

72 Parry, *Rise and Fall of Liberal Government*, p. 221.

73 Ann Robson, 'Founding of the National Society', 17–22; Rosen, 'Emily Davies and the Women's Movement', 120–1.

society followed it in April.[74] The *Englishwoman's Review* recorded the first women's suffrage petition from Ireland, from Dublin, in April 1868, and the existence of a Belfast Women's Suffrage Society with Isabella Tod as secretary, in 1870. Anne Robertson, from Blackrock, County Dublin, a correspondent of Lydia Becker's, co-ordinated Dublin activity from 1868.[75]

Throughout the autumn of 1867 the desirability of continuing the petitioning campaign was assumed. Lydia Becker wrote to Helen Taylor on 27 September that a paid canvasser, a Miss Knott, 'an intelligent superior person of her class' working in Liverpool, was having great success, securing about sixty names a day to the petition. But the next immediate consequence of the Reform Act was the revision of the electoral register according to the complex new criteria. This suggested an alternative strategy. Lydia Becker suggested that, instead of petitioning, qualified women should be encouraged to put forward their claims to a vote, in the approved way, before the overseers and revising barristers. By October, it had become evident that there would be an inconsistency between petitioning to change the law, and the argument that women were already entitled to the vote. Steinthal and others in the Manchester group were strongly of the view that the petitioning campaign should be abandoned.[76] Throughout November these alternatives were debated, but the issue was to be determined by a remarkably opportune event in the by-election held in November 1867 in Manchester.

The by-election, which took place on the death of the sitting member Edward James, was also undertaken in the immediate aftermath of the execution of three Irish Fenians in Manchester on 23 November, for their part in the rescue of two prisoners from a prison van. In the winter of 1867, the growth of Fenianism, the severe winter, and the activities of Protestant demagogues like the virulently anti-Catholic William Murphy of the Protestant Electoral Union, brought serious religious tensions in Manchester as throughout Lancashire. The radical Liberals of Manchester opposed the executions and anti-Catholic demagoguery, though among these sympathisers for Garibaldi and Italian unification there was little empathy for the position of a Catholic church identified as reactionary and unprogressive.[77]

[74] *EWR* 9 (October 1868); Helen Blackburn, *Women's Suffrage*, pp. 63–5.

[75] Marie O'Neill, 'The Dublin Women's Suffrage Association and Its Successors', *Dublin Historical Record* 38 (1985), 126–40; Cullen, 'Anna Maria Haslam', pp. 173–4; and Maria Luddy, 'Isabella M. S. Tod', in Cullen and Luddy, *Women, Power and Consciousness*, pp. 197–230; *EWR* 7 (April 1868), 466, and 1 (n.s.) (January 1870), 19.

[76] Correspondence between Lydia Becker and Helen Taylor, August–November 1867, MT, vol. XII, ff. 43–63.

[77] Neville Kirk, *The Growth of Working-Class Reformism in Mid-Victorian England* (London

Jacob Bright stood against two candidates of moderate Liberal or Liberal Conservative loyalties, as the candidate of the United Liberal party, a 'progressive' alliance between the Manchester leaders of the National Reform Union, the old Anti-Corn Law League political machine and campaigners for manhood suffrage like Ernest Jones. It was an election fought with unusual warmth, in which the politics of identity and interest were significant.[78] Bright was the candidate endorsed by the Irish Electors Association, as by the Manchester Trades Council. However, an incautious and anti-semitic remark which he made about Disraeli alienated many members of the Manchester Jewish community, and he strove to restore his credibility within it.[79] Temperance and the politics of education were also important issues; and members of the Manchester Committee for the Promotion of Women's Suffrage asked all three candidates to state their views. All three agreed to votes for qualified single or widowed householders, though only Bright resoundingly endorsed women's suffrage.[80]

The Manchester electorate had expanded rapidly even before the Reform Act, as it adopted a system of automatic and 'meticulous' registration after 1860. In this election Bright's backers, the National Reform Union, called for all its members and friends to take an active part in ward canvassing, since a minor clause in the new act rendered paid canvassing invalid.[81] The turnout of electors was high, Bright achieving more personal votes than any previous candidate in Manchester except one.[82]

It was under these circumstances that, on 26 November 1867, a woman called Lily Maxwell cast a parliamentary vote on the hustings in Manchester. Her name on the electoral register had first been discovered by Jacob Bright's canvassing team who then contacted Becker. 'She was

and Sydney: Croom Helm, 1985), pp. 323–4; Patrick Quinlivan and Paul Rose, *The Fenians in England 1865–1872: A Sense of Insecurity* (London: John Calder, 1982), pp. 56–67; H. J. Hanham, *Elections and Party Management: Politics in the Time of Disraeli and Gladstone* (1959; repr. Hassocks: Harvester, 1978), p. 421; Bruce Kinzer, 'J. S. Mill and Irish Land: A Reassessment', *Historical Journal* 27 (1984), 113–14.

[78] For the background to this election, see Hanham, *Elections and Party Management*, pp. 310–11; Antony Taylor, 'Modes of Political Expression', vol. II, pp. 417–24 and 490–504; for a more detailed discussion of these issues, see Jane Rendall, 'Who Was Lily Maxwell?: Women's Suffrage and Manchester Politics, 1866–1867', in Sandra Holton and June Purvis (eds.), *Votes for Women* (London: UCL Press, 1999), pp. 57–83.

[79] *ME*, 13, 15, 20 and 23 November 1867; A Member of the Manchester and Salford Trades Council Executive, *Manchester Election: To the Members of Trade Societies* (n.p. [1867]), MCL Broadsides; Bill Williams, *The Making of Manchester Jewry, 1740–1875* (1976; repr. Manchester University Press, 1985), p. 335; *Jewish Chronicle*, 29 November, 6 and 20 December, 10 January 1867.

[80] *ME*, 16, 18, 20 and 21 November 1867.

[81] Antony Taylor, 'Modes of Political Expression', pp. 101–3; *ME*, 13 November 1867.

[82] *ME*, 27 November 1867.

rather timid at first', Becker wrote, 'I believe I should never have got her to come only that she was so strongly in favour of Mr Bright.'[83] Lily Maxwell's vote was a fortuitous clerical error, a lucky gift opportunistically and enthusiastically exploited by Becker and Bright. Though strictly irrelevant to the cause, the response from the canvasser, Miss Knott, was immediate:

> Miss Knott was engaged in the canvass of Stockport when the news came of this vote. She immediately began to feel that she must wait for instructions, lest it should not be right to go on collecting signatures, and she said people refused to sign because they said women could vote now.

Thomas Hare drafted a new petition form, asking for a declaratory act to clarify the state of the law on women's suffrage.[84] By the end of 1867 Lydia Becker had already begun to try to convince the overseer and town clerk of Manchester to put qualified women on the register.[85] In the first week of January the overwhelming opinion in the MNSWS was to discontinue petitioning, even for a declaratory act. The decision was taken to embark on a new campaign, to place qualified women on the parliamentary register.[86]

The two grounds on which the case was to be made were set out by the constitutional lawyer, Thomas Chisholm Anstey. First, he reiterated that the 1832 Reform Act had been superseded by Romilly's Act of 1850, in which the term 'man' included 'woman' except where otherwise specified. Yet the definition of the voter in the 1867 act began 'every man of full age'. Secondly, and independently of Romilly's Act, he suggested there was a case for a broader interpretation of the spirit of the constitution. The appeal to the history of freeholding voters suggested that rights had been based on property rather than sex since at least the days of Henry VI. The House of Commons had chosen to rely only on the hostile evidence of Sir Edward Coke, who in 1644 had stated that all women were excluded from participation in parliamentary elections, although no law or statute explicitly stated this. Anstey accumulated precedents, including that of Dame Dorothy Packyngton who in 1572 returned two members to Parliament to serve in her name, as the only voter in Aylesbury. And he argued that women with the status of *feme sole* had customarily held a range of public offices. Their rights had been confirmed

[83] Lydia Becker to Mary Smith of Carlisle, 20 May 1868, Lydia Becker's Letter-Book, M50/1/3, MCL.

[84] Becker to Helen Taylor, 5 December [1867], MT, vol. XII, ff. 66–73; Katharine Hare to Helen Taylor, 14 January [1868], MT, vol. XIII, f. 206.

[85] *EWR* 6 (January 1868), 393–4; Becker to Taylor, 27 December [1867], MT, vol. XII, ff. 75–9.

[86] Becker to Taylor, 8 January 1868, MT, vol. XII, ff. 80–3.

by two important eighteenth-century cases, *Olive* v. *Ingram* (1739), which upheld the right of ratepaying women to stand for and elect to the post of sexton, and *R.* v. *Stubbs* (1788), which similarly determined that women who were substantial householders might act as overseers of the poor.[87]

The publicity given to the vote of Lily Maxwell had stressed the qualities of citizenship expected, qualities which had much in common with those of the 'independent artisan': independence, respectability and political commitment. To the MNSWS, it was her vote which 'removed women's suffrage from the region of theoretical possibilities to that of actual occurrences, and thereby gave a powerful impetus to the whole movement'.[88] Though that vote was apparently fortuitous, the campaign of 1868 was to develop a momentum far beyond that of 1867 as it drew upon Radical and Liberal allies. In February 1868, Alice Wilson intervened at a meeting of the National Reform Union, to call for support for the vote for all qualified women. She was sympathetically received, to 'unanimous approval' according to Becker; leading figures of the Union, like R. D. Rusden, had already signalled sympathy. Though Jacob Bright supported striking out the word 'male' from the programme of the Union, the chair ruled that the rules of the association could not be altered without notice, and the resolution was amicably withdrawn, in spite of Bright's view that it might have been carried.[89] A general election focused on the politics of Ireland was widely anticipated in the course of 1868, although it was recognised that it would have to wait for the completion of the new electoral register.

As work was done on the register, the full implications of the new rating regulations for women householders were recognised, as a wave of hostility to the personal payment of rates swept the larger towns. In Hulme, on 25 March, a large meeting was called by local councillors, with Jacob Bright's backing, to consider the impact of the abolition of compounding and petition against it. Female householders were specifically invited, and attended in large numbers. In Hulme 11,000 of 16,000 householders had compounded their rates before the act, and of these 1,601 were women.

[87] This paragraph is based on Thomas Chisholm Anstey, *Notes upon 'The Representation of the People Act, 1867' (30 & 31 Vict. c. 102). With Appendices* . . . (London, 1867), pp. 74–104, and his *On Some Supposed Constitutional Restraints upon the Parliamentary Franchise* (London, 1867), pp. 18–27, 48; see also Catherine S. Williams, 'The Public Law and Women's Rights: The Nineteenth-Century Experience', *Cambrian Law Review* 23 (1992), 80–103; Hilda L. Smith, 'Women as Sexton and Electors: King's Bench and Precedents for Women's Citizenship', in Hilda L. Smith (ed.), *Women Writers and the Early Modern British Political Tradition* (Cambridge University Press, 1998), pp. 324–42.

[88] MNSWS, *First Annual Report of the Executive Committee* (Manchester, 1868), pp. 4–5.

[89] *ME*, 12 February 1868, and other unidentified newspaper cuttings in M50/1/9/1, MCL; Lydia Becker to Helen Taylor, 12 February [1868], MT, vol. XII, ff. 11–12; Lydia Becker to Jessie Boucherett, 1 April 1868, M50/1/3, ff. 40–1, MCL.

One speaker suggested that the consequences of the act, and the abolition of compounding, for these women would be an extra 4d a week, for rents would not be lowered:

> There were 81,428 women throughout the country placed in a similar position, and an increase of 4d per week would produce £70,527. That was the amount the women of England were called upon to pay to allay the fears of a small and miserable faction in parliament. (*Cheers.*)

Lydia Becker attended the meeting and thought the agitation would strengthen the call for 'no taxation without representation'. The extent of the increased costs for poorer householders are unknown, though Becker noted orders for the payment of rates being made on a great many poor women in Salford.[90]

The plan adopted, co-ordinated from Manchester by Lydia Becker, was for a systematic endeavour, by all the suffrage societies, 'to procure the insertion of women all over England on the register of electors under the new Reform Act'. Boards of overseers were to be asked to insert in the list of voters all women householders who had paid their rates, and several hundred letters were sent out to boards of overseers in England.[91] Two major meetings, in Manchester and Birmingham, first gave publicity to the scheme. The mayor of Salford, the industrialist Henry Pochin, who with his wife was a long-established supporter of women's suffrage, chaired the meeting held in the Free-Trade Hall in Manchester on 14 April 1868. The platform included the MPs Jacob Bright and Thomas Bayley Potter, with Thomas Chisholm Anstey, Richard Pankhurst and R. D. Rusden, as well as the women members of the committee. Lydia Becker, Anne Robertson from Dublin and Mrs Pochin spoke, as did Bright and Pankhurst. Though Mrs Pochin's reference to women as 'spiritual Godivas' was thought to be unfortunate for the cause, the meeting was widely reported, and viewed as successful.[92] There was more nervousness about the Birmingham meeting on 8 May, since, lacking the local political muscle of the Manchester committee, activists there needed help and encouragement. Becker persuaded them to withdraw from the main Town Hall, a room '4 times as large as ours' and to book the Exchange Room for 600 people instead; but she ultimately judged that meeting also a 'triumphant success' with standing room only.[93]

[90] *ME*, 25 March 1868, in M50/1/9/1, MCL; Lydia Becker to Jacob Bright, 27 March 1868, M50/1/3, ff. 21–2, MCL.

[91] MNSWS, *First Annual Report*, pp. 4–6.

[92] *Ibid.*, p. 5; Becker to Jacob Bright, 16 April 1868, MF2675, ff. 61–2, MCL; cuttings from *ME*, *Manchester Guardian*, *Manchester Courier* and *Daily News*, 16 April 1868, M50/1/9/1, MCL. Mrs Pochin's invocation of Godiva could have been drawn from Kingsley, 'Women and Politics', 558.

[93] Becker to Annie Robertson, 25 April, to Ursula Bright, 27 April and 8 May, to Esther

In these months, Becker was at the heart of a network of correspondents across the United Kingdom, co-ordinating the women's suffrage campaign, encouraging, persuading and cajoling both committed supporters and more tentative recruits. She encouraged a similar campaign in Scotland, 'should the Scotch Bill be similarly worded', and corresponded with Anne Robertson in Dublin on the women's suffrage and the married women's property movements.[94] Throughout 1868 Becker also worked very closely with Elizabeth Wolstenholme, in the new Married Women's Property Committee. At the same time, the London committee continued to organise the presentation of petitions for a declaratory act, and on 14 May 1868 Mill presented one with 21,783 signatures, praying that qualified women should be declared entitled to vote. In total seventy-five petitions with almost 50,000 signatures were presented between February and June 1868.[95]

In Manchester and the surrounding area, members of the committee first waited on different boards of overseers, to whom Richard Pankhurst put their case. When Lydia Becker, Alice Wilson and Pankhurst met the overseers of Cheetham, Chorlton-on-Medlock and elsewhere in June 1868, they explored not only the historical grounds on which the claim was made but the competence of women to act as voters, and their claims on the grounds of intelligence, rationality and responsibility. Manchester and Cheetham overseers were not convinced, though those in Hulme were split.[96] The overseers of Salford agreed to draw up the registers to include all qualified women, as did those of Aberdeen, Finsbury in London and Southwark in Middlesex, a number of Lancashire townships and a few southern parishes.[97]

Refusal by the overseers meant that the task which then faced the suffrage societies was the identification and canvassing of qualified women, to persuade them to stake a claim. There is much to suggest that the methods used by the society drew upon the canvassing practices of the political parties. The MNSWS directed its paid organisers to shift their energies from the collection of signatures for petitions to the identification of potential voters from the directories. Becker liaised with representatives of the Liberal Registration Societies, but recognised that

Becker, 28 April and 2 May, in Becker's Letter-Book, MCL, ff. 69–70, 73, 76–8, 100–1, 108–9; cuttings from *Birmingham Daily Post* and *Aris's Birmingham Gazette* (9 May), *Birmingham Daily Gazette* (11 May), *Birmingham Journal* (16 May), M50/1/9/1, MCL.

94 See Becker's Letter-Book, esp. Becker to Grierson, 28 March 1868, to Annie Robertson, 2 and 24 May 1868, Letter-Book, ff. 27–8, 95–6, and 166–7, M50/1/3, MCL.

95 *EWR* 9 (October 1868), 67.

96 Cuttings from *ME*, 2, 12 and 20 June 1868, in M50/1/9/1, MCL; MNSWS, *First Annual Report*, pp. 6–8.

97 Newspaper cuttings, May–June 1868, M50/1/9/1, MCL; *EWR* 8 (July 1868), 530–1; 9 (October 1968), 37–9.

Conservative members too could potentially benefit from the registration of women voters. She warned the London committee of the dangers of approaching Liberal party agents, given the need to be above party.[98] Of over 4,000 qualified voters in the township of Manchester, 93 per cent signed the claim to be put on the register, as did 59 per cent of those qualified in Chorlton-on-Medlock.[99] While much of this was orchestrated by branches of the National Society for Women's Suffrage, the *Englishwoman's Review* suggested that many claims were made by women quite independently of the campaign. In Manchester, for instance, 400 women of 5,750 had sent in their claims independently.[100]

In September 1868, appeals by claimants were heard by revising barristers in registration courts across Britain, though the most active debates were clearly in Lancashire. The statutes of Henry VI, the details of *Olive* v. *Ingram* (1739) and the meaning of 'man' versus 'male person' were endlessly rehearsed. And the battle does appear to have had something of a party character, though much further local research is needed here. The claimants themselves could not be represented by counsel. In Manchester the case for 5,750 female claimants was put forward by counsel instructed by the Liberals and opposed by the representative of the Conservative Association, who claimed to be there 'more to watch than to oppose'. In east Kent there were no objections by either party to thirty-three female voters being included on the register. In Birmingham on the revision of the list for North Warwickshire, the Liberal representative suggested that something like 4,000 women were qualified to vote, though he was opposed by the agent of the Conservative party. In Leeds the solicitor appearing on behalf of the Liberal Association claimed the vote for a Quaker widow, Mary Howell, and was opposed by the Conservative representative. The barrister, T. Campbell Foster, after a long and hostile speech, fined the claimant 10s for her frivolity. Most revising barristers appear to have followed not historical precedent but the Commons vote on Mill's amendment.[101]

Similar arguments were put in Scottish courts. In Edinburgh, John McLaren, agent for the Independent Liberal Committee, supported the case of Elizabeth Pease Nichol, former Chartist and anti-slavery campaigner, on the grounds of 'the interest she took in every movement

[98] Becker to Mary Johnson, 19 and 29 May 1868, Becker's Letter-Book, ff. 132–4 and 193–4, M50/1/3, MCL.

[99] MNSWS, *First Annual Report*, p. 7; the precise figures were 3,924 of 4,215 qualified voters in the township of Manchester, and 1,106 of the 1,859 qualified in Chorlton-on-Medlock.

[100] *EWR* 9 (October 1868), 59.

[101] *Ibid.*, 57–64; MNSWS, *First Annual Report*, pp. 7–13; Helen Blackburn, *Women's Suffrage*, pp. 74–88 and appendix E. The most extensive reports of these events are in the newspaper cuttings for the period 15–30 September 1868, M50/1/9/1, MCL.

tending to the social and moral elevation of the community'. He argued that the common law of Scotland had permitted women to act as heritors, and in some cases with the right to vote for commissioners of police, and with responsibility for Poor Law assessment. In the old Scottish burghs women had been entitled to act as burgesses, and therefore take part in the election of the town councils who returned parliamentary representatives. And the Scottish Reform Act of 1868, like the English act, was drafted on the basis of 'men' not 'male persons'. The representative of the Edinburgh Conservative Association successfully objected to this as to the 239 other female claimants in Edinburgh.[102] However, in Aberdeen, the city assessor, John Duguid Milne, a man with a long interest in women's rights, upheld the claims of 1,088 female householders and 9,376 other householders, mainly lodgers, to a vote. As the *Aberdeen Journal* put it, in an article entitled 'Who Is a Man, and What Is a Lodger?': 'Why might not the ladies, and the advocates who plead their cause, take a wider sweep, and shew that whether a woman be a man or not, in a zoological sense, and within the meaning of the act, she at least ought to be?' In Aberdeen, as elsewhere, however, this decision was overturned in the Sheriff's Court.[103] There is no evidence of such a movement in Ireland.

By October 1868 only some 230 women remained on the electoral roll for England and Wales. The campaigners determined to appeal to higher courts, and four cases, including claims from Manchester and Salford, were put before the Court of Common Pleas on 7 November, defended by Sir John Coleridge and Richard Pankhurst, with the Pochins of Salford contributing to the costs. In each case the appeals were rejected.[104] In Scotland the equivalent case of *Brown* v. *Ingrame* was heard in the Court of Session on 30 October 1868, with the decision resting on 'the fact that there was a long and uninterrupted custom in Scotland limiting the franchise to males'.[105]

Nevertheless, the decision in the Court of Common Pleas did not affect the register in those few cases where women had been placed or left on the register by revising barristers, with no subsequent objections. Lydia

[102] Unidentified cutting of report of proceedings in Edinburgh Registration Court, September 1868 in M50/1/9/1, MCL.

[103] 'Who Is a Man and What Is a Lodger?', *Aberdeen Journal*, 23 September 1868, and 'Aberdeen – Registration of Voters', unidentified cutting, in M50/1/9/1, MCL; *EWR* 9 (October 1868), 74; for Duguid Milne's career, see Lindy Moore, *Bajanellas and Seminellas: Aberdeen University and the Education of Women 1860–1920* (Aberdeen University Press, 1991), pp. 5–36.

[104] MNSWS, *First Annual Report*, pp. 11–12; MNSWS, *Second Annual Report of the Executive Committee* (Manchester, 1869), pp. 3–5.

[105] Leah Leneman, *A Guid Cause: The Women's Suffrage Movement in Scotland* (Aberdeen University Press, 1991), p. 14.

Plate 6 'Revised – and Corrected'. *Punch*, 26 September 1868. In September 1868, appeals by ratepaying women, single or widowed, to be included on the electoral register were heard throughout Britain. Most were defeated. The reference is to Hamlet's words to Ophelia in *Hamlet*, Act III, Scene i, 'Get thee to a nunnery.'

Becker contacted all identified potential women voters, exhorting them to vote in the election of 1868.[106] The *Englishwoman's Review* reported several doing so in east Kent, and in Finsbury, London, with nine voting in Manchester, thirteen in Salford, twelve in Gorton, ten in Levenshulme and scattered individuals elsewhere, including two in Dublin.[107]

The election of 1868 was fought centrally on the issue of the Irish church. To campaigners for women's suffrage, however, it was perceived rather as an opportunity for contrasting the significance of the political debates sweeping the country with 'three great social questions', the education and the enfranchisement of women and the laws relating to married women. The *Englishwoman's Review* argued that women's enfranchisement was 'the greatest question brought before the public for many years', and that its readers should disregard party loyalties and vote on this basis. To the *Review* all other questions were 'trifling' by contrast, including the disestablishment of the Irish church. Twenty candidates had already promised support for the women's cause and should therefore be supported.[108]

But in some constituencies women's suffrage *was* a party question. Support for the movement in Manchester, for instance, can be to some extent identified, though by no means exclusively, with the Liberal political machine inherited from the Anti-Corn Law League. Of the three Liberal candidates in Manchester in 1868 – the Palmerstonian Sir Thomas Bazley, the radical Liberal Jacob Bright and Ernest Jones the ex-Chartist – Bright and Jones were both strongly committed supporters of women's suffrage, and Bazley agreed to the claims of qualified women. So too, however, did the Conservative Manchester employer, Hugh Birley, who defeated Ernest Jones.[109] The same pattern, of a greater degree of support, though not exclusively, from the Liberal party, can be identified in other urban areas, especially in northern towns. The *Englishwoman's Review* noted the 'generous assistance' of Liberal newspapers and the hostility of the Conservative press, as well as the higher level of Liberal support in the Commons. It advised 'women electors', or any other elector, that support should be given to the party or parties whose registration agents had endeavoured to place women's names on the register, and should be withdrawn from those who had attempted to dislodge the names of women voters.[110]

[106] *EWR* 9 (October 1868), 74; Helen Blackburn, *Women's Suffrage*, p. 87; MNSWS, *Second Annual Report*, p. 5.

[107] MNSWS, *Second Annual Report*, pp. 6–7; *EWR* 10 (January 1869), 137–40.

[108] *EWR* 9 (October 1868), 64–8.

[109] Birley voted for Jacob Bright's Women's Disabilities Bill in 1870.

[110] *EWR* 9 (October 1868), 65–6.

Plate 7 'Miss Mill Joins the Ladies'. *Judy*, 2 November 1868. Mill's defeat at Westminster in the general election is here associated with his campaigns for women's suffrage and the bringing of Governer Eyre to justice. Mill is shown out by the Conservative W. H. Smith, who defeated him at Westminster, while R. W. Grosvenor, the Whig–Liberal who was elected, studies his wine. Reproduced courtesy of the British Library.

Though the campaign had failed, it had succeeded in focusing attention, especially though not exclusively among urban Liberals and Radicals, on the position of the single woman householder who was also a ratepayer, and also perhaps if a tenant who had formerly compounded for her rates was a personal ratepayer for the first time. The result of the election of 1868 was of course a Liberal triumph for Gladstone and for his party. But reviewing the election from a different perspective, the *Englishwoman's Review* noted a total of ninety-two sympathetic members now in the House of Commons. Although this could not, of course, compensate for the loss of Mill himself, defeated in Westminster, it was to prove an underestimate of overall support.[111] The next two years were to demonstrate how far the Liberal triumph could assist the women's cause.

From the general election to the Women's Disabilities Bill: gains and losses, December 1868–May 1870

After the election the Manchester committee reviewed the prospects for the future. Petitioning would continue. And, ambitiously, it was hoped to prepare a bill to introduce women's suffrage, to be presented by the radical Jacob Bright and the Conservative Russell Gurney, the strongest supporters of the cause in the House of Commons. Bright and Gurney counselled a longer-term view, and a year spent campaigning, influencing public opinion and fundraising before any further parliamentary action. That advice was taken, though parliamentary action continued in relation to married women's property legislation.[112]

The peculiarities of the local franchise in the towns and cities of England and Wales were thought to offer more immediate scope. The Municipal Corporations Act of 1835 had, like the Reform Act, specifically excluded women for the first time. The process of incorporation, creating a new borough council, therefore had the consequence of excluding women ratepayers as voters. It is not known how far women had exercised the municipal vote, but the anomaly attracted attention. Manchester female ratepayers, who were excluded, could compare the rights to vote of women in the unincorporated suburbs with their own position.[113] Women might also, depending on local custom, be eligible to vote for Boards of Health and Improvement Commissions.[114]

111 *Ibid.* 10 (January 1869), 140–3.

112 Helen Blackburn, *Women's Suffrage*, p. 89.

113 For the rights of women to vote under a variety of local franchises, see Keith-Lucas, *English Local Government Franchise*, pp. 164–6; *The Echo* (London), 20 May 1869, in M50/1/9/2, MCL.

114 MNSWS, *Second Annual Report*; *Newcastle Daily Chronicle*, 20 May 1869, and *Bury Times*, 26 June 1869, in M50/1/9/2, MCL.

Plate 8 'Don Jacob Rideth His Hobby, to —?' Manchester Central Library, 1869. This undated caricature of Jacob Bright, which alludes to the chivalry of Don Quixote, may refer to Bright's success in introducing women's suffrage into municipal elections in May 1869. In the background his brother, John Bright, an opponent of women's suffrage, salutes him.

In May 1869 Jacob Bright of Manchester and John Hibbert of Oldham, both longstanding supporters of the women's cause, rose to amend the Municipal Franchise Bill for England and Wales in its committee stage:

wherever words occur which import the masculine gender, the same shall be held to include females for all purposes connected with and having reference to the election of or power to elect representatives of any municipal corporation.[115]

The bill had been introduced in the aftermath of the Reform Act to extend the principle of household suffrage to local government, and to reform corruption in municipal elections. Bright's tactics were to stress the conservative intention of his amendment, to suggest that the previous act, of 1835, had been innovatory in its exclusion of women, an invasion

[115] *Hansard*, vol. 196 (o.s.), vol. 1 (n.s.), appendix, cols. 1973–6, 7 June 1869; *EWR* 12 (July 1869), 275–9.

of established right. In noncorporate towns, which were not parliamentary boroughs, women could vote, as they could in parish vestries. When towns were incorporated, women were disfranchised, as recently had happened in Darlington and Southport. Southport in 1866 had had 2,085 qualified voters, 588 of whom were women. Once the town was incorporated, women voters were excluded. He also suggested – and further research is needed here – that, where such provision existed, in such boroughs, women exercised it in the same proportion as men did. Henry Austin Bruce, Gladstone's home secretary, who had already shown himself a sympathiser with the cause, rose to say:

> the hon. member had shown conclusively that this proposition was no novelty and that in every form of local government, except under the Municipal Corporations Act, females were allowed to vote. The clause introduced no anomaly, and he should give it his cordial support.

To those who watched, surprised by Bright's success, it was a demonstration that 'the tide of opinion in the House of Commons [was] beginning to turn'.[116]

At the same time, throughout 1869 and early 1870, the movement gave itself to organisation and agitation. There were 257 petitions with nearly 62,000 signatures presented in the parliamentary session, including nine petitions from Ireland, with two from Women's Suffrage Societies in Dublin and Belfast.[117] A series of major public meetings were held throughout the country and in London. Lydia Becker launched a demanding lecture tour in Mechanics Institutes, Town Halls and dissenting chapels across the north of England in April 1869. In Newcastle she spoke to 'a respectable and attentive audience of both sexes' supported by Joseph Cowen sen., his son and two local Unitarian ministers, who helped to form the new Newcastle Committee of the National Society for Women's Suffrage. In Leeds, with the backing of Edward Baines, she had a good audience, 'many of whom were working people', and defended her society's policy against hostile objections: 'women in lodgings should have votes in the same way as men in lodgings had votes; and if there was a humanity suffrage . . . the suffrage should include women'.[118]

[116] *EWR* 12 (July 1869), 279; for discussion of the support for this bill, see Martin Pugh, 'The Limits of Liberalism: Liberals and Women's Suffrage 1867–1914', in Eugenio Biagini (ed.), *Citizenship and Community: Liberals, Radicals and Collective Identities in British History 1865–1931* (Cambridge University Press, 1996), pp. 45–65.

[117] *EWR* 1 (n.s.) (January 1870), 19.

[118] *Northern Daily Express*, 1 April 1869; *Newcastle Daily Chronicle*, 1 April 1869; *Newcastle Daily Journal*, 1 and 2 April 1869; *Leeds Mercury*, 6 April 1869. For other accounts, see *ME*, 13 February 1869; *The Tribune*, 3 April 1869; *Carlisle Journal*, 6 April 1869; *Manchester City News*, 17 April 1869. Extracts are in M50 1/9/2, MCL.

The London committee began to develop its activities rather more forcefully than it had done in the previous year. In July 1869 its first public meeting demonstrated the support given by Liberal MPs, intellectuals and academics to the cause. The platform speakers included Mill and Fawcett, the MPs Sir Charles Dilke and James Stansfeld, Charles Kingsley, and Professor David Masson from Edinburgh. Clementia Taylor took the chair and the 22-year-old Millicent Fawcett and Caroline Biggs were the only woman speakers to a daunting audience.[119] At this and later meetings it was clear that the London society drew its support to a much greater extent from the London- and university-based intelligentsia. It was at some distance both from the Liberal political organisations from which Lydia Becker drew strength and from the women who had played such an active role in the *English Woman's Journal*.

The position of the London society was greatly strengthened by the publication of John Stuart Mill's *Subjection of Women*, greeted with immense enthusiasm by a number of those women, including Barbara Bodichon, Elizabeth Garrett and Lady Amberley. Elizabeth Garrett perhaps spoke for them when she wrote to Helen Taylor:

> I have read it with very great pleasure and with heartfelt sympathy & gratitude. I am so glad its tone is aggressive against slavery rather than apologetic for freedom, it will excite far more discussion & do far more good than any more cautious statement of the case on the side of women wd have done.[120]

The year 1869 also saw the publication of the important collection edited by Josephine Butler, *Woman's Work and Woman's Culture*, to which so many women and men active in the women's suffrage movement contributed. Julia Wedgwood, writing in that collection, urged the claims of women to develop their powers of self-cultivation and growth to the full.[121] She drew heavily upon Mill's conception of marriage, yet also went beyond it to stress arguments as relevant to married women as to single householders. To the hostile *Times*, this article provided confirmation that female suffrage was indeed a 'Trojan horse', with implications that were far more extensive than they seemed.[122]

In the autumn of 1869, a major concern was preparation for the municipal elections in which women voted for the first time, though in most places in a significantly lower proportion than male voters. The innova-

[119] *EWR* 1 (n.s.) (January 1870), 18–20.

[120] Elizabeth Garrett Anderson to Helen Taylor, 4 June 1869, MT, vol. XIV, no. 13, ff. 30–2; Barbara Bodichon to Helen Taylor, 1 August 1869, MT, vol. XII, no. 50, ff. 127–32; Lady Amberley to Helen Taylor, 9 July 1869, MT, vol. XIX, no. 19, ff. 41–2.

[121] Julia Wedgwood, 'Female Suffrage, Considered Chiefly with Regard to its Indirect Results', in Josephine Butler (ed.), *Woman's Work and Woman's Culture* (London, 1869), p. 248.

[122] *The Times*, 21 August 1869.

tion appears to have attracted considerable attention, as yet unstudied. In Bury in June Conservative 'Blue' agents had offered to pay the rates of poor women householders if they would cast their votes for Conservative candidates in the election to the Improvement Commission.[123] In Liverpool, the Liverpool Toxteth Association claimed a degree of gallantry for its initiative 'in introducing the ladies of Liverpool to a knowledge of practical politics'. The meeting was chaired by P. H. Holt, a member of one of the leading Liberal families, and the reporter of the *Liverpool Mercury* noted that it 'fairly represented the middle-class female population of Liverpool', and that the 'bluestocking woman's rights' element was absent.[124]

Becker commented on the results of the election: 'it is so new an idea for women to vote that many would doubtless be prevented by timidity, as the votes had to be given in person'.[125] The *Manchester Examiner and Times* analysed the impact of women's voting in different wards of the city, and the MNSWS carefully tabulated the national results. In Bristol, there was a higher proportionate turnout of female than male householders to vote, 242 out of a total of 1,355. In Bolton over 1,100 women voted, and in Manchester nearly 1,900.[126]

From January 1870 a concerted series of public meetings were held, by all the branches of the National Society, to mark the beginning of the campaign for the introduction of a new bill, and high hopes were expressed for a larger number of supporters than for Mill's amendment.[127] In Edinburgh over 1,200 attended a packed meeting chaired by the MP Duncan McLaren, with powerful speeches by Jacob Bright, Professor David Masson and Lyon Playfair MP, though no woman spoke.[128] Between January and March major meetings were held in London, Bath, Bristol, Crewe, Newcastle, South Shields, Lincoln, Ipswich, Leicester, Sunderland and many smaller places. In March Millicent Fawcett delivered her first major speech in Brighton. It was followed by one on 23 March in Birmingham, where her discussion of the 'Electoral Disabilities of Women' in the Town Hall drew what was described as 'the largest audience that has ever probably assembled in that room'.[129] On 18 April both Millicent and Henry Fawcett spoke again

123 *Bury Times*, 26 June 1869, in M50/1/9/2, MCL.

124 *Liverpool Mercury*, 23 October 1869, in M50/1/9/2, MCL.

125 *EWR* 1 (n.s.) (January 1870), 34.

126 *ME*, 2 November 1869, in M50/1/9/2, MCL; MNSWS, *Second Annual Report*, pp. 21–2; see also *Leeds Mercury*, 24 November 1869, in M50/1/9/2, MCL.

127 *EWR* 1 (n.s.) (January 1870), 37; Helen Blackburn, *Women's Suffrage*, pp. 103–4.

128 *EWR* 2 (n.s.) (April 1870), 91–7.

129 *Ibid.*, 97–101; David Rubinstein, *A Different World for Women: The Life of Millicent Garrett Fawcett* (Hemel Hempstead: Harvester-Wheatsheaf, 1991), pp. 38–9.

at a large and apparently very successful meeting held in Dublin, attended by Irish MPs, including powerful Irish Liberals like Sir John Gray, editor of the Dublin *Freeman's Journal*, and by the provost and academics of Trinity College Dublin and the Archdeacon of Dublin. Most support came from the Protestant community, although the *Englishwoman's Review* recorded that: 'A remarkable feature of this meeting was that persons of such opposite political and religious opinions took part in it. Every daily morning and evening paper in Dublin gave full and favourable reports of the proceedings.'[130] Petitioning too continued in the 1870 session, when a total of 663 petitions were presented to the House of Commons, with over 134,000 signatures.[131]

The second reading of the Women's Disabilities Bill, which was apparently applicable to the whole of the United Kingdom, was introduced by Jacob Bright on 4 May 1870, and was passed by 33 votes, with 124 in favour and 91 against. The government spokesman, Henry Bruce, who had positively endorsed Bright's amendment to the Municipal Franchise Bill, here equivocated to delay the bill going into committee:

> He was sure there were many members prepared to support the second reading who would not wish to go further, and that was a good ground for delay. It was for these reasons that he was not able to give his personal support to the Bill, at the same time that he was desirous of having it understood that neither personally, nor as a member of the government, was he giving any opinion on its merits.[132]

That motion provided the opportunity for the first of a number of hostile speeches by Gladstone on the subject, on 12 May 1870. The bill was defeated a week later at its committee stage, with Gladstone, at 2.00 in the morning, leading a solid majority of 220, against 94 committed supporters, 60 Liberals and 34 Conservatives.

Jacob Bright had put a cautious case, based on the rights of women ratepayers, who would indeed be a small minority of the electorate and were in England and Wales already qualified for the municipal franchise. He won support from some members prepared to consider the question on the grounds of property rather than of sex. His 148 still included members with strong links to Victorian intellectual life, and a solid group of radical urban Liberals, with strong links to militant dissent. Thirty-two Conservatives had supported Bright, a larger proportion than in 1867, perhaps because of the freedom of opposition. Twelve of twenty-one sup-

130 *EWR* 3 (n.s.) (July 1870), 193–5.

131 MNSWS, *Third Annual Report*, pp. 8–9.

132 *Hansard*, 3rd ser., vol. 201, cols. 237–9, 4 May 1870; for a more detailed discussion of the vote, see Rendall, '"The Real Father of the Whole Movement"'.

porters holding Irish seats were Home Rulers, with eighteen supporters, a significant increase, holding Scottish seats.[133]

The women's movement was encouraged rather than despondent. Bright, a month later, suggested that the bill had advanced towards the realm of practical politics, and that it should be introduced again in the next session. Mill himself reflected that such a defeat 'cannot be fairly called a check' but marked 'enormous progress'.[134] The bill was introduced again each year by Bright until 1874, though it never again reached the same level of support. The previous four years, from May 1866 to May 1870, had nevertheless appeared to transform the practical political possibilities.

The aftermath: women and the limits of citizenship, c. 1870–1900

In practice, the movement for the parliamentary franchise was to take much, much longer, and was not completed until 1928. The tensions already apparent in the years between 1867 and 1870 were to bring a series of damaging splits in the Victorian women's suffrage movement. The rivalry between London and Manchester grew sharper and in 1871 the Manchester committee set up a new national committee, the Central Committee of the National Society for Women's Suffrage, with Jacob Bright in the chair, which the London group refused to join. The split lasted until 1879. Meanwhile, the failure to pass an effective Married Women's Property Act in 1870 brought conflicts over the enfranchisement of married women to a head. In 1874 Lydia Becker supported a Conservative bill which explicitly excluded married women, in direct opposition to the Radical–Liberal circle around Jacob Bright. Ultimately, this conflict was to lead to the founding of the Women's Franchise League in 1889, and the Women's Emancipation Union in 1891, both of which associated the rights of married women with the pursuit of full citizenship. The foundation of the National Union of Women's Suffrage Societies in 1897 finally provided a central umbrella for campaigns, though it did not heal fundamental political differences.

In the area of local government, however, there were to be continuing if variable developments across the United Kingdom, after the granting of the municipal franchise to women in England and Wales in 1869. But the timetable was determined as much by that for the reform of local government in the different nations of the UK as by the demands of the women's

133 Rendall, '"The Real Father of the Whole Movement"'; MNSWS, *Third Annual Report*, pp. 4–9.

134 MNSWS, *Third Annual Report*, p. 6; *EWR* 3 (n.s.) (July 1870), 191; Mill to Charles Kingsley, 9 July 1870, in Mill, *Later Letters*, vol. XVII, p. 1744.

movement. In England and Wales single and widowed women ratepayers were able to vote for all local bodies after 1869. The experience of the municipal elections there in 1870 was constantly cited by speakers for the movement to demonstrate both that women wanted the vote and that they would use it. It had not been clear at this election whether married women were excluded, though a subsequent High Court ruling, in *R.* v. *Harrold* in 1872, determined that they were. They were nevertheless soon to represent nearly a fifth of the municipal electorate.[135] The Education Act of 1870 for England and Wales provided that women who were municipal and parish voters could also vote in the school board elections. Any woman, married or not, could stand as a candidate, since no qualifications were required, as Elizabeth Garrett and Emily Davies in London and Lydia Becker in Manchester did successfully in 1870, setting important precedents for the holding of public office. In Wales, Rose Mary Crawshay, wife of the Merthyr ironmaster, Robert Thompson Crawshay, and an active supporter of the women's suffrage campaign, was elected a member of the Merthyr School Board in March 1871.[136] The first woman to be elected to such an office in Scotland, under the Scottish Education Act of 1872, was Mrs Jane Arthur, in Paisley in 1873.[137] There was no equivalent legislation in Ireland.

The timetable for further steps in local enfranchisement varied considerably. In England and Wales, single or widowed women ratepayers were qualified to vote for and to become Poor Law guardians, though none stood for office until 1875, when Martha Merrington was elected to the Poor Law Board in Kensington. But a high property qualification meant that only the affluent were able to serve; the abolition of the qualification in 1894 had immediate effects.[138] Ratepaying women began to use their vote, although the franchise was also heavily biased towards property until 1894. In Ireland, qualified women were also able to vote for Poor Law guardians, though as Anna Haslam wrote: '*that* was so commonly carried out upon exclusively party lines, and with so little regard to the well-being of our destitute poor, that we were fairly excusable for taking little interest in it'. The Presbyterian Isabella Tod and the Quaker Anna

[135] Patricia Hollis, *Ladies Elect: Women in English Local Government, 1865–1914* (Oxford: Clarendon Press, 1987), pp. 29–34; Keith-Lucas, *English Local Government Franchise*, pp. 165–8.

[136] Ryland Wallace, *Organise! Organise! Organise!: A Study of Reform Agitations in Wales, 1840–1886* (Cardiff: University of Wales Press, 1991), p. 167.

[137] Elspeth King, 'The Scottish Women's Suffrage Movement', in Esther Breitenbach and Eleanor Gordon (eds.), *Out of Bounds: Women in Scottish Society 1800–1945* (Edinburgh University Press, 1992), p. 131; Hollis, *Ladies Elect*, p. 35.

[138] Hollis, *Ladies Elect*, ch. 4; guardians had to be not only ratepayers but rated up to a minimum of £15 outside London, and up to £40 in London, before 1894.

Haslam campaigned for the same role for women as Poor Law guardians as in England, with particular reference to the limited resources and rigidity of the Irish Poor Law. This was achieved only in William Johnston's Poor Law Guardians Act of 1896.[139]

The Scottish Poor Law was based upon an entirely different structure. Propertied women in local parishes may have played some part in the kirk sessions, which were responsible for poor relief before 1845, though very little is known of the extent to which they did so.[140] Poor Law legislation of 1845 had established parochial boards, which added ratepayers' representatives, elected by a system of plural voting dependent on wealth, to the kirk sessions and heritors. It is not clear whether women could stand, though the *Englishwoman's Review* recorded in 1876, one year after the election of Martha Merrington in Kensington, the election of Margaret Foulton to the managing committee of the Inverkeithing Parochial Board, and also noted subsequent elections.[141]

Women in Scotland were granted municipal enfranchisement only in 1882. In England and Wales from 1888, women ratepayers were admitted to vote for county councils, and in Scotland from 1889, though on a basis slightly different from that for England, since marriage did not there form an absolute bar as in England. In 1894 separate legislation for both England and Scotland allowed women to vote for their parish councils, and, in England, district councils.[142]

In Ireland, where the municipal franchise was far more limited, the situation was particularly complex. In 1871, the Conservative Belfast MP, William Johnston, had pointed out the inconsistency in women's voting rights between England and Ireland and hoped that, when the Municipal Corporation Amendment Act (Ireland) was reintroduced in the next session, the anomaly would be redressed.[143] However, no such bill was introduced, and a campaign to win the municipal vote for women in Ireland began in 1873. In 1875, the Presbyterian suffragist Isabella Tod pointed out that some Irishwomen had the vote for Poor Law guardians

139 Anna Haslam, 'Irishwomen and the Local Government Act', *EWR* 239 (n.s.) (15 October 1898), 221; Isabella Tod, 'The Place of Women in the Administration of the Irish Poor Law', *EWR* 103 (15 November 1881), 481–9; Virginia Crossman, *Local Government in Nineteenth-Century Ireland* (Institute of Irish Studies, Queens University of Belfast, 1994), pp. 43–64.

140 R. A. Houston, 'Women in the Economy and Society of Scotland, 1500–1800', in Houston and I. D. Whyte (eds.), *Scottish Society 1500–1800* (Cambridge University Press, 1989), p. 137.

141 *EWR* 36 (May 1876), 228; 190 (March 1889), 128; Mabel Atkinson, *Local Government in Scotland* (Edinburgh and London, 1904), pp. 104–12.

142 *EWR* 193 (June 1889), 269–70; Leneman, *A Guid Cause*, p. 26; Hollis, *Ladies Elect*, pp. 306, 356–8; Keith-Lucas, *English Local Government Franchise*, p. 167; Atkinson, *Local Government in Scotland*, pp. 30–4.

143 *EWR* 8 (n.s.) (October 1871), 281.

and harbour and water board commissioners; in unincorporated towns they could vote for town commissioners, but not for municipal councillors; and nowhere could they stand for office.[144] In 1885 a local act was introduced for Dublin, which, as Isabella Tod pointed out, unjustly ignored women. But when a similar local act was passed for Belfast in 1887, William Johnston intervened to secure the vote for 8,000 Belfast women householders. There was, however, fierce opposition, in the midst of the Home Rule debates, to any extension of household suffrage to all Irish boroughs. By 1895 the total number of women voters in Belfast was not far less than that of the total number of male voters in Dublin. Women were enfranchised in the two Dublin townships of Kingstown and Blackrock in 1894, but other Irishwomen had to wait until the reforms of the Local Government Act of 1898 for the municipal, district and county franchise, and the right to stand as district councillors.[145]

Defining women's citizenship

> if there was a humanity suffrage . . . the suffrage should include women.
> (Lydia Becker, Leeds, April 1869)[146]

Women and men campaigning for women's enfranchisement expressed as they did so their sense of the extent to which the roles of women and men should be shifted, how radically and at what pace. Though a gendered contrast between the public and private lives of men and women often provided a powerful rhetorical framework to spoken and written arguments, it is clear from the complex and varied lives of the women described here that such a contrast cannot be literally interpreted. And the political identities shaped in these campaigns were not rooted simply in an assault on masculine power, although many of the women who figure here took an active and uncompromising part in other parallel campaigns, including the movement to reform the laws of marriage and that against the Contagious Diseases Acts.

The different cultural and political histories related above included women and men of the liberal intelligentsia of London and Cambridge, Edinburgh philanthropists, Manchester radicals and Belfast ratepayers, Irish Quakers and many others, all of whom, to our knowledge, were white. Almost all were Protestant or secularist. The arguments which

144 *Women's Suffrage Journal*, 1 March 1875, quoted in Luddy, 'Isabella M. S. Tod', p. 216.

145 Isabella M. S. Tod, 'Municipal Franchise for Women in Ireland', *EWR* 170 (15 July 1887), 291–3; Haslam, 'Irishwomen and the Local Government Act'; Crossman, *Local Government in Nineteenth-Century Ireland*, pp. 83–5.

146 *Leeds Mercury*, 6 April 1869, in M50/1/9/2, MCL.

they put varied not only with reference to marital status, but also in relation to boundaries of class, religion, nationality and race. Those arguments could exclude as well as include. Suffragists often in private expressed the desire for a 'humanity suffrage', yet in public compromised according to the tactical needs of the moment, and drew upon the political language and practice with which they could most easily identify. Suffragists, like other participants in the reform crisis, drew their own boundaries for citizenship of that British nation of which they imagined themselves a part.

Yet in private, at the height of the campaign of 1868 to enfranchise single women and widows who were qualified ratepayers, Lydia Becker wrote to Richard Pankhurst in terms which spoke of the equality of all individuals:

> the ultimate end to which all efforts at partial enfranchisement are subsidiary. The principle that every human soul is an independent kingdom – nay a universe – over which the individual is sole sovereign – The notion that any one owes subjection or subordination to another is fatal to the higher life of both rulers and subject.[147]

In her correspondence she made it clear that in principle she did not believe in differentiating between husbands and wives, for 'justice is the truest expediency', and the absurdity of the loss of the franchise on marriage would soon be apparent.[148] Richard Pankhurst set at the heart of his own radical commitment a similar belief in 'the right to vote in the character of a human being, possessing intelligence and adequate reasoning power'.[149]

However, one important construction of women's citizenship upon which Becker drew was very different from 'humanity suffrage'. The demand that women should be enfranchised on precisely the same terms as men was tactically attractive and superficially consonant with liberal principles, and placed suffragist arguments within a long individualist tradition of male radicalism. The vote was constituted as a moral responsibility of the individual, who was in the terms of the seventeenth-century Levellers an independent individual, with a property in labour. Manhood suffrage was still the suffrage of the 'independent' man.[150] By the 1860s, as Keith McClelland suggests (chapter 2 in this volume), such older radical arguments were supplemented by the concept of the rational, respectable

147 Becker to Pankhurst, 24 May 1868, Becker's Letter-Book, f. 161, M50/1/3, MCL.
148 Becker to Professor Jack, 22 March 1868, *ibid.*, ff. 11–12.
149 Richard Pankhurst, 'The Right of Women to Vote Under the Reform Act, 1867', *Fortnightly Review* 10 (o.s.), 4 (n.s.) (September 1868), 250–4.
150 Biagini, *Liberty, Retrenchment and Reform*, pp. 272–5 and 286–8.

working man as household head and breadwinner. This version of citizenship had at its centre the implicit exclusion of all married women.

The *Englishwoman's Review* wrote of 'lady householders' and speculated on the likelihood of working-class women, likely to be 'innkeepers, lodging house keepers, small shopkeepers and washerwomen', possessing the vote.[151] The publicity which Lydia Becker gave to potential or actual women voters suggested the qualities of citizenship that could be emphasised, qualities which had much in common with the 'independent artisan'. Women voters, like Lily Maxwell, were respectable, intelligent and engaged in useful, though not necessarily paid, labour. The *Englishwoman's Review* reported that she was 'an intelligent person of respectable appearance . . . [who] keeps a small shop for the sale of crockery ware', 'a woman of strong political opinions . . . delighted to have a chance of expressing them' in voting for Jacob Bright, the Liberal, as her candidate, publicly at the hustings.[152] The women who voted in Manchester in 1868 were described as ranging 'in social grade from the rank of well-to-do shopkeepers down to that of the very poorest labourer' and as displaying genuine political feeling, intelligence and interest, 'a fair sample of the 10,000 eligible women ratepayers of Manchester'.[153]

There were considerable tactical advantages in the movement's initial focus on customary rights and the enfranchisement of women householders, apparent in the ease with which the municipal franchise was granted, and the extent of male support gained by the limitations of the demand. Many of the parliamentarians who acquiesced in the granting of the municipal franchise in 1869, and who supported Bright in 1870, were reassured by such moderation. Equally, some sections of the labour movement were also prepared to contemplate women's suffrage, within limits 'so far as working women paying their lot and earning their independent livelihood, womanhood suffrage too'.[154]

A few of the liberals and radicals who built bridges with working-class politics in 1866–8, like Joseph Cowen jun. and George Holyoake, were committed to continuing support for the women's cause as well as to manhood suffrage. In May 1871, Cowen's *Newcastle Daily Chronicle* called for the right of all women to vote in parliamentary elections.[155] But, in general, male working-class leaders were not prepared to add female

[151] [Jessie Boucherett (?)], 'Some Probable Consequences of Extending the Franchise to Female Householders', *EWR* 1 (October 1866), 26–34.

[152] *EWR* 6 (January 1868), 359–69.

[153] MNSWS, *Second Annual Report*, pp. 6–7; *EWR* 10 (January 1869), 137–40.

[154] *Reynolds's News*, 20 April 1873, quoted in Biagini, *Liberty, Retrenchment and Reform*, p. 293.

[155] Nigel Todd, *The Militant Democracy: Joseph Cowen and Victorian Radicalism* (Whitley Bay: Bewick Press, 1991), p. 101.

franchise to their platforms, many fearing that the enfranchisement of women would strengthen the Conservative party.[156]

The consequences of a position which excluded married women of all classes from virtually all formal rights of citizenship were far-reaching, and were to split the movement for the rest of the century. An emphasis on the qualities of the respectable artisan, in the spirit of the Reform Act of 1867, failed to bring common ground between the labour and the women's movements. But the attractiveness of the appeal to custom and a 'golden age' for women in the historic past of the nation did strengthen the conservative and nationalist strand within suffragist rhetoric which is further discussed below (pp. 169–72).

However, the arguments for the citizenship of women went beyond the British radical tradition, and differed significantly from the demands of working men. They drew upon the familiarity of middle-class women with a rhetoric of 'woman's mission', a rhetoric which had its origins in a language of sexual difference, and in the extensive growth of middle-class women's philanthropic activity in the nineteenth century. So in 1870 Rose Crawshay, the wife of the leading ironmaster of Merthyr Tydfil, suggested to an audience there that: 'Possession of a vote will tend to ennoble women's characters . . . and a high standard of morality [will be] introduced throughout the world.'[157]

That sense of sexual difference could be relocated in a new and public setting, and women of the liberal elite found it possible to rewrite that 'mission' in their case for enfranchisement. Most suffragists shared an antipathy towards claiming rights in a spirit of self-interest. They preferred to stress, in different degrees, that commitment to altruism found in the writings of advanced liberalism which Stefan Collini has explored.[158] Rights were conceived in relationship to a duty or a responsibility to others. In her early pamphlet of 1867, Barbara Bodichon saw enfranchisement for women as enhancing public spirit more generally, instilling a 'healthy, lively, intelligent' patriotism, and 'an unselfish devotedness to the public service'.[159] A new form of civic humanism here could justify a public role for educated and responsible women through a sense of mission to the uneducated and the poor, excluded by that very definition from the political nation.[160] Such a role rested, to varying degrees, on both class and sexual difference.

156 Biagini, *Liberty, Retrenchment and Reform*, pp. 308–12.
157 Quoted in Wallace, *Organise! Organise! Organise!*, p. 165.
158 Collini, *Public Moralists: Political Thought and Intellectual Life in Britain 1850–1930* (Oxford: Clarendon Press, 1991), ch. 2.
159 Bodichon, *Reasons for the Enfranchisement of Women*, p. 108.
160 Jane Lewis, *Women and Social Action in Victorian and Edwardian England* (Aldershot: Edward Elgar, 1991), pp. 1–13.

That sense of political mission rooted in responsibility to the nation was reinforced through awareness, partly through interest in nationalist issues, of the ideas of Joseph Mazzini. His *Duties of Man* (1858; first English translation by Emilie Venturi, 1862) set duty to others, to one's own society and to humanity, and to a world of future social harmony and the reconciliation of classes against the pursuit of rights. The impact of Mazzini's writing and of the struggle for Italian unification on both working-class and women's movements in Britain has only recently been appreciated.[161] His views could apparently accommodate sexual difference while also offering women a breadth of activity within a public setting. The *Women's Suffrage Journal* in November 1870 conveyed his view that the question of women's suffrage was also that of the moral education of society, never to be narrowed down to 'what is called a right or an interest': 'let duty be your ground, both in protecting your unhappy sisters and in urging your political claims'.[162]

Christian Socialists like Charles Kingsley, Frederick Denison Maurice and Thomas Hughes and others influenced by their ideas were equally committed to the potential mission of middle-class women. Kingsley, Hughes and Llewellyn Davies, brother of Emily Davies, were all signatories to the petition presented for women's enfranchisement in 1867, and all attended women's suffrage meetings in the late 1860s and early 1870s. They shared an exalted conception of the complementarity of women and men, and of the 'purity and earnestness' that women might bring to the political process.[163] F. D. Maurice wholeheartedly supported women's suffrage in the debates of the late 1860s 'as a positive strength to the moral life of England'.[164] Charles Kingsley's position was ambivalent. In 1869, welcoming Mill's *Subjection of Women*, he acknowledged that there were those – and the implication is that they included himself – who had held similar views for many years. He suggested that the Reform Act of 1867 had indeed created a new peril for 'refined and educated women', who might well seek to defend themselves and 'their lowlier sisters' from the tyranny of uneducated men. Kingsley, as a supporter of Governor

[161] Emilie Venturi took an active part in the women's movement, especially the campaigns for reform of the law affecting married women's property, and the repeal of the Contagious Diseases Acts. For Mazzini's popularity, see Biagini, *Liberty, Retrenchment and Reform*, pp. 46–50, and Finn, *After Chartism*, pp. 159–72.

[162] Mazzini, 'Mazzini on the Franchise for Women', *Women's Suffrage Journal* 9 (1 November 1871), 95. See also Kate Amberley, 'The Claims of Women', *Fortnightly Review* 15 (o.s.), 9 (n.s.) (January 1871), 110; she quotes from Venturi's translation of Mazzini's *The Duties of Man* (London, 1862), ch. 6.

[163] Kingsley, 'Women and Politics', 557.

[164] Maurice, *The Rev. F. D. Maurice on Female Suffrage* (from the *Spectator* of 5 March 1870; pamphlet at Fawcett Library, London Guildhall University), p. 2; Frank Maulden McLain, *Maurice, Man and Moralist* (London: SPCK, 1972), pp. 101–13.

Eyre, was here in an unlikely alliance with Mill, in defending what the essential qualities of women – but especially middle-class women – could bring to the political order to combat the new majority. 'The State commits an injustice in debarring a woman from the rights of a citizen because she chooses over and above them, to perform the good works of a saint.'[165] Deeply unhappy at the involvement of women in the campaign against the Contagious Diseases Acts, he expressed himself committed to 'woman as the teacher, the natural and therefore divine, guide, purifier, inspirer of the man'.[166] Mill's diplomatic but perhaps not insincere response was to agree: 'Cannot we associate the cause with quiet, upright and ladylike women as well as with vulgar, questionable, and pushing ones?'[167] Many suffragists wholeheartedly rebutted the implications of such arguments, whether from Kingsley or from Mill.

Most significantly, John Stuart Mill's stress on citizenship as a means to individuality and self-cultivation could be compatible with different gender roles for women and men, and could be entirely appropriate for married women as well as single ones. In *On Liberty* (1859), as in the *Subjection of Women* (1869), John Stuart Mill's goal was self-development, the highest cultivation of individual faculties, in all their variety and diversity. The right kind of marriage offered the continuous pleasures of such development.[168] But such citizenship was unlikely to be for all; the uneducated and the mediocre in his own society would need help, though the women of the liberal elite might draw upon Mill's views of public duties as offering enlarged horizons, social functions and practical disciplines.

The language of individuality undoubtedly shaped the political outlook of early suffragists. Millicent Fawcett wrote, in the aftermath of the Paris Commune, that no country was so safe from revolution as one in which its citizens enjoyed perfect freedom, and for her: 'Freedom is nothing but power to exercise the faculties, and how can the faculties be exercised if they are not cultured?'[169] Education and cultivation were to these liberals the keys to citizenship. To Julia Wedgwood, describing the narrowness of and lack of opportunity in the life of the middle-class woman, female

[165] Kingsley, 'Women and Politics', 554–5, 557.

[166] Charles Kingsley to Mrs Peter Taylor, 27 May 1870, and to John Stuart Mill, n.d., in *Charles Kingsley: His Letters and Memories of His Life*, edited by his wife, 2 vols. (London, 1877), pp. 326–8.

[167] Mill to Charles Kingsley, 9 July 1870, in Mill, *Later Letters*, vol. XVII, pp. 1742–4.

[168] Susan Mendus, 'The Marriage of True Minds: The Ideal of Marriage in the Philosophy of John Stuart Mill', in Mendus and Jane Rendall (eds.), *Sexuality and Subordination: Interdisciplinary Studies of Gender in the Nineteenth Century* (London: Routledge, 1989), pp. 171–91.

[169] Millicent Fawcett, 'The Education of Women: A Lecture Delivered at Newcastle, November 13th, 1871', in Henry Fawcett and Millicent Garrett Fawcett, *Essays and Lectures on Social and Political Subjects* (London, 1872), p. 226.

suffrage was to be claimed not as a right, and not as an end in itself alone, but rather as a means: 'we seek to be numbered among citizens quite as much from our need of being awakened to higher duties as from a demand for extended rights. We desire it more for what it would make us than for what it would give us'.[170]

One duty for women as potential voters lay in the shaping of a different kind of marriage, for women of all classes, one which would permit such self-development. To those disinclined to claim their rights, the appeal was to their sense of obligation to such sisters – as in that by Millicent Fawcett at Bristol in a lecture in 1871:

> If you don't want rights because you have so many privileges, remember the fate of those among your country-women who are associated with men base enough to avail themselves of the power which the law places so unreservedly in their hands.

She condemned the 'domestic selfishness' of indolent wealthy women, and recalled the fate of so many of her countrywomen, desperate for education, locked into brutal marriages, a situation which only legislation could change. Gladstone had asked about working men, 'Are they not our own flesh and blood?', and Fawcett put that same question about women.[171]

Anne Robertson spoke at a packed meeting in Dublin in 1872 of the inequities of the law's treatment of mothers, reviewing two recent cases. In one, the courts had ruled the daughter of a Catholic father, who died young, and Protestant mother, had to be brought up a Catholic according to the wishes of the father's relatives. In another, a Catholic widow of a Protestant husband, had had to flee her native country, Ireland, to bring up her children in her own faith. Anne Robertson saw this as a question not 'of religious intolerance, but of an utter forgetfulness of woman's claims to justice or fair dealing, even in her so called sacred sphere of wife and mother'.[172] There was a close relationship, and a considerable overlap among the activists, between the Manchester suffrage movement and the campaign for the improvement of married women's legal position. Suffrage writers in the late 1860s and early 1870s were entirely united on this, an issue which most clearly indicated the absence of any female voice in the legislature, and the partiality and self-interest of existing legislation.

170 Julia Wedgwood, 'Female Suffrage in Its Influence on Married Life', *Contemporary Review* 20 (August 1872), 370, and 'Female Suffrage, . . . with Regard to Its Indirect Results', p. 255.

171 Fawcett, 'Why Women Require the Franchise. A Lecture Delivered in the Colston Hall, Bristol, in March 1871', in Fawcett and Fawcett, *Essays and Lectures*, p. 270.

172 Anne I. Robertson, *Women's Need of Parliamentary Representation: A Lecture upon the Necessity of Giving Women the Parliamentary Franchise* (Dublin, 1872), pp. 6–9.

Suffragists agreed that not all members of a society would be ready for a form of citizenship that encouraged individuality. Many initially shared Mill's distrust of democracy and, influenced by him, noted the ways in which he proposed to limit its effects. In his *Considerations on Representative Government* (1861), Mill suggested a simple test of literacy and numeracy for voters, with plural votes for the better educated, as well as the disqualification of paupers and non-taxpayers. Another solution was the proposal for proportional representation put forward by Thomas Hare, based on a national list of candidates and a quota preference system, as a means of ensuring the representation of minorities, and in particular the election not of local notables or party hacks, but 'men of talent and character', clearly men like Mill and his friends.[173] Helen Taylor, unsurprisingly, actively supported an educational qualification, plural voting and Thomas Hare's scheme for proportional representation.[174] Millicent Fawcett published two articles on Hare's complex scheme in *Macmillan's Magazine*.[175] Barbara Bodichon and Jessie Boucherett also expressed interest.[176] Suffragists shared the same anxieties about democracy, and about enfranchising the illiterate and those dependent on poor relief as their fellow liberals and radicals.

Although they reclaimed a sense of sexual difference where appropriate, leading suffragist writers at the same time tended to disassociate themselves from the language of philanthropy and 'woman's mission', associating it as Millicent Fawcett did with the 'spurious philanthropy' of charity.[177] They looked rather for a framework of social responsibility, which rested on an informed, scientific base, and to the kind of social science practised and debated at the National Association for the Promotion of Social Science. Lawrence Goldman has indicated how the association represented the different elements of the political nation that may be associated with the mid-Victorian process of liberal coalescence. It brought together hard-working Liberal MPs, professional administrators, co-operators, advanced

173 See Thomas Hare, *The Election of Representatives, Parliamentary and Municipal: A Treatise* (1859), 3rd edn, with a preface, appendix, and other additions (London, 1865); F. B. Smith, *Making of the Second Reform Bill*, pp. 212–13.

174 Mill to Chapman, 21 November 1866, in Mill, *Later Letters*, vol. XVII, p. 1216; Helen Taylor, 'The Ladies' Petition', 67n.

175 Millicent Fawcett, 'Proportional Representation', *Macmillan's Magazine* 22 (September 1870), 376–82; and her 'Short Explanation of Mr Hare's Scheme of Representation', *Macmillan's Magazine* 23 (April 1871), 816–26. Both are reprinted together in *Essays and Lectures*, pp. 336–68.

176 Barbara Bodichon, 'Authorities and Precedents for Giving the Suffrage to Qualified Women', *EWR* 2 (January 1867), 64–72; Jessie Boucherett to Helen Taylor, 4 June [1867], MT, vol. XII, ff. 162–5; [Jessie Boucherett (?)],'Debate on the Enfranchisement of Women', *EWR* 4 (1867), 207.

177 Millicent Fawcett, 'Free Education in its Economic Aspects', in Fawcett and Fawcett, *Essays and Lectures*, p. 64.

employers, Christian socialists and academic liberals.[178] Its secretary George Hastings was one of the most active male supporters of the women's movement, including women's suffrage from the mid-1850s onwards, as was his successor, John Westlake, with his wife and daughters. The association also of course included others, including positivists and some trade unionists, rather less sympathetic to women's suffrage. But, as Goldman suggests, the association offers a different perspective on mid-Victorian liberalism than one which focuses on the figure of Gladstone. It also perhaps demonstrates how proposals for women's suffrage could divide that liberalism, yet win from it an important degree of support.

Julia Wedgwood, writing of women who might mistakenly encourage pauperism out of an overly feminised and sentimentally Christian compassion, spoke of a woman's perception of political economy as belonging 'to a secular male world, with which she has nothing to do'. Citizenship should bring a sense of responsibility to replace the easy pleasures of charity, an involvement in the national life and an understanding of laws of political economy that might end through 'beneficent discipline' the 'rot of pauperism'. To Wedgwood, the incomprehension of the poor shown by the legislators of the House of Commons could be very obviously remedied by the special qualifications which women might bring to such work, once informed by a sense of responsibility and by 'intellectual training'.[179]

Similarly, Millicent Fawcett wrote of the consequences of pauperism, on the importance of working-class payment for education and on the encouragement of self-help and independence among the poor. She wrote of the 'luxurious unemployed and the pauperised unemployed' as more numerous proportionately in England than elsewhere, a situation to be remedied only by harsh measures to encourage Malthusian self-restraint and curb population increases.[180] Isabella Tod, the Belfast suffragist, echoed her on Irish pauperism, where though 'the laxity of the English Poor Law' was not desired, the rigidity of regulations dealing with women and children required discretion and flexibility: 'the economy of a workhouse is the economy of a house, only less various, but dealing with larger sums and quantities'.[181]

178 See esp. Goldman, 'Social Science Association, 1857–1886', and his 'Peculiarity of the English?: The Social Science Association and the Absence of Sociology in Nineteenth-Century Britain', *Past & Present* 114 (1987), 133–71; also Kathleen McCrone, 'National Association for the Promotion of Social Science', and Yeo, *Contest for Social Science*, ch. 6.

179 Wedgwood, 'Female Suffrage in Its Influence on Married Life', 365–6; Wedgwood, 'Female Suffrage, Considered Chiefly with Regard to Its Indirect Results', pp. 278–89.

180 Fawcett, 'Free Education', p. 59, and her 'National Debts and National Prosperity', in Fawcett and Fawcett, *Essays and Lectures*, pp. 144–5; see also her *Political Economy for Beginners* (London, 1870), and her *Tales in Political Economy* (London, 1874).

181 Tod, 'Place of Women', 483–6.

Liberal arguments for women's suffrage did include the educated and cultivated married woman, but tended to erect barriers against the uneducated, both men and women, representing their continuing fears of the tyranny of the majority. The working-class woman in whose name the suffrage was claimed and to whom protection was promised was not, in this language, the autonomous individual who might benefit from the kind of citizenship which rested on the fullest cultivation of individual potential.

Within the women's suffrage movement, citizenship was expressed not only through claims to rights and to duties. It was also inseparable from expressions of collective identity. Mid-Victorian suffragists often appealed to a national past and a constitutional heritage, frequently conflating British and English histories.[182] In 1867 Helen Taylor chose to write tactically, appealing to the Whig principles of the British constitution, to the rights of property and the claims of taxpayers. As Mill said, she chose to emphasise 'some novel and especially national characteristics', and a 'peculiarly English point of view'. She grounded the request in 'the principles of the British constitution' and the claims of English women to share in the 'birthright' of an Englishman, the right to preserve his property. She appealed to a Whig of 1688, Lord Somers, and contrasted that authority with the abstractions of natural rights and 'woman's mission'. Mill echoed many of her arguments in introducing his amendment to the Reform Bill in June 1867.[183]

Particular and gendered versions of English history were invoked. The working-class radicals' appeal to Anglo-Saxon democracy could be paralleled by the notion of early Anglo-Saxon and even early Germanic societies as ones particularly favourable to women. Hints contained in the works of the Roman historian Tacitus on the freedom of women of the ancient Britons, who participated in public councils with Boudicca, and on the participation of women in the councils of early German tribes were developed in the spirit of the rewriting of early medieval British history by Victorian historians.[184] By the middle of the nineteenth century the emphasis on the essential qualities of the Anglo-Saxon peoples as the

[182] Antoinette Burton, *Burdens of History: British Feminists, Indian Women, and Imperial Culture, 1865–1915* (Chapel Hill and London: University of North Carolina Press, 1994), pp. 52–9.

[183] Helen Taylor, 'The Ladies' Petition'; Mill to Chapman, 21 November 1866, in Mill, *Later Letters*, vol. XVII, p. 1216; Mill, *Speech . . . on the Admission of Women to the Electoral Franchise*.

[184] On working-class radicals' view of the Anglo-Saxon past, see Biagini, *Liberty, Retrenchment and Reform*, pp. 54–6; on Victorian historians of medieval England, see John W. Burrow, *A Liberal Descent: Victorian Historians and the English Past* (Cambridge University Press, 1981), esp. pts II–III; Reginald Horsman, *Race and Manifest Destiny: The Origins of American Racial Anglo-Saxonism* (Cambridge, Mass.: Harvard University Press, 1981), ch. 4.

greatest of all branches of the Teutons had been spread most effectively by Charles Kingsley, as in his *Hereward the Wake* (1866). To Kingsley, 'the welfare of the Teutonic race is the welfare of the world'.[185] Frances Power Cobbe could write in 1868 that:

> Our Teuton race from the days of Tacitus, has borne women whose moral nature has been in more than equipoise with their passions; and who have both deserved and obtained a freedom and a respect unknown to their sisters of the south.[186]

The movement had its Anglo-Saxon heroines. Mary Smith of Carlisle, suffragist, autobiographer, and schoolmistress and nonconformist, included in her book of poems, entitled *Progress*, written between 1865 and 1873, not only poems on 'Oliver Cromwell' and 'Gladstone's Axe' but 'Ethelflaed Queen of Mercia', clearly the female equivalent of King Alfred, who had brought prosperity, peace and Christianity to Mercia.[187]

In the debates over the granting of the municipal franchise to women, much was made of women's part in local government as an essential part of an immemorial constitution, governed by customary law alone. Increasingly the appeal was made to the rights to local officeholding anciently enjoyed by women. They could be churchwardens, waywardens, overseers of the poor, before they were barred by nineteenth-century legislation.[188] There were strong elements here of a 'golden age' of the past, with the loss of the parliamentary vote for women seen as a kind of accidental and temporary deviation from the true principles of the constitution, rooted in local self-government and lost at some point in the seventeenth century. Such a language marked out boundaries, with the potential to exclude not only the married and the dependent, but also those without access to that Anglo-Saxon past, carrying a potent message in relation to other parts of the United Kingdom.

The British nation with which suffragists identified rested on profoundly Protestant assumptions. These assumptions could be rooted in the kind of histories of Anglo-Saxon nationhood told by Kingsley, through which the Reformation became a key event in the raising of women's status.[189] They were also forged through close associations with campaigning and Liberal nonconformity, evident across the United Kingdom, in Scotland and in Wales as in England. In Wales noncon-

[185] Charles Kingsley, *The Roman and the Teuton: A Series of Lectures Delivered Before the University of Cambridge* (Cambridge and London, 1864), p. 338.

[186] Frances Power Cobbe, 'Criminals, Idiots, Women and Minors', *Fraser's Magazine* 78 (December 1868), 791.

[187] Mary Smith, *Progress and Other Poems*... (London, 1873), pp. 172–3.

[188] *Women's Suffrage Journal* 33 (1 November 1872), 141; Lydia Becker, *The Rights and Duties of Women in Local Government* (Manchester, 1879).

[189] Kingsley, 'Women and Politics', 552–3.

formist ministers and their wives were notably active on committees for women's suffrage by the early 1870s. Some, like the Reverend Alfred Tilly of Swansea, a temperance campaigner, called for female suffrage in anticipation of greater sobriety, for 'women would favour those laws which tended to restrict the temptation to drunkenness which exists now'.[190] The nonconformist base of Welsh Liberalism could also create distrust of the potentially Conservative and 'clerical' impact of the effects of women's suffrage in England, for, as Thomas Love Jones-Parry suggested to Lydia Becker in 1870: 'in England, and particularly in boroughs such as Bath, women are Conservative under great clerical influence, which always tends to fetter freedom of thought'.[191]

Yet it would be entirely misleading to identify the varied and complex women's suffrage movement with a dogmatic Protestantism. Much of its support in all parts of the United Kingdom also came from those small but influential sects which had maintained for so long a position apart from such intolerance, Quakerism and Unitarianism. Among Anglicans the movement noticeably drew on a Broad Church following, and also attracted some with no strong religious loyalties, whether committed freethinkers or not. Suffragists were committed to religious liberty and to toleration. The *Englishwoman's Review* and after 1870 the *Women's Suffrage Journal* wrote optimistically of developments in the Irish women's movement as appealing to both religious communities, and early meetings strove to attract representatives from both those communities.

Early women's suffrage activists in Ireland in the 1860s and 1870s were, however, drawn almost entirely from the Protestant middle classes. Women like the Quaker Anna Haslam and the Presbyterian Isabella Tod had comparable interests to their English, Scottish and Welsh fellows, and like many others were deeply involved in campaigns to improve women's education, in married women's property legislation and in moral reform movements. Like other suffragists also, Irish feminists were able to mobilise some influential Liberal support. Much of this still awaits further research. Although parliamentary support for women's suffrage included a number of Irish nationalist MPs, it does not appear that any connections were established between the women's suffrage movement and the case for Home Rule. The limited aims of the movement were not to appeal to Anna Parnell, who made a far more direct intervention in the politics of Ireland through the Ladies Land League from 1879. Only in the early twentieth century did a more nationalist-oriented movement for

190 Quoted in Wallace, *Organise! Organise! Organise!*, pp. 165–8.
191 Quoted *ibid.*, p. 170.

women's suffrage appear, although even then there were tensions over the priorities to be established.[192]

Among Protestant suffragists, there remained a profound distrust of Catholicism, a distrust borne not necessarily of a militant Anglo-Saxon nationalism, but from that sense of history as a movement of rationally informed progress within which the Catholic church played a reactionary and hostile role, as it did in so many Enlightenment and Whig narratives of women's history. That distrust was shared by Mill himself.[193] Josephine Butler, herself a devout evangelical Anglican, was in later years to recognise the difficulties which Home Rule for Ireland posed for many of her Liberal contemporaries. She too drew on a fundamentally Protestant historical sense:

> it will, I think, be found all through the history of Ireland, that at its happiest, and freest times, it was the most independent of Papal government and influence. Successive Coercion Acts have at intervals driven the people to look towards Rome, as they otherwise would not have done.[194]

Butler, though recognising how deeply such a sense of the reactionary nature of the papacy was entrenched, nevertheless called for a Christian spirit to do justice to Irish wrongs. Among Irish suffragists the leading figures in the early years were Protestants like Anne Robertson and Isabella Tod, who identified themselves actively with the cause of political, social and economic improvement in Ireland. Isabella Tod was in the 1880s to become both a convinced Unionist and a pacifist internationalist in her commitment to that cause of improvement.[195] Millicent Fawcett's patriotism was to lead her into strong opposition to Irish Home Rule, and with Kate Courtney she founded the Women's Liberal Unionist Association in 1888, and split the loyalties of women of the Liberal party.

192 See Mary Cullen, 'How Radical Was Irish Feminism Between 1860 and 1920?', in Patrick J. Corish (ed.), *Radicals, Rebels and Establishments: Papers Read Before the Irish Conference of Historians, Maynooth, 16–19 June 1983*, Historical Studies, vol. XV (Belfast: Appletree, 1985), pp. 185–20; Cullen and Luddy, *Women, Power and Consciousness*, for essays on Anna Haslam, Isabella Tod and Anna Parnell; Cliona Murphy, *The Women's Suffrage Movement and Irish Society in the Early Twentieth Century* (New York: Harvester Wheatsheaf, 1989); Rosemary Cullen Owens, *Smashing Times: A History of the Irish Suffrage Movement 1899–1922* (Dublin: Attic Press, 1984).

193 Kinzer, 'J. S. Mill and Irish Land', 113–14; E. D. Steele, 'J. S. Mill and the Irish Question: Reform and the Integrity of the Empire, 1865–1870', *Historical Journal* 12 (1970), repr. in Alan O'Day (ed.), *Reactions to Irish Nationalism 1865–1914* (London: Hambledon Press, 1987), pp. 220–2.

194 Josephine E. Butler, *Our Christianity Tested by the Irish Question* (London, [1887?]), p. 8.

195 See Anne Robertson's *The Story of Nelly Dillon*, 2 vols. (London, 1866); Heloise Brown, 'An Alternative Imperialism: Isabella Tod, Internationalist and "Good Liberal Unionist"', *Gender & History* 10 (1998), 358–80.

The narratives which they employed drew not only upon national and Protestant histories, but upon broader histories of gender relations in civil society, histories in which women had not a marginal or antiquarian but a central role. The theme that united virtually all writing and campaigning on the suffrage in these years was a consciousness of participating in the progressive movement of civilisation, and, in the words of the *Englishwoman's Review* in July 1867, 'that great onward march which is at last to place woman in the position for which heaven intended her'.[196] That onward march was the history of the modernity and improvement of civil society, of Western civilisation, a history also of an increasing improvement in gender relations, which could only be measured comparatively. This theme had been familiar to radical Unitarians of the 1830s and 1840s as to Harriet Taylor and John Stuart Mill in 1851. In Mill's *Subjection of Women*, as in his earlier work, the conditions of marriage and the legal disabilities of women were clearly the last survivals of a feudal past, inappropriate to the modern and advanced society of the nineteenth century.

The years in which the claim for the suffrage were being formulated were also years of active development in the field of anthropology, in the work of scholars such as Henry Maine, John McLennan, John Lubbock and E. B. Tylor. Marriage and the history of the human family were major concerns of these writers, who wrote and reviewed in the same journals as Millicent Fawcett and Lydia Becker, though their political commitments were varied. They shared assumptions of progressive development, and the view that civilisation brought with it increasing personal freedom and independence for women from the promiscuous, polyandrous or patriarchal families of the different pasts they were constructing.[197]

In the pages of the *Englishwoman's Review* and elsewhere, suffragists never ceased to assault the conditions of English marriage as outmoded and 'barbaric' inheritances of a past world. Speaking of and denying differences in male and female intellect to the Manchester Ladies Literary Society in March 1868, Lydia Becker spoke of 'the long dark night of ignorance and superstition which represents the past history of our race' and of 'the dawn of a brighter day'. In private she wrote that the paper 'made quite a commotion' in the Manchester Anthropological Society.[198] In the *Englishwoman's Review* in January 1867, Barbara Bodichon recalled Harriet Mill's frequently quoted differentiation of

196 *EWR* 1 (July 1867), 239.

197 See George Stocking, *Victorian Anthropology* (New York: Free Press, 1987), ch. 6.

198 Lydia Becker, 'Is There Any Specific Distinction Between Male and Female Intellect?', *EWR* 8 (July 1868), 483–91; Becker to Jessie Boucherett, 31 March 1868, M50/1/3, MCL.

European women from 'the habits of submission' of 'Asiatic women', and of the 'savages of the forest', and Serjeant Manning's writing of the exclusion of women from the suffrage as 'a remnant of savage life, which the improvements of modern civilization have not yet dealt with'.[199]

In February 1868, the editorial of the Radical–Liberal newspaper, the *Manchester Examiner and Times*, wrote of arguments against women's suffrage as 'not distinguishable in principle from those which have held rule for ages in the mountains of Circassia, in the slave markets of Constantinople, and in the plantations of the southern states of America'. The paper called for 'the development of feminine character in its social and political relations' and argued directly that 'it is desirable that wives and mothers should know what citizenship means'.[200] The rhetoric was predictable, the 'orientalism' in Edward Said's sense commonplace, the images of savage women familiar tropes.

Similarly the collection of essays edited by Josephine Butler, *Woman's Work and Woman's Culture* (1869), included two historical essays by contributors to the *Essays on Reform*, Charles Pearson and John Boyd Kinnear. Both were regular attendees at women's suffrage meetings after 1869. Their essays suggest the significance of an evolutionary, yet Whiggish, historical context for the movement, combining assumptions of historical progress with a view of the distinctiveness of the Anglo-Saxon or Teutonic inheritance. Pearson wrote in his essay both of 'the legal relations of husband and wife [as] . . . a relic of primitive times' and of 'courage, and strong will, and pure morals, characteristics for which the women of the Teutonic races were noted at an early period'.[201] Boyd Kinnear referred in his essay on women's work and their participation in politics to 'the surviving barbarism of our laws'.[202] In her introduction, Butler noted the similarities between their work and Mill's, but pointed out that each of these essays had been written before the *Subjection of Women* appeared. This framework was already a commonplace one for the women and men active in the women's suffrage movement.

There were broader imperial issues. A relationship between subordination on the grounds of gender and that of race was perceived by many participants in and observers of the women's suffrage movement. Helen Taylor suggested in 1866 that the Eyre prosecution should 'concern

199 Bodichon, 'Authorities and Precedents', 66–8, 71–2.

200 *ME*, 12 February 1868.

201 Charles Pearson, 'On Some Historical Aspects of Family Life', in Butler, *Women's Work and Women's Culture*, pp. 154 and 167.

202 John Boyd Kinnear, 'The Social Position of Women in the Present Age', in Butler, *Women's Work and Women's Culture*, pp. 363–4; on Kinnear, see Christopher Harvie, 'John Boyd Kinnear, 1828–1920', *Journal of the Scottish Labour History Society* 3 (1970), 25–33.

women even more nearly than the franchise, for no one will suffer more than women, if arbitrary authority of any sort is to be left without any legal responsibility'.[203] But in 1868 Mill wrote to Priscilla McLaren of his disappointment at the response of women to the story of Morant Bay, though he was not here referring specifically to suffragists:

it has been with especial sorrow that I have seen so many women cold and unmoved at the recital of sufferings which it might have been supposed would at least have aroused some womanly pity & generous indignation against the perpetrators.[204]

The Times used their public exchange of letters to link Mill's feminism with his pursuit of Governor Eyre, as exemplifying that extremism which had led the electors of Westminster to reject him.[205] For many associated with Mill, like Peter and Clementia Taylor, active in the Jamaica Committee, women's suffrage was one of a variety of radical causes to be supported, and sometimes combined. Clementia Taylor found it hard to see Charles Kingsley as an ally in the women's suffrage cause, given his support for Governor Eyre (though Mill and Taylor recruited him nevertheless).[206] The enfranchisement of black populations, as of working men, could be employed rhetorically in the interests of women's suffrage. In the debate on the Women's Disabilities Bill of 1870, Jacob Bright pointed to the enfranchisement of 'a negro population of 4,000,000' in the Southern USA, securing those states 'peace and prosperity', in the face of the same arguments that were being applied to women. Charles Dilke heightened the inconsistency of passing over one class of the adult population in Britain: 'You do not pass over negroes, for there are negro voters in almost every borough in the country; but you pass over one class – the class of women.'[207] Yet John Stuart Mill's commitment to the Jamaica Committee was coupled with a reluctance to contemplate the extension of citizenship to those who were not yet civilised, as Catherine Hall suggests below (chapter 4).

Many suffragists were entirely clear on the priority of the politics of gender. Emily Davies's concern lest the movement should be associated

[203] Draft letter from Helen Taylor to Clementia Taylor, 2 November 1866, vol. XIII, f. 262, MT.

[204] John Stuart Mill to Priscilla McLaren, 12 December 1868, in Mill, *Later Letters*, vol. XVI, pp. 1521–2.

[205] Kinzer, Robson and Robson, *A Moralist in and out of Parliament*, p. 271.

[206] Clementia Taylor to Helen Taylor, 15 and 23 July 1867, and Helen Taylor to Clementia Taylor, draft, 25 July 1867, vol. XIII, ff. 279 and 284–5, MT; Charles Kingsley to Helen Taylor, 3 June 1867, and Helen Taylor to Kingsley, draft, 8 June 1867, vol. XVII, ff. 24–5, MT; Mill to Kingsley, July 9 1870, in Mill, *Later Letters*, vol. XVII, pp. 1742–4.

[207] *Hansard*, 3rd ser., vol. 201, cols. 203, 220.

too closely with other 'crotchets' of John Stuart Mill, like 'Jamaica & the Reform League', indicated the limits of her political commitment. Yet as Antoinette Burton has so clearly illustrated, the female other – and especially the woman of the East – was constantly deployed in the pamphlets, periodicals and speeches of the women's suffrage movement, linking the significance of women's emancipation to the continuing progress of the West.[208] The contrasts drawn implied both the backwardness of this area of British life, and the essential qualities of British civilisation with which British women might identify. So Mrs William Grey wrote in 1867 of opposition to women voting in public:

> Softly, ladies. Surely we are in England, not in Turkey. It is of Englishwomen we are speaking, not of the secluded inhabitants of an Oriental zenana, and it seems strange to hear that English women are afraid of mingling in crowds and public places.[209]

Conclusion

The women who pursued their claims in the late 1860s made political choices in a rapidly changing situation. By 1870, they had, for England and Wales, gained much more than Helen Taylor could possibly have expected in 1866. The debates surrounding the Reform Act had brought some women to the gates of the political nation, though those gates remained barred to the great majority. The boundaries of gender had formally been breached in England and Wales, in that single ratepaying women could now vote in municipal elections, and for the school board. Similar advances would follow without too much delay for Scotland. In Ireland, though the initial history of the women's suffrage movement has a superficial similarity to events in the rest of the United Kingdom, that movement was to take a very different course, and one that cannot be told without reference to a developing nationalist politics.

The account given above may have indicated how much still remains to be known of the early history of the women's suffrage movement in the context of the political history of the 1860s. Support for the cause among members of Parliament was in many respects greater than might have been expected, for a relatively short-lived period. The convergence of middle-class Radical–Liberal politics, and academic and intellectual liberalism in this brief moment made women's suffrage appear a practical possibility to some observers. More research and a closer understanding

[208] Emily Davies to Barbara Bodichon, 21 August 1866, Bodichon Papers, Girton College, Cambridge; Burton, *Burdens of History*, ch. 3 and *passim*.

[209] Mrs William Grey, *Is the Exercise of the Suffrage Unfeminine?* (London, 1870), p. 6, quoted in Burton, *Burdens of History*, p. 88.

of such expectations might also indicate the temporary nature and the limitations of the success achieved. Much support had rested on the cautious nature of what was sought, and most of Jacob Bright's parliamentary supporters in 1870 would not have voted for a more radical measure.

Developments in the 1870s were to be less favourable, even as the relationship between advanced liberalism, radicalism and the leadership of the working-class movement grew closer. The increasing place of trade union concerns within that leadership did not encourage claims for women's suffrage.[210] Nor did Gladstone's ministry encourage the cause, for Gladstone, the 'Arch-Enemy' to Lydia Becker, was unwavering in his opposition to women's suffrage. And the retreat of Lancashire Liberalism and the discarding of older political machines dating from the Anti-Corn Law League may also have affected this heartland of the women's suffrage movement.[211] From this perspective, the changing priorities of Victorian Radical–Liberalism were becoming less sympathetic to women seeking to enter the political nation than they had been in the 1860s. Nevertheless, women's presence on the margins of the political nation was not insignificant. And many suffragists, especially those from the Victorian intelligentsia, participated actively in the debates and concerns of that nation in the last quarter of the nineteenth century. They too helped to define its boundaries, although in very different ways.

As I write today, the only detailed history of the women's suffrage movement of 1865–70 remains that of a participant, and its first historian, Helen Blackburn. It is a painstaking and meticulous record, and one which may be very clearly identified with her pride in a nation's past. Blackburn drew upon a very lengthy tradition of Anglo-Saxonism, one which looked back to the uses of Tacitus' *Germania* but also drew upon Sir Henry Maine, when she wrote:

> of all the great Indo-Germanic races, the Anglo-Saxon has kept closest to the free and open life of the early Aryans and has preserved best that idea of companionship between men and women of which traces remain in prehistoric times of other races.[212]

She contrasted that Anglo-Saxon inheritance, which had ensured to women 'their share of personal independence', with a history of early

[210] For discussion of developments in the 1870s and later, see Jonathan Spain, 'Trade Unionists, Gladstonian Liberals and the Labour Law Reforms of 1875', in Eugenio F. Biagini and Alastair J. Reid (eds.), *Currents of Radicalism: Popular Radicalism, Organised Labour and Party Politics in Britain, 1850–1914* (Cambridge University Press, 1991), pp. 109–33; Pugh, 'Limits of Liberalism'.

[211] Ann Robson, 'A Birds' Eye View of Gladstone', in Bruce L. Kinzer (ed.), *The Gladstonian Turn of Mind: Essays Presented to J. B. Conacher* (University of Toronto Press, 1985), pp. 63–96.

[212] Helen Blackburn, *Women's Suffrage*, p. 2.

Roman law which had subjected 'the will and the possessions of the wife'. Reviewing the situation of women as she found it around 1900, she found the claim for women's suffrage 'most insistent in lands peopled by the Anglo-Saxon race' and this to be 'an inevitable result' of the 'historical evolution' of

> a race which has worked out its faith along lines of Christian teaching that encourage independence of thought, and has worked out its political institutions on the lines of looking to the judgment of each to bear on the common concerns of all.[213]

Of course there were many different versions of the growth of the women's suffrage movement. It is not here suggested that this Anglo-Saxon and Protestant version was by any means the only or most characteristic viewpoint. Yet Blackburn's *Record of the Women's Suffrage Movement* has remained the only major published source for the early history of this movement; it is time to rewrite its story.

[213] *Ibid.*, p. 228.

4 The nation within and without

Catherine Hall

This chapter locates the imagined nation of 1867 within a wider frame of empire. It utilises postcolonial perspectives to rethink the nation and to grasp the ways in which Britain was constituted through its colonial 'others'. My intention is not to make an argument about the determination of the terms of the Reform Act itself. Rather I suggest that a full understanding of the meaning of the nation as constituted in 1867 depends on a grasp of the imagined nation in both its political and its cultural forms. The reconstitution of the nation in 1867 was in part focused on the reconfiguration of forms of belonging that were internal to that nation – which men might now vote – but it was also focused on the constitution of the nation's 'others'. Discussions apparently peripheral to the act itself – over events in Jamaica and their meanings in Britain between 1865 and 1867, and relations between Ireland and Britain from 1865 to 1868 – give insight into the ways in which different notions of citizen and subject were constituted, notions that were not formally incorporated into the act but that framed it in such a way as to demarcate some of the different boundaries of nation and empire, citizen and subject. The boundaries that concern me here are those constructed through racial and ethnic categories. The essay aims to question existing historiographical paradigms and open up a way of thinking about the British nation and British domestic politics that focuses on the interconnections between Britain, Jamaica and Ireland and the impact such relations had on how national politics and national identities were constituted. The moment of 1867 offers an opportunity to reflect on the nation as it was framed at that point, how citizens were defined, who belonged and in what ways, who were the imagined insiders and who were the outsiders. John Saville in his study *1848* uses official records to locate British domestic politics within the triangle of revolutionary Paris, insurgent Ireland and a revitalised Chartist movement in London and the industrial north.[1] This chapter, in

[1] John Saville, *1848: The British State and the Chartist Movement* (Cambridge University Press, 1987).

a different but related mode, utilises a focus on the construction of political and cultural identities, those of the Englishman (for I am particularly interested in that hegemonic formation), 'the negro' and the Irishman, identities which were always gendered, in an attempt to explicate the construction of an imagined nation and empire with its hierarchical forms of belonging.[2]

The debates of 1866–7, which took place inside and outside Parliament, were concerned with defining the different ways of belonging to nation and empire, who were subjects and who were citizens, and what the hierarchies were within those categories.[3] There was no legal category 'citizen' until 1981 when the British Nationality Act created a number of different forms of British citizenship.[4] From 1986 citizenship would only be accorded to UK-born or -naturalised people and their UK-born or -naturalised children, and three categories of citizenship were established: British citizenship, British Dependent Territories citizenship and British Overseas citizenship.[5] Prior to the legislation of the late twentieth century all peoples of the British Empire enjoyed the status of subject, subject to the laws and rule of the state, sharing the so-called ancient liberties of the protection of the crown. In the mid-1860s the mark of citizenship was clearly seen to be the vote, the right to participate in the political community. In the debates as to who was to have that vote, configurations of property, class, race, ethnicity and gender were all in play. They provided the lines on which boundaries could be drawn up, different social groups included or excluded from the imagined community of the nation. But the debates over nation can also be seen as framed by empire, for it was impossible to think about the 'mother country' and its specificities without reference to the colonies. The colonies provided some of the benchmarks which allowed the English, and here I am referring to English as the hegemonic identity, English/British, to determine what they did not want to be and who they thought they were. Through the construction of imagined others in Australia, in Canada, in New Zealand, in the ex-colony of the United States and most significantly in 1866–7 in Jamaica and Ireland, that most particular colony which was also a part of the United Kingdom, the English achieved a temporary settlement, as to who was to belong

[2] This chapter clearly does not take a 'four nations' approach. I am aware of the limitations of not dealing with Scotland and Wales but here I am focusing on the imagined 'Englishman' who was supposed to stand for the nation.

[3] Some of these issues are discussed in the introduction, pp. 57–62.

[4] For a very helpful introduction to the literature on immigration and nationality legislation, see Robin Cohen, *Frontiers of Identity: The British and the Others* (London: Longman, 1994).

[5] Gail Lewis, 'Citizenship', in Gordon Hughes (ed.), *Imagining Welfare Futures* (London: Routledge in association with the Open University, 1998), pp. 103–50.

politically to the new nation. Other benchmarks were provided by European nations, particularly France, and by the ancient empires of the past, especially Greece and Rome. All these societies provided a way of measuring England against others, but there was a deep-rooted and widely shared set of assumptions which cut across radical, liberal and Tory that England was the greatest and most civilised nation of all time. The colonies demonstrated this, for they were possessed and civilised by the English. Europe demonstrated this, for it had not reached the heights of freedom and liberty enjoyed by the English. The lessons of History demonstrated this, for the great empires of Greece and Rome had decayed while the British went on from strength to strength. The Anglo-Saxon race was demonstrably supreme.[6] The English regularly thanked God for their prosperity and blessings, for their high place among the peoples of the earth. As Dr Miller, Birmingham's leading Anglican clergyman, put it in a typical opening prayer at a civic occasion,

> We thank Thee, we praise Thee, for the many blessings which we enjoy in this land, and for the prosperity which Thou continuest to us, notwithstanding our shortcomings and sins. The earth is Thine and the fulness thereof. It is of Thy will that England has been raised to her high place among the peoples of the earth.[7]

In this view England was the freest and most vigorous nation, the Imperial Parliament the most enlightened and most powerful assembly in the world.

The events of the year 1867, with its reform of the franchise, point attention to changes in the definition of political citizenship: who was categorised as able to participate in the election of governments. The more inclusive definition which was established at that time suggests that the political nation of Britain was increasingly being conceptualised in terms that linked those of kindred race. Substantial numbers of Irish in England and Wales were enfranchised for the first time in 1867, thus solidifying the particular colonial relationship between those who were classified as Anglo-Saxon and Celt. While all those born in Britain, and indeed in the British Empire, supposedly enjoyed the rights of the subject, the ancient liberties of the free Briton, only some subjects were granted the rights of citizen. In 1867 there were no formal distinctions between imperial subjects and British subjects. Those men who enjoyed the franchise either in Britain, the white settler colonies or those dependencies that had representative forms of government had the rights of citizens but were not legally defined as such. The absence of a legal framework, however, did

[6] For examples of this kind of thinking, see the collection of essays from liberal intellectuals in *Essays on Reform* (London, 1867).

[7] *Birmingham Daily Post*, 3 January 1865.

not prevent informal hierarchies being firmly in place and laying the ground for the explicitly differentiated treatment of the Irish and other imperial subjects in a later period. It was not until the reaction against east European Jewish immigration in the late nineteenth century that migration into Britain was first regulated with the Aliens Act of 1905.[8] In 1914 it was felt necessary to pass a British Nationality and Status of Aliens Act, designed to ensure that a British subject anywhere was a British subject everywhere. The beginnings of decolonisation in the post-war era inspired the 1948 Nationality Act, which reaffirmed the rights of subjecthood to all members of the British Empire. This was an act designed, as Kathleen Paul argues, to maintain Britain's unique position as the 'metropolitan motherland' and demonstrate to the world that the United Kingdom was still the centre of a great commonwealth of nations despite the claims to independence from some quarters.[9] This definition of all citizens of empire states as first and foremost British subjects opened the way to the arrival of large numbers of West Indian, South Asian and Irish migrants in the 1950s and 1960s, which led in turn to the Immigration Act of 1962 that differentiated on racial grounds who had the right to enter Britain.

These formal demarcations of the twentieth century were mapped, however, on to a well-established frame of hierarchical difference. The Reform Act of 1867, I suggest, looked at alongside the new Canadian settlement of the same year and the Jamaica Act of the preceding year can be read as formally differentiating black Jamaicans from white British, white Canadians or white Australians (who had been granted representative government from the early 1850s) from brown Indians (ruled directly by the crown from 1858 following the 'Mutiny', informally differentiating Anglo-Saxons from Celts. Metropolis and colonies, nation and empire, were demarcated by racially defined difference: some races, it was thought, were more advanced than others. At one moment Anglo-Saxons and Celts were discursively constructed as belonging to Britain, 'the people', sharing a special history, able to tolerate religious difference, united in their membership of the most advanced and civilised culture, with a mission to imperialise others. At the very same moment there were discordant constructions of Celt as barbaric and inferior, locked in pagan Catholicism, and of Celts as a race with a particular myth of origin and nationalist tradition, linked intimately to Fenianism. All of these elements

[8] David Feldman, 'The Importance of Being English: Jewish Immigration and the Decay of Liberal England', in Feldman and Gareth Stedman Jones (eds.), *Metropolis. London Histories and Representations Since 1800* (London: Routledge, 1989), pp. 56–84.

[9] Kathleen Paul, *Whitewashing Britain: Race and Citizenship in the Postwar Era* (Ithaca, N.Y., and London: Cornell University Press, 1997), pp. xii, 10.

coexisted in 1867, reminding us of the complexity of nation-building projects and the fragility and impermanence of any settlement. Beyond the nation yet within the empire, 'white settlers' in Australia, Canada, the Cape and New Zealand were granted forms of self-government which were rejected as totally out of the question in India or Jamaica because the majority population was not white. This racially and ethnically differentiated map of nation and empire was part of the imagined world of nineteenth-century British men and women.[10]

I will explore these propositions, but first let me sketch in a skeleton form the sequence of events across Jamaica, Ireland and Britain that culminated in the passing of the second Reform Act in July 1867.

In October 1865 a black rebellion broke out at Morant Bay in Jamaica and martial law was declared by the British governor, Edward John Eyre. By November the news of the repression had reached England and critics of Eyre were organising themselves and pressuring the government to establish an inquiry. A Royal Commission was set up which reported in April 1866 but the parliamentary debate resulted in no serious consequences for the government. Meanwhile, by March 1866 the Jamaican House of Assembly had surrendered its powers to the crown and Jamaica had become a crown colony. At the same time the Liberal government had suspended habeas corpus in Ireland on account of the serious disturbances associated with Fenianism. It was also attempting to get a Reform Bill through Parliament which would have significantly extended the franchise – but this was rejected. The defeat of the Liberal Reform Bill and the spectre of a new Tory government led to huge demonstrations, led by the Reform League. At one large demonstration in July 1866 the railings of Hyde Park were knocked down and peace was restored only through the good offices of the Reform League – a humiliation for the government. The end of 1866 and the beginnings of 1867 saw a preoccupation with political violence as the critics of Eyre, dissatisfied with government action, tried to prosecute privately both Eyre and a number of army and navy officers. The first of the Fenian 'outrages' took place in Manchester and political trials were held, and a series of large reform demonstrations were held at which political violence began to be discussed openly. By this time Disraeli had realised that parliamentary reform was unavoidable and that the key question was on what terms. He bowed to the inevitable and introduced a Tory bill which was strenuously resisted by many on his own side. In May 1867 the Reform League decided on another great demonstration in Hyde Park; the government refused permission and mobilised troops and the police.

[10] Kathleen Paul describes the 'competing communities of "Britishness"' in post-war Britain, the English, Irish, Afro-Caribbean etc.: *ibid.*, p. xii. My point is that these contemporary hierarchies have a long set of histories.

Nevertheless, the League successfully occupied the park with a crowd of 100,000–150,000, the government was seriously humiliated and the home secretary forced to resign. Later in the month, John Stuart Mill proposed an unsuccessful amendment to the government bill which deleted 'man' and inserted 'person'. In June serious riots erupted in Birmingham with Irish Catholics and extreme Protestants locked in conflict.

During this period the House of Commons was debating Fenian violence, the excesses of the army in Jamaica and the question of reform, and it was in this climate that the Reform Act for England and Wales was passed, giving the vote to substantial numbers of working men. At the end of 1867 fears over Fenianism were at their height and anti-Catholic riots erupted across the Midlands and the north in 1868. That same year Reform Bills were passed for both Scotland and Ireland and in 1870 the movement began for Home Rule in Ireland.

In 1867–8 three influential texts were published by major public figures that reflected on the new political and cultural scene. Each of those texts reminds us of the ways in which the English imagination was nationally and racially inflected. One was the trumpet blast of doom from Carlyle, the Scot who contributed so much to definitions of what it meant to be English, 'Shooting Niagara and After'. The second was Matthew Arnold's more tempered but nevertheless powerful critique of contemporary culture – *Culture and Anarchy*. The third was John Stuart Mill's controversial pamphlet *England and Ireland*, which was an uncharacteristically intemperate reflection on Fenianism and its impact.

In 'Shooting Niagara', elements which had been key to Carlyle's thought since the 1830s were brought to vitriolic fruition. His critique of democracy, his insistence on natural leadership and strong government, his preoccupation with empire and with racial difference produced a text that is remarkable for its sense of rage and vitriol, its disturbances erupting into the narrative. Carlyle had never believed in democracy; as he put it in *Chartism*: 'Surely of all "rights of men", this right of the ignorant man to be led by the wiser, to be, gently or forcibly, held in the true course by him, is the indisputablest . . . [democracy] is the summation of no-government and *laissez-faire*.'[11] For him, therefore, an extension of the franchise was a disaster. There never was, he argued, 'so hugely critical an epoch in the history of England as this we have now entered upon, with universal self-congratulation and flinging-up of caps'.[12] The cancer at the heart of this

[11] Thomas Carlyle, *Chartism* (1840), reprinted in *Selected Writings of Thomas Carlyle*, (Harmondsworth: Penguin, 1971), p. 189.

[12] Thomas Carlyle, 'Shooting Niagara: and After?' (1867), reprinted in Carlyle, *Critical and Miscellaneous Essays*, 7 vols. (London, 1899), vol. V, p. 299.

crisis was the notion of democracy, which brought with it, 'blockheadism, gullibility, bribeability, amenability to beer and balderdash'.[13] In his view it was ludicrous to talk of the equality of uneducated with educated, female with male, black with white. It was the 'Nigger-Philanthropists', as he described the critics of Eyre, the abolitionists, the supporters of the North in the American Civil War, who were the real enemy within, sapping the vital energies of Englishmen with their crazy comparisons of 'Quashee Nigger' with Socrates or Shakespeare. 'The Nigger', for Carlyle, was 'a poor blockhead with good dispositions, with affections, attachments'. It was a sign of the madness of the times for him that in the US Civil War 'half a million of excellent White Men, full of gifts and faculty, have torn and slashed one another into horrid death . . . and three million absurd Blacks, men and brothers (of a sort), are completely "emancipated"'.[14] Servantship, like wedlock, he believed, must be a condition for life for such people. Races were different: 'blacks' were not brothers, the Irish were stupid.[15] It was the collapse of the government in the face of 'Nigger-Philanthropists' and reformers of the franchise which resulted, for him, in the mad rush towards Niagara. He singled out for calumny the Jamaica Committee, for their attacks on martial law, their idea that 'any Governor, commanded soldier, or official person, putting down the frightfulest Mob-insurrection Black or White, shall do it with the rope round *his* neck, by way of encouragement to him'.[16] He was also enraged with the Lord Chief Justice, who had argued in the High Court that in his view there was a legal case that Eyre must answer (a judgement which had absolutely no effect), and with the home secretary, for his cowardly collapse in the face of the Reform League. He was disgusted with the weakness and ineffectiveness of the government: 'no Fenian taken with the reddest hand is to be meddled with'.[17] The character of the times was 'cheap and nasty', as English goods had become with the absence of proper labour. He looked for a form of aristocratic government, led by heroes, like his great heroes Cromwell and Frederick the Great, who could instil a proper authority. Such men were particularly needed to deal with the colonies: 'all ungoverned, and nine-tenths of them full of jungles, boa-constrictors, rattlesnakes, Parliamentary Eloquences and Emancipated Niggers ripening towards nothing but destruction'.[18] The hierarchy of difference was critical to Carlyle: one race must govern another, one class another, one sex another. Social order depended on the maintenance of these differences.

[13] *Ibid.*, p. 306. [14] *Ibid.*, p. 304.
[15] See, for example, the stereotype of the stupid Irishman: *ibid.*, p. 311.
[16] *Ibid.*, p. 308. [17] *Ibid.*, p. 305. [18] *Ibid.*, p. 312.

Matthew Arnold was similarly concerned with what he saw as the breakdown of good government and the turn to anarchy. His analysis was significantly different from Carlyle's in that he focused on the emptiness of wealth and industry and looked for a revival of cultural values amongst the educated rather than hoping for strong authoritarian leadership. But like Carlyle, he turned to 'race' as part of the explanation of the malaise which was at work. His critique of liberal individualism, personified for him by John Bright, the Liberal member for Birmingham who was the extra-parliamentary leader of the reform movement in its widest manifestations, a critic of Eyre and a defender of Irish rights, focused on its assumption that personal liberty was the key to English freedom and always the ultimate goal. The major right, he argued, could not be for everyone to do what they wanted:

> this and that body of men, all over the country, are beginning to assert and put in practice an Englishman's right to do what he likes; his right to march where he likes, meet where he likes, enter where he likes, hoot as he likes, threaten as he likes . . . [what can Liberals do] when the man who gives an inflammatory lecture, or breaks down the park railings, or invades a Secretary of State's office is only following an Englishman's impulse to do as he likes.[19]

His critique of individualism and of a certain kind of Englishness was linked to his perception of the philistinism of that creed: the limitations of a doctrine of personal liberty, narrow-minded Christianity and worship of machinery. Nonconformists, he believed, 'had developed one side of their humanity at the expense of all others, and have become incomplete and mutilated men in consequence'. What they needed was a new totality, an infusion of 'sweetness and light'.[20] There was a lack of 'general intelligence' in the culture, a need for a new balance.

Arnold connected this to his theory of race. Influenced particularly by Renan, the French philologist who was to develop a concept of nation in the 1870s, Arnold drew together elements of contemporary racial and social thought in his analysis of the crisis of English culture represented by 1867.[21] In his account the English race combined elements of what he defined as the great rival forces, Hebraism and Hellenism. Hebraism, the Semitic tradition, was marked by strictness of conscience and what he constructed as a masculine and muscular relation to the world, focused on doing. Hellenism, the Aryan tradition, was characterised by spontaneity of conscience and feminised, flexible thinking. Thus, as Robert Young

[19] Matthew Arnold, *Culture and Anarchy* (1867), repr. ed. J. Dover Wilson (Cambridge University Press, 1963), pp. 76–7. [20] *Ibid.*, pp. 10–11.

[21] On Renan's influence on Arnold, see Robert J. C. Young, *Colonial Desire: Hybridity in Theory, Culture and Race* (London: Routledge, 1995), esp. pp. 68–72.

argues, Arnold constructed racial difference allied to sexual difference as the basis of culture. The struggle between racial forces provided the motor of history.[22] The 'English race', in his mind, was marked by its search for moral perfection. Puritanism was the most powerful manifestation of that search for 'moral development and self-conquest'. But the nineteenth-century version of Puritanism, provincial nonconformity, represented by Bright and characterised by the search for personal assertion, endangered the nation. With heavy irony he caricatured the Englishman's conviction of his own liberties at the expense of others and argued,

> We are not in danger from Fenianism, fierce and turbulent as it may show itself: for against this our conscience is free enough to let us act resolutely and put forth our overwhelming strength the moment there is any real need for it. In the first place, it never was any part of our creed that the great right and blessedness of an Irishman, or, indeed, of anybody on earth except an Englishman, is to do as he likes; and we can have no scruple at all about abridging, if necessary, a non-Englishman's assertion of personal liberty.

The British constitution, he continued, its checks and balances, were for Englishmen. Englishmen, however rough, and Fenians simply could not be compared. The Fenian was 'desperate and dangerous, a man of a conquered race, a Papist, with centuries of ill-usage to inflame him against us, with an alien religion established in his country by us at his expense, with no admiration of our institutions, no love of our virtues'.[23]

The Hyde Park rioter, on the other hand, was a deeply familiar being, for whom the most important issue was that of wages.[24] *He* constituted the danger, alongside the extreme Protestants who encouraged fanatical religious bigotry, and the Colonel Wilsons of this world (Wilson had instructed his troops not to interfere in Hyde Park when threatened by 'roughs'). The dangers were within, not without. External threats such as Fenians could be dealt with: internal disharmony was a more serious problem. In his later writing Arnold was to focus on the need for a fusion of Celt and Saxon, to make one 'homogeneous, English-speaking whole'.[25] In 1867 he sought a balance between Hellenic and Hebraic, not constructing certain races (Indo-European and Semitic) as totally distinct but as permeable and capable of transformation. The 'barbarians' (or aristocracy), 'philistines' (middle classes) and 'populace', who made up the population, were all part of one nation, each with elements of the other. In each of these classes there were a certain number of 'aliens', led by their love of human perfection. Their desire for 'sweetness and light', for more Hellenic elements, needed to be mobilised. We now know,

[22] *Ibid.*, p. 62. [23] Arnold, *Culture and Anarchy*, pp. 56, 79–80. [24] *Ibid.*, p. 80.
[25] Arnold, *On the Study of Celtic Literature*, quoted in Young, *Colonial Desire*, p. 71.

thanks to science, he argued, 'the great and pregnant elements of difference which lie in race, and in how signal a manner they make the genius and history of an Indo-European people vary from those of a Semitic people'. The English were a nation of Indo-European stock, but 'nothing more strongly marks the essential unity of man than the affinities we can perceive . . . between members of one family of peoples and members of another'.[26] The English race had a great future to his mind, but that future required racial regeneration.

Mill penned his pamphlet *England and Ireland* in the last months of 1867 when the country was in a state of serious agitation over the 'Manchester Martyrs', the three Fenians who were finally hanged for their part in the escape of the Irish nationalist prisoners, Kelly and Deasy, from Manchester Gaol in September 1867, and the ensuing death of a prison guard. In December the widespread public sympathy for the Fenians was undermined by the explosion at Clerkenwell which killed four and injured over one hundred, in the botched attempt to secure the release of two further Fenian prisoners. Mill was still engaged at this time in his efforts to secure justice over the events in Jamaica, was representing Westminster in the House of Commons and had been involved with the debates over the franchise. It was the most publicly political period of his life. Retrospectively, in his *Autobiography*, Mill remarked that, when he wrote the pamphlet,

> there were few who did not feel that if there was still any chance of reconciling Ireland to the British connexion, it could only be by the adoption of much more thorough reforms in the territorial and social relations of the country than had yet been contemplated.[27]

The key points of the pamphlet in Mill's mind were 'to show the undesirableness, for Ireland as well as for England, of separation between the countries, and . . . a proposal for settling the land question by giving to the existing tenants a permanent tenure, at a fixed rate, to be assessed after due inquiry by the State'.[28] Fenianism, he argued, had made the English (including himself) understand that Irish grievances had not disappeared despite Catholic representation and the opening up of employment, the abolition of tithes and a rise in prosperity. Fenianism had created in Britain a line of division between those who were sympathetic to Irish aspirations and those who were not. 'Repressed by force in Ireland itself, the rebellion visits us in our own homes, scattering death among those

26 Arnold, *Culture and Anarchy*, pp. 141–2.

27 John Stuart Mill, *Autobiography* (London, 1873), repr. in *Collected Works of John Stuart Mill* [*CW*], gen. ed. J. M. Robson, 33 vols. (University of Toronto Press, 1962–91), vol. I, *Autobiography and Literary Essays*, ed. J. M. Robson and Jack Stillinger (1981), pp. 279–80.

28 *Ibid.*

who have given no provocation but that of being English-born.' English people, particularly the upper and middle classes, argued Mill, must try and understand Irish antipathy to England and the governing classes must recognise that institutions that 'they thought must suit all mankind since they suited us' might be most unsuitable for Ireland.[29] Most significantly Mill linked political changes in Britain with a greater sympathy for Irish grievances. 'The rising power in our affairs, the democracy of Great Britain, is opposed on principle, to holding any people in subjection against their will . . . The time is come', he predicted, 'when the democracy of one country will join hands with the democracy of another, rather than back their own ruling authorities in putting it down.' Such sentiments were alarming in the immediate wake of the Reform Act.[30] Mill was convinced that an attack on the tyrannical power of the landlords was essential if the Union was to be stabilised. The level of American support for the Fenians, in terms of leadership, money, skills and military discipline, made Irish disaffection dangerous and 'a people like the Irish, always ready to trust implicitly those who they think hardy in their cause', would be only too ready to take up these opportunities. The English nation, he insisted, must reflect on their rule. They had been compelled in India to shake off their 'insular prejudices' and not govern simply according to 'common English habits and notions'. It was those who understood India, he suggested, presumably referring to himself and his long experience with the East India Company, who understood Ireland best. There were many points of comparison to his mind between the 'Hindoo' and Irish characters and between the agricultural economies of the two societies. India, he believed, was governed at that time with a full 'recognition of its differences from England'. What had been done for India must be done for Ireland.[31] The unmentioned difference was that Fenianism had not yet delivered a full-scale 'Mutiny', as had happened in India in 1857.

Mill was resolutely against any separation between England and Ireland, convinced that this was in the interests of neither country. Celt and Saxon, he was convinced, were 'the two races, perhaps the most fitted of any two in the world to be the completing counterpart of one another'.[32] Liberal opinion had been seriously disturbed by Fenianism. Some forms of nationalism were, after all, the great passion of many liberals in the middle of the nineteenth century. It was not possible, Mill believed, to hold Ireland by military force. That would make British

[29] John Stuart Mill, *England and Ireland* (London, 1868), repr. in *CW*, vol. VI, *Essays on England, Ireland and the Empire*, ed. J. M. Robson (1982), pp. 508–11.

[30] *Ibid.*, pp. 520–1. [31] *Ibid.*, pp. 518–19.

[32] J. S. Mill, *Considerations on Representative Government* (London, 1861), repr. in *CW*, vol. XIX, *Essays on Politics and Society*, ed. J. M. Robson (1977), p. 551.

support for Poles, Hungarians and Italians in their struggles for national independence quite nonsensical.[33] Mill joined in the public outcry against the treatment of Fenian prisoners on the grounds that their action stemmed from their belief in the misgovernment of their country: they were men who were 'certainly not likely to be guilty of ordinary crime and vice . . . rather . . . capable of heroic actions and lofty virtue'.[34] But idealistic nationalism did not make their case right. The Irish as a race, Mill thought, had not yet demonstrated, as had the Hungarians, 'a measure of the qualities which fit a people for self-government'. Small nations, he thought, needed their nationalist aspirations to be reconciled with absorption into their larger neighbours who must govern them justly. The question was raised as to why Ireland could not have self-government like Canada. Mill argued that Ireland's position, with representation in the Imperial Parliament, was superior to that of Canada, 'a dependency with a provincial government, allowed to make its own laws and impose its taxes, but subject to the veto of the mother-country, and not consulted at all about alliances or wars, in which nevertheless it is compelled to join'.[35]

As E. D. Steele notes, Mill was convinced of England's special role in the progress of humanity, 'the Power' as he put it in *Considerations on Representative Government*, 'which of all in existence best understands liberty and . . . has attained to more of conscience and moral principle in its dealings with foreigners than any other great nation seems to conceive as possible or recognise as desirable'.[36] Such assumptions allowed him to place England at the apex of a hierarchy of nations: the wealthiest, the freest, the most civilised, the most powerful, the most able to govern others. From this perspective 'races' were judged as more or less worthy of representative government, more or less able to become nations. Governmental institutions needed to be radically different according to the 'stage of advancement' of the society. Those who had only recently come under 'civilised influences' required guidance and 'leading strings' in government. Thus India and Jamaica, for example, were clearly not ready in Mill's view for self-government. There were plenty of circumstances in which peoples were 'unfit for liberty'. In these instances government would require to be in 'a considerable degree despotic'.[37] Ireland was a very special case. Like India, but not like India. For despite

[33] Mill, *England and Ireland*, p. 520.

[34] Cited in E. D. Steele, 'J. S. Mill and the Irish Question: Reform and the Integrity of the Empire 1865–1870', *Historical Journal* 12 (1970), repr. in Alan O'Day (ed.), *Reactions to Irish Nationalism 1865–1914* (London: Hambledon Press, 1987), p. 210. This article has greatly helped me to think about Mill's writing on Ireland.

[35] Mill, *England and Ireland*, pp. 524–6.

[36] Steele, 'J. S. Mill and the Irish Question'; Mill, *Considerations*, p. 565.

[37] Mill, *Considerations*, p. 377.

the similar characteristics of 'Hindoo' and Irish in Mill's mind, the Irish were white and lived just across the water from England. Furthermore, many of them now lived in England and Scotland and in the wake of the Reform Act could vote. The Irish were backward yet had to be incorporated in the Union.

Mill's pamphlet was received with shock and horror for its attack on property rights. His conversion to peasant proprietorship, security of tenure and fair rents were seen as an appalling departure from classical political economy.[38] Mill himself soon retreated from his own description of the Irish land system as tyrannical.[39] But his interest in the special relationship between Irish and English, Celt and Anglo-Saxon, was redolent of the ways in which race and nation were reflected upon and linked in his mind.

Carlyle, Arnold and Mill, in their very different ways, were reflecting on the connections between 'race' and nation, connections that had become very significant by the mid-1860s. All focused on dangers within (for Ireland was constructed as necessarily 'within' in Mill's mind), and were not seriously troubled by external threats, their confidence in British strength holding firm. While Carlyle vented his spleen on 'Nigger-Philanthropists', in other words those who wrongly constituted themselves as brothers to lesser races, Arnold constructed the danger in terms of racial imbalance. Both saw race as critical to nation. Mill, meanwhile, was concerned with the dangers attached to Irish nationalism and regarded thoroughgoing reform of British rule in Ireland as necessary. Celts and Anglo-Saxons must cohere. He did not want Ireland to become another India, as it had been before the 'Mutiny', or indeed another Jamaica.

The turn to race as an explanatory category was part of the development of scientific and philosophical thought in this period. As Nancy Stepan argues, from the end of the eighteenth century in Britain, '"race" increasingly became a primary form of self and group identification'.[40] Scientific orthodoxy in Britain in 1800 was convinced that the different races had originated from one family. By the 1840s these arguments were being undermined and the emphasis moved to the fundamental heterogeneity of mankind, the natural differences between men, fixed by immutable biological laws. Alongside this went the notion that races

38 For a discussion of Mill on the Irish question, see Thomas C. Holt, *The Problem of Freedom: Race, Labor and Politics in Jamaica and Britain, 1823–1938* (Baltimore: Johns Hopkins University Press, 1992), pp. 323–29.

39 Steele, 'J. S. Mill and the Irish Question', p. 233.

40 Nancy Stepan, *The Idea of Race in Science: Great Britain 1800–1960* (Basingstoke: Macmillan, 1982), p. xii.

formed a hierarchy, with Europeans at the top and negroes at the bottom. Much attention was given to the ways in which these differences could be measured by a focus on the skull and the brain, for example. Symptomatic of this new approach to 'race' and the ways in which it was popularised was the work of Robert Knox. Knox, a Scot who became convinced of the superiority of the Saxon race, started his professional life as an anatomist. In the 1840s he turned to more general theories of racial science and visited the great industrial centres of England in the 1840s, giving lectures which later became *The Races of Men*. He noted that he was reported in the provincial press but received no national attention. 'The world was so *national* and *race* had been so utterly forgotten . . . that I had the whole question to myself.' By 1850, however, when the book was published, the revolutions of 1848, Knox believed, had clarified to the world at large how race had something to do with the history of nations.[41] For him it was clear that races were suited to their own regions and that race was deeper than nationality: it was the Saxons who would inevitably dominate the future of the British Isles. 'History', as Stepan puts it, 'was a matter of each race attempting to dominate its own homeland and construct its own government, laws and civilisation according to its distinct, inner nature.'[42] 'Race' and nation, in other words, were inextricably connected.

Jamaica

Jamaica provided a crucial testing ground for ideas about race and nation from the late eighteenth century. The largest and wealthiest of the British Caribbean islands, Jamaica dominated debates in Britain about West Indian slavery and its abolition. The anti-slavery movement emerged as a powerful force in Britain in the 1780s, was fairly quiescent in the late 1790s as a result of the Napoleonic Wars and the dangerous associations between radicalism and emancipation, revived in the 1800s and won the abolition of the slave trade in 1806.[43] By the 1820s it was clear that slavery as an institution was not dying away and a new campaign began for abolition. The immensely popular campaigns for the abolition of slavery in British colonies and subsequently for the abolition of apprenticeship (the system introduced to provide forced labour for the planters for a fixed

41 Robert Knox, *The Races of Men: A Philosophical Inquiry into the Influence of Race over the Destiny of Nations* (2nd edn, London, 1852), p. 20.

42 Stepan, *Idea of Race in Science*, p. 43.

43 There is a vast literature on anti-slavery. Two key texts are David Brion Davis, *The Problem of Slavery in the Age of Revolution 1770–1832* (London: Cornell University Press, 1975); and Robin Blackburn, *The Overthrow of Colonial Slavery 1776–1848* (London: Verso, 1988).

Plate 9 'The town of Morant, Morant Bay, Jamaica'. *Illustrated London News*, 25 November 1865 (University of London Library).

term) were marked by a vision of the universal family of man, and of different races as the branches of that linked family. In the vision of the abolitionists, the nation was stained by the national sin of slavery; abolition would make possible the expiation of that crime. The act that emancipated slaves in British colonies was represented by its supporters as a triumph for British justice and mercy. Britain led the world as a liberty-loving nation, a nation which loved liberty so much that it was prepared to grant it to others who were much less privileged. Britain was characterised by might and mercy, a capacity for generosity to those who were less fortunate. 'Pity for Poor Africans', exhorted the poet Cowper, and his words were circulated widely, shaping the imagination of a generation alongside the image of the poor slave kneeling and asking whether he/she were indeed a man and a brother, a woman and a sister.[44] Black people were the victims of white greed, who could be rescued from the barbarism of slavery, worse even than the barbarism of Africa since it had been made by white people, people who by nature knew better. These representations of 'negroes', the polite, abolitionist term for black people, as passive victims asking for help, came to dominate debates on race in the 1830s

[44] William Cowper, *The Poetical Works of William Cowper* (London, 1872), p. 408.

Plate 10 'Coaling a Royal Mail steam-packet at Kingston, Jamaica'. *Illustrated London News*, 25 November 1865 (University of London Library).

and early 1840s.[45] It characterised official thinking as well as the views of the abolitionist public.

By the mid-1840s the mood was shifting: the abortive expedition to the Niger organised by Buxton in the hopes of promoting commerce, Christianity and civilisation, the arguments amongst the abolitionists as to the rights and wrongs of the protection of West Indian sugar, and the gradual realisation that the abolitionist dream of a prosperous, productive West Indies, peopled with free labour, with disciplined industrious workers and domesticated wives, was not going to happen in the way that had been imagined all conspired to reduce enthusiasm for and interest in the emancipated negro.[46] It was in this context that Carlyle broke the dis-

[45] For a much longer version of these arguments, see Catherine Hall, *Civilizing Subjects: Race and Empire in the English Imagination 1830–1867* (Cambridge: Polity Press, forthcoming), esp. pt II.

[46] Howard Temperley, *British Antislavery 1833–1870* (London: Longman, 1972), and his *White Dreams, Black Africa: The Antislavery Expedition to the River Niger 1841–1842* (New Haven and London: Yale University Press, 1991); Douglas Lorimer, *Colour, Class and the Victorians: English Attitudes to the Negro in the Mid-Nineteenth Century* (Leicester University Press, 1978); Catherine Hall, 'White Visions, Black Lives: The Free Villages of Jamaica', *History Workshop Journal* 36 (1993), 100–32.

Plate 11 'The Jamaica Question'. *Punch*, 23 December 1865. The planter's ironic question here is counterposed to the racist description of the slouching black worker.

cursive frame established by abolitionism and published his 'Occasional Discourse on the Negro Question', an essay which decisively shifted the regime of benign, if profoundly unequal, abolitionist representation and displaced pity with its close relation, contempt. Planter and abolitionist discourse, as Emilia da Costa has noted, always shared some characteristics. Both believed in industry and self-discipline, in education, progress and civilisation. Both were confident of the power of ideas to change the world, had deep respect for human reason and claimed to defend the interests of empire. Both shared a commitment to property rights and profit, and a fear of the people, whether black or white. Those similarities were buried under a powerful rhetoric on both sides. But as da Costa argues, it was the shared ground that made the hostilities and resentments so deep.[47] Planters and abolitionists hated each other and Carlyle's contempt for 'Nigger-Philanthropists' was more bitter than his contempt for 'niggers'. But neither planter nor abolitionist discourse was predicated on equality. Abolitionism envisioned negroes as potentially the same as white people, that they could become such if free and with the right support. There was no recognition of any black identity having a value of its own, no recognition of diversity as a positive value, in other words.[48] Planter discourse, which Carlyle rearticulated in 1849 from the heart of the metropolis, insisted on immutable racial difference and constructed that difference hierarchically: black men must always be ruled by white.

In 1843 Carlyle had published *Past and Present*, his essay on the condition of England, in which he responded to the social and political crises of the 1840s by arguing for a form of white kinship. Describing the horrors of poverty and the workhouse, a society in which parents were driven to poison their own children, where starvation ruled in a land of riches and plenty, he dreamt, as Cora Kaplan has argued, of an England where racial unity could be the 'sign though which the divided social body could be repaired'.[49] Even the 'depraved', 'savage' and 'degraded' Irish must be brought into the new family of England, for they were human mothers and fathers, of white skin and professing the Christian religion, and as such belonged to the island story.[50]

For Carlyle that dream of a new England was combined with a dream of empire. The English, Saxon inheritors of Teutonic strength and enter-

[47] Emilia Viotti da Costa, *Crowns of Glory, Tears of Blood: The Demerara Slave Rebellion of 1823* (Oxford University Press, 1994), p. 34.

[48] Thanks to Gail Lewis for drawing my attention to the distinction that can be made between 'difference', used in the hierarchical sense, and 'diversity', meaning an acceptance of or indeed attachment of value to differences between peoples.

[49] Cora Kaplan, 'White Skin: Ethnology, Nationalism and Feminism in the 1840s', unpublished paper (1993).

[50] Thomas Carlyle, *Past and Present* (1843; London: J. M. Dent, 1960), p. 2.

prise, must follow in the footsteps of their heroic forefathers, occupy the 'uninhabited' world and spread their racial seed.[51] Such a vision was premised upon assumptions of racial superiority profoundly at odds with abolitionist thinking. In the 1830s and early 1840s Carlyle had not come out publicly against the abolitionists, though he did not hide his prejudices in his private circle.[52] By 1849, however, after a visit to Ireland, which deeply disturbed him since it confronted him with what he interpreted as white degeneration and degradation, Carlyle was ready to publish his 'Occasional Discourse on the Negro Question'.[53] It argued that the emancipated were idle, that their incapacity to labour demonstrated that they were incapable of civilisation: they were born to be servants and slaves. They should be made to grow goods for the rest of the world, by the use of the whip if necessary. For Carlyle the West Indies had been purchased with British blood: it was not there for black people to lie indolently under pumpkin plants waiting for the fruits of the earth to disgorge themselves into their animal-like mouths.[54]

Carlyle was thinking across the boundaries of conservatism and radicalism, seeking to rebuild an organic community around new forms of racial purity. The weight which he carried as a cultural critic ensured him an audience, even when publishing anonymously. But more significant was the way in which he had read 'the signs of the times', put his finger on the national pulse and discerned a shift in mood which he articulated, in the process setting the agenda for debates on the West Indies in Britain in the 1850s and 1860s. It was not that everyone agreed with Carlyle – far from it – but even those most sympathetic to the emancipated soon felt obliged to engage with his arguments and to disprove his views. Mill published an immediate refutation but the damage had been done.[55] The assumption that black men and women were part of the same universal family as white people, an assumption that many did not share but few would openly debate in the high moment of abolitionism, no longer held a position of hegemonic power.

[51] On the central importance of Anglo-Saxonism to English racial thinking, see Reginald Horsman, *Race and Manifest Destiny: The Origins of American Radical Anglo-Saxonism* (Cambridge, Mass.: Harvard University Press, 1981).

[52] See, for example, Lucretia Mott, *Lucretia Mott's Diary of Her Visit to Great Britain to Attend the World's Anti-Slavery Convention of 1840*, ed. F. B. Tolles (London: Friends Historical Society, 1952), p. 54.

[53] On Carlyle's inner turmoil in this period, see Norma Clarke, 'Deep Glooms and Bottomless Dubitations', *History Workshop Journal* 45 (1998), 278–82.

[54] Thomas Carlyle, 'Occasional Discourse on the Negro Question', *Fraser's Magazine* 40 (December 1849), 670–8.

[55] Mill, 'The Negro Question', *Fraser's Magazine* 41 (January 1850), 25–31, repr. in *CW*, vol. XXI, *Essays on Equality, Law and Education*, ed. Stefan Collini (1984), pp. 85–96. This was published anonymously.

That shift was apparent in official thinking as well as in the field of cultural representation. On the eve of the abolition of apprenticeship in 1838 the assumption at the Colonial Office was that freed apprentices would enjoy the same rights as other subjects of the British crown: they would have the same access to the law and the same voting rights. As Lord Glenelg put it, 'the apprenticeship of the emancipated slaves is to be immediately succeeded by personal freedom, in that full and unlimited sense of the term in which it is used in reference to the other subjects of the British crown'.[56] As Thomas Holt argues, however, that doctrine had been effectively abandoned by the 1850s and the political process in Jamaica had come to be viewed in racial terms, that black men were inevitably politically immature.[57] Carlyle's friend Henry Taylor, who worked at the Colonial Office, was one of the architects of this shift. As early as 1839, faced with a constitutional crisis over Jamaica, Taylor had argued that the island should become a crown colony. Exasperated with the antics of the planters on the one hand, and fearful of the black majority that would emerge in due course on the other, Taylor judged that direct rule from the Colonial Office would be preferable to either.[58] Such thinking came to dominate official discourse. The emancipated did not behave with the docility that had been expected and black and 'coloured' (the contemporary term for mixed-race) men had become increasingly present in Jamaican politics from the 1840s, challenging white hegemony. It was all too apparent that the white population was in decline and the black population an ever larger majority: 'personal freedom' in the 'unlimited sense' would inevitably mean black rule. The Colonial Office, as Holt demonstrates, endeavoured between 1849 and 1865 to maintain forms of democratic practice whilst denying its substance. In the process, 'racism became an essential solvent for dissolving the otherwise blatant contradictions between liberal democratic ideology and colonial practice'.[59] Fear of a black majority stalked debates over Jamaican politics, and solutions to the ever-present tensions between planters and the 'mother country' over control of the island were increasingly resolved at the expense of black people. While in the 1830s the Colonial Office had been centrally concerned with protecting the rights of apprentices and freed slaves, by the late 1850s the limited black and coloured representation in the House of Assembly had been significantly reduced.

This shift contrasted sharply with developments in the so-called white settler colonies, where (with the exception of South Africa) the decima-

[56] Quoted in Holt, *Problem of Freedom*, p. 179. [57] *Ibid.*, p. 182.

[58] C. V. Gocking, 'Early Constitutional History of Jamaica (with Special Reference to the Period 1838–1866)', *Caribbean Quarterly* 6 (1960), 114–33.

[59] Holt, *Problem of Freedom*, p. 214.

tion of the indigenous populations seemed to preclude the possibility of black majorities. By 1850 key British policy-makers had begun to make distinctions between the future of what were being seen as black and white colonies. A colony's fitness for self-government was crucially connected with its demographic make-up and with the character of the white settlers. In the tropics, it was thought, they were only 'temporary sojourners', whereas in Canada, Australia and New Zealand they had gone to stay.[60] As Sir James Stephen, humanitarian, abolitionist and key figure in the Colonial Office for many years, put it in a private letter after his retirement:

> England ought never to give up a single colony: the course taken in Canada was the only right course. It was that of cheerfully relaxing, one after another, the bonds of authority, as soon as the colony itself clearly desired that relaxation . . . so substituting a federal for a colonial relation – no national pride wounded, or national greatness diminished, or national duty abandoned. It remains for the Canadians to cut to the last cable which anchors them to us. But it is for them, not for us, to take that step and to assume the consequent responsibility. The same process is in progress in the Australian colonies. The rest are unfit for it – detached islands with heterogeneous populations – wretched burdens which in an evil hour we assumed and have no right to lay down again.[61]

Stephen had spent his early years in the West Indies and, in the period after emancipation, he supported the granting of political freedoms to black people and insisted that personal freedom was only a part of the settlement.[62] Yet he came to make the conventional distinction between a colony, a new growth from the mother country with Britons who settled and created the seeds of a new nation, and a dependency, which it could never be expected would be self-governing. The sugar colonies were dependencies. Those dependencies were not an asset; rather they were a burden, a responsibility which the more civilised British had to endure in the interests of those less privileged than themselves. Dependencies were not nations. The twist with Jamaica was that it had had a form of representative government with its own House of Assembly since 1662. That House of Assembly had been totally dominated by the planters until the 1840s, but a limited property franchise and the expectation of an expansion in voting rights meant the spectre of black majority rule. Eventually this was to provoke the planters to abolish their own form of representative government and turn to direct rule from London.

[60] The phrase is Colonial Official James Stephen's, quoted *ibid.*, p. 235.

[61] Quoted in Kenneth N. Bell and W. P. Morrell, *Select Documents on British Colonial Policy 1830–1860* (Oxford: Clarendon Press, 1928), p. xxiv.

[62] Paul Knaplund, *James Stephen and the British Colonial System 1813–1847* (Madison: University of Wisconsin Press, 1953), p. 120.

In 1837 there was a crisis in Canada over French Canada's demand for independence from Britain. Lord Durham was sent to sort it out and his report, while not immediately adopted, provided the model for the forms of 'responsible government' that were subsequently established in the white settler colonies. The principle of this 'responsible government' was that the governor should act solely on the advice of a Cabinet which was supported by a majority of an elected legislature. Durham also believed that ethnic differences in Lower Canada, the differences between the French and the British, could be solved through Anglicisation of the French. In the late 1830s the tensions between French agriculturists and British commercial interests in Canada were interpreted in *racial* terms, the British became Anglo-Saxons, locked in ancient hostilities with the French, but inter-European differences came to be subsumed as the black/white dichotomy was sharpened and intensified. At the end of the 1840s it was proposed that the Jamaican constitution should be remodelled in the same way as the Canadian, but the Colonial Office argued that this would be quite inappropriate since Canada was 'in a totally different state from Jamaica as to political elements'.[63] What was meant by this was that Canada would grow more British: Jamaica, on the contrary, would grow more black.

'The friends of the negro', as the anti-slavery enthusiasts called themselves, kept a watchful eye on Jamaica after emancipation and tried to protect the interests of the black peasantry against both the planters and the Colonial Office. But they themselves lost confidence in their vision of an emancipated peasantry, industrious, familial and Christian, as the evidence mounted of economic decline on the island and of what missionaries regarded as 'backsliding', which included the decline of marriage and the re-emergence of 'superstitions'. While totally refuting Carlyle's account of the island, they had to battle constantly against the agenda he had set. Furthermore, the change in climate in Britain associated with the rise of racial science – accentuated by the reaction to the 'Indian Mutiny' in 1857 and the hysteria over the events at Cawnpore and elsewhere, and the debate over the American Civil War, which saw Britain split between support for the North and the South with more open support of a pro-slavery rhetoric and practice – all contributed to a sense of disillusion and disappointment over the 'great experiment' of emancipation.[64]

This was the mood when news of the rebellion at Morant Bay arrived in

[63] Quoted in Holt, *Problem of Freedom*, p. 243.

[64] On the shift in the atmosphere in this period, see Lorimer, *Colour, Class and the Victorians*; Temperley, *British Antislavery*; Christine Bolt, *Victorian Attitudes to Race* (London: Routledge and Kegan Paul, 1971).

Britain in November 1865.[65] In October crowds had gathered outside the courthouse in Morant Bay, a small town on the east coast of the island, to protest about a disputed fine. The protest had turned to violence and a number of people were killed, both by the rioters and by the volunteers. Governor Eyre, fearful of a general rising, proclaimed martial law and sent in the troops. In the subsequent reprisals 439 black and coloured people were killed, 600 men and women were flogged and over 1,000 huts (as they were described at the time) and houses were burnt. First accounts came from the press, then Governor Eyre's reports arrived, which dwelt on the horrors of the actions of the rebels. 'The blacks have risen', as Eyre put it.[66] A potentially catastrophic rebellion had broken out on an island with a population of 350,000 black people, but only 13,000 white people. The fear was that all white people would be massacred and it was this which justified the rapid reprisals. The events in Jamaica were viewed through the lens of the Haitian rebellion of the 1790s, when all white people had been driven from the island, and the 'Indian Mutiny' which had transfixed the British in 1857. Morant Bay, in Eyre's fevered imagination, would be another Cawnpore.[67]

This version of events, planter discourse rearticulated, was soon challenged by the 'friends of the negro' on the island, mainly missionaries, who speedily provided a counter-narrative. Their focus was on the small scale of the local riots that had erupted and the brutality of the response from the British army, the excesses of martial law. The regime of representation associated with abolitionism, of meek negroes waiting for guidance from white people, was reworked. Negroes were the victims, the excesses of particular officers and of the Maroons (the descendants of escaped slaves from the Spanish period who had lived in freedom in the interior and struck deals with the British) the source of the problem. The anti-slavery lobby refuted any notion of black leadership or agency, denied any conspiracy against white people and emphasised the long history of injustice on the island. Their martyr was George William Gordon, illegitimate son of a slaveholder and a slave, politician and elected member of the House of Assembly, married to a white woman, who had been the victim of Eyre's misuse of the powers of martial law.

[65] On Morant Bay and its aftermath, see Bernard Semmel, *The Governor Eyre Controversy* (London: MacGibbon and Kee, 1962); Lorimer, *Colour, Class and the Victorians*; Gad Heuman, *'The Killing Time': The Morant Bay Rebellion in Jamaica* (Basingstoke: Macmillan, 1994); Holt, *Problem of Freedom*.

[66] Parliamentary Papers [PP], 1866, vol. LI, *Papers Relating to the Disturbances in Jamaica*, pt I, no. 251, Eyre to Caldwell, p. 152.

[67] On Eyre, see Catherine Hall, 'Imperial Man: Edward John Eyre in Australasia and the West Indies, 1833–1866', in Bill Schwarz (ed.), *The Expansion of England: Race, Ethnicity and Cultural History* (London: Routledge, 1996), pp. 130–70.

Their central concern, and that of the Jamaica Committee (which was set up to take up the issues around Morant Bay), was that British subjects must be protected by the law wherever they were and that the 'military massacres' that had taken place were a stain on Britain's reputation for justice and humanity. 'We are tempted to inquire', as the British and Foreign Anti-Slavery Society put it, 'on which side are the bloodthirstiness and savagery so recklessly ascribed to the long-suffering and badly governed negro population of Jamaica.'[68] Questions were asked in Parliament, meetings organised, letters sent to the press, deputations despatched to the secretary of state for the colonies, the stalwarts of the anti-slavery movement mobilised support across the country and the Jamaica Committee orchestrated the protests, produced information and put pressure on the government. The Liberal government responded by establishing a Royal Commission to investigate what had happened.

The debate in England as to the rights and wrongs of what had happened in Jamaica continued for well over two years.[69] The Jamaica Committee was led in the House of Commons by Thomas Hughes, the author of *Tom Brown's Schooldays*, Charles Buxton, long-established anti-slavery activist, and John Stuart Mill, who had been elected as Liberal MP for Westminster in 1865. By April 1866 the findings of the Royal Commission were made public. They declared that there had been a genuine danger and that Eyre had been right to react vigorously. They also argued, however, that martial law had been maintained in Jamaica for too long and that the punishment meted out had been excessive and barbarous, the burning of houses wanton and cruel.[70] The Liberal government felt that this criticism was enough and would have been happy to let the matter drop. Soon after the appearance of the Royal Commission Prime Minister Russell resigned when the House of Lords rejected his Reform Bill. With the Tories in power, led by Lord Derby, the radical critics of Eyre were much less worried about embarrassing the government. Disappointed by the failure to condemn Eyre and take action against him and other key military figures who had been involved in the suppression, they prepared to press the issue of the prosecution of individuals responsible. Failing government action, Mill and the Jamaica Committee were prepared to proceed with a private prosecution.[71]

[68] *Anti-Slavery Reporter*, 1 December 1865. This journal gives detailed reports of the British reaction to Morant Bay.

[69] For a longer discussion of this, see Catherine Hall, 'Competing Masculinities: Thomas Carlyle, John Stuart Mill and the Case of Governor Eyre', in her *White, Male and Middle Class: Explorations in Feminism and History* (Cambridge: Polity Press, 1992), pp. 255–95.

[70] PP, 1866 [3683] XXX, *Report of the Jamaica Royal Commission (1866)*, Part I, Report.

[71] Jamaica Committee, *Jamaica Committee Papers*, 6 vols. (London, 1866–7), vols. I–III.

The increasingly militant activity of the Jamaica Committee provoked a backlash and a growing public sympathy for Eyre. This sympathy for the wronged British governor, as he was seen, linked into the growing fears of working-class activity on the issue of reform and generalised fears about the Irish.[72] The Jamaica Committee was having to rely heavily on radicals and on working-class support. Eyre was burnt in effigy at Clerkenwell Green, for example, at a reform demonstration in September 1866.[73] The dangers of democracy seemed all too imminent and anxieties about potential anarchy at home suffused the conservative discourses on the heroic Eyre who had saved the beleaguered white people. In this context a number of prominent public figures, led by Thomas Carlyle, organised a pro-Eyre defence group and a public debate was conducted over the events in Jamaica. For the Jamaica Committee the two central questions were those of the rule of law and of England's relation to its foreign dependencies. Martial law had been misused in Jamaica, particularly in the scandalous proceedings of the court that ordered the hanging of Gordon. It was not only the subject-races of the empire that were threatened by this but freeborn Englishmen themselves. As Mill put it in his *Autobiography*,

> there was much more at stake than only justice to the Negroes, imperative as was that consideration. The question was whether the British dependencies, and eventually, perhaps Great Britain itself, were to be under the government of law, or of military licence.[74]

The rule of law must reach across the empire and ensure formal equality before its majesty. This was not, however, to suggest that subjects were the same as citizens, that negroes or Indians should have the same political rights as Englishmen.

For Carlyle and the supporters of Eyre it was absurd to compare a negro insurrection with anything that might happen in England. Negroes were uncivilised, excitable, superstitious: Eyre was a hero for effectively suppressing what might have been a most dangerous rebellion. For Carlyle, Eyre had shown 'some of the very highest qualities that ever in a man . . . have been considered meritorious'.[75] He had sustained natural law against the lawlessness of the rebels. 'The English nation', he trumpeted, 'never loved anarchy; nor was wont to spend its sympathy on miserable mad seditions, especially of this inhuman and half-brutish type; but always loved order, and the prompt suppression of sedition.' 'Niggers'

[72] Semmel, *Governor Eyre*, focuses on the connections between class issues and the Jamaica debate. [73] *Ibid.*, p. 97. [74] Mill, *Autobiography*, p. 281.

[75] Quoted in Sidney S. Olivier, *The Myth of Governor Eyre* (London: Leonard and Virginia Woolf, 1933), pp. 336–8.

were a lower order for Carlyle. 'If Eyre had shot the whole Nigger population and flung them into the sea', he wrote, 'would it probably have been much harm to them, not to speak of us.'[76] It is not possible to estimate how many in Britain shared this view. What can be said is that, while public opinion was on the side of the critics of Eyre in the first months of 1866, a backlash had formed after the publication of the Royal Commission and the decision of the Jamaica Committee to try and prosecute Eyre. 'It was clear', wrote Mill retrospectively, 'that to bring English functionaries to the bar of a criminal court for abuses of power committed against negroes and mulattoes was not a popular proceeding with the English middle classes.'[77] Similarly *The Spectator*, in an article in June 1868 analysing why the middle classes had supported Eyre, noted that they were 'positively enraged at the demand of negroes for equal consideration with Irishmen, Scotchmen and Englishmen'.[78] This was an ironic judgement given the meaning of Irishness at that moment.

Ireland

Jamaica provided one site for an experiment over the relation between 'race' and forms of political representation which framed the debates of 1866–7. But black people lived in colonies far away and at this time did not constitute a significant population 'at home'.[79] The Irish, however, were a presence in both England and Scotland and that presence was crucial to the rethinking of 'race' and nation in the middle of the nineteenth century. Britain was not a homogeneous society in the middle of the nineteenth century and the most visible outsiders in England were the Irish. The constitution of the Irish as 'a race apart', a process which reached a crisis point in the mid-1860s in the context of Fenian troubles, was central to the debate as to what Englishness/Britishness was, who were its 'others', who deserved the privilege of citizenship and what were the acceptable forms of political masculinity. The 1830s and 1840s were decades dominated by questions of class antagonism at home, and questions of race were primarily articulated through the universalism of abolitionist rhetoric, a particular form of racial thinking. There were other racial discourses, as, for example, the critique of 'white slavery' by radi-

[76] Carlyle quoted in William F. Finlason, *The History of the Jamaica Case: Being an Account Founded upon Official Documents of the Rebellion of the Negroes in Jamaica* (London, 1869), p. 369; Jane Welsh Carlyle, *Letters and Memorials of Jane Welsh Carlyle*, ed. James Anthony Froude (London, 1883), p. 381. [77] Mill, *Autobiography*, p. 282.

[78] Quoted in Semmel, *Governor Eyre*, p. 171.

[79] The significant black population of eighteenth-century London had substantially disappeared by the middle of the nineteenth century; see James Walvin, *Black and White: The Negro and English Society 1555–1945* (London: Allen Lane, 1973), p. 189.

Plate 12 'Attack on the prison van at Manchester, and rescue of the Fenian leaders'. *Illustrated London News*, 28 September 1867 (University of London Library)

cals who insisted on the hypocrisy of the abolitionists and turned attention to the condition of workers at home, with a rhetoric that was always potentially racist.[80] There was no war with France, Britain's traditional enemy, to mobilise the nation around issues of patriotism, and it was a period of relative peace for Britain in the wider world.[81] The language of class provided a frame with which to make sense of the divisions *within*, the divisions associated with poverty, disease and unemployment. As attention focused on the new urban centres and on Chartism, class, signifying the differences between capital and labour, masters and men, aristocrats, gentry and others, seemed to capture the crucial differences. In 1844 Engels wanted to characterise the new epoch that Manchester, and England, symbolised for him. He explained what he saw as the key changes in class relations, the emergence of the proletariat and of the bourgeoisie as two great classes facing each other in antagonistic

[80] Patricia Hollis, 'Anti-Slavery and British Working-Class Radicalism in the Years of Reform', in Christine Bolt and Seymour Drescher (eds.), *Anti-Slavery, Religion and Reform: Essays in Memory of Roger Anstey* (Folkestone: Dawson, 1980), pp. 294–315.

[81] Linda Colley, *Britons: Forging the Nation 1707–1837* (New Haven and London: Yale University Press, 1992); C. A. Bayly, *Imperial Meridian: The British Empire and the World, 1780–1830* (London: Longman, 1989).

Plate 13 'Fenian prisoners at Manchester conveyed through Mosley Street on their way to the Bellevue Prison'. *Illustrated London News*, 28 September 1867 (University of London Library).

relations, as a result of technological change. It was the language of class which provided one way of articulating the changes in social relations associated with the development of industrial capitalism. In the analysis of Marx and Engels it also provided a route for change: these fundamental antagonisms would be dramatically resolved.[82] Utilised in somewhat different ways by political economists, by analysts and cultural critics, by working-class radicals in the Chartist movement, it provided a way of describing what was new and different about English society in the early nineteenth century. In focusing the middle-class mind on the dangers associated with these divisions, as in the debate over 'the Condition of England', class had threatening connotations, ones which could be deflected by attention to other 'enemies within'.

The focus on class did not mean that questions of ethnicity disappeared, and the Irish question was never absent from the mid-1820s. The peculiar status of Ireland in relation to Britain was marked by the long history of colonialism and brutality. Ireland was part of the United Kingdom once the Act of Union had been passed in 1800, represented by

[82] Frederick Engels, 'The Condition of the Working Class in England', in K. Marx and F. Engels, *On Britain* (2nd edn, Moscow: Foreign Languages Publishing House, 1962), pp. 6–338.

Plate 14 'The Fenian Guy Fawkes'. *Punch*, 28 December 1867. Here the Irishman, characterised by stereotypical features and surrounded by the children of 'excessive breeding', is posed as a threat to parliamentary government but also as likely to blow himself up.

100 MPs in the House of Commons and with its landowners constituting a significant force in the House of Lords. Yet at the same time it was a colony, not part of Britain, its Catholic population fiercely hostile to English occupation, English control of land, English Protestantism and English brutality. Ireland, as Mary Hickman argues, 'was a constituent part of the United Kingdom but continued to be ruled as a colony', its people constructed as both inferior and alien, the fact that both peoples were subjects of the same monarch carrying no notion of common rights or shared national identity.[83] Like India, it provided cheap food and cheap labour for the mother country. But Irish cheap labour was in Britain as well as in Ireland. There had been seasonal migration for centuries but the growth of a permanent Irish population in Britain, associated in part with the decline of industrial employment in Ireland after the Union, meant that there was an Irish presence 'at home'. The Irish had long been represented in England as uncivilised barbarians: violent, wild and treacherous on the one hand, contemptible, stupid and inferior on the other. Their presence in the new industrial towns was deeply disturbing, at least to some middle-class commentators.

Take James Phillips Kay, a senior physician in Manchester in the 1830s. He began research into the causes of infection in the area of Ardwick and Ancoates where he was working and where the population was largely Irish, migrants who had come into Manchester to work in the mills. His analysis of his findings drew on utilitarian assumptions that the health and strength of the population was crucial to good government and social order.

While secretary to the Manchester Board of Health, Kay produced a report in 1832 on *The Moral and Physical Condition of the Working Classes Employed in the Cotton Manufactories in Manchester*. It was inspired by the serious outbreak of cholera that had occurred in Manchester and elsewhere. His conviction was that 'the fatal visitations of cholera' were made in the 'houses of squalid poverty and reckless vice'. 'He whose duty it is', he argued,

> to follow the steps of this messenger of death, must descend to the abodes of poverty, must frequent the close alleys, the crowded courts, the overpeopled habitations of wretchedness, where pauperism and disease congregate round the social cause of discontent and political disorder in the centre of our large towns, and behold with alarm, in the hot-bed of pestilence, ills that fester in secret, at the very heart of society.[84]

[83] Mary J. Hickman, *Religion, Class and Identity: The State, the Catholic Church and the Education of the Irish in Britain* (Aldershot: Avebury, 1995), pp. 2, 24, 83.

[84] James Phillips Kay, *The Moral and Physical Condition of the Working Classes Employed in the Cotton Manufactories in Manchester* (1832; repr. London: Cass, 1970), p. 8.

Cholera provided a metaphor for Kay, a way of linking pauperism, disease and disorder and defining them all as 'ills' which required a cure. As Mary Poovey argues, everyone belonged to the same 'social body', the body of society and the nation, but the term 'social body' had a double meaning – the society as an organic whole and the poor in isolation from the rest of the society:

> The ambiguity that this double usage produced was crucial to the process of cultural formation . . . for it allowed social analysts to treat one segment of the population as a special problem at the same time that they could gesture towards the mutual interests that (theoretically) united all parts of the social whole. The phrase *social body* therefore promised full membership in a whole (and held out the image *of* that whole) to a part identified as needing both discipline and care.[85]

Cholera, Kay was convinced, could be eradicated only by raising the physical and moral condition of the working community, for it was their immorality and depravity which made them subject to illness. Cholera, in other words, was a moral, not a physical problem, and it was the demoralisation of particular groups that made them subject to poverty and ill-health.

In this account it was the failings of particular groups, their moral inadequacies, that underpinned the problems of the nation. England's condition was represented as a kind of disease, and the unruly poor as victims in need of aid. Class conflict was explained as a function of ignorance and education was the cure. Social reform, not political reform, was the answer. Working-class homes Kay represented as *not* home, a place where children were neglected, women were employed outside and men were living off the wages of their children. But domestic disorder was not read in this instance in terms of class; rather it was read in terms of race. In Kay's argument it was the Irish who were to blame for the fatal contagion which was poisoning the nation and producing a debilitated race of workers, workers who might become an infinitely more threatening 'race apart'. The illness of the social body could be cured if the noxious elements were removed, and those elements were Irish. The ills that afflicted England were rooted in Ireland. The failure of the English to take pride in their homes was caused by the increase in the Irish population. The English were in danger of becoming like the Irish, who were presented as a cross between matter and beast. Almost every problem Kay identified he saw as being caused by the Irish. The exclusion of this 'enemy within', who were constructed as racialised,

[85] Mary Poovey, 'Making a Social Body: British Cultural Formation, 1830–1864', in Poovey, *Making a Social Body: British Cultural Formation, 1830–1864* (University of Chicago Press, 1995), p. 8. I have been much influenced by Poovey's reading of Kay in her 'Curing the Social Body in 1832: James Phillips Kay and the Irish in Manchester', in Poovey, *Making a Social Body*, pp. 55–72.

was one imagined way to solve the problem. His answer (to the problem he had himself constructed) was that the migrants should 'go home'.

Kay was deeply shocked by his forays into the 'bowels' of Manchester. The problem which he immediately identified was the 'destitute hordes' who had 'poured' in; the problem, in other words, came from somewhere else. Irish 'savagery' in his view was rooted in their being accustomed to living on the margins of subsistence. They had no access to the pleasures of civilisation, which in the minds of political economists were the commodities with which a house could be properly furnished, a varied and nourishing diet provided, decent clothes worn. Civilisation encouraged wants which were artificial, and it was this which distinguished man from beast. 'Barbarism' was life without those commodities. 'Savages' knew the 'fatal secret of subsisting on what is barely necessary to life' and the Irish example of this was dangerously 'contagious', a word associated with infection and disease.[86] The toil of the mill-workers was a form of drudgery that was potentially damaging since it deadened the intellect and threatened to make men into animals. But the Irish presence was accentuating all these problems, and the creation of a healthy body politic would depend on ejecting this contamination. Then it would be possible to re-educate English working people. This differentiation of the Irish from the English, in terms not only of contagion but of fears of crime and a potential threat to political stability, informed government efforts in the 1830s and 1840s on the one hand to create boundaries around the Irish, demarcate them as different, and on the other to denationalise them, deprive them of their Irishness.[87] By the 1840s Peel was fully aware that in Ireland coercion could not be an adequate strategy and had embarked on his attempt to redress grievances in relation to land, the church and education, an agenda that was disrupted by the famine but that Gladstone was to take up at the end of the 1860s.[88]

Kay's racialisation of the Irish – his conviction that they were a separate race with characteristics different from those of the English, yet that they had at the same time the power to pollute the English – drew on a long history between England and Ireland and on well-established traditions of representation. The link between Irishness and Catholicism was central. Catholic emancipation, as Best has noted, far from providing a settlement between Protestants and Catholics, increased conflict over Catholicism

[86] Kay, *Moral and Physical Condition*, pp. 21, 27, 82.

[87] Mary J. Hickman, 'Education for "Minorities": Irish Catholics in Britain', in Gail Lewis (ed.), *Forming Nation: Framing Welfare* (London: Routledge in association with the Open University, 1998), pp. 139–80.

[88] D. G. Boyce, *The Irish Question and British Politics 1868–1986* (Basingstoke: Macmillan, 1988), pp. 1, 6.

and convinced Protestants that they must defend their position. Irish Protestant orators began to lecture up and down England and Scotland stoking the fires of anti-Catholicism now that their ascendancy was no longer constitutionally guaranteed in Ireland.[89] Anti-Catholicism was endemic in nineteenth-century Britain, erupting periodically as in the troubles over Catholic emancipation, the uproar over Peel's grant to the Catholic college at Maynooth in 1845, the outrage at the restoration of the Catholic hierarchy in 1850, the Murphy riots of the mid-1860s. The themes were persistent: objections to a sacrificial priesthood claiming to mediate between self and salvation and to the 'sacrifice of the mass', objections to the power of Rome which was seen as a threat to the liberties of the individual and of the nation, the notion that Catholicism was inimical to the truth and the belief that celibacy was un-English, unmanly and unnatural.[90] The extent of anti-Catholicism was connected to the widespread fears that the faith was spreading, its extensive missionary activities bearing fruit as in the Oxford Movement, that the body politic, the 'natural language' of which was Protestantism, was under threat.[91]

In the 1830s, however, working-class solidarity cut across ethnic or racial divisions. The Catholic church was hostile to Chartism, but the flock did not always follow the clergy. Dorothy Thompson argues that there was a very considerable Irish presence in the Chartist movement and that one of the starting points for that movement was the response to the draconian Coercion Act passed for Ireland in 1833. The shared consciousness of exclusion from the constitution, of being under attack from government and employers and of having no access to political power united Irish and British workers. Many British radicals, furthermore, had enormous admiration for the tradition of Irish nationalism. In Barnsley, for example, the Irish worked with others in trade societies and radical organisations with apparently little awareness of ethnic divisions. Conflicts between Irish and British working men in the Chartist period were, she suggests, unusual.[92] Liverpool, however, was the scene of sporadic violence between English and Irish in the late 1830s and early 1840s, violence which was sparked off by the growth of Orangeism (for

[89] G. F. A. Best, 'Popular Protestantism in Victorian Britain', in Robert Robson (ed.), *Ideas and Institutions of Victorian Britain. Essays in Honour of George Kitson Clark* (London: G. Bell and Sons, 1967), p. 139. [90] *Ibid.*, pp. 117–25.

[91] The analogy is Newman's: see E. R. Norman, *Anti-Catholicism in Victorian England* (London: George Allen and Unwin, 1968), p. 19; Walter L. Arnstein, *Protestant Versus Catholic in Mid-Victorian England: Mr Newdegate and the Nuns* (Columbia: University of Missouri Press, 1982).

[92] Dorothy Thompson, 'Ireland and the Irish in English Radicalism Before 1850', in James Epstein and Dorothy Thompson (eds.), *The Chartist Experience: Studies in Working-Class Radicalism and Culture, 1830–1860* (Basingstoke: Macmillan, 1982), pp. 123, 128, 140, 144.

Orange lodges were established in places where there were extensive Irish settlement) and strong anti-Catholic campaigns within the city.[93]

In 1837 Daniel O'Connell, the celebrated leader and brilliant rhetorician of the movement for Catholic emancipation, who had subsequently focused on questions of reform of the Union, split with Feargus O'Connor, the radical nationalist and Chartist, and Chartism. This increased tensions, for O'Connell tried to take the Irish in Britain with him. But associations between Chartists and repealers were again close in 1848 and Saville argues that the connections between British and Irish radicals in the context of revolution in France was one of the galvanising factors for the coercive response to troubles at home and in Ireland.[94]

Post-1848, however, increasing tension marked relations between British and Irish, and these tensions took a racial form. John Belchem suggests that the upsurges in ultra-Protestantism and anti-Irish riots after 1848 were linked to the strengthening of the supposed characteristics of the Irish as disloyal and prone to rebellion – characteristics that had been felt as dangerously present in the year of revolutions.[95] From the 1840s there was more emphasis on the imputed racial characteristics of the Irish Celt. Violent class prejudice against the working classes was endemic, but it was not racialised in the ways that anti-Irish feelings were. Carlyle's much quoted characterisation of the Irish, for example, in his pamphlet on *Chartism*, utilised racial categories to draw sharp boundaries between Saxon and Celt:

> Crowds of miserable Irish darken our towns. The wild Milesian features, looking false ingenuity, restlessness, unreason, misery and mockery, salute you on all highways and byways. The English coachman, as he whirls past, lashes the Milesian with his whip, curses him with his tongue; the Milesian is holding out his hat to beg. He is the sorest evil this country has to strive with. In his rags and laughing savagery, he is there to undertake all work that can be done by mere strength of hand and back; for wages that will purchase him potatoes . . . The Saxon man, if he cannot work on those terms, finds no work . . . he has not sunk from decent manhood to squalid apehood . . . the uncivilised Irishman drives out the Saxon native, takes possession of his room. There abides he, in his squalor and unreason, in his falsity and drunken violence, as the ready-made nucleus of degradation and disorder.[96]

Ironically, Carlyle was a hero of the Young Ireland movement in the 1840s. His translation of German philosophical romanticism, with its cel-

[93] Panikos Panayi, 'Anti-Immigrant Violence in Nineteenth- and Twentieth-Century Britain', in Panayi (ed.), *Racial Violence in Britain, 1840–1950* (revised edn, Leicester University Press, 1996), p. 9.

[94] Saville, *1848*, p. 14.

[95] John Belchem, 'English Working-Class Radicalism and the Irish', in Roger Swift and Sheridan Gilley (eds.), *The Irish in the Victorian City* (London: Croom Helm, 1985), pp. 85–97.

[96] Carlyle, *Chartism*, p. 171.

ebration of spiritual rebirth through nationhood and focus on the nation's history as a shared story of a racial community struggling against foreign domination, found ready ears amongst journalists and publicists in Dublin.[97] Racial stereotypes always have double potential: positive and negative. While Young Irelanders celebrated 'the race', Carlyle despised it. At a time when Carlyle was presumably formulating his ideas for 'Occasional Discourse on the Negro Question', after his second visit to Ireland, Carlyle wrote to his friend Emerson in April 1849. The Irish would have to learn, he insisted, 'that man does need government, and that an able-bodied starving beggar is and remains (whatever Exeter Hall may say to it) a SLAVE destitute of a MASTER'. The Irish shared their savagery with black people, yet 'having a white skin and European features, [they] cannot be prevented from circulating among us at discretion, and to all manner of lengths and breadths'.[98] Yet the Irish slipped, for Carlyle, between being as barbarous as black people and belonging, in however attenuated and troubling a way, to the nation: their whiteness the warning sign, for the English, of possible degradation.

Cartoonists translated such images visually, developing a set of racial characteristics, focusing on a bulge in the lower part of the face, a prominent chin, big mouth, receding forehead, short nose and upturned nostrils, all of which became the racialised signs of 'Paddy'. Tenniel, who joined *Punch* in 1851 led this trend.[99] 'There was an almost universal tendency', notes O'Tuathaigh, 'from the 1840s onwards to describe the immigrant Irish and their problems in distinctly racial terms.'[100] The widely accepted stereotype of 'Paddy' was brutalised, intemperate, improvident, unclean, mendacious and menacingly savage. All of this was understood as national character. The decline of radicalism after 1850 left the way open, as Saville and others have noted, for more aggressive discrimination against the Irish, and more straightforward racism, visible, for example, in the coverage from *The Times* in this period.[101] The sharpening of ethnic antagonisms, and their racialisation, was associated with the increasing numbers of Irish coming to Britain in the period of the Famine and its aftermath. In 1841 there were over 400,000 Irish in England, Scotland and Wales with the Irish constituting 1.8 per cent of the population of England and Wales, 4.8 per cent in Scotland. Between

[97] R. F. Foster, *Modern Ireland 1600–1972* (London: Allen Lane, 1988), p. 313

[98] Quoted in Holt, *Problem of Freedom*, pp. 281–2.

[99] See R. F. Foster, 'Paddy and Mr Punch', in his *Paddy and Mr Punch: Connections in Irish and English History* (Harmondsworth: Penguin, 1995), pp. 171–94, for an account of the different representations of the Irish in *Punch* in the middle to late nineteenth century.

[100] M. A. G. O'Tuathaigh, 'The Irish in Nineteenth-Century Britain: Problems of Integration', *Transactions of the Royal Historical Society*, 5th ser., 31 (1981), 161.

[101] Saville, *1848*, p. 39.

1841 and 1851 the number of Irish in England and Wales had increased by 79 per cent and nearly a quarter of the population of Liverpool was Irish.[102] By 1861 the census recorded 601,634 Irish born in England and Wales, undoubtedly an underestimate but nevertheless marking at 3 per cent their highest percentage of the population of England and Wales ever recorded.[103]

Neville Kirk argues that there was persistent British–Irish tension between 1850 and 1870, tension which erupted most violently in 1852 and 1868.[104] Increased migration, ethnic clustering, competition in the labour market and energetic middle-class Protestant organisations fostering anti-Catholic sentiment all combined with the demise of Chartism to unleash virulent anti-Irish spleen. There were serious anti-popery disturbances in London, Cheltenham and Birkenhead in the wake of the restoration of the Catholic hierarchy, and anti-Irish disturbances in a number of towns in 1852, most notably Stockport. One man was killed and a hundred injured, Irish homes were broken into with the slogan 'England for Ever', and English rioters marched to the tune of 'Rule Britannia'. 'We very much doubt', announced a leader in *The Times*, 'whether in England, or indeed in any free Protestant country, a true Papist can be a good subject.'[105] For how could a double allegiance be maintained, to England and to Rome? Wolverhampton was the scene of another anti-Irish riot in 1858, stirred up by one of the many anti-Catholic lecturers who travelled the country.[106] The late 1850s and early 1860s may have seen a lessening of ethnic tension in some areas, but the volatility of relations between migrants and 'natives' was apparent.

In the early 1860s tensions between Irish Catholics and secularist supporters of Garibaldi and his struggle for an Italian nation erupted in several places. There was much sympathy amongst British radicals and Liberals for European nationalisms. At times this was inclusive of Irish aspirations for nationhood, but the linkage of anti-Catholicism with sympathy for the Italian cause sharpened contradictions for the Irish. Garibaldi's secularism and the turn of the papacy against Italian nationalism had coincided with the growth of anti-Catholic sentiment in Britain. Garibaldi was an impossible hero for any Catholic. Italian nationalist

102 R. F. Foster, *Modern Ireland*, p. 362.

103 John A. Jackson, *The Irish in Britain* (London: Routledge and Kegan Paul, 1963), pp. 7, 11.

104 Neville Kirk, *The Growth of Working-Class Reformism in Mid-Victorian England* (London: Croom Helm, 1985), p. 310. The following paragraph relies heavily on Kirk's work.

105 *The Times*, 3 March 1853, cited in Jackson, *The Irish in Britain*, p. 155.

106 Roger Swift, '"Another Stafford Street Row": Law, Order and the Irish Presence in Mid-Victorian Wolverhampton', in Swift and Gilley, *The Irish in the Victorian City*, pp. 179–206.

refugees in London raged against the power of the pope, who was seen as a serious obstacle to a united Italy. In 1860 the pope appealed for troops and an Irish brigade was formed to fight against the Risorgimento. In September 1862 these tensions culminated in the 'Hyde Park Aspromonte' (named after the famous battle in Italy) when thousands of Irish Catholics, singing for 'God and Rome', attacked secularist supporters of Garibaldi. A week later more than 100,000 Garibaldians and Irishmen staged a pitched battle in the park, with the Guardsmen attempting hopelessly to keep control. Similar disturbances took place in Birkenhead and Chesterfield.[107] It was in this context that *Punch* found the 'missing link' between the 'Gorilla' and the 'Negro' in the 'Irish Yahoo' of the 'lowest districts of London'.[108] In Ireland and across the Irish diaspora the rioters were celebrated. They had proved that 'the Irish in England are now a force not to be despised by . . . the British Empire'. The Dublin *Nation* had a graphic drawing 'executed in the first style of art' of 'Pat skinning the British Lion, in Hyde Park, 1862'. As Sheridan Gilley argues, the riots were significant in consolidating Irish nationalist organisation and sentiment and contributing to the development of Fenianism.[109]

By 1867 the rise of Fenianism, economic distress and the success that extreme Protestant groups had in exploiting anti-Catholic feeling together resulted in a period of acute hostilities, coinciding with events in Jamaica and the agitation over reform.

Fenianism, named after the mythic hero Finn Macumhall and carrying the nationalist dream embodied in that ancient tradition, was the movement associated with the Irish Republican Brotherhood, and was founded in the United States in the mid-1850s. The Brotherhood had been established in Dublin in 1858 and was committed to the overthrow of British rule in Ireland and the setting up of a republic.[110] The links between Ireland and the United States were crucial to the Fenians and many of the key activists in Britain had spent time there. Fenianism was a secular and republican movement and it linked the demand for the return of the land to the demand for an independent Ireland. Its advocates were prepared to use violence, whether in Ireland, Canada or England. It was a powerful diasporan movement with its strongest bases in the United States and Australia, and it was the threat of military action from abroad that made Fenianism so serious a concern to the governing classes: 'British rule in Ireland was threatened for the first time by a world-wide

[107] Sheridan Gilley, 'The Garibaldi Riots of 1862', *Historical Journal* 16 (1973), 697–732; Panayi, 'Anti-Immigrant Violence', p. 9.
[108] *Punch*, 18 October 1862.
[109] Gilley, 'Garibaldi Riots', 725.
[110] Patrick Quinlivan and Paul Rose, *The Fenians in England 1865–1872: A Sense of Insecurity* (London: John Calder, 1982).

organization with a secure base.' Queen Victoria commented on the dangers in her diary and Charles Dickens wrote fearfully of his 'strong apprehensions' of a war with the United States given the strength of Fenian sympathy there.[111] Anxiety about Fenianism reached its peak between 1865 and 1868. The Fenian aim was to seize power in Ireland, using actions in Canada or England as ways of destabilising the British government. John Devoy, a leading activist who was responsible for the Fenian organisation of the British army in Ireland, argues in his *Recollections* that the British government realised the extent of the danger in the summer of 1865 and acted effectively, drafting Irish regiments to distant parts of the empire and making use of courts martial to deal with Fenians in the army.[112] At the same time leaders in Ireland were arrested. In March 1867 there was an abortive rising in Ireland followed by an attempt to seize arms stored in Chester Castle.

There was significant support for Fenianism within Britain, amongst the Irish and some radicals. In the words of Devoy,

> The Irish in Great Britain were at that time even more intensely Irish than their fellow-countrymen who had remained at home. They lived a life of incessant combat among a people who hated them, and there was not a man among them who had not had several personal encounters with insolent Englishmen, while there were many instances of fights on a larger scale . . . they were in the full sense of the term in an enemy's country.[113]

Simply being Irish meant being associated with Fenianism, whether there was any evidence of nationalist sentiment or not.[114] This suited the Fenians well: Irishness and Fenianism went together. Stephens, the Fenian commander-in-chief to 1866, claimed a membership of around 80,000 in Ireland, England, Scotland and Wales, plus 15,000 in the army.[115] This was probably a gross overestimate but it was certainly the case that the potential for a pincer movement on England from Ireland, the United States and Canada created extensive fear.[116] But there was also deep hostility to the movement, a hostility that became more widespread in the aftermath of the 'outrages' on the mainland. The majority of Irish immigrants had a political objective, argues O'Tuathaigh, to redefine Britain's constitutional relations with Ireland, and when this

111 *Ibid.*, p. 5.

112 John Devoy, *Recollections of an Irish Rebel* (New York: Charles P. Young and Co., 1929), p. 65. 113 *Ibid.*, p. 114.

114 Jennifer Davis, 'Jennings Buildings and the Royal Boroughs: The Construction of the Underclass in Mid-Victorian Britain', in Feldman and Stedman Jones, *Metropolis*, p. 27.

115 Devoy, *Recollections*, p. 33.

116 See, for example, Gladstone's fears cited in R. F. Foster, *Modern Ireland*, p. 395; for a judgement of the revolutionary potential of Fenianism and its aftermath, see Marx and Engels, 'Letters on Britain', in their *On Britain*, pp. 533–84.

intruded violently, as with Fenianism, it was deeply resented.[117] Fenianism fostered that most inflammatory image of the Irish, the subversive within, the terrorist potentially rotting the vitals of the nation.

In May 1867 John Bright, the MP for Birmingham, had presented a petition to the House of Commons on behalf of Fenian prisoners. The petition began by condemning secret associations and violence and hoped that order might be restored in Ireland with the judicious use of power. Bright argued that the history of Ireland was one of neglect, injustice, repression and dispossession and that the present distribution of political power meant that the Irish nation could not make their wishes felt. 'There is a legitimate ground', he maintained, 'for the chronic discontent of which Fenianism is the expression.' He asked on behalf of the petitioners, well-known gentlemen with first-rate educations and good positions (who included Beesly and Harrison), that the Fenians should not be treated as common prisoners. Alarmed by 'their recollection of the conduct of the English army and its officers in India and Jamaica', they asked for the 'utmost moderation' and 'strict adherence to the laws of fair and humane warfare' in handling disturbances in Ireland.[118]

But Bright's support for the Fenian prisoners was controversial. Anti-Irish sentiment was widespread in Birmingham and there was a major riot in the town in June 1867, sparked off by the rhetoric of William Murphy. Birmingham had a strong Irish and Fenian presence. As the centre of the gun trade it had a strategic significance, and a key Fenian figure, Richard O'Sullivan Burke, was based there as an incognito arms dealer.[119] Murphy had been born and baptised a Catholic in Limerick but his father had been converted to Protestantism and became a Protestant lecturer. William arrived in Liverpool in 1862, walked to London and offered his services as an evangelist. The anti-Catholic was a stock public orator and entertainer and Murphy was only one of many, but one who was particularly effective in the context of the mid-1860s. He joined the Protestant Evangelical Mission and Electoral Union, committed to the maintenance of 'the Protestantism of the Bible and the LIBERTY OF BRITAIN'.[120] The first incident of rioting after one of his sermons was in Plymouth in 1866.[121]

117 O'Tuathaigh, 'Irish in Nineteenth-Century Britain', 170.

118 *Hansard*, 3rd ser., vol. 186, cols. 1929–31.

119 John Denvir in his memoirs described Birmingham as 'one of the most active centres of the movement': cited in Quinlivan and Rose, *Fenians*, pp. 33–4.

120 Walter L. Arnstein, 'The Murphy Riots: A Victorian Dilemma', *Victorian Studies* 19 (1975–6), 53.

121 D. M. MacRaild, 'William Murphy, the Orange Order and Communal Violence: The Irish in West Cumberland, 1871–1874', in Panayi, *Racial Violence*, pp. 44–64. See also Alan O'Day, 'Varieties of Anti-Irish Behaviour in Britain 1846–1922', in the same volume, pp. 26–43.

His lectures were dramatic and incendiarist, deliberately courting controversy, playing on the rhetoric of anti-Catholicism and channelling the fears of working-class Protestants. He associated the papacy, political despotism and Fenianism, and linked sexual danger with celibacy, the confessional and convent life. In 1864 the case of Mary Ryan, an Irish orphan who had been placed in a convent and then forcibly abducted to Belgium to receive treatment for lunacy, had mobilised terrors of physical seduction and moral corruption amongst extreme Protestants. In 1865 the Protestant Electoral Union had published the sensational *Confessional Unmasked*, articulating the anxieties felt by Protestant husbands and fathers on account of their mothers, daughters and wives.[122] Murphy used simple homely images and was building on fertile ground. As Arnold stated somewhat ironically in *Culture and Anarchy*, 'What I wish to say to you as Protestant husbands is, *take care of your wives*.'[123] 'Murphyism', as Quinlivan and Rose argue, 'reflected the reaction to Fenianism at the grass roots level.'[124] His meetings, in the words of MacRaild, 'gave form and shape to the popular Victorian stereotype of the aggressive "Paddy"'.[125] Popular Protestantism, dominated by the middle classes in the 1850s, found significant working-class support in the 1860s.

In September 1865 the *Birmingham Journal*, a solidly liberal paper, commented on that 'plague', Fenianism. It was, they argued, 'an impenetrable mystery':

> Who they are, what they want, what grievances they labour under, what remedies they propose nobody knows. All that is known is that, chiefly in the south and west of Ireland, numbers of insane people, of the very lowest class, get together stealthily, in out of way places for the purposes of drill. 'Death to the Saxon' is, of course, supposed to be their watchword and their object; but of what they would do after the killing neither they, nor anybody else, have the least idea.[126]

But such ignorance could not be maintained in the face of Fenian actions 'at home', and the British public had to learn what it was that Fenians wanted. Fenianism became, for the *Birmingham Journal*, this 'treasonable conspiracy, baffled and repressed in Ireland', which had assumed the form of organised violence and assassination in England and needed to be firmly put down.[127] Murphy's lectures took place in that context. His series on the 'errors of Roman Catholicism' were delivered in Birmingham in June 1867 in a specially erected wooden building, a 'tabernacle', holding 3,000 to 4,000 people, since the mayor had refused

122 Best, 'Popular Protestantism', pp. 128–9, 133.
123 Arnold, *Culture and Anarchy*, p. 91.
124 Quinlivan and Rose, *Fenians*, p. 33.
125 MacRaild, 'William Murphy', p. 46.
126 *Birmingham Journal*, 16 September 1865.
127 *Ibid.*, 23 November 1867.

use of the Town Hall after disturbances in Wolverhampton and elsewhere. The atmosphere was electric, with a large crowd outside battering on the doors while Murphy declaimed on the dangers of popery as worse than the devil and invited his audience to 'Stand firm to your principles: say within yourselves, we will not give up the Bible, the glory of old England, and the bulwark of our Sunday schools.' 'We have given you liberty of conscience', argued Murphy,

> You can go to your chapels, and worship God on the top of your heads if you like, but if you interfere with the rights of an Englishman, then John Bull will . . . send them to Garibaldi, or to 'Paddy Land' . . . Romanism was despotism, Protestantism was liberty: Romanism was death, Protestantism was life . . . every Popish priest was a murderer, a cannibal, a liar and a pickpocket.

While Murphy ranted in the building the crowd erupted outside and began to fight with the police. A large number of rioters identified as Irish were sighted and it was asserted that the women were particularly hostile to the forces of law and order. There were also large numbers of 'roughs', those sections of the working classes seen as not aspiring to respectability. Serious disturbances that day and the reading of the Riot Act and the swearing-in of special constables were followed by Protestant retaliation the following day, when it was estimated that between 50,000 and 100,000 were on the streets. In the evening a band of Murphy's supporters marched to the Irish district of the town armed with staves. They broke into houses and damaged a Catholic chapel while singing 'Glory, Glory Hallelujah' and 'John Brown's Body'. Park Street, an almost exclusively Irish street, was left in ruins.[128] There were dozens of casualties and many arrests, mainly Irish. *The Times* regretted the 'sad and even portentous sight', not in Belfast but in Birmingham, 'one of the most flourishing and not the least enlightened of English manufacturing towns'.[129] Despite this, Murphy's series continued and debate raged in the local papers on the events and the coverage of them. Murphy depended on the right to freedom of speech and claimed that, should he be prevented from continuing, 30,000 Birmingham men would want to know why. He recommended Orangeism to his audience and exhorted the men to save their wives and daughters from the contamination of priestcraft and tyranny.[130] The nation, in Murphy's mind, should never have included Catholics.

In September 1867, by which time the new Reform Act had received the royal assent, an attempt was made to rescue Fenian prisoners from

[128] *Birmingham Daily Post*, 18 June 1867.
[129] *The Times*, 20 June 1867, quoted in Arnstein, 'Murphy Riots', 58.
[130] *Birmingham Daily Post*, 3 July 1867.

Manchester Gaol in the course of which a prison van guard was unintentionally killed. By the end of 1867 the manufacturing districts of the north were full of rumours of imminent insurrection.[131] In Manchester, where one-tenth of the population was Irish, operatives were armed to protect properties and special constables were sworn in.[132] Demonstrations of sympathy with the convicted Fenians in London and Birmingham were met with great hostility and in Birmingham a rival mob of several hundreds demonstrated in favour of hanging them.[133] Amongst some radicals there was serious unease at the way in which the trial was conducted. Ernest Jones, a long-time Chartist, was working with the defence but left in disgust at the proceedings: *Reynolds's News* described it as a 'deep and everlasting disgrace' to the English government.[134] *The Spectator* in October argued that only 'occasion' was needed to transform the 'inextinguishable feud' between immigrant and native workers into 'a fatal war of races and creeds'.[135] This was a language inflected by Morant Bay. In November the 'Manchester Martyrs' were executed and in December a second attempt was made to engineer the escape of Fenian prisoners from Clerkenwell. In the process four civilians were killed and many injured. Those who had been sympathetic became more critical. Many Irish in Britain disassociated themselves from Fenianism as, for example, the 22,000 who sent an address to the queen condemning the Clerkenwell massacre.[136] The Catholic hierarchy took the lead in condemning what had happened. With this backdrop Murphy started a new lecture tour and disturbances erupted throughout 1868, particularly in the north-west. Orange lodges and other extreme Protestant organisations were very active in this period, and Irish Catholics were enraged by what they saw as his blasphemy: the conflict was explosive. Murphy himself was badly injured in one such clash in 1871 and died in his adopted town of Birmingham the following year.

Anti-Irish and anti-Catholic feeling was endemic in the England of the mid-1860s. Irish Catholics were castigated at all levels of the social hierarchy and were defended by few. The association with Fenianism was explosive. In the imagined nation as it was reconstituted in 1867, 'Paddy', the racialised Irishman, stood as a potent 'other' to the respectable Englishman, who had proved his worth and deserved a vote.

131 Kirk, *Working-Class Reformism*, p. 321.

132 Paul Rose, *The Manchester Martyrs: The Story of a Fenian Tragedy* (London: Lawrence and Wishart, 1970), p. 22.

133 Quinlivan and Rose, *Fenians*, p. 69.

134 Quoted in Paul Rose, *Manchester Martyrs*, p. 53.

135 *The Spectator*, 5 October 1867, cited in Kirk, *Working-Class Reformism*, p. 321.

136 O'Day, 'Varieties of Anti-Irish Behaviour', p. 38.

The parliamentary debates

Debates in both the House of Commons and the House of Lords over the extension of the franchise 'at home', Fenianism, and Morant Bay and its aftermath were infused with racial discourse. Notions of English national characteristics, Irishness and blackness informed the ways in which members of both houses thought about the forms of government appropriate to the different sites of the empire. The metropolis was constituted differently from the colonies and the colonies themselves were clearly differentiated according to their populations with their distinctive imputed racial characteristics. Increasing numbers of Englishmen and even Irishmen might be ready for the privilege of the vote; Jamaicans were certainly not.

The debate over reform in the 1860s had been framed by reference to questions of race and empire from the beginning, for it was the American Civil War which gave the impetus to working-class men to demand the vote again. As Marx noted, 'As in the eighteenth century, the American War of Independence sounded the tocsin for the European middle class, so, in the nineteenth century, the American Civil War sounded it for the European working class.'[137] Support for the North had been very strong amongst the male working-class rank and file and this had provided a bond between them and the middle-class liberal abolitionists, some of whom, like John Bright, had been traditionally opposed by old Chartists as representatives of capital. In the aftermath of the Crimean War, of which he had been a critic, to the horror of many of his erstwhile middle-class radical supporters, Bright had turned to the theme of 'the people' versus privilege and was appealing strongly to 'the nation'.[138] In his mind the nation should correspond with 'the people', that body of responsible male public opinion which provided a bedrock of good sense and could be counterpoised to monopolists and aristocrats. Older class affiliations were beginning to be displaced by newly articulated ethnic and racial identities, as Englishmen, as Anglo-Saxons, as members of the nation. As Bright argued as early as 1861,

> England is the living mother of great nations on the American and on the Australian continents, which promise to endow the world with all her knowledge and all her civilization and with even something more than the freedom she herself enjoys.[139]

[137] Karl Marx, *Capital*, vol. II (1938 edn), p. xviii, cited in Royden Harrison, *Before the Socialists: Studies in Labour and Politics 1861–1881* (London: Routledge and Kegan Paul, 1965), p. 67.

[138] Patrick Joyce, *Democratic Subjects: The Self and the Social in Nineteenth-Century England* (Cambridge University Press, 1994), p. 134.

[139] Quoted in William Robertson, *Life and Times of the Right Honourable John Bright* (London: Cassell, 1883), p. 396.

The idea of the constitution was vital to him, alongside the notion that England's story was that of the advance of liberty. For him and for other radicals male suffrage in the Australian states and the eventual enfranchisement of black men in the aftermath of the US Civil War in 1867 marked instances of the triumph of the best of the imperial spirit. Manhood suffrage, at this stage, however, was best left to the white settler colonies, to Australia, Canada and New Zealand and that great former colony, the United States. A powerful supporter of the North, Bright was convinced that 'America' (as he and virtually everyone else called the United States), the child of England, had much to offer the English. A brilliant speaker, he was regularly able to attract thousands to his meetings on reform and he linked the liberation of slaves with the proper recognition of the political rights of respectable working men. Bright represented himself as a typical Englishman, with Saxon qualities and basic human passions. In his oratory, as Patrick Joyce argues, he was able to articulate the elemental feelings of 'the people'. English provided a 'natural language' for this.[140] For Bright the Anglo-Saxon race was one race across the empire. 'You know the boast we have', he told a Birmingham audience in 1865,

> of what takes place when the negro slave lands in England; you know what one of our best poets said, that if their lungs but breathed our air, that moment they are free; they touch our country and their shackles fall. But how is it with an Englishman? Why an Englishman, if he goes to the Cape, he can vote; if he goes farther, to Australia, to the nascent empires of the New World, he can there vote; if he goes to the Canadian federation, he can there vote; and if he goes to those grandest colonies of England not dependent upon the English crown . . . there . . . can give his free and independent vote. (*Loud cheers.*) It is only in his own country, on his own soil, where he was born, the very soil which he has enriched with his labour and with the sweat of his brow, that he is denied this right which in every other community of Englishmen in the world would be freely accorded to him. (*Much cheering.*)[141]

Englishmen, Bright concluded, were 'to live like the coolies or Chinese imported into the West Indies', denied the rights that Anglo-Saxons deserved.[142] Similarly, the radical Henry Fawcett drew on ideas about the empire and its glories when arguing for an increase in male suffrage:

> Why, every time I look at Australia or any other part of our colonial Empire, I am the more proud of being an Englishman; for I think that our colonies are the centres of a civilization equal to our own. Greece had achieved many of the greatest intellectual triumphs of modern civilization; Rome had an Empire as vast as

[140] Joyce, *Democratic Subjects*, pp. 94–8. [141] *Birmingham Daily Post*, 19 January 1865.

[142] Quoted in John Breuilly, Gottfried Niedhart and Antony Taylor (eds.), *The Era of the Reform League: English Labour and Radical Politics 1857–1872. Documents Selected by Gustav Mayer* (Mannheim: Palatium Verlag im J. and J. Verlag, 1995), p. 194.

ours; but the freedom, the greatness and the glory of those countries have departed, and have left no living testimony behind. But what seems likely to be the destiny of this country? We in every quarter of the globe are founding nations which image our greatness, which inherit our institutions, and which in ages yet to come will reflect the greatness and glory of the nation from which they have sprung.[143]

Other contenders in the debate on reform took a less benevolent view of these experiments in the empire and the ex-colony of the USA. John Bright's most powerful antagonist within Parliament and the most systematic critic of an extension of the franchise throughout 1866–7 was Robert Lowe, who had lived in Australia in the 1840s and was passionately opposed to the male franchise which had been established there. He refuted the notion that every citizen of a state had a right to share in government, arguing that, if these rights existed, 'they are as much the property of the Australian savage and the Hottentot of the Cape as of the educated and refined Englishman'. 'Those who uphold this doctrine', he insisted, 'must apply it to the lowest as well as to the highest grades of civilization.'[144] Lowe believed that the granting of the occupational franchise would 'revolutionize the institutions of this country for all time to come'.[145] If Parliament wanted to embrace venality, ignorance and drunkenness then certainly they should extend the franchise, and could look to the white settler colonies for evidence as to the likely results: 'I do not want to say anything disagreeable, but if you want to see the result of democratic constituencies, you will find them in all the assemblies of Australia, and in all the assemblies of North America.'[146]

Lowe did not need to remind his audience of the large numbers of Irish migrants now represented in those assemblies in Australia and North America. He drew upon his version of colonial events to terrify the House of Commons with the spectre of losing all that was 'dear to us as Englishmen'.[147] Queensland, he argued, provided a horrifying example of what happened when an ignorant electorate were given the vote. Only the other day, he claimed, 'the people were nearly murdering the House of Assembly' on the grounds that they did not like one of their decisions.[148] In his last-ditch attempt in 1867 to stop the Reform Bill Lowe threatened the House with anarchy on the basis of the colonial experience: 'In the colonies . . . they have got Democratic Assemblies. And what is the result? Why, responsible Government becomes a curse not a blessing . . . It tends

143 *Hansard*, 3rd ser., vol. 182, col. 204, March–April 1866.
144 *Ibid.*, vol. 178, col. 1424, March–May 1865.
145 *Ibid.*, vol. 187, col. 785, May–June 1867. 146 *Ibid.*, vol. 182, cols. 787, 791.
147 On Lowe's career as a popular politician in New South Wales, see A. Patchett Martin, *Life and Letters of the Right Honourable Robert Lowe, Viscount Sherbrooke*, 2 vols. (London, 1893). 148 *Hansard*, 3rd ser., vol. 187, cols. 787, 791.

to anarchy.'[149] Similarly, Lowe drew on the American experience and contrasted it most unfavourably to England:

> Did you ever hear of a man who was ostracised from public life in America in consequence of his having committed a murder, a forgery, a perjury, or anything of that kind? Things which would not be tolerated for an instant in England are passed by without notice in America.[150]

Drawing on the historically short fuse of English rage about American interference on the subject of Ireland, he evoked the image of the American Congress supporting the Fenians – surely the Honourable Members did not want the House of Commons to be like that? The chief property of the United States, he claimed, was 'its gift of nature', its 'fertile land', 'noble rivers' and 'boundless extent of territory'. All this meant that turbulent political demagogues could become 'contented cultivators of the land'. In England, on the contrary, property was 'the work of art and of time' and had been 'piled up century after century by the industry of successive generations of Englishmen'. Such distinctions must be maintained.[151] Sustaining his defence of the rights of property, Lowe was to be the most significant critic of Mill's proposals for land reform in Ireland.[152]

In February and March 1866 a decision had been taken in the House of Commons, with very brief debate, that cleared the way, as it were, for the months of discussion as to which kinds of men were to become citizens. In March 1866 Jamaica had been declared a crown colony, to be governed directly by London. This followed the political suicide which the Jamaican House of Assembly, granted representative government in 1662, committed in the wake of Morant Bay. Terrified by the spectre of black power, the predominantly white House voluntarily gave up power after only two weeks of debate, enthusiastically supported by Eyre – a move which was resisted by only ten 'coloured' (the contemporary term for mixed-'race') and Jewish members. Jamaican representative government had long been criticised as unsatisfactory, both by the majority black population, whose interests were not represented by the limited and corrupt system of franchise, and by the Colonial Office, who were contemptuous of white planter mentality in the colony and angry at the constant blocking of any reforms initiated by London, usually under pressure from the abolitionists. The House of Assembly had few friends, but had been strenuously defended by the planters as the instrument of their political power. They themselves, however, were aware that they could

149 *Ibid.*, vol. 182, col. 2108. 150 *Ibid.*, col. 160.
151 *Ibid.*, vol. 187, col. 795; vol. 178, col. 1438.
152 Steele, 'J. S. Mill and the Irish Question', pp. 231–2.

not stem the tide of black voters for ever, given the importance of black peasant proprietorship, and in the wake of Morant Bay preferred to protect their interests through an even more restricted franchise and a Legislative Council, in which they knew they would be adequately represented.[153] Eyre would have preferred a Legislative Council entirely nominated by the governor, since he regarded the people as 'incompetent to judge for themselves'.[154] He had to be content, however, with a raised property franchise and a council half nominated, half elected. With crocodile tears he wept over the loss of 'institutions so deservedly dear to every British heart'.[155] His comfort was that the Jamaicans were not British.

There were protests within Jamaica as, for example, from the parish of St Catherine, where petitioners were most alarmed at the effective concentration of power in the hands of the governor. 'The measure', they argued,

> is against the spirit of the age, against the spirit of English legislation, and against everything that is politic and just. That under the provisions of this Bill almost the entire black, and nineteen twentieths of the white and coloured population will be disfranchised, without committing any offence against society, or the laws of the land; a measure against which your Petitioners, as loyal subjects, solemnly protest, being utterly inconsistent with the genius of the British constitution, which is based upon taxation and representation.[156]

Many of the progressives in Jamaica believed that their chances of a better future were improved under the protection of direct British rule – but protection was what was at issue. As subjects of the crown they could look forward to the rule of law British-style, a right which they had not been able to enjoy. There was no question, however, of their rights as citizens, the right to vote for a government and participate directly in the political affairs of their nation. Male subjects, however, continued to enjoy, if that is the right term, the right to enlist in the British army and fight colonial wars on behalf of the metropolis.

Neither the 'genius of the British constitution' nor the spirit of the age could protect the democratic rights of the inhabitants of St Catherine. British radicals and many Liberals were prepared to exert themselves

153 The increasing scale of the ownership of land by black peasant proprietors in the wake of emancipation meant that both the planters and the British government were agreed in the view that in the end black electors would predominate. On black peasant proprietorship, see Sidney W. Mintz, *Caribbean Transformations* (Chicago: Aldine Publishing, 1974).

154 Eyre to Caldwell, 7 December 1865, PP, 1866, vol. LI, Part 1, *Papers Relating to the Disturbances in Jamaica*, p. 353.

155 Governor Eyre's Address to the House of Assembly and the Legislative Council, 22 December 1865, PP, 1866, vol. LI, Part 2, *Further Papers Relevant to the Disturbances in Jamaica*, p. 444.

156 *Ibid.*, p. 424.

energetically on behalf of the oppressed white peoples of Europe in their struggle for nationhood. Solidarity with Italian, Hungarian and Polish nationalisms had become the popular causes of the 1850s and 1860s, displacing the abolitionist cause and privileging the white brotherhood of Europe over the Indian, Maori or Jamaican rebels in the English imagination. Radicals were certainly prepared to defend the rights of Jamaican black people to the rule of law in the aftermath of Morant Bay, though few of them had anything to say as to those same rights in the case of the Indian 'mutineers'. But they were not interested in the defence of representative government in Jamaica. While making arguments for the extension of the franchise 'at home' they were quite content for this colonial franchise to be reduced.

John Stuart Mill made what he regarded as his most significant political speech in the House of Commons in the debate over the Royal Commission on Jamaica, but he did not speak when crown colony status was agreed.[157] Mill, as we have seen, was convinced that representative government was the best form of government, but he was also firmly of the view that only some societies were ready for it. The decades after emancipation in the British West Indies had demonstrated in his mind that the planters were not fit for representative government, for they had not even sustained the rule of law. Indeed, it was the collapse of the rule of law in the wake of Morant Bay that was at the heart of his critique of Eyre.[158]

Furthermore, the problems of representative government did not rest only with the planters. Peoples who had recently emerged from slavery needed political education, and the protection of crown colony status would provide appropriate conditions for that process. If Mill, the champion of the anti-Eyre campaign and a veteran of abolitionist causes, had no interest in challenging the demise of representative government in Jamaica, it was hardly likely that anyone else in the British Parliament would. Indeed both the House of Commons and the House of Lords showed so little interest in the issue that the three readings of the bill and royal assent were all achieved within less than five weeks.

The general consensus in both Houses was that 'there now remains in the island neither material for a free representative Assembly nor the basis upon which a free representative Assembly could be founded'. The 'excitable', which meant black, population needed strong government; the old representative system had been an 'absurd burlesque' of the British constitution.[159] As one of the supporters of Eyre put it, emancipation had meant that

[157] Mill, *Autobiography*, p. 281. [158] *Hansard*, 3rd ser., vol. 184, cols. 1797–1806, July 1866.
[159] *Ibid.*, vol. 181, cols. 921, 927, February–March 1866.

> a constituency was introduced which rendered representative institutions no longer practicable. He could hardly conceive that the most sanguine democrat who would be ready to compose the constituency of the House of Commons chiefly of working men, or of those who could barely read and write, would defend the sudden introduction of that half-civilized, and but recently emancipated antagonistic population into a constituency of old representatives.

'Representative institutions', he feared, 'could never be re-established.' Meanwhile, Stephen Cave, a well-established member of the West India interest and long-time defender of the planters in Britain, argued that the constitution of Jamaica had been a great barrier to prosperity, for 'the frequent elections which took place turned away the people from habits of industry to political excitement'.[160] Speaker after speaker referred to the conventional wisdom that the real problem in Jamaica was 'the want of continuous labour'. This was the marker of difference from Britain; it was this which signified lack of civilisation not only for Mill but for majority opinion across the political boundaries: men who were not proper labourers did not deserve a vote or the possibility of participating in representative government. Baines, for example, the Liberal MP for Leeds, based his demand for the extension of the borough franchise on the demonstration that these men had made of their efficacy and utility. 'These are the men', he argued,

> who carry on the vast and varied industry of the country; they till your soil, they work your mines and machinery, they manufacture the products which command the markets of the world; their labour and skill make all your capital available, and produce all your comforts and luxuries; they navigate your ships of war and trade, and they fill the ranks of your armies. Their sinews are strong, their energies are not surpassed, their courage is high, their natural abilities are as good as those of the classes above them, they are now an educated people who daily read the news of all the world.

It was dangerous, he insisted, to leave such men unrepresented.[161] Such claims would not be made for the negro: their capacity to labour was questioned in terms of their racial characteristics.

Even principled Liberals and lifetime supporters of emancipation such as the erstwhile secretary of state for the colonies, Lord Grey, were resigning themselves to the view that 'From all the evidence I have been able to collect, I have come to the conclusion that for many years to come the negroes will be unfit to exercise political power.' Grey insisted 'that the very unsatisfactory results of the abolition of slavery in Jamaica should not be attributed to any inherent fault of the negro race'. In his view the failure of the 'great experiment' was the fault of the Jamaican legislature,

[160] *Ibid.*, cols. 1174–5, 927. [161] *Ibid.*, vol. 178, cols. 1378–9.

which 'was utterly opposed to all the dictates of political science and political economy' and, therefore, bound to fail. The House of Assembly had persistently resisted the mother country and used its unchecked powers to mismanage the country. Its most responsible act was to commit legislative suicide. The explanation for that he saw as the inevitable move towards the extension of black people's power as they gradually gained property and political influence. Faced with such a spectre the planters were quite correct in his view to assume that the best they could hope for was to be ruled by the crown. 'From all the evidence brought before me', he repeated, asserting his right to speak on these matters and to make definitive judgements on peoples thousands of miles away from the fastness of the House of Lords, 'I am persuaded that there is no peculiarity in the black race which will prevent their improvement; they are a people capable of great industry, although, doubtless, very excitable, and having certain faults that in time will disappear.' Their lordships discussed the parlous state of Ireland the same day as that of Jamaica, and Grey argued there was 'something amiss which requires to be remedied'. Houses were 'hardly fit for the habitation of civilized creatures', agriculture was in a very poor state, trade was limited and emigration continued apace. Emigrants were becoming involved with Fenianism and contributing large amounts of money in the United States and Australia. Furthermore, there was a high level of support for Fenianism in Ireland, despite its obvious strategic failures. At the root of the problem, argued Grey, was political disaffection and it was essential to win the affection of the people. Lord Dufferin, on the other hand, argued that the troubles in Ireland came from without. In 1798 the French had stirred rebellion; in 1848 it was the example of the European revolutions. Now it was only the lowest and most ignorant who were disaffected. Their lordships bemoaned the connections between the Irish unrest and the American Civil War. Jamaica occupied a different space in their political imaginations, however, for a black majority population meant a different political landscape. No one ever suggested that the white male labouring population of Ireland should be excluded from the extension of the franchise, for on the imperial scale Celts were always part of the brotherhood of Britain, albeit in a racialised and unequal position. There were 'certain peculiarities in the national character' which needed to be taken into account when deciding what to do with the Irish.[162] But such peculiarities did not legitimate disenfranchisement. Excluding large numbers of the Irish population in England from the franchise through restrictions about stable residence was one thing; simply excluding them from rights of democratic

162 *Ibid.*, vol. 182, cols. 124–405.

participation because they were Irish would have been quite another. The Irish were indeed both within and without.

The electoral reform legislation went through after the second Hyde Park demonstration and debacle had finally convinced all but the most hard-line of the conservatives that a new settlement was inevitable. The consensual lines of inclusion were drawn around those who had demonstrated 'regularity of life and general trustworthiness of conduct', men who were 'worthy of it', not 'migratory paupers' (who undoubtedly included many of the Irish) or 'the wandering and passing population'.[163] The 1867 act gave the vote to men who were household heads and had been in residence in rented property for a minimum of twelve months (see appendix D, pp. 241–2, for more details on the act's provisions). It was *independence* that gave some working-class men the status to become part of the gendered world of the political nation, members of the fraternity of England, privy to the rational discourse of politics, freed from the sphere of passion and emotion which was intimately linked to the status of dependant. Such men would not threaten the fabric of the national culture, would not 'make us any less English, or less national than we are now'.[164] Citizens, it was decreed, were men with homes, men with families, men with jobs.

In the Commons Mill had argued that 'martial law is the total suspension of all law'. He insisted that, if Eyre and other responsible persons were not prosecuted, 'we are giving up altogether the principle of government by law, and resigning ourselves to arbitrary power'. However, the imposition of crown colony status, a form of arbitrary power since control was held by the governor, a crown appointee, did not strike him or his supporters in that way. For the protection of British rule was a better bet, in their view and indeed in the view of the massed ranks of Lords and Commons, than the dangers of Jamaican self-government. Planters, as abolitionists had long argued, did not represent the right kind of whiteness, and were certainly not English.[165] In the same debate, W. E. Forster, the only official at the Colonial Office to be critical of the new settlement, raised the awkward question: why were Eyre and the British troops prepared to commit atrocities

> from which they would have shrunk had the victims been white people? The reason was that they were not free, and he did not know that he himself or any Member of the House would have been free from the race feeling – the feeling of contempt for what was regarded as an inferior race. This, however, only made it

[163] *Ibid.*, vol. 186, cols. 7–51, March–May 1867.
[164] R. H. Hutton, 'The Political Character of the Working Class', in *Essays on Reform*, p. 36.
[165] Catherine Hall, 'Missionary Stories: Gender and Ethnicity in England in the 1830s and 1840s', in her *White, Male and Middle Class*, pp. 205–54.

> the more incumbent upon Parliament, able as it was to sit calmly in judgement upon these things, to affirm that there ought not to be one code of morality for one colour, and another code for another.[166]

Forster, however, represented the minority. The Jamaica Bill, originally proposed for three years, became permanent on the nod. As Carlyle put it so succinctly, 'blacks', as he and many others referred to black men and women, were not white Anglo-Saxons and could not expect the same rights – neither as subjects nor as citizens.

The Irish both could and could not expect the same rights. Many Irish in England were enfranchised in the Reform Act of 1867 and the Reform Acts of the following year for Ireland and Scotland extended that representation, though the absence of an urban working class in Ireland made the Irish Reform Act of 1868 'extremely mouse-like'.[167] It was not until the legislation of 1884–5 that there was a single electoral reforming package for the four countries of the United Kingdom. Celts might be 'the missing link' in the minds of some, but they were also Britons. The presence of a potentially significant Irish vote within the UK meant the transformation of nationalist politics, for now there was always the possibility of substantially influencing Westminster. Parnell saw this clearly and in 1878 echoed some of Devoy's earlier sentiments but in a new political context: 'we have a great force in England . . . composed of men who have been scourged and driven from this country – driven to earn their bread in a foreign land under many circumstances of disadvantage'.[168] After 1867 the Irish electorate always might vote ethnically. As Isaac Butt, the leader of the first Home Rule organisation in Britain, put it in 1873,

> there were towns in England in which the Irish vote was a third of the whole, and it would be given to no enemy of Ireland. That was a great power. There were towns in England in which he was told the Irish vote was in the majority. That was a greater power . . . The first element of success was a just and righteous cause, and the next was that they would be able to command an overwhelming majority of Irish members and a powerful influence in English representation, and if these elements were properly worked they were sufficient to carry the cause.[169]

The Irish represented 15–30 per cent of the population in many English urban centres, especially in the north. In the event this potential was never fully realised, as Alan O'Day argues. The combination of insufficient con-

[166] *Hansard*, 3rd ser., vol. 184, cols. 1797–1813.

[167] K. Theodore Hoppen, 'The Franchise and Electoral Politics in England and Ireland 1832–1885', *History* 70 (1985), 215. See appendix D, pp. 241–2, for more details on the Irish Reform Act of 1868.

[168] Cited in Alan O'Day, 'The Political Organization of the Irish in Britain 1867–1890', in Roger Swift and Sheridan Gilley (eds.), *The Irish in Britain 1815–1939* (London: Pinter, 1989), p. 183.

[169] *Ibid.*, p. 185.

centrations in particular constituencies, alongside over-representation in seats which were secure for either Liberals or Tories, the refusal by many Irish to participate in British elections because of their hostility to mainstream politics, and the poor organisation of the Irish vote all meant that the vote delivered was never what the nationalists hoped. Furthermore, there were still many Irishmen who were not enfranchised.

Nevertheless, the potential for electoral influence was vital. In the 1868 election Irish activity was channelled into support for Gladstone, who had been moved by the spectre of Fenianism to the view that Ireland must be pacified. His Peelite policy of reconciliation, which included church disestablishment and land reform, was classically combined with a Coercion Act. But many Irish in England and Scotland were not satisfied with the Liberals, and in May 1870 the first of a series of meetings was held in Birmingham to discuss the issues over Ireland. In the same month Isaac Butt, the Orangeman and Tory who was also a nationalist, founded the Home Government Association. Butt had a long history as a defender of the Union but had come to the conclusion in the wake of Fenianism that Home Rule would be the most effective defence. He had been involved with the defence of Fenian prisoners between 1865 and 1868 and from 1871 to 1879 he sat as a Home Rule MP for Limerick.[170] As the chair of a Home Rule meeting in Middlesbrough noted, 'one of the greatest difficulties the Irish people had to contend with in England was being regarded with a certain amount of suspicion as dangerous characters'.[171] Regular electoral politics, however, provided a different kind of context from that of Fenianism, and Roy Foster estimates that moderate Home Rule mobilised far more of the Irish in England than Fenianism ever had.[172] It did not, however, banish the link between the Irish and terrorism, a link that has haunted the representation of the Irish in England into the present.

Meanwhile the white settlers of Canada achieved a new settlement too. The British North America Act of March 1867 created Canada as a new nation, with its founding provinces New Brunswick, Nova Scotia, Quebec and Ontario. The course of the bill was unexciting. It had support from both sides in the House of Commons but there was very little interest. Gladstone had long been a great enthusiast; Bright argued against it on the grounds that the will of the people of the Maritime Provinces had been overridden.[173] The Durham Report of 1839 had recommended

[170] R. F. Foster, *Modern Ireland*, p. 305.

[171] Cited in O'Day, 'Political Organization of the Irish', p. 189.

[172] R. F. Foster, *Modern Ireland*, p. 367.

[173] R. G. Trotter, 'The Coming of Federation', in J. H. Rose, A. P. Newton and E. A. Benians (eds.), *The Cambridge History of the British Empire*, 9 vols. (Cambridge University Press, 1929–59), vol. VI (1930), *Canada*, pp. 438–64; Paul Knaplund, *The British Empire 1815–1939* (2nd edn, New York: Howard Fertig, 1969), pp. 217–33.

responsible government for the provinces dominated by English settlers and this had set the pattern for the white settler colonies. Australia, New Zealand and the Cape had achieved responsible government with a propertied male franchise by the 1850s. Canada now set the pace again by becoming a nation, a dominion of the empire.

That same year of 1867 an interesting development took place in New Zealand. The wars of the 1860s between Maori and the British Empire had died down, Maori having been defeated by colonial troops with the support of 'native auxiliaries' rather than by imperial forces. The disengagement of imperial troops, Belich argues, which was more or less complete by 1866, meant that the colonial government was more dependent on local allies and more willing to make deals with them. One such deal was the provision of four Maori seats in the New Zealand Parliament in 1867: a reward for the increasing number of Maori who had been prepared to fight with Pakeha. In the election of 1868 the seats went to kupapa (Maori supporters of the Europeans) chiefs. It was only four seats of seventy, but it marked the recognition that Parliament could not be a place only for white settlers. The Treaty of Waitingi had acknowledged Maori sovereignty, but that autonomy had been lost by the end of the century. 'Maori cultural autonomy and identity survived the impact of Europe; Maori political independence did not.'[174] Maori became part of the new nation of New Zealand, represented, albeit unequally, in the government. Race did not act as a straightforward bar to political representation, any more than it did in the other settler colonies. That was not part of the British way and would be 'opposed to all our feelings'.[175] Race was, however, a part of the equation in the complex political settlements across the empire.

In the wake of the destruction of the Hyde Park railings, anyone who could be identified as having been involved was arrested and severely punished. Marx railed against the 'thick headed John Bulls of the Reform League' whose reformist politics he despised, and noted that the 'cur Knox, the police magistrate of Marylebone, snaps out summary judgement in a way that shows what would happen if London were Jamaica'.[176] If London had been Jamaica the agitators would have been summarily

[174] James Belich, *Making Peoples: A History of the New Zealanders from Polynesian Settlement to the End of the Nineteenth Century* (Auckland and London: Allen Lane, 1996), pp. 244, 265, 270.

[175] The phrase is Trollope's, in relation to Natal and the problem which the majority black population represented. Trollope was convinced that a franchise based explicitly on racial belonging was impossible, as was the prospect of black men ruling white: Anthony Trollope, *South Africa*, 2 vols. (London, 1878), vol. II, p. 261.

[176] Marx to Engels, 27 July 1866, in their *On Britain*, p. 541.

executed or flogged. But England was not Jamaica. In 1866 white male radicals saw their interests as closely linked to those Jamaican black people persecuted in the wake of Morant Bay. But, by July 1867, ironically because of the pressure they had been able collectively to exert, they had been received within the brotherhood of the nation, whilst black Jamaican males had been condemned to a racialised form of subjecthood, and white British women, of every social class, had been firmly positioned within their separate sphere. Irish men in England had been received into the nation on the same terms as Anglo-Saxons; but their equal legal status did not prevent either their cultural exclusion from the nation or their own identification as different. The nation was a family, as was the empire, but families, as everyone knew, had rules of belonging and the British Parliament had decided how the lines should be drawn, the white brotherhood of Britain reconstituted, at least for the moment. Race, gender, property, labour and purported level of civilisation now determined who was included in and excluded from the political nation, how groups belonged to the social body.

Appendix A. England, Wales and Scotland: the Reform Acts of 1832

1. England and Wales

Franchise qualifications

Boroughs

1. Adult males over twenty-one owning or occupying as tenant property (a house, warehouse, office or shop) assessed for rating at £10 per annum or more were enfranchised, provided that
   a. They had been in possession or residence of the property for at least one year;
   b. They had paid all poor rates and assessed taxes on the property; and
   c. They had not been in receipt of poor relief during the previous year.
2. Those who had previously had the vote under a variety of local provisions, but did not qualify as £10 owners or occupiers under the 1832 reform, retained the right to vote during their lifetimes, as 'ancient rights' voters, so long as they lived in the borough or within seven miles of it. This right could not be left to their heirs.

Counties Those enfranchised were:

1. Adult males over twenty-one owning freehold property assessed for the land tax at 40s (£2) or more. (This had been the qualification since 1430.) If such property was not owned directly but held for life only,

Information in Appendices A–D is taken from: Michael Dyer, *Men of Property and Intelligence: The Scottish Electoral System Prior to 1884* (Aberdeen: Scottish Cultural Press, 1996); Norman Gash, *Politics in the Age of Peel: A Study in the Technique of Parliamentary Representation, 1830–1850* (2nd edn, Hassocks: Harvester, 1977), pt I; H. J. Hanham, 'Introduction', to Charles R. Dod, *Electoral Facts from 1832 to 1853 Impartially Stated . . .* (1853), ed. H. J. Hanham (Brighton: Harvester Press, 1972); K. T. Hoppen, 'The Franchise and Electoral Politics in England and Ireland, 1832–1885', *History* 70 (1985), 202–17; Hoppen, *Elections, Politics and Society in Ireland, 1832–1885* (Oxford: Clarendon Press, 1984); John Prest, *Politics in the Age of Cobden* (Basingstoke: Macmillan, 1977), ch. 2; Charles Seymour, *Electoral Reform in England and Wales* (New Haven: Yale Historical Publications, 1915); F. B. Smith, *The Making of the Second Reform Bill* (Cambridge University Press, 1966); Eric J. Evans, *The Forging of the Modern State: Early Industrial Britain, 1783–1870* (2nd edn, London: Longman, 1996); Evans, *The Great Reform Act of 1832* (2nd edn, London: Routledge, 1994).

holders could qualify only by occupation, marriage, bequest, officeholding or by the property being worth £10. A freehold did not necessarily have to be in land, but could include annuities, offices, shareholdings in enterprises which managed real estate, and life-interests in schools, almshouses and hospitals.
2. Adult males holding land assessed for the land tax as £10 copyholders (a leaseholder by manorial custom).
3. Leaseholders for sixty years or more.
4. Adult males leasing or renting land worth £50 or more per annum. (This was a result of the 'Chandos Amendment'.)
5. Freeholders and copyholders who had occupied property for six months, leaseholders and tenants for twelve months.

Registration

All qualified voters in both counties and boroughs had to be entered on the register of electors, revised annually, in order to cast a vote; in the boroughs this was done automatically, though in the counties electors had to claim their votes.

Distribution

Boroughs

1. Fifty-six lost seats.
2. Thirty lost one of two members.
3. Twenty-two new seats created, each with two members.
4. Nineteen new seats created, each with one member.

Counties

1. Yorkshire to have six members.
2. Twenty-six to elect four members each instead of two.
3. Seven to elect three members each instead of two.
4. Isle of Wight became separate county constituency.

2. Scotland

Franchise qualifications

Burghs

1. Adult males over twenty-one owning or occupying as tenant property (a house, warehouse, office or shop) assessed for rating at £10 per annum or more were enfranchised, provided that

a. They had been in possession or residence of the property for at least one year;
b. They had paid all poor rates and assessed taxes on the property; and
c. They had not been in receipt of poor relief during the previous year.

Counties Under 1832 the vote was extended to those who were:
1. £10 owners of land, houses, feu duties or other property to the annual value of £10.
2. Tenants with leases of over fifty-seven years worth £10, and of over nineteen years for those worth £50.
3. Tenants and occupiers who paid yearly rent of no less than £50.
4. Those who were already voters in under the pre-1832 system, who retained the vote for their lifetimes.
5. Life-rent office holders of offices worth £10 or more (where the holding of property, by appointment, yielded a life-rent, such as the manses and glebes of ministers and schoolmasters).

Registration

All qualified voters in both counties and burghs had to be entered on the register of electors, revised annually, in order to cast a vote; in the burghs this was done automatically by town clerks, though in the counties the responsibility lay with parish ministers, and it was the responsibility of electors, until the County Voters Registration Act of 1861, to claim their votes.

Distribution

Burghs
1. Eight new seats created (increasing the total from fifteen to twenty-three).
2. Edinburgh and Glasgow to return two members each.
3. Aberdeen, Dundee, Greenock, Paisley and Perth to return one member each.
4. The other fourteen seats were elected by districts (groupings of burghs): each district to elect one member.

Counties The number of county seats remained at thirty: twenty-seven counties each elected one member; three groups of two counties each elected one member: Elgin and Nairn; Ross and Cromarty; Clackmannan and Kinross.

Appendix B. Ireland: the Catholic Emancipation Act (1829), the 1832 Reform Act and the Irish Reform Act (1850)

Catholic Emancipation Act (1829)

1. Disenfranchised 40s (£2) freeholders.
2. Raised the property qualification in the counties to a £10 a year freehold. The Irish freeholder normally held land subject to the payment of a nominal sum as a tenant for life or succession of lives, and the act of 1829 required the freeholder to swear as a 'solvent tenant' that he could afford an extra £10 in rent.

1832 Reform Act (Ireland)

Franchise qualifications

Boroughs £10 occupier and 'ancient rights' franchise, as in England and Wales.

Counties

1. Enfranchised owners of property with an annual value of at least £10 (as under Catholic Emancipation Act).
2. Added leaseholders with leaseholds to the value of £10 with leases of at least twenty years.

Since the leaseholders' position was endangered by the 'solvent tenant' test described above, which could have left them vulnerable to higher rent demands, the act substituted for the freeholder's oath a declaration that he had a 'beneficial interest' of £10 a year in the holding. This phrase was subject to conflicting interpretation, as to whether it simply implied profit or income of £10 a year, or should be identified with the 'solvent tenant' test. This uncertainty, added to the problems of the registration system (noted below), limited the size of the Irish electorate significantly between 1832 and 1850.

3. Continued a registration system dating from 1727. Voters were required to register their title but having once registered obtained a

'certificate' entitling them to vote for eight years without further investigation. The number of voters at any one time was therefore unknown.

Distribution

Boroughs and universities

1. Thirty-five original seats: Belfast, Galway, Limerick and Waterford each gained one seat.
2. Dublin University gained a second seat. (The franchise was for all holders of MA and higher degrees.)

The Irish Reform Act of 1850

This act was made possible by the introduction in 1838 of an Irish Poor Law and the resultant valuations of property for ratepaying purposes. It transformed the situation in Ireland in two ways:

1. Both county and borough voters qualified through the simple occupation of premises valued for the Poor Law as worth £12 and £8 respectively.
2. Voters' lists were to be maintained automatically, and it was not necessary for voters to claim individually.

Appendix C. Reform proposals for England and Wales, 1852–66

The name(s) in parentheses after the date indicates the main sponsor(s) of the bill, with political affiliation. All proposals refer to those who would obtain the vote.

February 1852 (Lord John Russell, Whig–Liberal)

1. All occupiers to the value of £5 (boroughs) and £20 (counties).
2. Those paying 40s a year in direct taxes (in both counties and boroughs).

February 1854 (Lord John Russell, Whig–Liberal)

1. £6 occupiers resident for more than two and a half years (boroughs) and £10 occupiers (counties).
2. Those paying 40s a year in direct taxes in both counties and boroughs (as in 1852).
3. Men with a minimum yearly salary of £100 paid at least quarterly.
4. Those possessing £10 a year income from funds, bank stock or East India Company shares.
5. Graduates of any UK university.
6. Any man with £50 deposited for at least three years in a savings bank in his borough of residence.

   Redistribution of seats to include: sixty-six small boroughs to be disenfranchised; addition of seventeen seats to the boroughs, two to the Inns of Court, one to London University and forty-six to the counties.

February 1859 (Lord Derby and Benjamin Disraeli, Conservative)

1. £10 occupiers in both counties and boroughs.
2. Lodgers worth £20 a year.

3. 40s (£2) freeholder living in a borough must vote in the borough and not in the adjacent county.
4. Members of certain professions, government pensioners, university graduates and those with at least £60 in savings banks. (These were what John Bright called the 'fancy franchises'.)

   Redistribution of seats to include: seventy small boroughs to be disenfranchised; additions of eighteen seats to large boroughs; fifty-two seats to go to counties.

March 1860 (Lord John Russell, Whig–Liberal)

£6 rental qualification (borough occupiers) and £10 (county occupiers).

Some small redistribution of seats was included.

March 1866 (W. E. Gladstone, Liberal – for Lord Russell's government)

Franchise qualiWcations

Boroughs

1. £7 rental qualification. This was intended to suggest a rather higher outlay by the potential voter. A £7 rental implied the 'gross estimated rental exclusive of local rates and surcharges for furniture and repair'. Gladstone's calculation was that the gross outlay would be approximately £11/4/0d, suggesting an annual income of £67/4/0d or 26s a week.[1]
2. Lodger franchise of £10.
3. Those with at least £50 in savings banks.

Counties

1. £14 rental qualification.
2. Those with at least £50 in savings banks.

Redistribution

Forty-nine small boroughs (populations less than 8,000) to be disenfranchised with boroughs grouped:

a. Twenty-six seats to go to the counties.
b. Twenty-two seats to go to the boroughs.
c. One seat to go to London University.

[1] F. B. Smith, *Making of the Second Reform Bill*, p. 67. £67/4/0d = £67.20; 26s = £1.30.

Appendix D. The Reform Acts of 1867–8: England and Wales, and Scotland

The Reform Act for England and Wales, June 1867

Franchise qualifications

Boroughs Those enfranchised were:

1. All ratepaying adult male occupiers.
2. Lodgers in lodgings 'of annual value' of at least £10 a year, resident for at least 12 months.[2] The practice of 'compounding', by which lodgers paid their rates through their landlord, was abolished, though this was reversed in 1869.

Counties Those enfranchised were:

1. Occupiers – as owners, leaseholders, or copyholders on a sixty-year lease – of lands to a yearly value of £5.
2. Ratepaying tenants who occupied lands to a rateable value of £12 a year.

Redistribution

Boroughs

1. One single-member and three double-member constituencies disenfranchised for corruption.
2. Forty-two small boroughs (populations of less than 10,000) lost some or all of their representation:
   a. Three lost both members.
   b. Thirty-five lost one of two members.
   c. Four lost a single member.
3. Two new double-member and nine new single-member borough constituencies created.

[2] The term 'of annual value', suggested by John Bright, followed that in the Liberal Bill of 1866, and is defined by F. B. Smith as 'the rating value of the unfurnished lodging, representing an actual rental of almost £15 when charges for furnishings and services were added' (*ibid.*, p. 194).

4. Four cities increased from double-member to triple-member constituencies: Birmingham, Leeds, Liverpool, Manchester.
5. Two towns increased from single-member to double-member constituencies: Merthyr Tydfil and Salford.

Counties

1. Ten counties to elect two additional members each.
2. Lancashire to elect three additional members.
3. West Riding of Yorkshire to elect two additional members.

Universities University of London to elect one member.

Reform Act for Scotland, June 1868

Franchise qualifications

Burghs In general this provided for the same qualifications as those of England and Wales: the £10 occupier franchise was introduced, except that no specific lodger franchise was included since there lodgers were legally tenants.

Counties The qualification for owners fell to £5 and that for tenants to £14.

Reform Act for Ireland, June 1868

Franchise qualifications

Boroughs Reduced qualification from £8 to £4.

Counties Franchise maintained at £12.

Appendix E. The number of borough and county seats in the UK, 1832–68

		England	Wales	Scotland	Ireland	Total
1833	Counties	144	15	30	64	253
	Boroughs	323	14	23	39	399
	Universities	4			2	6
	Total	471	29	53	105	658
1868	Counties	169	15	32	64	280
	Boroughs	290	14	26	39	369
	Universities	5		2	2	9
	Total	464	29	60	105	658
Changes, 1833–1868						
		England	Wales	Scotland	Ireland	Total
	Counties	25	0	2	0	27
	Boroughs	–33	0	3	0	–30
	Universities	1	0	2	0	3
	Total	–7	0	7	0	0

Source: Eric J. Evans, *The Forging of the Modern State: Early Industrial Britain, 1783–1870* (2nd edn, London: Longman, 1996), Table B.iv, p. 401.

Appendix F. The size of the electorate in the UK, 1866–8

	Boroughs	Counties	Total
1. 1866			
England and Wales	514,026	542,633	1,056,659
Scotland	55,515	49,979	105,494
Ireland	30,958	164,408	195,366
UK	600,499	757,020	1,357,519
2. 1868			
England and Wales	1,225,042	791,253	2,016,295
Scotland	152,312	74,978	227,290
Ireland	53,070	180,090	233,160
UK	1,430,424	1,046,321	2,476,745

Increases, 1866–1868

	Boroughs	Counties	Total
England and Wales	711,016	248,620	959,636
Scotland	96,797	24,999	121,796
Ireland	22,112	15,682	37,794
UK	829,925	289,301	1,119,226

% changes (1866 = 100)

	Boroughs	Counties	Total
England and Wales	138.3	45.8	90.8
Scotland	174.4	50.0	115.5
Ireland	71.4	9.5	19.3
UK	138.2	38.2	82.4

Figure 3. *The electorate of the United Kingdom, 1866–8*

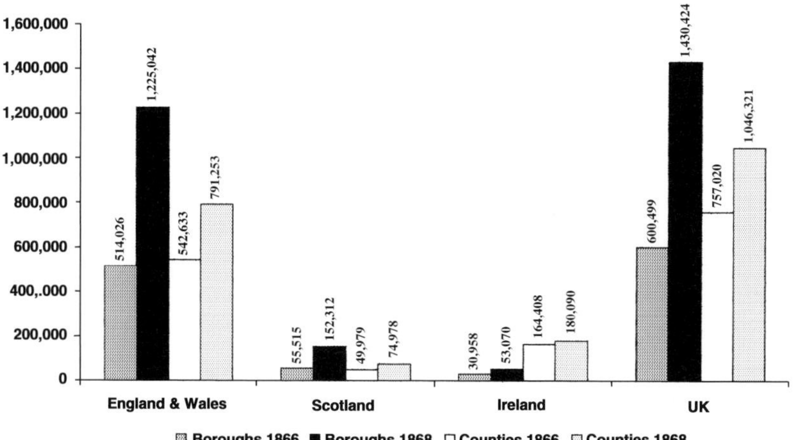

Source: F. B. Smith, *The Making of the Second Reform Bill* (Cambridge University Press, 1966), p. 236.

Appendix G. Cast of characters

WILLIAM ALLAN (1813–74)

Junta member (see Junta entry). Born in Ulster, then worked in Liverpool and Crewe. Secretary of the Journeymen Steam Engine Makers' Society 1847–50 and then the general secretary of the Amalgamated Society of Engineers (estab. 1851) 1851–74. Treasurer of the Parliamentary Committee of the Trades Union Congress, 1871–4.

VISCOUNTESS AMBERLEY (1842–74)

The daughter of a Liberal politician, Lord Stanley of Alderley, and of Lady Stanley, Kate Amberley married a fellow admirer of John Stuart Mill and Harriet Taylor, John Russell, Viscount Amberley, in 1864. She became a close friend of Helen Taylor, and supported the work of Emily Davies and Elizabeth Garrett in education and medicine. In 1870 she gave her first lecture on women's suffrage, and from then until her early death was an active organiser and speaker in the cause, and president of the Bristol and West of England Women's Suffrage Society.

ROBERT APPLEGARTH (1834–1924)

Junta member (see Junta entry). Born in Hull then worked as a joiner in Sheffield. General secretary of the Amalgamated Society of Carpenters and Joiners 1861–71 and representative of the ASCJ on the London Trades Council from 1863. On the general council of the International Working Men's Association 1865 and again 1868–72. Committee member of the Reform League. Member of the Royal Commission on Contagious Diseases (1871–3), as a result of which he resigned as general secretary of the ASCJ because of criticisms of his appointment. Became secretary to Edward Jenkins of the National Education League and later an agent for a mining equipment company.

MATTHEW ARNOLD (1822–88)

Eldest son of Thomas Arnold, he was educated at Winchester, Rugby and Balliol College, Oxford. In 1847 he became private secretary to the Marquis of Lansdowne and in 1851 was appointed inspector of schools, a post which he held for thirty-five years. His personal preoccupation was, however, with cultural initiatives directed against the mediocrity and philistinism of the English middle classes, through his poetry, his literary criticism and his most famous essay, *Culture and Anarchy* (1867).

EDMOND BEALES (1803–81)

Son of the Cambridgeshire corn merchant and radical, Samuel Pickering Beales, he was educated at Eton and Trinity College, Cambridge, and became a barrister. Politically active in the cause of Poland from the 1830s, and the anti-Russian campaigns of the 1850s, he organised the Garibaldi Reception Committee in 1864 and supported the North during the American Civil War. He spoke on behalf of parliamentary reform in the early 1860s, was instrumental in the formation of the Reform League in 1865 and became its leader, 1865–9. He stood unsuccessfully for Tower Hamlets as a Reform League candidate in 1868.

LYDIA BECKER (1827–90)

Daughter of a Manchester chemical manufacturer whose family had come from Germany a generation earlier, she was educated mainly at home in England and Germany. Hearing Barbara Bodichon's paper at the meeting of the National Association for the Promotion of Social Science in Manchester in October 1866 converted her to the movement for women's suffrage, of which she became a leading figure, dominating the Manchester Women's Suffrage Society for many years. In 1870 she founded the *Women's Suffrage Journal* and continued to edit it until her death. She was also elected to the Manchester School Board in 1870.

EDWARD SPENCER BEESLY (1831–1915)

Son of a clergyman, he was educated at Wadham College, Oxford, taught at Marlborough College from 1854 and became professor of history and principal of University College Hall, London, in 1860. Greatly influenced by the work of the French positivist Auguste Comte, his vision was of a moralistic, capitalist utopia. He drew increasingly close to trade unionism in the 1860s, becoming a close associate of the leaders of the London Trades Council, a frequent contributor to the *Bee-Hive*, and an active campaigner on behalf of the Reform League. He also sought to foster international contacts between British trade unionists and their European counterparts from the 1860s.

BARBARA LEIGH SMITH BODICHON (1827–91)

Daughter of a Unitarian radical MP, she studied at the new Ladies College in Bedford Square from 1849, and in 1854 published *A Brief Summary in Plain Language of the Most Important Laws Concerning Women*. In 1856 she drew up the petition advocating the reform of married women's property laws, and, with Bessie Rayner Parkes, established the *English Woman's Journal* in 1858. She was influential in the early phases of the women's suffrage movement, organising with Emily Davies and Helen Taylor the first petition to the House of Commons in June 1866, and was also involved in the foundation of Girton College, Cambridge. Her feminist interests were shared with a career as a successful artist and her marriage to Eugène Bodichon, with whom she shared a home in Algeria for part of every year.

JACOB BRIGHT (1821–99)

From a Rochdale millowning family, like his brother John Bright, he was educated as a Quaker, and worked for the family firm in Rochdale. Though he was committed to the politics of the Anti-Corn Law League in the 1840s, he also had links to local Chartist groups in Rochdale, and supported the Complete Suffrage Union of Joseph Sturge, which attempted to link the two movements. In the 1860s he advocated a reforming Irish policy, and was an officer of the Union and Emancipation Society. With his wife, formerly Ursula Mellor, he was a leading campaigner for women's suffrage, and one of its most important spokesmen in the House of Commons. He was MP for Manchester, 1867–74 and 1876–85, and for Manchester South, 1886–95.

JOHN BRIGHT (1811–89)

Like his brother Jacob, John Bright was educated as a Quaker and first worked in the family business. A leading campaigner for the Anti-Corn Law League, he became MP for Durham in 1843, and for Manchester between 1847 and 1857. In the 1850s he was a leading advocate of parliamentary and financial reform, and opponent of the Crimean War. Defeated at Manchester in 1857, he was MP for Birmingham from 1857 to 1885, and for Birmingham Central 1885 to 1889. He was an active supporter of the North in the US Civil War, and one of the most important campaigners and orators on parliamentary reform outside the House of Commons in 1866–7. He entered Gladstone's cabinet in 1868 as president of the Board of Trade.

HENRY AUSTIN BRUCE (BARON ABERDARE FROM 1873) (1815–95)

Heir to a coalmining fortune, he pursued a legal career from 1837, and was MP for Merthyr Tydfil between 1852 and 1868, and for Renfrewshire 1869–73. He was actively interested in the work of the Social Science Association, and, as education minister 1864–6 and home secretary 1868–73, was able to put some of his reforming ideals into practice.

JOSEPHINE BUTLER (1828–1906)

From a landed Northumbrian family with Whig connections, the Greys, she married George Butler, an Oxford-based Anglican clergyman and educationist, in 1852. They moved to Liverpool in 1864, and in 1866 Butler began workhouse visiting in Liverpool, and established a refuge for prostitutes. George and Josephine Butler were both involved in the work of the North of England Council for the Higher Education of Women. Her published works included *The Education and Employment of Women* (1868), and her edited *Woman's Work and Woman's Culture* (1869). In 1869, Butler became involved in the work for which she is best remembered, the campaign to repeal the Contagious Diseases Acts, which were finally repealed in 1886.

THOMAS CARLYLE (1795–1881)

Son of a Dumfriesshire mason, educated at the parish school and Edinburgh University, he abandoned his first plan to become a Presbyterian minister, and made a career by reviewing and translating Goethe from the German. He moved to Chelsea in 1834, and in his historical writing focused especially on the careers of great men, the 'heroes' of his work, *On Heroes, Hero-Worship and the Heroic in History* (1841). He also warned of the dangers of revolution, democracy and laissez-faire, as in *The French Revolution* (1837), *Chartism* (1839) and *Past and Present* (1843). In 1849 he published anonymously his 'Occasional Discourse on the Negro Question', which argued that black men were born to be mastered. The essay was republished in 1853 with the more inflammatory title of 'Occasional Discourse on the Nigger Question'. After the events at Morant Bay in 1865 Carlyle led the support for Governor Eyre and celebrated him as a hero. In his 'Shooting Niagara: and After?' (1867), Carlyle's fear of democracy was linked with his contempt for black people and their white supporters.

FRANCES POWER COBBE (1822–1904)

From an Anglo-Irish landowning background, Cobbe was mainly educated at home. Deciding, after the death of her father in 1857, to find some way to maintain herself independently, Cobbe took an active interest in the work of Mary Carpenter for delinquent children. Moving to London, she earned her living as a journalist for the *Echo, Standard and Daily News* in the 1860s and 1870s. Her article 'Criminals, Idiots, Women and Minors' (1868) argued for women's legal right to divorce, child custody and economic independence. She was also an active campaigner against vivisection. In 1884, Cobbe retired to Wales with her close friend Mary Lloyd.

EDWIN COULSON (?–1893)

Junta member (see Junta entry). Secretary of the London Order of the Operative Bricklayers' Society, 1860–90.

JOSEPH COWEN JUN. (1829–1900)

The eldest son of the industrialist and Liberal MP for Newcastle 1865–72, Joseph Cowen sen., Joseph Cowen jun. was active in the cause of revolutionary and national movements from an early age. A friend of Mazzini and Kossuth, he strongly supported the Society of the Friends of Italy, 1853–5. He financed a number of northern reform periodicals including the *English Republic* (1851–5) and the *Northern Tribune* (1854–5). He established the Northern Reform Union in 1858 to campaign for manhood suffrage, vote by ballot and the abolition of property qualifications for MPs, and purchased the *Newcastle Daily Chronicle* in 1860 as its mouthpiece. He was treasurer of the Northern Reform League, 1866–7, also active in the campaigns for a free Sunday, for women's suffrage and in the co-operative and republican movements. He was MP for Newcastle 1874–86.

EMILY DAVIES (1830–1921)

Daughter of an evangelical clergyman and schoolmaster, she received, unlike her brothers, a very limited education, in Gateshead from 1840. Introduced to the women's movement through a meeting with Barbara

Leigh Smith Bodichon, she became actively involved with the *English Woman's Journal*. After moving to London in 1861, she worked successfully to improve the educational position of women, ensuring the inclusion of girls in the Schools Enquiry Commission of 1867–8, and establishing the future Girton College in 1869. A leading member of the Kensington Society, she, with Bodichon and Helen Taylor, organised the first petition for women's suffrage to the House of Commons in June 1866. Though a member of the first London Committee, she retreated from the women's suffrage movement after conflict with Helen Taylor and Mill. In 1919 she was one of the few members of the early women's movement to cast her vote.

CHARLES WENTWORTH DILKE (1843–1911)

The second baronet, he was educated at Trinity Hall, Cambridge, and graduated in law in 1866. After a period of travel in the British colonies in 1866–7 he was elected MP for Chelsea in 1868. An advanced radical, he opposed W. E. Forster's Education Bill of 1870 calling for directly elected school boards in place of committees of boards of guardians. In 1871 he toured the country speaking on republican issues leading to riots at Bristol, Bolton, Derby and Birmingham. Despite sustained opposition he was returned as Liberal MP for Chelsea in 1874. He later became, with Joseph Chamberlain, an acknowledged leader of the radical section of the Liberal party in Parliament, and a committed Home Ruler; his career was ruined by an affair with Mrs Crawford, wife of the Liberal MP for Lanark. He retired from public life in 1885, though he returned to the Commons in 1892.

BENJAMIN DISRAELI (CREATED EARL OF BEACONSFIELD, 1876) (1804–81)

Son of Isaac D'Israeli, a man of letters, he was descended from an Italian Jewish family, but was baptised an Anglican in 1817. A novelist and journalist in the 1820s, he stood for Parliament for the first time in 1832. Elected in 1837, he became part of a small Conservative backbench group known as 'Young England', which combined the Conservative politics of the landed interest with a concern for social reform that was also evident in his novels *Coningsby* (1844) and *Sybil* (1845). When in 1845 Robert Peel determined to repeal the Corn Laws, Disraeli's fierce attacks helped to overthrow Peel. As a major political force, he became Chancellor of the Exchequer and leader of the House of Commons in Lord Derby's governments of 1852, 1858–9 and 1866–8. He became prime minister briefly on Derby's retirement in 1868 and again, and most importantly, between 1874 and 1880.

EDWARD JOHN EYRE (1815–1901)

Third son of a Yorkshire vicar, and originally destined for the army, he chose instead to seek his fortune in Australia in 1833, where he became well-known as an explorer of South Australia. Sympathetic to Aboriginal peoples, he became their first named protector in South Australia. In 1846 he returned to England; he was appointed as lieutenant governor of southern New Zealand in 1847 but quarrelled with his superior, and returned home. In 1854 he was appointed lieutenant governor of St Vincent, then of Antigua and in 1862 Jamaica. When rebellion broke out at Morant Bay in 1865, he was convinced that it was part of a black conspiracy to massacre all white people and reacted accordingly, imposing martial law and pursuing all those seen as rebels with brutality. The Liberal government removed him from his post and on his return to England he was deeply shocked by the condemnation of his conduct from a vociferous minority. He retired to Devon where he lived quietly until his death.

HENRY FAWCETT (1833–84)

Son of a Salisbury draper, he was educated at Peterhouse, Cambridge, and became a fellow of Trinity Hall. He was blinded in 1858, but continued his political and academic career, with the support of Millicent Garrett Fawcett whom he married in 1867. He was appointed professor of political economy at Cambridge in 1863, and lectured and wrote extensively on economic matters. As a longstanding friend of John Stuart Mill, his interests included proportional representation, suffrage reform and the enfranchisement of women. He secured election as an MP for Brighton in 1865. As a radical MP he supported the Reform Bill of 1867 and the abolition of religious tests at the university, and recommended extension of the Factory Acts to agricultural labourers. He was to become postmaster general in Gladstone's second ministry.

MILLICENT GARRETT FAWCETT (1847–1929)

One of ten children of an Aldeburgh merchant, Millicent Garrett encountered the early women's movement through her sister, Elizabeth, then fighting to enter the medical profession, and through Emily Davies. In 1867 she married Henry Fawcett, whom she had come to know through the liberal circle around John Stuart Mill. Actively committed to women's suffrage from 1867, and an early member of the London Committee, she was a powerful speaker for the cause. She was also interested in political economy, publishing *Political Economy for Beginners* (1870) and, with Henry Fawcett, *Essays and Lectures on Political Subjects* (1872). A committed Liberal, and also a Unionist, in 1889 she contributed to a split in the ranks of Liberal women suffragists over Home Rule for Ireland. From 1897 she became leader of the National Union of Women's Suffrage Societies, until 1919 when the principle of votes for women was won.

WILLIAM EWART GLADSTONE (1809–98)

From a family of Liverpool merchants and slaveowners, he was educated at Eton and Oxford, and entered the Commons as a Tory in 1832. President of the Board of Trade under Sir Robert Peel, he remained as a Peelite after the split in the Conservative party caused by the repeal of the Corn Laws. He joined Palmerston's ministry as Chancellor of the Exchequer in 1852–5, and his role as Chancellor in Palmerston's last ministry, 1859–65, marked his new career in the united Liberal party after 1859. In Earl Russell's ministry of 1865–6, Gladstone, still Chancellor, dominated the Commons debates. He led the Liberal party to victory in the general election of 1868, speaking widely and powerfully in the country on the question of disestablishing the Irish church. He led subsequent Liberal ministries of 1868–74, 1880–5, 1886 and 1892–4.

GEORGE WILLIAM GORDON (C. 1820–65)

Son of a Jamaican planter and an enslaved woman, Gordon was helped by his father to establish himself in business and became a prosperous landowner. Sitting in the Jamaican House of Assembly, one of the small group of 'coloured' men in that predominantly white body, he became a significant opponent of the administration of Governor Eyre. When the rebellion broke out at Morant Bay, Eyre was convinced that Gordon was to blame and he was arrested, tried and hanged. A Baptist, a gentleman and married to a white woman, he became a martyr for the opponents of Eyre in England.

DANIEL GUILE (1814–83)

Junta member (see Junta entry). Born near Liverpool. Joined the Friendly Society of Iron Moulders in 1834 and was secretary of the Friendly Society of Iron Founders, 1863–81. Member of the London Trades Council, 1864–7 and of the Parliamentary Committee of the Trades Union Congress, 1875–6.

RUSSELL GURNEY (1804–78)

Son of a baron of the Court of Exchequer, a barrister and QC, he became recorder of the City of London in 1857 and entered Parliament as the Conservative member for Southampton in 1865. In that year he was sent out by the Liberal government to investigate the conduct of Governor Eyre. He was also an important spokesman for the women's suffrage movement and actively involved in the campaign for married women's property legislation, with his wife, Emelia Batten Gurney. He introduced the Married Women's Property Bill in 1869 and again in 1870, though the latter was fundamentally transformed by the House of Lords before passing into law. Emelia Gurney was strongly committed to the admission of women into medicine, and served on the council of Girton College.

FREDERIC HARRISON (1831–1923)

While a student and then Fellow of Wadham College, Oxford, 1851–6, Harrison was strongly influenced by Richard Congreve and became an advocate of Positivist doctrines. With other leading Positivists, including E. S. Beesly, Harrison was part of the group of intellectuals who were closest to the leaders of trade unions and working-class politicians in the 1860s and 1870s. He was a member of the Royal Commission on Trade Unions (1867–9) and with Thomas Hughes wrote the Minority Report, which defended the principles of trade unionism and provided the programmatic basis for the trade unions' campaign for full legal recognition of unionism in the early 1870s. A barrister, Harrison was also active in legal education as well as being a prolific writer on historical and political subjects. In his later years he became increasingly conservative, especially on imperial questions. He published his *Autobiographic Memoirs* in two volumes in 1911.

GEORGE HOWELL (1833–1910)

Son of a mason and builder, he was variously employed as a ploughboy, journeyman shoemaker, bricklayer and deputy foreman, and was also a practising Methodist and vigorous temperance advocate. He was active in London radical clubs and Benjamin Lucraft's North London Political Union, and an organiser in the London builders' strike, 1859–60. Elected to the London Trades Council in 1861, he promoted the Trades Unionists' Manhood Suffrage and Vote by Ballot Association in 1862. His international interests included membership of the Garibaldi Reception Committee and the International Working Men's Association in 1864. In 1865 he was elected permanent secretary to the Reform

League. In the election of 1868 he stood unsuccessfully for Aylesbury in 1868. He was secretary of the Parliamentary Committee of the Trades Union Congress 1871–6, and was elected MP for Bethnal Green in 1885.

THOMAS HUGHES (1822–96)

Son of the classical scholar, John Hughes, he was educated at Rugby and Oxford and called to the Bar in 1848. Strongly influenced by the Christian Socialist doctrines of F. D. Maurice and J. M. Ludlow, he was a vigorous exponent of Christian Socialist-inspired co-operative ventures. He was influential in the foundation of the Working Men's College at Great Ormond Street, and was its principal 1872–83. He was elected for Lambeth in 1865 and for Frome in 1868 on a manhood suffrage platform. In the Commons he gained a reputation as an independent social reformer, proposing an unsuccessful trade union bill in 1869 following on his membership of the Royal Commission on Trade Unions (1867–9). With Frederic Harrison he wrote the Minority Report of the Commission, which advocated the recognition of trade union rights. He left the House after an unsuccessful candidature for Marylebone in 1874. He was chairman of the first Co-operative Congress in 1869. He is chiefly known for his authorship of *Tom Brown's Schooldays* (1857).

ERNEST JONES (1819–69)

From an aristocratic German family background, in 1838, he moved to England and trained as a barrister. After bankruptcy in 1844, he became increasingly involved with Chartist politics and the world of international exiles. Imprisoned for two years for inflammatory speeches, 1848–50, he became the leading figure in the Chartism of the 1850s. In 1861 he moved to Manchester to take up his legal career and was active in a range of reforming associations, including the Union and Emancipation Society and the Northern Department of the Reform League. He acted as one of the lawyers in defence of the Fenians in the Manchester trials of 1867. He was also a supporter of women's suffrage. He stood unsuccessfully as a candidate for the United Liberal party in Manchester in 1868.

'JUNTA' OF TRADE UNIONISTS

The Junta was the term applied by Sidney and Beatrice Webb to five leading London unionists who played a key role in the labour politics in the 1860s: William Allan, Robert Applegarth, Edwin Coulson, Daniel Guile and George Odger (see individual entries for each man).

CHARLES KINGSLEY (1819–75)

Son of a Devonshire clergyman, after attending the University of Cambridge, Kingsley obtained a curacy at Eversley in Hampshire where he became rector in 1846. During the 1840s he had some sympathy with radical politics, especially Chartism, and helped to found the movement of Christian Socialism in 1848, as well as Queens College for young women in 1848. His novels include works of social reform, like *Yeast* and *Alton Locke* (1850), and historical novels such as *Westward Ho!* (1855) and *Hereward the Wake* (1866). From 1860 to 1869 he was professor of modern history at Cambridge, and increasingly he appealed to a Protestant and Anglo-Saxon nationalism, evident in his support of the Confederate South and Governor Eyre. He continued to be interested in women's education, and was a moderate supporter of the movement for women's suffrage.

WILLIAM JAMES LINTON (1812–98)

Apprenticed as a wood engraver, Linton was a leading internationalist and republican and prominent English supporter of Giuseppe Mazzini. With Mazzini and others Linton founded the Peoples' International League in 1847, a body established to further the rights of every people to self-government and maintenance of their own nationality. In March 1848 Linton was also a founder, with other 'moderate' London Chartists, of the People's Charter Union. He played an important part in shaping the PCU's concern with foreign affairs. Subsequently he was a keen supporter of Italian nationalism through the 'Friends of Italy' (1851–5) and was also a leading figure in the republican movement, mainly through his journal, *English Republic* (1851–5). He married Eliza Lynn, the novelist and woman of letters, in 1858 (although they subsequently separated). In 1866 Linton emigrated to New Haven, Connecticut, where he worked as a printer and engraver and published a number of works on engraving, including his *History of Wood Engraving in America* (1882), as well as his *Memories*, an autobiography, in 1895.

ROBERT LOWE (CREATED VISCOUNT SHERBROOKE, 1880) (1811–92)

Educated at Winchester and Oxford he became a barrister and politician in Australia, 1842–50. On his return to London in 1850 he acted as leader-writer for *The Times*, and entered the Commons in 1852 (holding the seat for Kidderminster 1852–9, Calne 1859–67 and London University 1868–80). After holding junior office, he became education minister 1859–64, and Chancellor of the Exchequer 1868–73. He was the first MP for London University 1868–80. Committed to strict financial control of educational expenditure, he was the outstanding opponent of democracy in the Commons, drawing in his speeches on his Australian experience. He led the group of Liberals known as the Cave of Adullam to vote with the Conservatives against the Liberal bill of 1866.

FREDERICK DENISON MAURICE (1805–72)

Born a Unitarian, Maurice reacted against Unitarian teaching, hoping to read for the Bar after attending Cambridge. However in 1831 he attended Exeter College, Oxford, to take Anglican orders, and in 1834 was ordained to a curacy near Leamington. In 1840 he was appointed to the chair of English literature and modern history at King's College, London, and acquired friends, including J. M. Ludlow, Charles Kingsley and Thomas Hughes, who were to form the Christian Socialist movement. In 1848 he helped to establish Queen's College for Women for the education of young women. From 1854 he focused less on Christian Socialism than on the Working Men's College which he founded in that year. In 1866 he was elected to the chair of casuistry, moral theology and moral philosophy at Cambridge. His many publications included *The Workman and the Franchise: Chapters from English History on the Representation and Education of the People* (1866).

JOHN STUART MILL (1806–73)

The young Mill's education, at home with his utilitarian father, and his reaction against it were famously recorded in his *Autobiography* (1873). He first met Harriet Taylor in 1830 and their relationship increased his interest in the position of women. In support of the Philosophic Radicals in the House of Commons he edited the *London Review* (later *London and Westminster Review*) from 1835 to 1840. From 1840 onwards he concentrated on writing on philosophical and political subjects. His major works were: *A System of Logic* (1843); *Principles of Political Economy* (1848); *On Liberty* (1859); *Considerations on Representative Government* (1861); and *The Subjection of Women* (1869). In the 1860s Mill was an active supporter of the North in the American Civil War, and the central public figure in the Jamaica Committee, set up in 1866 to campaign for the prosecution of Edward Eyre for his responsibility for the massacre at Morant Bay, Jamaica. From 1865 to 1868 he was elected as MP for Westminster; there he spoke many times on parliamentary reform, introduced the subject of women's suffrage to the House of Commons and intervened influentially on the debate about the future of Ireland, partly through *England and Ireland* (1868). After 1868 he continued, through his stepdaughter, Helen Taylor, to take an active interest in the campaign for women's suffrage.

DANIEL O'DONOGHUE (OR THE O'DONOGHUE) (1833–89)

As the son of Charles O'Donoghue and nephew of Daniel O'Connell, he sought to inherit the mantle of O'Connell, but failed in his bid to reunite the repeal movement. Educated at Stonyhurst, he was elected as a Whig for Tipperary 1857–63, expelled from the House of Commons 1863 for impropriety and re-elected for Tralee 1865–85. He spoke widely on parliamentary reform during the 1860s, and was president of the Irish branch of the Reform League, 1866–7, and elected vice-president of the Reform League and of the Scottish National Reform League in 1867. He was declared bankrupt in 1870 and retired from the House in 1885.

GEORGE ODGER (1813–77)

Junta member (see Junta entry). Born near Plymouth. Chartist and then republican. A London West End ladies' shoemaker and secretary of the London Trades Council 1862–72. Member of the General Council of the International Working Men's Association, 1864–71. Stood unsuccessfully for Parliament many times between 1868 and 1874.

BESSIE RAYNER PARKES (1829–1925)

Daughter of the radical Whig and Unitarian Joseph Parkes, and from the 1840s a close friend of Barbara Leigh Smith Bodichon, she shared Bodichon's commitment to legal reform, and in 1856 published her *Remarks on the Education of Girls*. With Bodichon she founded the *English Woman's Journal*, which she edited, and in 1866 published her *Essays on Women's Work*, which drew heavily on her contributions to the *Journal*. Her conversion to Roman Catholicism in 1864 reflected her own interest in the work of Sisters of Charity as a model for women's action. In 1867 she married a Frenchman, Louis Belloc, and had two children, Hilaire Belloc and Marie Belloc Lowndes. She was never active in the campaign for women's suffrage, though continued to show sympathy for feminist politics in her long later life.

JAMES STANSFELD (1820–98)

The son of a Halifax lawyer, and a Unitarian, he was educated at University College, London. A close friend of Mazzini, he was actively involved in support for national movements in Europe in the 1840s and 1850s. He was MP for Halifax 1859–65, held junior office 1863–4, 1866 and 1868–71, and was president of the Local Government Board 1871–4. He was a consistent supporter of women's suffrage and the main parliamentary leader of the campaign to repeal the Contagious Diseases Acts.

CLEMENTIA TAYLOR (1810–1908)

Clementia Doughty met her husband Peter Alfred Taylor while employed as a governess to his sisters. Their home, Aubrey House in Notting Hill, became a favourite centre for a wide range of radical causes, including sympathy for European nationalism in the 1850s, and support for the North in the American Civil War and those involved with the Jamaica Committee to prosecute Governor Eyre. Clementia Taylor was a member of the first women's suffrage committee of 1866, and secretary of the committee of the London National Society for Women's Suffrage established with Helen Taylor in 1867.

HARRIET TAYLOR (1807–58)

The daughter of a London surgeon, she married John Taylor, a Unitarian, in 1825. The marriage was initially happy, but in 1830 Harriet met John Stuart Mill, who shared many of her feminist ideas, and in 1833 she separated from her husband. Harriet and Mill lived apart, but spent much of their time with one another and travelled abroad together. In 1851, after the death of John Taylor, she married Mill. Throughout the 1830s and 1840s, they productively shared their ideas on the position of women. In 1851, the article published as Mill's work in the *Westminster Review*, 'The Enfranchisement of Women', was largely by Harriet Taylor. She was influenced by the Owenite socialists in her political and feminist ideas, arguing for the reform of marriage laws and women's economic independence. Mill acknowledged her inspiration underlying the *Subjection of Women* (1869).

HELEN TAYLOR (1831–1907)

The youngest of the three children of Harriet Taylor, she had begun a career as an actress, but on Harriet's death in France in 1858, she replaced her in many respects by Mill's side, sharing his work and commitment to the women's cause. Acting as his hostess, she also dealt with much of his correspondence. In the early 1860s she joined Emily Davies in the Kensington Society, and in 1866 she co-operated with Barbara

Leigh Smith Bodichon in collecting signatures for the petition of June 1866. In the same year she was one of the founders of the second London committee for women's suffrage. She continued to work and write for the cause throughout the 1860s and 1870s, after Mill's death in 1873. In 1876 she was elected to the London School Board by the borough of Southwark and in the 1880s remained active in many radical causes.

PETER ALFRED TAYLOR (1819–91)

A partner in Samuel Courtauld and Co., the silk manufacturers, he was a practising Unitarian and in the 1840s a follower of the Manchester School, who was also inspired by European revolutionary and nationalist movements. He was a friend of Joseph Cowen jun., chairman of the Society of the Friends of Italy, treasurer of the London Emancipation Society during the American Civil War and a champion of the cause of international arbitration. He helped to convene the Jamaica Committee and was one of the leaders of the campaign for the impeachment of Governor Eyre in 1864. He was vice-president of the Reform League, and, with Clementia Taylor his wife, an early and committed supporter of women's suffrage. He sat as MP for Leicester, 1862–84, and in his last years became a Liberal Unionist.

FRANCES JULIA WEDGWOOD (1833–1913)

Daughter of the philologist Hensleigh Wedgwood, and niece of Charles Darwin, she was a minor writer and novelist, who contributed on a wide range of literary topics to the *Contemporary Review*, *Macmillan's Magazine* and other periodicals. Though she never took an active part in the organised women's suffrage movement, her articles on 'Female Suffrage in Its Influence on Married Life', *Contemporary Review* 20 (1872), and 'Female Suffrage, Considered Chiefly with Regard to Its Indirect Results', in Butler's *Woman's Work and Woman's Culture* (1869), attracted much attention.

ELIZABETH WOLSTENHOLME ELMY (1834?–1913)

Daughter of a Methodist minister from Eccles, she established a school of her own near Manchester at nineteen, and was by 1865 sufficiently successful to establish the Manchester Schoolmistresses Association. She was involved in the North of England Council for the Higher Education of Women, and the Married Women's Property Committee active from 1868 to 1882 to secure possession of property and earnings for married women. She worked closely with Manchester women's suffrage campaigners, and was also energetically committed to the campaign against the Contagious Diseases Acts. In 1874 she married Benjamin Elmy, and she and her husband, both freethinkers, continued to work to improve the legal situation of women, and to campaign for women's suffrage.

Bibliography

MANUSCRIPT SOURCES

Lydia Becker Papers, Manchester Central Library [MCL].
Bodichon Papers, Girton College, Cambridge.
Cowen Collection, Tyne and Wear County Record Office, Newcastle upon Tyne [CC].
Davies Papers, Girton College, Cambridge [FCD].
Mill–Taylor Papers, British Library of Political and Economic Science, London School of Economics [MT].
Parkes Papers, Girton College, Cambridge [PPG].

GOVERNMENT PUBLICATIONS

Hansard's Parliamentary Debates.
Journal of the House of Commons.
Parliamentary Papers, 1866, LI, Part 1, *Papers Relating to the Disturbances in Jamaica.*
Parliamentary Papers, 1866, LI, Part 2, *Further Papers Relevant to the Disturbances in Jamaica.*
Parliamentary Papers, 1866 [3683] XXX and [3683–I] XXXI, *Report of the Jamaica Royal Commission (1866)*, Part I, Report, and Part II, Minutes of Evidence and Appendix.
Parliamentary Papers, 1867–8 [3980–I] XXXIX, *Royal Commission on Trade Unions and Other Organisations*, 5th Report.
'Petition for Extension of the Electoral Franchise to All Householders, Without Distinction of Sex . . . (7 June 1866, No. 8501)', *Reports of the Select Committee of the House of Commons on Public Petitions, Session 1866*, appendix.

NEWSPAPERS AND PERIODICALS

Anti-Slavery Reporter
Aris's Birmingham Gazette
Bee-Hive
Birmingham Daily Gazette
Birmingham Daily Post
Birmingham Journal
Cabinet Newspaper

Chain Makers' Journal
Contemporary Review
Daily Telegraph
English Woman's Journal
Englishwoman's Review [*EWR*]
Fortnightly Review
Fraser's Magazine
Jersey Independent
Jewish Chronicle
Macmillan's Magazine
Manchester City News
Manchester Examiner and Times [*ME*]
Manchester Guardian
Morning Star
Newcastle Daily Chronicle
Newcastle Daily Journal
Newcastle Weekly Chronicle
Northern Daily Express
Northern Reform Record
Northern Star
Punch
Reynolds's Newspaper
The Times
Tribune
Westminster Review
Women's Suffrage Journal

CONTEMPORARY ARTICLES, BOOKS, PAMPHLETS AND SPEECHES

Adams, W. E., *Tyrannicide: Is It Justifiable?*, London, 1858.
An Argument for Complete Suffrage, London, Manchester and Newcastle upon Tyne, 1860.
The Slaveholders' War: An Argument for the North and the Negro, Manchester, 1863.
Bonaparte's Challenge to Tyrannicides by the Author of 'Tyrannicide: Is It Justifiable?', 'A Suppressed Pamphlet', 1867 (copy in British Library).
Memoirs of a Social Atom, London, 1903; repr. with intro. by John Saville, New York: Augustus M. Kelley, 1968.
Amberley, Kate, 'The Claims of Women', *Fortnightly Review* 15 (o.s.), 9 (n.s.) (January 1871), 95–110.
Anstey, Thomas Chisholm, *Notes upon 'The Representation of the People Act, 1867' (30 & 31 Vict. c. 102): With Appendices . . .*, London, 1867.
On Some Supposed Constitutional Restraints upon the Parliamentary Franchise, London, 1867.
Arnold, Matthew, *Culture and Anarchy* (1867); repr. ed. J. Dover Wilson, Cambridge University Press, 1963.
Atkinson, Mabel, *Local Government in Scotland*, Edinburgh and London, 1904.

Baxter, R. Dudley, *The Results of the General Election*, London, 1869.

Becker, Lydia, 'Is There Any Specific Distinction Between Male and Female Intellect?', *English Woman's Journal* 8 (July 1868), 483–91.

'The Political Disabilities of Women', *Westminster Review* 97 (o.s.), 41 (n.s.) (January 1872), 50–70.

The Rights and Duties of Women in Local Government, Manchester, 1879.

Blackburn, Helen, *Women's Suffrage: A Record of the Women's Suffrage Movement in the British Isles with Biographical Sketches of Miss Becker*, London and Oxford, 1902; repr. New York: Source Book Press, 1970.

Bodichon, Barbara, *Objections to the Enfranchisement of Women Considered*, London, 1866.

Reasons for the Enfranchisement of Women, London, 1866; repr. in Jane Lewis, *Before the Vote Was Won*, pp. 38–46.

'Authorities and Precedents for Giving the Suffrage to Qualified Women', *English Woman's Journal* 2 (January 1867), 64–72.

Boilermakers' Society, *Annual Report*, 1881.

[Boucherett, Jessie (?)], 'Some Probable Consequences of Extending the Franchise to Female Householders', *EWR* 1 (October 1866), 26–34.

'Debate on the Enfranchisement of Women', *EWR* 4 (1867), 199–208.

Bourn, William, *History of the Parish of Ryton*, Carlisle, 1896.

Butler, Josephine E., *Our Christianity Tested by the Irish Question*, London, [1887?].

Butler, Josephine E. (ed.), *Woman's Work and Woman's Culture*, London, 1869.

Carlyle, Jane Welsh, *Letters and Memorials of Jane Welsh Carlyle*, ed. James Anthony Froude, London, 1883.

Carlyle, Thomas, *Chartism* (1840); repr. in *Selected Writings of Thomas Carlyle*, Harmondsworth: Penguin, 1971, pp. 151–232.

Past and Present (1843); repr. London: J. M. Dent, 1960.

'Occasional Discourse on the Negro Question', *Fraser's Magazine* 40 (December 1849), 670–8.

'The Negro Question', *Fraser's Magazine* 41 (January 1850), 25–31.

'Shooting Niagara: and After?' (1867), in Carlyle, *Critical and Miscellaneous Essays*, 7 vols., London, 1899, vol. V, pp. 299–339.

Cobbe, Frances Power, 'Criminals, Idiots, Women and Minors', *Fraser's Magazine* 78 (December 1868), 777–94.

Cobbett, James Paul and Doubleday, Thomas, *A Hand-Book for Reformers*, London, Manchester and Newcastle upon Tyne, 1859 (copy in Mitchell Library, Glasgow).

Cooper, Thomas, *The Life of Thomas Cooper*, London, 1873.

The Council of the Manchester Chartist Association to the Democratic Reformers of Great Britain, 1851 (pamphlet in Lovett Collection, Goldsmith's Library, University of London).

Cowper, William, *The Poetical Works of William Cowper*, London, 1872.

Dod, Charles R., *Electoral Facts from 1832 to 1853 Impartially Stated* ... (1853), ed. H. J. Hanham, Brighton: Harvester Press, 1972.

Duncan, W., *Life of Joseph Cowen*, London and Newcastle upon Tyne, 1904.

Engels, Friedrich, 'The Condition of the Working Class in England' (1845), in Marx and Engels, *On Britain*, pp. 6–338.

Essays on Reform, London, 1867.

Fawcett, Henry and Fawcett, Millicent Garrett, *Essays and Lectures on Social and Political Subjects*, London, 1872.

Fawcett, Millicent, *Political Economy for Beginners*, London, 1870.

'Proportional Representation', *Macmillan's Magazine* 22 (September 1870), 376–82; repr. in Fawcett and Fawcett, *Essays and Lectures*, pp. 336–52.

'A Short Explanation of Mr Hare's Scheme of Representation', *Macmillan's Magazine* 23 (April 1871), 816–26; repr. in Fawcett and Fawcett, *Essays and Lectures*, pp. 353–68.

'The Education of Women: A Lecture Delivered at Newcastle, November 13th, 1871', in Fawcett and Fawcett, *Essays and Lectures*, pp. 206–29.

'Free Education in Its Economic Aspects', in Fawcett and Fawcett, *Essays and Lectures*, pp. 50–69.

'National Debts and National Prosperity', in Fawcett and Fawcett, *Essays and Lectures*, pp. 125–53.

'Why Women Require the Franchise: A Lecture Delivered in the Colston Hall, Bristol in March 1871', in Fawcett and Fawcett, *Essays and Lectures*, pp. 262–91.

Tales in Political Economy, London, 1874.

Finlason, William F., *The History of the Jamaica Case: Being an Account Founded upon Official Documents of the Rebellion of the Negroes in Jamaica*, London, 1869.

Gammage, R. G., *History of the Chartist Movement, 1837–1854* (1894 edn); repr. London: Merlin Press, 1969.

Grey, Earl, *Parliamentary Government Considered with Reference to a Reform of Parliament: An Essay* (1858); revised edn, London, 1864.

Hare, Thomas, *The Machinery of Representation*, 2nd edn, London, 1857.

The Election of Representatives, Parliamentary and Municipal: A Treatise (1859), 3rd edn, with preface, appendix, and other additions, London, 1865.

Haslam, Anna, 'Irishwomen and the Local Government Act', *EWR* 239 (n.s.) (15 October 1898), 221–5.

Jamaica Committee, *Jamaica Committee Papers*, 6 vols., London, 1866–7.

Jones, E. R., *The Life and Speeches of Joseph Cowen*, London, 1885.

Kay, James Phillips, *The Moral and Physical Condition of the Working Classes Employed in the Cotton Manufactories in Manchester* (1832); repr. London: Cass, 1970.

Kingsley, Charles, *The Roman and the Teuton: A Series of Lectures Delivered Before the University of Cambridge*, Cambridge and London, 1864.

'Women and Politics', *Macmillan's Magazine* 20 (1869), 552–61.

Charles Kingsley: His Letters and Memories of His Life, edited by his wife, 2 vols., London, 1877.

Kinnear, John Boyd, 'The Social Position of Women in the Present Age', in Butler, *Woman's Work and Woman's Culture*, pp. 331–67.

Knox, Robert, *The Races of Men: A Philosophical Inquiry into the Influence of Race over the Destiny of Nations*, 2nd edn, London, 1852.

Ludlow, J. M. and Jones, Lloyd, 'The Progress of the Working Classes 1832–1867', in *Questions for a Reformed Parliament*, pp. 277–328.

The Progress of the Working Classes 1832–1867, London, 1867.

Manchester National Society for Women's Suffrage, *First Annual Report of the Executive Committee*, Manchester, 1868.

Second Annual Report of the Executive Committee, Manchester, 1869.

Third Annual Report of the Executive Committee, Manchester, 1870.

Martin, A. Patchett, *Life and Letters of the Right Honourable Robert Lowe, Viscount Sherbrooke*, 2 vols., London, 1893.

Marx, Karl, *The Class Struggles in France: 1848–1850* (1850), in Marx, *Surveys from Exile*, pp. 13–142.

The Eighteenth Brumaire of Louis Bonaparte (1852), in Marx, *Surveys from Exile*, pp. 143–249.

A Contribution to the Critique of Political Economy (1859); ed. with intro. by Maurice Dobb, London: Lawrence and Wishart, 1971.

Capital: A Critique of Political Economy, vol. I (1867), trans. Ben Fowkes, Harmondsworth: Penguin, 1976.

Karl Marx: Political Writings, vol. II, Surveys from Exile, ed. David Fernbach, Harmondsworth: Penguin, 1973.

Marx, Karl and Engels, Friedrich, 'Letters on Britain', in Marx and Engels, *On Britain*, pp. 533–84.

On Britain, 2nd edn, Moscow: Foreign Languages Publishing House, 1962.

Maurice, F. D., *The Rev. F. D. Maurice on Female Suffrage* (1870); repr. from the *Spectator*, 5 March 1870 (pamphlet at Fawcett Library, London Guildhall University).

Mazzini, G., *The Duties of Man*, trans. Emilie Venturi, London, 1862.

'Mazzini on the Franchise for Women', *Women's Suffrage Journal* 9 (1 November 1871), 95.

A Member of the Manchester and Salford Trades Council Executive, *Manchester Election: To the Members of Trade Societies*, n.d. [1867] (pamphlet in Manchester Central Library Broadsides).

Mill, Harriet Taylor, 'Enfranchisement of Women', *Westminster Review* 55 (July 1851), 289–311.

Mill, John Stuart, *Collected Works of John Stuart Mill* [*CW*], gen. ed. J. M. Robson, 33 vols., University of Toronto Press, 1962–91.

'Modern French Historical Works – Age of Chivalry', *Westminster Review* 6 (July 1826), 62–103; repr. in *CW*, vol. XX, *Essays on French History and Historians*, ed. J. M. Robson (1985), pp. 15–52.

'Civilization: Signs of the Times', *London and Westminster Review* 3 and 25 (April 1836), 1–28; repr. in *CW*, vol. XVIII, *Essays on Politics and Society*, ed. J. M. Robson (1977), pp. 117–48.

A System of Logic, Ratiocinative and Inductive (London, 1843); repr. in *CW*, vols. VII–VIII, ed. J. M. Robson (1973).

Principles of Political Economy, with Some of their Applications to Social Philosophy (London, 1848); repr. in *CW*, vols. II–III, ed. J. M. Robson (1965).

'The Negro Question', *Fraser's Magazine* 41 (January 1850), 25–31; repr. in *CW*, vol. XXI, *Essays on Equality, Law and Education*, ed. Stefan Collini (1984), pp. 85–96.

On Liberty (London, 1859); repr. in *CW*, vol. XVIII, *Essays on Politics and Society*, ed. J. M. Robson (1977), pp. 213–310.

Thoughts on Parliamentary Reform (2nd edn, London, 1859); repr. in *CW*, vol. XIX, *Essays on Politics and Society*, ed. J. M. Robson (1977), pp. 311–39.

Considerations on Representative Government (London, 1861); repr. in *CW*, vol. XIX, *Essays on Politics and Society*, ed. J. M. Robson (1977), pp. 371–577.

August Comte and Positivism (London, 1865); repr. in *CW*, vol. X, *Essays on Ethics, Religion and Society*, ed. J. M. Robson (1969), pp. 261–368.

Speech of John Stuart Mill, MP on the Admission of Women to the Electoral Franchise: Spoken in the House of Commons, May 20th 1867 (London, 1867); repr. in *Public and Parliamentary Speeches*, pp. 151–62.

England and Ireland (London, 1868); repr. in *CW*, vol. VI, *Essays on England, Ireland and the Empire*, ed. J. M. Robson (1982), pp. 505–32.

The Subjection of Women (London, 1869); repr. in *Essays on Equality, Law and Education*, pp. 259–340.

Autobiography (London, 1873); repr. in *CW*, vol. I, *Autobiography and Literary Essays*, ed. J. M. Robson and Jack Stillinger (1981), pp. 1–290.

The Later Letters of John Stuart Mill, 1849–1873, ed. Francis Mineka and Dwight N. Lindley, *CW*, vols. XIV–XVII (1972).

Essays on Equality, Law and Education, ed. J. M. Robson, *CW*, vol. XXI (1984).

Public and Parliamentary Speeches, ed. J. M. Robson and Bruce Kinzer, *CW*, vol. XXVIII (1988).

Mott, Lucretia, *Lucretia Mott's Diary of Her Visit to Great Britain to Attend the World's Anti-Slavery Convention of 1840*, ed. F. B. Tolles, London: Friends Historical Society, 1952.

Mylne, Margaret, *Woman and Her Social Position: An Article Reprinted from the Westminster Review, No. LXVIII, 1841*, London: C. Green and Son, 1872.

Northern Reform Union, *To the People of Great Britain and Ireland*, 4 pp., Newcastle upon Tyne, 1 March 1858; repr. in *Newcastle Daily Chronicle*, 12 March 1858.

Paine, Tom, *Common Sense* (1776), in *The Essential Thomas Paine*, intro. Sidney Hook, London: New English Library, 1969, pp. 23–72.

Pankhurst, Richard, 'The Right of Women to Vote Under the Reform Act, 1867', *Fortnightly Review* 10 (o.s.), 4 (n.s.) (September 1868), 250–4.

Parkes, Bessie Rayner, *Summer Sketches and Other Poems*, London, 1854; repr. in Parkes, *Poems*, London, 1855.

Pearson, Charles, 'On Some Historical Aspects of Family Life', in Butler, *Woman's Work and Woman's Culture*, pp. 152–85.

Questions for a Reformed Parliament, London, 1867.

Reid, Marion, *A Plea for Woman* (1843); repr. Edinburgh: Polygon, 1988.

Robertson, Anne I., *Myself and My Relatives: A Story of Home Life*, London, 1863.

The Story of Nelly Dillon, 2 vols., London, 1866.

Women's Need of Parliamentary Representation: A Lecture upon the Necessity of Giving Women the Parliamentary Franchise, Dublin, 1872.

Robertson, William, *Life and Times of the Right Honourable John Bright*, London, 1883.

Smiles, Samuel, *Self-Help*, London, 1859.

Character, London, 1871.

Smith, Mary, *Progress and Other Poems . . .*, London, 1873.

Stubbs, William, *Lectures on Early English History*, ed. Arthur Hassall, London, 1906.

Taylor, Helen, 'The Ladies' Petition, Presented to the House of Commons by Mr J. Stuart Mill, June 7th 1866', *Westminster Review* 31 (n.s.) (January 1867),

63–79; subsequently published as *The Claims of Englishwomen to the Franchise Constitutionally Considered*, London, 1867; repr. in Jane Lewis, *Before the Vote Was Won*, pp. 21–37.

Tod, Isabella M. S., 'The Place of Women in the Administration of the Irish Poor Law', *EWR* 103 (15 November 1881), 481–9.

'Municipal Franchise for Women in Ireland', *EWR* 170 (15 July 1887), 291–3.

Trollope, Anthony, *South Africa*, 2 vols., London, 1878.

Webb, Sidney and Webb, Beatrice, *Industrial Democracy*, London, 1898.

Wedgwood, Julia, 'Female Suffrage, Considered Chiefly with Regard to Its Indirect Results', in Butler, *Woman's Work and Woman's Culture*, pp. 247–89.

'Female Suffrage in Its Influence on Married Life', *Contemporary Review* 20 (August 1872), 360–70.

Wollstonecraft, Mary, *A Vindication of the Rights of Woman* (1792); repr. in *The Works of Mary Wollstonecraft*, ed. Janet Todd and Marilyn Butler, 7 vols., London: William Pickering, 1989, vol. V, pp. 79–266.

Wright, Thomas [The Journeyman Engineer], *Our New Masters*, London, 1873.

PUBLISHED SECONDARY SOURCES

Abrams, Philip, *Historical Sociology*, Shepton Mallet: Open Books, 1982.

Abramsky, Chimen and Collins, Henry, *Karl Marx and the British Labour Movement: Years of the First International*, Basingstoke: Macmillan, 1965.

Alexander, Sally, 'Women, Class and Sexual Difference in the 1830s and 1840s', *History Workshop Journal* 17 (1984), 125–49.

Becoming a Woman and Other Essays in Nineteenth- and Twentieth-Century Feminist History, London: Virago, 1994.

Anderson, Benedict, *Imagined Communities: Reflections on the Origin and Spread of Nationalism*, London: Verso, 1983.

Anderson, Olive, *A Liberal State at War*, Basingstoke: Macmillan, 1967.

Anderson, Perry, *Arguments Within English Marxism*, London: Verso, 1980.

Annas, Julia, 'Mill and the Subjection of Women', *Philosophy* 52 (1977), 179–94.

Appleby, Joyce, Hunt, Lynn and Jacob, Margaret, *Telling the Truth About History*, New York: W. W. Norton, 1994.

Armstrong, Nancy, *Desire and Domestic Fiction: A Political History of the Novel*, New York: Oxford University Press, 1987.

Arnstein, Walter L., 'The Murphy Riots: A Victorian Dilemma', *Victorian Studies* 19 (1975–6), 51–72.

Protestant Versus Catholic in Mid-Victorian England: Mr. Newdegate and the Nuns, Columbia: University of Missouri Press, 1982.

Badran, Margot, *Feminists, Islam and Nation: Gender and the Making of Modern Egypt*, Princeton University Press, 1993.

Barker, Hannah and Chalus, Elaine, 'Introduction', in Barker and Chalus, *Gender in Eighteenth-Century England*, pp. 1–28.

Barker, Hannah and Chalus, Elaine (eds.), *Gender in Eighteenth-Century England: Roles, Representations and Responsibilities*, London: Addison-Wesley Longman, 1997.

Barlow, Paul, 'Grotesque Obscenities: Thomas Woolner's *Civilization* and Its Discontents', in Colin Trodd, Barlow and David Amigoni (eds.), *Victorian*

Culture and the Idea of the Grotesque, Aldershot: Ashgate Press, 1999, pp. 97–118.

Barth, Frederick, *Ethnic Groups and Boundaries: The Social Organization of Cultural Difference*, London: Allen and Unwin, 1969.

Bayly, C. A., *Imperial Meridian: The British Empire and the World, 1780–1830*, London: Longman, 1989.

Behagg, Clive, *Labour and Reform: Working-Class Movements 1815–1914*, London: Hodder and Stoughton, 1991.

Belchem, John, 'Chartism and the Trades, 1848–1850', *English Historical Review* 98 (1983), 558–87.

'English Working-Class Radicalism and the Irish', in Swift and Gilley, *The Irish in the Victorian City*, pp. 85–97.

'Radical Language and Ideology in Early Nineteenth-Century England: The Challenge of the Platform', *Albion* 20 (1988), 247–59.

Belich, James, *Making Peoples: A History of the New Zealanders from Polynesian Settlement to the End of the Nineteenth Century*, Auckland and London: Allen Lane, 1996.

Bell, Kenneth N. and Morrell, W. P., *Select Documents on British Colonial Policy 1830–1860*, Oxford: Clarendon Press, 1928.

Benenson, Harold, 'Victorian Sexual Ideology and Marx's Theory of the Working Class', *International Labor and Working-Class History* 25 (1984), 1–23.

Berridge, Virginia, 'Popular Sunday Papers and Mid-Victorian Society', in George Boyce, James Curran and Pauline Wingate (eds.), *Newspaper History: From the Seventeenth Century to the Present Day*, London: Methuen, 1978, pp. 247–64.

Best, G. F. A., 'Popular Protestantism in Victorian Britain', in Robert Robson (ed.), *Ideas and Institutions of Victorian Britain: Essays in Honour of George Kitson Clark*, London: G. Bell and Sons, 1967, pp. 115–42.

Bhabha, Homi K. (ed.), *Nation and Narration*, London: Routledge, 1990.

Biagini, E. F., 'British Trade Unions and Popular Political Economy, 1860–1880', *Historical Journal* 30 (1987), 811–40.

Liberty, Retrenchment and Reform: Popular Liberalism in the Age of Gladstone, 1860–1880, Cambridge University Press, 1992.

Biagini, Eugenio F. and Reid, Alastair J., 'Currents of Radicalism, 1850–1914', in Biagini and Reid, *Currents of Radicalism*, pp. 1–19.

Biagini, Eugenio F. and Reid, Alastair J. (eds.), *Currents of Radicalism: Popular Radicalism, Organised Labour and Party Politics in Britain, 1850–1914*, Cambridge University Press, 1991.

Blackburn, Robin, *The Overthrow of Colonial Slavery 1776–1848*, London: Verso, 1988.

Blewett, Neal, 'The Franchise in the United Kingdom, 1885–1918', *Past & Present* 32 (1965), 27–56.

Bolt, Christine, *Victorian Attitudes to Race*, London: Routledge and Kegan Paul, 1971.

Bolt, Christine and Drescher, Seymour (eds.), *Anti-Slavery, Religion and Reform: Essays in Memory of Roger Anstey*, Folkestone: Dawson, 1980.

Bottomore, T. B. (ed.), *A Dictionary of Marxist Thought*, 2nd edn, Oxford: Blackwell, 1991.

Boyce, D. G., *The Irish Question and British Politics 1868–1986*, Basingstoke: Macmillan, 1988.

Brent, Richard, *Liberal Anglican Politics: Whiggery, Religion and Reform 1830–1841*, Oxford: Clarendon Press, 1987.

Breuilly, John, Niedhart, Gottfried and Taylor, Antony (eds.), *The Era of the Reform League: English Labour and Radical Politics 1857–1872. Documents Selected by Gustav Mayer*, Mannheim: Palatium Verlag im J. & J. Verlag, 1995.

Brown, Heloise, 'An Alternative Imperialism: Isabella Tod, Internationalist and "Good Liberal Unionist"', *Gender & History* 10 (1998), 358–80.

Burgess, Keith, *The Origins of British Industrial Relations*, London: Croom Helm, 1975.

Burn, W. L., *The Age of Equipoise*, London: George Allen and Unwin, 1964.

Burns, J. H., 'John Stuart Mill and Democracy, 1829–1861', in J. B. Schneewind (ed.), *Mill: A Collection of Critical Essays*, Basingstoke: Macmillan, 1969, pp. 280–328.

'The Light of Reason: Philosophical History in the Two Mills', in John M. Robson and Michael Laine (eds.), *James and John Stuart Mill/Papers of the Centenary Conference*, University of Toronto Press, 1976, pp. 3–20.

Burrow, John, *A Liberal Descent: Victorian Historians and the English Past*, Cambridge University Press, 1981.

Whigs and Liberals: Continuity and Change in English Political Thought, Oxford: Clarendon Press, 1988.

Burton, Antoinette, *Burdens of History: British Feminists, Indian Women, and Imperial Culture, 1865–1915*, Chapel Hill and London: University of North Carolina Press, 1994.

'Rules of Thumb: British History and "Imperial Culture" in Nineteenth- and Twentieth-Century Britain', *Women's History Review* 3 (1994), 483–500.

Caine, Barbara, 'John Stuart Mill and the English Women's Movement', *Historical Studies* 18 (1978), 52–67.

'Feminism, Suffrage and the Nineteenth-Century English Women's Movement', *Women's Studies International Forum* 5 (1982), 537–50.

Victorian Feminists, Oxford University Press, 1992.

Calhoun, Craig (ed.), *Habermas and the Public Sphere*, Cambridge, Mass.: MIT Press, 1992.

Cannadine, David, 'British History as a "New Subject": Politics, Perspectives and Prospects', in Grant and Stringer, *Uniting the Kingdom?*, pp. 12–30.

Chalus, Elaine, '"That Epidemical Madness": Women and Electoral Politics in the Late Eighteenth Century', in Barker and Chalus, *Gender in Eighteenth-Century England*, pp. 151–78.

Chatterjee, Partha, *The Nation and Its Fragments: Colonial and Postcolonial Histories*, Princeton University Press, 1993.

Nationalist Thought and the Colonial World, Minneapolis: University of Minnesota Press, 1993.

Claeys, Gregory, 'Language, Class and Historical Consciousness in Nineteenth-Century Britain', *Economy and Society* 14 (1985), 239–63.

'Mazzini, Kossuth, and British Radicalism, 1848–1854', *Journal of British Studies* 28 (1989), 225–61.

Clark, Anna, 'The Rhetoric of Chartist Domesticity: Gender, Language, and Class in the 1830s and 1840s', *Journal of British Studies* 31 (1992), 62–88.

'Gender, Class, and the Nation: Franchise Reform in England, 1832–1928', in Vernon, *Re-reading the Constitution*, pp. 230–53.

'Manhood, Womanhood, and the Politics of Class in Britain, 1790–1845', in Frader and Rose, *Gender and Class in Modern Europe*, pp. 263–79.

Clarke, Norma, 'Deep Glooms and Bottomless Dubitations', *History Workshop Journal* 45 (1998), 278–82.

Clements, R. V., 'British Trade Unions and Popular Political Economy, 1850–1875', *Economic History Review* 14 (1961–2), 93–104.

Cohen, G. A., *Karl Marx's Theory of History: A Defence*, Oxford: Clarendon Press, 1978.

Cohen, Robin, *Frontiers of Identity: The British and the Others*, London: Longman, 1994.

Cole, G. D. H., 'Some Notes on British Trade Unions in the Third Quarter of the Nineteenth Century', *International Review of Social History* 2 (1937); repr. in E. M. Carus-Wilson (ed.), *Essays in Economic History*, 3 vols., London: Edward Arnold, 1962, vol. III, pp. 202–21.

Colley, Linda, 'Britishness and Otherness: An Argument', *Journal of British Studies* 31 (1992), 309–29.

Britons: Forging the Nation 1707–1837, New Haven and London: Yale University Press, 1992.

Collini, Stefan, 'Political Theory and the "Science of Society" in Victorian Britain', *Historical Journal* 23 (1980), 203–31.

Public Moralists: Political Thought and Intellectual Life in Britain 1850–1930, Oxford: Clarendon Press, 1991.

Collini, Stefan, Winch, Donald and Burrow, John, *That Noble Science of Politics: A Study in Nineteenth-Century Intellectual History*, Cambridge University Press, 1983.

Colls, Robert, 'Englishness and the Political Culture', in Colls and Dodd, *Englishness*, pp. 29–61.

Colls, Robert, and Dodd, Philip (eds.), *Englishness: Politics and Culture 1880–1920*, London: Croom Helm, 1986.

Coltham, Stephen, 'The *Bee-Hive* Newspaper: Its Origins and Early Struggles', in Asa Briggs and John Saville (eds.), *Essays in Labour History*, Basingstoke: Macmillan, 1960, pp. 174–204.

'George Potter, the Junta and the *Bee-Hive*', *International Review of Social History* 9 (1964), 390–432, and 10 (1965), 23–65.

Cooper, Frederick and Stoler, Ann Laura (eds.), *Tensions of Empire: Colonial Cultures in a Bourgeois World*, Berkeley: University of California Press, 1997.

Corfield, Penelope, 'Introduction: Historians and Language', in Corfield (ed.), *Language, History and Class*, Oxford: Basil Blackwell, 1991, pp. 1–29.

Costa, Emilia Viotti da, *Crowns of Glory, Tears of Blood: The Demerara Slave Rebellion of 1823*, Oxford University Press, 1994.

Cott, Nancy, *The Bonds of Womanhood: Woman's Sphere in New England, 1780–1835*, New Haven: Yale University Press, 1977.

Cowling, Maurice, *Mill and Liberalism*, Cambridge University Press, 1963.
1867: Disraeli, Gladstone and Revolution, Cambridge University Press, 1967.
Cronin, J. E., 'Language, Politics and the Critique of Social History', *Journal of Social History* 20 (1986–7), 177–84.
Crossick, Geoffrey, *An Artisan Elite in Victorian Society: Kentish London 1840–1880*, London: Croom Helm, 1978.
Crossman, Virginia, *Local Government in Nineteenth-Century Ireland*, Institute of Irish Studies, Queens University of Belfast, 1994.
Cullen, Mary, 'How Radical Was Irish Feminism Between 1860 and 1920?', in Patrick J. Corish (ed.), *Radicals, Rebels and Establishments: Papers Read Before the Irish Conference of Historians, Maynooth, 16–19 June 1983*, Historical Studies, vol. XV (Belfast: Appletree, 1985), pp. 185–20.
'Anna Maria Haslam', in Cullen and Luddy, *Women, Power and Consciousness*, pp. 161–96.
Cullen, Mary and Luddy, Maria (eds.), *Women, Power and Consciousness in Nineteenth-Century Ireland*, Dublin: Attic Press, 1995.
Cunningham, Hugh, 'The Language of Patriotism', in Samuel, *Patriotism*, vol. I, pp. 57–89.
Daunton, Martin and Halpern, Rick (eds.), *Empire and Others: British Encounters with Indigenous Peoples, 1600–1850*, London: UCL Press, 1998.
Dauphin, Cécile, et al., 'Women's Culture and Women's Power: Issues in French Women's History', in Karen Offen, Ruth Roach Pierson and Jane Rendall (eds.), *Writing Women's History: International Perspectives*, Bloomington: Indiana University Press, 1991, pp. 107–34.
Davidoff, Leonore and Hall, Catherine, *Family Fortunes: Men and Women of the English Middle Class 1780–1850*, London: Hutchinson, 1987.
Davin, Anna, 'Imperialism and Motherhood', *History Workshop Journal* 5 (1978), 9–65.
Davis, David Brion, *The Problem of Slavery in the Age of Revolution 1770–1832*, London: Cornell University Press, 1975.
Davis, Jennifer, 'Jennings Buildings and the Royal Boroughs: The Construction of the Underclass in Mid-Victorian Britain', in Feldman and Stedman Jones, *Metropolis*, pp. 11–39.
Davis, John, 'Slums and the Vote', *Historical Research* 64 (1991), 375–88.
Davis, John and Tanner, Duncan, 'The Borough Franchise After 1867', *Historical Research* 69 (1996), 306–27.
Davis, John A., 'Garibaldi and England', *History Today*, December 1982, 21–6.
Davis, R. W., *Political Change and Continuity 1760–1885: A Buckinghamshire Study*, Newton Abbot: David and Charles, 1972.
Dawson, Graham, *Soldier Heroes: British Adventure, Empire and the Imagining of Masculinities*, London: Routledge, 1994.
de Groot, Joanna, 'The Dialectics of Gender: Women, Men and Political Discourses in Iran c. 1890–1930', *Gender & History* 5 (1993), 256–68.
Devoy, John, *Recollections of an Irish Rebel*, New York: Charles P. Young and Co., 1929.
Dinwiddy, John, *Bentham*, Oxford University Press, 1989.
Dodd, Philip, 'Englishness and the National Culture', in Colls and Dodd, *Englishness*, pp. 1–28.

Dubois, Ellen Carol, *Feminism and Suffrage: The Emergence of an Independent Women's Movement in America, 1848–1969*, Ithaca, N.Y.: Cornell University Press, 1978.

Dworkin, Dennis L., *Cultural Marxism in Postwar Britain*, Durham, N.C.: Duke University Press, 1997.

Dyer, Michael, *Men of Property and Intelligence: The Scottish Electoral System Prior to 1884*, Aberdeen: Scottish Cultural Press, 1996.

Easthope, Anthony, *British Post-Structuralism Since 1968*, 2nd edn, London: Routledge, 1991.

Eley, Geoff, 'Reading Gramsci in English: Observations on the Reception of Antonio Gramsci in the English-Speaking World, 1957–1982', *European History Quarterly* 14 (1984), 441–78.

'Edward Thompson, Social History and Political Culture: The Making of a Working-Class Public, 1780–1850', in Kaye and McClelland, *E. P. Thompson*, pp. 12–49.

'Nations, Publics, and Political Cultures: Placing Habermas in the Nineteenth Century', in Calhoun, *Habermas and the Public Sphere*, pp. 289–339.

Ellison, Mary, *Support for Secession: Lancashire and the American Civil War*, University of Chicago Press, 1972.

Epstein, James, 'Rethinking the Categories of Working-Class History', *Labour/Le Travail* 18 (1986), 195–208.

Epstein, James, and Thompson, Dorothy (eds.), *The Chartist Experience: Studies in Working-Class Radicalism and Culture, 1830–1860*, Basingstoke: Macmillan, 1982.

Evans, Eric J., *The Great Reform Act of 1832*, 2nd edn, London: Routledge, 1994.

'Englishness and Britishness: National Identities, c. 1790–c. 1870', in Grant and Stringer, *Uniting the Kingdom?*, pp. 223–44.

The Forging of the Modern State: Early Industrial Britain, 1783–1870, 2nd edn, London: Longman, 1996.

Fanon, Frantz, *The Wretched of the Earth*, Harmondsworth: Penguin, 1967.

Black Skin, White Masks, London: Pluto, 1986.

Feldman, David, 'The Importance of Being English: Jewish Immigration and the Decay of Liberal England', in Feldman and Stedman Jones, *Metropolis*, pp. 56–84.

Englishmen and Jews: Social Relations and Political Culture 1840–1914, New Haven: Yale University Press, 1994.

Feldman, David, and Jones, Gareth Stedman (eds.), *Metropolis. London Histories and Representations Since 1800*, London: Routledge, 1989.

'Feminism and Nationalism', special issue, *Journal of Women's History* 7 (1995).

Fenn, Robert A., *James Mill's Political Thought*, New York and London: Garland, 1987.

Finn, Margot C., *After Chartism: Class and Nation in English Radical Politics, 1848–1874*, Cambridge University Press, 1993.

Foner, Philip S., *British Labor and the American Civil War*, New York and London: Holmes and Meier, 1981.

Foster, John, *Class Struggle and the Industrial Revolution*, London: Weidenfeld and Nicolson, 1974.

'The Declassing of Language', *New Left Review* 150 (1985), 29–46.

Foster, R. F., *Modern Ireland 1600–1972*, London: Allen Lane, 1988.
Paddy and Mr Punch: Connections in Irish and English History, Harmondsworth: Penguin, 1995.
Frader, Laura and Rose, Sonya O. (eds.), *Gender and Class in Modern Europe*, Ithaca, N.Y., and London: Cornell University Press, 1996.
Fraser, W. H., *Trade Unions and Society: The Struggle for Acceptance 1850–1880*, London: George Allen and Unwin, 1974.
Fryer, Peter, *Staying Power: The History of Black People in Britain*, London: Pluto, 1984.
Gallagher, Thomas, 'The Second Reform Movement, 1848–1867', *Albion* 12 (1980), 147–63.
Garrard, John, *Leadership and Power in Victorian Industrial Towns, 1830–1880*, Manchester University Press, 1983.
Gash, Norman, *Reaction and Reconstruction in English Politics, 1832–1852*, Oxford: Clarendon Press, 1965.
Politics in the Age of Peel: A Study in the Technique of Parliamentary Representation 1830–1850, London: Longmans Green, 1953; 2nd edn, Hassocks: Harvester, 1977.
Gellner, Ernest, *Nations and Nationalism*, Oxford: Basil Blackwell, 1983.
'Gender, Nationalisms, and National Identities', special issue, *Gender & History* 5 (1994).
Gibbins, John, 'J. S. Mill, Liberalism, and Progress', in Richard Bellamy (ed.), *Victorian Liberalism: Nineteenth-Century Political Thought and Practice*, London and New York: Routledge, 1990, pp. 91–109.
Giddens, Anthony, *Capitalism and Modern Social Theory*, Cambridge University Press, 1971.
Gillespie, F. E., *Labor and Politics in England 1850–1867*, Durham, N.C.: Duke University Press, 1927; repr. London: Frank Cass, 1966.
Gilley, Sheridan, 'The Garibaldi Riots of 1862', *Historical Journal* 16 (1973), 697–732.
Gilroy, Paul, *There Ain't No Black in the Union Jack*, London: Hutchinson, 1987.
'Nationalism, History and Ethnic Absolutism', *History Workshop Journal* 30 (1990), 114–19.
The Black Atlantic: Modernity and Double Consciousness, London: Verso, 1993.
Gleadle, Kathryn, *The Early Feminists: Radical Unitarians and the Emergence of the Women's Rights Movement, 1831–1851*, Basingstoke: Macmillan, 1995.
Gocking, C. V., 'Early Constitutional History of Jamaica (with Special Reference to the Period 1838–1866)', *Caribbean Quarterly* 6 (1960), 114–33.
Goldman, Lawrence, 'The Social Science Association, 1857–1886: A Context for Mid-Victorian Liberalism', *English Historical Review* 101 (1986), 95–134.
'A Peculiarity of the English?: The Social Science Association and the Absence of Sociology in Nineteenth-Century Britain', *Past & Present* 114 (1987), 133–71.
Grant, Alexander and Stringer, Keith (eds.), *Uniting the Kingdom? The Making of British History*, London and New York: Routledge, 1995.
Gray, John, *Mill on Liberty: A Defence*, London: Routledge and Kegan Paul, 1983.

Gray, Robert Q., *The Labour Aristocracy in Victorian Edinburgh*, Oxford: Clarendon Press, 1976.

'Bourgeois Hegemony in Victorian Britain', in Jon Bloomfield (ed.), *Class, Hegemony and Party*, London: Lawrence and Wishart, 1977, pp. 73–93.

The Aristocracy of Labour in Nineteenth-Century Britain, Basingstoke: Macmillan, 1981.

'Deconstructing the English Working Class', *Social History* 11 (1986), 363–74.

Grimshaw, Patricia, Lake, Marilyn, McGrath, Ann and Quartly, Marian, *Creating a Nation: 1788 to 1990*, Melbourne: McPhee Gribble, 1994.

Habermas, Jürgen, *The Structural Transformation of the Public Sphere: An Inquiry into a Category of Bourgeois Society* (first published 1962 in German), trans. Thomas Burger with Frederick Lawrence, and intro. Thomas McCarthy, Cambridge, Mass.: MIT Press, 1989.

Hall, Catherine, 'The Tale of Samuel and Jemima: Gender and Working-Class Culture in Nineteenth-Century England', in Kaye and McClelland, *E. P. Thompson*, pp. 78–102.

'Competing Masculinities: Thomas Carlyle, John Stuart Mill and the Case of Governor Eyre', in Catherine Hall, *White, Male and Middle Class*, pp. 255–95.

'Missionary Stories: Gender and Ethnicity in England in the 1830s and 1840s', in Catherine Hall, *White, Male and Middle Class*, pp. 205–54.

White, Male and Middle Class: Explorations in Feminism and History, Cambridge: Polity Press, 1992.

'"From Greenland's Icy Mountains . . . to Afric's Golden Sand": Ethnicity, Race and Nation in Mid-Nineteenth-Century England', *Gender & History* 5 (1993), 212–30.

'White Visions, Black Lives: The Free Villages of Jamaica', *History Workshop Journal* 36 (1993), 100–32.

'Rethinking Imperial Histories: The Reform Act of 1867', *New Left Review* 208 (1994), 3–29.

'Imperial Man: Edward John Eyre in Australasia and the West Indies, 1833–1866', in Bill Schwarz (ed.), *The Expansion of England: Race, Ethnicity and Cultural History*, London: Routledge, 1996, pp. 130–70.

'Going a-Trolloping: Imperial Man Travels the Empire', in Midgley, *Gender and Imperialism*, pp. 180–99.

Civilizing Subjects: Race and Empire in the English Imagination 1830–1867, Cambridge: Polity Press, 2000.

Hall, Stuart, 'When was "the Post-Colonial"?: Thinking at the Limit', in Iain Chambers and Lidia Curti (eds.), *The Post-Colonial Question: Common Skies, Divided Horizons*, London: Routledge, 1996, pp. 242–60.

Hamburger, Joseph, *James Mill and the Art of Revolution*, New Haven and London: Yale University Press, 1963.

Intellectuals in Politics: John Stuart Mill and the Philosophic Radicals, New Haven and London: Yale University Press, 1965.

Hampsher-Monk, Iain, *A History of Modern Political Thought: Major Political Thinkers from Hobbes to Marx*, Oxford: Blackwell, 1992.

Hanham, H. J., *Elections and Party Management: Politics in the Time of Disraeli and Gladstone*, London: Longmans Green, 1959; repr. Hassocks: Harvester, 1978.

Hannam, June, '"An Enlarged Sphere of Usefulness": The Bristol Women's Movement c. 1860–1914', in Madge Dresser and Philip Ollerenshaw (eds.), *The Making of Modern Bristol*, Tiverton: Radcliffe Press, 1996, pp. 184–209.

Harris, José, 'Between Civic Virtue and Social Darwinism: The Concept of the Residuum', in David Englander and Rosemary O'Day (eds.), *Retrieved Riches: Social Investigation in England 1840–1914*, Aldershot: Scolar Press, 1995, pp. 67–87.

Harrison, Brian, *Drink and the Victorians: The Temperance Question in England 1815–1872*, London: Faber and Faber, 1971.

'A Genealogy of Reform in Modern Britain', in Bolt and Drescher, *Anti-Slavery, Religion and Reform*, pp. 118–48.

Harrison, Brian and Hollis, Patricia (eds.), *Robert Lowery: Radical and Chartist*, London: Europa, 1979.

Harrison, Ross, *Bentham*, London: Routledge and Kegan Paul, 1983.

Harrison, Royden, 'The British Labour Movement and the International in 1864', in Ralph Miliband and John Saville (eds.), *The Socialist Register 1964*, London: Merlin Press, 1964, pp. 293–308.

Before the Socialists: Studies in Labour and Politics 1861–1881, London: Routledge and Kegan Paul, 1965; 2nd edn, Aldershot: Gregg Revivals, 1994.

Harrison, Royden and Zeitlin, Jonathan (eds.), *Divisions of Labour: Skilled Workers and Technological Change in Nineteenth-Century Britain*, Brighton: Harvester Press, 1985.

Harvie, Christopher, 'John Boyd Kinnear, 1828–1920', *Journal of the Scottish Labour History Society* 3 (1970), 25–33.

The Lights of Liberalism: University Liberals and the Challenge of Democracy 1860–1886, London: Allen Lane, 1976.

Hechter, Michael, *Internal Colonialism: The Celtic Fringe in British National Development, 1536–1966*, London: Routledge and Kegan Paul, 1975.

Henriques, U. R. Q., *Before the Welfare State*, London: Longman, 1979.

Heuman, Gad, *'The Killing Time': The Morant Bay Rebellion in Jamaica*, Basingstoke: Macmillan, 1994.

Hewitt, Nancy, *Women's Activism and Social Change: Rochester, New York 1822–1872*, Ithaca, N.Y., and London: Cornell University Press, 1984.

'Beyond the Search for Sisterhood: American Women's History in the 1980s', *Social History* 10 (1985), 299–321.

Hickman, Mary J., *Religion, Class and Identity: The State, the Catholic Church and the Education of the Irish in Britain*, Aldershot: Avebury, 1995.

'Education for "Minorities": Irish Catholics in Britain', in Gail Lewis (ed.), *Forming Nation: Framing Welfare*, London: Routledge in association with the Open University, 1998, pp. 139–80.

Higginbotham, Evelyn Brooks, 'African-American Women's History and the Metalanguage of Race', *Signs* 17 (1992), 251–74.

Hill, Christopher, 'The Norman Yoke', in Hill, *Puritanism and Revolution*, London: Panther edn, 1968, pp. 58–125.

'The English Revolution and Patriotism'; repr. in Samuel, *Patriotism*, vol. I, pp. 159–68.

Hilton, Boyd, 'Peel: A Reappraisal', *Historical Journal* 22 (1979), 585–614.

Himmelfarb, Gertrude, 'Politics and Ideology: The Reform Act of 1867', in Himmelfarb, *Victorian Minds: Essays on Nineteenth-Century Intellectuals*, London: Weidenfeld and Nicolson, 1968, pp. 333–92 (first published as 'The Politics of Democracy: The English Reform Act of 1867', *Journal of British Studies* 6 (1966), 97–138).

'Reply to F. B. Smith', *Journal of British Studies* 7 (1967), 100–4.

On Liberty and Liberalism: The Case of John Stuart Mill, New York: Alfred Knopf, 1974.

The Idea of Poverty: England in the Early Industrial Age, London: Faber and Faber, 1984.

Hobsbawm, E. J., 'Custom, Wages and Work-load in Nineteenth-Century Industry', in Hobsbawm, *Labouring Men*, pp. 344–70.

'The Labour Aristocracy in Nineteenth-Century Britain', in Hobsbawm, *Labouring Men*, pp. 272–315.

Labouring Men, London: Weidenfeld and Nicolson, 1964.

Industry and Empire, Harmondsworth: Penguin, 1969.

'Karl Marx's Contribution to Historiography', in Robin Blackburn (ed.), *Ideology in Social Science*, Glasgow: Fontana, 1972, pp. 265–83.

The Age of Capital 1848–1875, London: Weidenfeld and Nicolson, 1975.

'The Aristocracy of Labour Reconsidered', in Hobsbawm, *Worlds of Labour*, pp. 227–51.

'Artisans and Labour Aristocrats', in Hobsbawm, *Worlds of Labour*, pp. 252–72.

'Debating the Labour Aristocracy', in Hobsbawm, *Worlds of Labour*, pp. 214–26.

'Marx and History', *New Left Review* 143 (1984), 39–50; repr. in Hobsbawm, *On History*, London: Weidenfeld and Nicolson, 1997, pp. 157–70.

Worlds of Labour, London: Weidenfeld and Nicolson, 1984.

Nations and Nationalism Since 1760: Programme, Myth, Reality, Cambridge University Press, 1990.

Hobsbawm, Eric and Ranger, Terence (eds.), *The Invention of Tradition*, Cambridge University Press, 1983.

Holcombe, Lee, *Wives and Property: Reform of the Married Women's Property Law in Nineteenth-Century England*, Oxford: Martin Robertson, 1983.

Hollis, Patricia, *The Pauper Press*, Oxford: Clarendon Press, 1970.

'Anti-Slavery and British Working-Class Radicalism in the Years of Reform', in Bolt and Drescher, *Anti-Slavery, Religion and Reform*, pp. 294–315.

Ladies Elect: Women in English Local Government, 1865–1914, Oxford: Clarendon Press, 1987.

Holt, Thomas C., *The Problem of Freedom: Race, Labor and Politics in Jamaica and Britain, 1823–1938*, Baltimore: Johns Hopkins University Press, 1992.

Holton, Sandra, *Suffrage Days: Stories for the Women's Suffrage Movement*, London: Routledge, 1996.

Hoppen, K. Theodore, *Elections, Politics and Society in Ireland 1832–1885*, Oxford: Clarendon Press, 1984.

'The Franchise and Electoral Politics in England and Ireland 1832–1885', *History* 70 (1985), 202–17.

The Mid-Victorian Generation, 1846–1886, Oxford: Clarendon Press, 1998.

Horsman, Reginald, *Race and Manifest Destiny: The Origins of American Racial Anglo-Saxonism*, Cambridge, Mass.: Harvard University Press, 1981.

Houston, R. A., 'Women in the Economy and Society of Scotland, 1500–1800', in Houston and I. D. Whyte (eds.), *Scottish Society 1500–1800*, Cambridge University Press, 1989, pp. 118–47.

Hulme, Peter, 'Including America', *Ariel* 26 (1995), 117–23.

Hunt, E. H., *Regional Wage Variations in Britain, 1850–1914*, Oxford: Clarendon Press, 1973.

British Labour History 1815–1914, London: Weidenfeld and Nicolson, 1981.

'Industrialization and Regional Inequality: Wages in Britain, 1760–1914', *Journal of Economic History* 46 (1986), 935–66.

Jackson, John A., *The Irish in Britain*, London: Routledge and Kegan Paul, 1963.

Jacob, Margaret, 'The Mental Landscape of the Public Sphere: A European Perspective', *Eighteenth-Century Studies* 28 (1994), 95–113.

Jalland, Pat, *Women, Marriage and Politics 1860–1914*, Oxford University Press, 1986.

James, C. L. R., *The Black Jacobins: Toussaint l'Ouverture and the San Domingo Revolution*, 2nd edn, New York: Vintage, 1963.

Jameson, Frederic, 'The Brick and the Balloon: Architecture, Idealism and Land Speculation', *New Left Review* 228 (1998), 25–46.

Jenkins, Keith, *Re-thinking History*, London: Routledge, 1991.

Jenkins, Keith (ed.), *The Postmodern History Reader*, London and New York: Routledge, 1997.

Jones, Gareth Stedman, *Outcast London: A Study of the Relationship Between Classes in Victorian Society*, Oxford: Clarendon Press, 1971.

'Rethinking Chartism', in Stedman Jones, *Languages of Class: Studies in English Working-Class History 1832–1982*, Cambridge University Press, 1983, pp. 90–178 (originally published as 'The Language of Chartism', in Epstein and Thompson, *The Chartist Experience*, pp. 3–58).

Joyce, Patrick, *Work, Society and Politics: The Culture of the Factory in Later Victorian England*, Brighton: Harvester Press, 1980.

Visions of the People: Industrial England and the Question of Class 1848–1914, Cambridge University Press, 1991.

Democratic Subjects: The Self and the Social in Nineteenth-Century England, Cambridge University Press, 1994.

Kaplan, Cora, 'Wild Nights: Pleasure/Sexuality/Feminism', in Kaplan, *Sea-Changes: Essays on Culture and Feminism*, London: Verso, 1986, pp. 31–56.

Kaye, H. J. and McClelland, Keith (eds.), *E. P. Thompson: Critical Perspectives*, Cambridge: Polity Press, 1990.

Kearney, Hugh, *The British Isles: A History of Four Nations*, Cambridge University Press, 1995.

Keith-Lucas, Brian, *The English Local Government Franchise: A Short History*, Oxford: Basil Blackwell, 1952.

Kelly, Audrey, *Lydia Becker and the Cause*, Centre for North-west Regional Studies, University of Lancaster, 1992.

Kent, Christopher, *Brains and Numbers: Elitism, Comtism, and Democracy in Mid-Victorian England*, University of Toronto Press, 1978.

Kerber, Linda, 'Separate Spheres, Female Worlds, Woman's Place: The Rhetoric of Women's History', *Journal of American History* 75 (1988), 9–39.

King, Elspeth, 'The Scottish Women's Suffrage Movement', in Esther Breitenbach and Eleanor Gordon (eds.), *Out of Bounds: Women in Scottish Society 1800–1945*, Edinburgh University Press, 1992, pp. 121–50.

Kinzer, Bruce, 'J. S. Mill and Irish Land: A Reassessment', *Historical Journal* 27 (1984), 111–27.

Kinzer, Bruce L., Robson, Ann P. and Robson, John M. (eds.), *A Moralist in and out of Parliament: John Stuart Mill at Westminster, 1865–1868*, University of Toronto Press, 1992.

Kirk, Neville, *The Growth of Working-Class Reformism in Mid-Victorian England*, London: Croom Helm, 1985.

'In Defence of Class: A Critique of Recent Revisionist Writing on the Nineteenth-Century Working Class', *International Review of Social History* 32 (1987), 2–47.

Knaplund, Paul, *James Stephen and the British Colonial System 1813–1847*, Madison: University of Wisconsin Press, 1953.

The British Empire 1815–1939, 2nd edn, New York: Howard Fertig, 1969.

Lake, Marilyn, 'Mission Impossible: How Men Gave Birth to the Australian Nation – Nationalism, Gender and Other Seminal Acts', *Gender & History* 4 (1992), 305–22.

Landes, Joan, *Women and the Public Sphere in the Age of the French Revolution*, Ithaca, N.Y.: Cornell University Press, 1988.

Lane, Michael (ed.), *Structuralism: A Reader*, London: Cape, 1970.

Lawrence, Jon and Taylor, Miles, 'Introduction: Electoral Sociology and the Historians', in Lawrence and Taylor (eds.), *Party, State and Society: Electoral Behaviour in Britain Since 1820*, Aldershot: Scolar Press, 1997, pp. 1–26.

Leneman, Leah, *A Guid Cause: The Women's Suffrage Movement in Scotland*, Aberdeen University Press, 1991.

Leventhal, F. M., *Respectable Radical: George Howell and Victorian Working-Class Politics*, London: Weidenfeld and Nicolson, 1971.

Levine, Philippa, *Feminist Lives in Victorian England: Private Roles and Public Commitment*, Oxford: Basil Blackwell, 1990.

Lewis, Gail, 'Citizenship', in Gordon Hughes (ed.), *Imagining Welfare Futures*, London: Routledge in association with the Open University, 1998, pp. 103–50.

Lewis, Jane, *Before the Vote Was Won: Arguments for and Against Women's Suffrage 1864–1896*, London and New York: Routledge and Kegan Paul, 1987.

'Separate Spheres: Threat or Promise?', *Journal of British Studies* 30 (1991), 105–15.

Women and Social Action in Victorian and Edwardian England, Aldershot: Edward Elgar, 1991.

Linebaugh, Peter, *The London Hanged: Crime and Civil Society in the Eighteenth Century*, Harmondsworth: Penguin, 1991.

'Links Across Difference: Gender, Ethnicity and Nationalism', special issue, *Women's Studies International Forum* 18 (1995).

Lorimer, Douglas, *Colour, Class and the Victorians: English Attitudes to the Negro in the Mid-Nineteenth Century*, Leicester University Press, 1978.

Luddy, Maria, 'Isabella M. S. Tod', in Cullen and Luddy, *Women, Power and Consciousness*, pp. 197–230.

McClelland, Keith, 'Time to Work, Time to Live: Some Aspects of Work and the Re-formation of Class in Britain, 1850–1880', in Patrick Joyce (ed.), *The Historical Meanings of Work*, Cambridge University Press, 1987, pp. 180–209.

'Masculinity and the "Representative Artisan" in Britain, 1850–1880', in Michael Roper and John Tosh (eds.), *Manful Assertions: Masculinities in Britain Since 1800*, London: Routledge, 1991, pp. 74–91.

'Rational and Respectable Men: Gender, the Working Class, and Citizenship in Britain, 1850–1867', in Frader and Rose, *Gender and Class in Modern Europe*, pp. 280–93.

McClelland, Keith and Reid, Alastair, 'Wood, Iron and Steel: Technology, Labour and Trade Union Organisation in the Shipbuilding Industry, 1840–1914', in Harrison and Zeitlin, *Divisions of Labour*, pp. 151–84.

McClintock, Anne, *Imperial Leather: Race, Gender and Sexuality in the Colonial Context*, London: Routledge, 1995.

McCrone, David, *Understanding Scotland: The Sociology of a Stateless Nation*, London and New York: Routledge, 1992.

McCrone, Kathleen, 'The National Association for the Promotion of Social Science and the Advancement of Victorian Women', *Atlantis* 8 (1982), 44–66.

MacKenzie, John, 'Occidentalism, Counterpoint and Counter-Polemic', *Journal of Historical Geography* 19 (1993), 339–44.

'Edward Said and the Historians', *Nineteenth-Century Contexts* 185 (1994), 9–25.

Orientalism: History, Theory and the Arts, Manchester University Press, 1995.

McKibbin, Ross, Matthew, Colin and Kay, John, 'The Franchise Factor in the Rise of the Labour Party', *English Historical Review* 91 (1976); repr. in McKibbin, *Ideologies of Class: Social Relations in Britain 1880–1950*, Oxford: Clarendon Press, 1990, pp. 66–100.

McLain, Frank Maulden, *Maurice, Man and Moralist*, London: SPCK, 1972.

MacRaild, D. M., 'William Murphy, the Orange Order and Communal Violence: The Irish in West Cumberland, 1871–1874', in Panayi, *Racial Violence*, pp. 44–64.

Maehl, W. H., 'The Northeastern Miners' Struggle for the Franchise, 1872–1874', *International Review of Social History* 20 (1975), 198–219.

Malmgreen, Gail, 'Anne Knight and the Radical Subculture', *Quaker History* 71 (1982), 100–13.

Mandler, Peter, *Aristocratic Government in the Age of Reform: Whigs and Liberals 1830–1852*, Oxford: Clarendon Press, 1990.

Manning, D., *The Mind of Jeremy Bentham*, London: Longmans, 1968.

Marks, Shula, 'History, the Nation and Empire: Sniping from the Periphery', *History Workshop Journal* 29 (1990), 111–19.

Marshall, P. J., *Imperial Britain*, Creighton Lecture, University of London, 1994.

Mason, John Hope, 'Creativity in Action', in Iain Hampsher-Monk (ed.), *Defending Politics: Bernard Crick and Pluralism*, London: British Academic Press, 1993, pp. 1–21.

Matthew, H. C. G., 'Disraeli, Gladstone and the Politics of Mid-Victorian Budgets', *Historical Journal* 22 (1979), 615–43.
Gladstone 1809–1874, Oxford: Clarendon Press, 1986.
Meehan, Joanna (ed.), *Feminists Read Habermas: Gendering the Subject of Discourse*, New York and London: Routledge, 1995.
Mendus, Susan, 'The Marriage of True Minds: The Ideal of Marriage in the Philosophy of John Stuart Mill', in Mendus and Jane Rendall (eds.), *Sexuality and Subordination: Interdisciplinary Studies of Gender in the Nineteenth Century*, London: Routledge, 1989, pp. 171–91.
Midgley, Clare, *Women Against Slavery: The British Campaigns, 1780–1870*, London and New York: Routledge, 1992.
'Anti-Slavery and Feminism in Nineteenth-Century Britain', *Gender & History* 5 (1993), 343–62.
'Anti-Slavery and the Roots of "Imperial Feminism"', in Midgley, *Gender and Imperialism*, pp. 161–79.
Midgley, Clare (ed.), *Gender and Imperialism*, Manchester University Press, 1998.
Mintz, Sidney W., *Caribbean Transformations*, Chicago: Aldine Publishing, 1974.
Monypenny, W. F. and Buckle, G. E., *The Life of Benjamin Disraeli, Earl of Beaconsfield*, 6 vols., London: John Murray, 1910–20.
Moore, D. C., *The Politics of Deference*, Brighton: Harvester Press, 1976.
Moore, Lindy, *Bajanellas and Seminellas: Aberdeen University and the Education of Women 1860–1920*, Aberdeen University Press, 1991.
Morris, R. J., *Class, Sect and Party: The Making of the British Middle Class, Leeds 1820–1850*, Manchester University Press, 1990.
Mort, Frank, *Dangerous Sexualities: Medico-Moral Politics in England Since 1830*, London: Routledge and Kegan Paul, 1987.
Mueller, Iris W., *John Stuart Mill and French Thought*, Urbana: University of Illinois Press, 1956.
Murphy, Cliona, *The Women's Suffrage Movement and Irish Society in the Early Twentieth Century*, New York: Harvester Wheatsheaf, 1989.
Nairn, Tom, *The Break-Up of Britain*, London: Verso, 1977.
'Nationalisms and National Identities', special issue, *Feminist Review* 44 (1993).
Newbould, Ian, *Whiggery and Reform, 1830–1841: The Politics of Government*, Basingstoke: Macmillan, 1990.
Norman, E. R., *Anti-Catholicism in Victorian England*, London: George Allen and Unwin, 1968.
Nossiter, T. J., *Influence, Opinion and Political Idioms in Reformed England: Case Studies from the North East 1832–1874*, Brighton: Harvester Press, 1975.
O'Brien, Patricia, 'Michel Foucault's History of Culture', in Lynn Hunt (ed.), *The New Cultural History*, Berkeley: University of California Press, 1989, pp. 25–46.
O'Day, Alan, 'The Political Organization of the Irish in Britain 1867–1890', in R. Swift and S. Gilley (eds.), *The Irish in Britain 1815–1939*, London: Pinter, 1989, pp. 98–105.
'Varieties of Anti-Irish Behaviour in Britain 1846–1922', in Panayi, *Racial Violence*, pp. 26–43.
O'Neill, Marie, 'The Dublin Women's Suffrage Association and Its Successors', *Dublin Historical Record* 38 (1985), 126–40.

O'Tuathaigh, M. A. G., 'The Irish in Nineteenth-Century Britain: Problems of Integration', *Transactions of the Royal Historical Society* 5th ser., 31 (1981), 149–74.

Offen, Karen, 'Defining Feminism: A Comparative Historical Approach', *Signs* 14 (1988), 119–57.

Oliver, Dawn and Heater, Derek, *The Foundations of Citizenship*, London: Harvester Wheatsheaf, 1994.

Olivier, Sidney S., *The Myth of Governor Eyre*, London: Leonard and Virginia Woolf, 1933.

Olney, R. J., *Lincolnshire Politics, 1832–1885*, Oxford University Press, 1973.

Omi, M. and Winant, H., *Racial Formation in the United States from the 1960s to the 1980s*, New York: Routledge, 1989.

Owens, Rosemary Cullen, *Smashing Times: A History of the Irish Suffrage Movement 1899–1922*, Dublin: Attic Press, 1984.

Palmer, Bryan D., *E. P. Thompson: Objections and Oppositions*, London: Verso, 1994.

Panayi, Panikos, 'Anti-Immigrant Violence in Nineteenth- and Twentieth-Century Britain', in Panayi, *Racial Violence*, pp. 1–26.

Panayi, Panikos (ed.), *Racial Violence in Britain, 1840–1950*, revised edn, Leicester University Press, 1996.

Pankhurst, R. K. P., *The Saint-Simonians, Mill, and Carlyle*, London: Sidgwick and Jackson, 1957.

Parker, Andrew, Russo, Mary, Sommer, Doris and Yaeger, Patricia (eds.), *Nationalisms and Sexualities*, London and New York: Routledge, 1992.

Parry, Jonathan, *The Rise and Fall of Liberal Government in Victorian Britain*, New Haven and London: Yale University Press, 1993.

Pateman, Carole, 'Feminist Critiques of the Public/Private Dichotomy', in Pateman, *Disorder of Women*, pp. 118–40 (orig. published in S. I. Benn and G. G. Gaus (eds.), *Public and Private in Social Life*, London: Croom Helm, 1983, pp. 281–306).

The Sexual Contract, Cambridge: Polity Press, 1988.

The Disorder of Women: Democratic Feminism and Political Theory, Stanford University Press, 1989.

Paul, Kathleen, *Whitewashing Britain: Race and Citizenship in the Postwar Era*, Ithaca, N.Y., and London: Cornell University Press, 1997.

Perkin, H. J., *The Origins of Modern English Society 1780–1880*, London: Routledge and Kegan Paul, 1969.

Peruga, Mónica Bolufer and Deusa, Isabel Morant, 'On Women's Reason, Education and Love', *Gender & History* 10 (1998), 183–216.

Pocock, J. G. A., 'British History: A Plea for a New Subject', *Journal of Modern History* 47 (1975), 601–21.

'The Limits and Divisions of British History: In Search of the Unknown Subject', *American Historical Review* 87 (1982), 311–36.

Pollard, Sidney and Robertson, Paul, *The British Shipbuilding Industry, 1870–1914*, Cambridge, Mass., and London: Harvard University Press, 1979.

Poovey, Mary, 'Curing the Social Body in 1832: James Phillips Kay and the Irish in Manchester', in Poovey, *Making a Social Body*, pp. 55–72.

'Domesticity and Class Formation: Chadwick's 1842 *Sanitary Report*', in Poovey, *Making a Social Body*, pp. 115–31.

'Making a Social Body: British Cultural Formation, 1830–1864', in Poovey, *Making a Social Body*, pp. 1–24.

Making A Social Body: British Cultural Formation, 1830–1864, University of Chicago Press, 1995.

'Thomas Chalmers, Edwin Chadwick, and the Sublime Revolution in Nineteenth-Century Government', in Poovey, *Making a Social Body*, pp. 98–114.

Porter, Bernard, *The Refugee Question in Mid-Victorian Politics*, Cambridge University Press, 1979.

Prest, John, *Politics in the Age of Cobden*, Basingstoke: Macmillan, 1977.

Prochaska, F. K., *Women and Philanthropy in Nineteenth-Century England*, Oxford: Clarendon Press, 1980.

Prothero, Iorwerth, 'William Benbow and the Concept of the "General Strike"', *Past & Present* 63 (1974), 132–71.

Radical Artisans in England and France, Cambridge University Press, 1997.

Pugh, Martin, 'The Limits of Liberalism: Liberals and Women's Suffrage 1867–1914', in Eugenio Biagini (ed.), *Citizenship and Community: Liberals, Radicals and Collective Identities in British History 1865–1931*, Cambridge University Press, 1996, pp. 45–65.

Pyle, Andrew (ed.), *Liberty: Contemporary Responses to John Stuart Mill*, Bristol: Thoemmes Press, 1994.

'The Subjection of Women': Contemporary Responses to John Stuart Mill, Bath: Thoemmes Press, 1995.

Quinlivan, Patrick and Rose, Paul, *The Fenians in England 1865–1872: A Sense of Insecurity*, London: John Calder, 1982.

Rabinow, Paul (ed.), *The Foucault Reader: An Introduction to Foucault's Thought*, Harmondsworth: Penguin, 1984.

Rediker, Marcus, *Between the Devil and the Deep Blue Sea*, Cambridge University Press, 1988.

Rendall, Jane, *The Origins of Modern Feminism: Women in Britain, France, and the United States 1780–1860*, Basingstoke: Macmillan, 1985.

'"A Moral Engine?": Feminism, Liberalism, and the *English Woman's Journal*', in Rendall, *Equal or Different*, pp. 112–38.

'Citizenship, Culture and Civilisation: The Languages of British Suffragists, 1866–1874', in Caroline Daley and Melanie Nolan (eds.), *Suffrage and Beyond: International Feminist Perspectives*, Auckland University Press, 1994, pp. 127–50.

'Who Was Lily Maxwell?: Women's Suffrage and Manchester Politics, 1866–1867', in Sandra Holton and June Purvis (eds.), *Votes for Women*, London: UCL Press, 1999, pp. 57–83.

'"The Real Father of the Whole Movement"?: John Stuart Mill, Liberal Politics, and the Movement for Women's Suffrage, 1865–1873', in Amanda Vickery (ed.), *Women, Power and Privilege*, Stanford University Press, forthcoming [2000].

Rendall, Jane (ed.), *Equal or Different: Women's Politics 1800–1914*, Oxford: Basil Blackwell, 1987.

Richardson, Sarah, 'The Role of Women in Electoral Politics in Yorkshire During the 1830s', *Northern History* 32 (1996), 133–51.

Ridley, Jasper, *Lord Palmerston*, London: Constable, 1970.

Rigby, S. H., *Marxism and History: A Critical Introduction*, Manchester University Press, 1987.

Riley, Denise, *'Am I That Name?': Feminism and the Category of Women in History*, Basingstoke: Macmillan, 1989.

Robbins, Keith, 'An Imperial and Multinational Polity: The Scene from the Centre, 1832–1922', in Grant and Stringer, *Uniting the Kingdom?*, pp. 244–54.

Great Britain: Identities, Institutions and the Idea of Britishness, Harlow: Longman, 1998.

Robson, Ann P., 'The Founding of the National Society for Women's Suffrage 1866–1867', *Canadian Journal of History* 8 (1973), 1–22.

'A Birds' Eye View of Gladstone', in Bruce L. Kinzer (ed.), *The Gladstonian Turn of Mind: Essays Presented to J. B. Conacher*, University of Toronto Press, 1985, pp. 63–96.

'No Laughing Matter: John Stuart Mill's Establishment of Women's Suffrage as a Parliamentary Question', *Utilitas* 2 (1990), 88–101.

'Mill's Second Prize in the Lottery of Life', in Michael Laine (ed.), *A Cultivated Mind: Essays on J. S. Mill Presented to John M. Robson*, University of Toronto Press, 1991, pp. 215–41.

Robson, Ann P. and Robson, John M. (eds.), *Sexual Equality: Writings by John Stuart Mill, Harriet Taylor Mill, and Helen Taylor*, University of Toronto Press, 1994.

Robson, J. M., *The Improvement of Mankind: The Social and Political Thought of John Stuart Mill*, University of Toronto Press, 1968.

'Mill in Parliament: The View from the Comic Papers', *Utilitas* 2 (1990), 120–43.

Roper, Lyndal, *Oedipus and the Devil: Witchcraft, Sexuality and Religion in Early Modern Europe*, London: Routledge, 1994.

Rose, Michael E., 'The Crisis of Poor Relief in England 1860–1890', in W. J. Mommsen in collaboration with Wolfgang Mock (eds.), *The Emergence of the Welfare State in Britain and Germany*, London: Croom Helm on behalf of the German Historical Institute, 1981, pp. 50–70.

'The Disappearing Pauper: Victorian Attitudes to the Relief of the Poor', in E. M. Sigsworth (ed.), *In Search of Victorian Values: Aspects of Nineteenth-Century Thought and Society*, Manchester University Press, 1988, pp. 56–72.

Rose, Paul, *The Manchester Martyrs: The Story of a Fenian Tragedy*, London: Lawrence and Wishart, 1970.

Rose, Sonya O., *Limited Livelihoods: Gender and Class in Nineteenth-Century England*, London: Routledge, 1992.

Rosen, Andrew, 'Emily Davies and the Women's Movement 1862–1867', *Journal of British Studies* 19 (1979), 101–21.

Royle, Edward, *Victorian Infidels: The Origins of the British Secularist Movement 1791–1866*, Manchester University Press, 1974.

Chartism, 3rd edn, London: Addison-Wesley Longman, 1996.

Rubinstein, David, *A Different World for Women: The Life of Millicent Garrett Fawcett*, Hemel Hempstead: Harvester-Wheatsheaf, 1991.

Ryan, Alan, *J. S. Mill*, London: Routledge, 1974.

Ryan, Mary, *Women in Public: Between Banners and Ballots 1825–1880*, Baltimore and London: Johns Hopkins University Press, 1990.

Said, Edward W., *Orientalism: Western Concepts of the Orient*, Harmondsworth: Penguin, 1985.

Culture and Imperialism, London: Chatto and Windus, 1993.

Salt, John, 'Local Manifestations of the Urquhartite Movement', *International Review of Social History* 13 (1968), 350–65.

'Isaac Ironside', in Joyce Bellamy and John Saville (eds.), *Dictionary of Labour Biography*, vol. II, Basingstoke: Macmillan, 1974, pp. 201–7.

Samuel, Raphael, 'The Workshop of the World: Steam Power and Hand Technology in Mid-Victorian Britain', *History Workshop Journal* 3 (1977), 6–72.

Island Stories: Unravelling Britain, London: Verso, 1998.

Samuel, Raphael (ed.), *Patriotism: The Making and Unmaking of British National Identity*, 3 vols., London: Routledge, 1989.

Savage, Mike and Miles, Andrew, *The Remaking of the British Working Class*, London: Routledge, 1994.

Saville, John, *Ernest Jones: Chartist*, London: Lawrence and Wishart, 1952.

'Trades Councils and the Labour Movement to 1900', *Bulletin of the Society for the Study of Labour History* 14 (1967), 29–34.

1848: The British State and the Chartist Movement, Cambridge University Press, 1987.

Schwarzkopf, Jutta, *Women in the Chartist Movement*, Basingstoke: Macmillan, 1991.

Scott, Joan Wallach, 'Gender: A Useful Category of Historical Analysis', in Scott, *Gender and the Politics of History*, pp. 28–50.

Gender and the Politics of History, New York: Columbia University Press, 1988.

'On Language, Gender and Working-Class History', in Scott, *Gender and the Politics of History*, pp. 53–67.

Semmel, Bernard, *The Governor Eyre Controversy*, London: MacGibbon and Kee, 1962.

Sewell, William H. jun., 'How Classes Are Made: Critical Reflections on E. P. Thompson's Theory of Working-Class Formation', in Kaye and McClelland, *E. P. Thompson*, pp. 50–77.

Seymour, Charles, *Electoral Reform in England and Wales*, New Haven: Yale Historical Publications, 1915.

Shanley, Mary Lyndon, *Feminism, Marriage and the Law in Victorian England, 1850–1895*, Princeton University Press, 1989.

Shannon, Richard, 'David Urquhart and the Foreign Affairs Committee', in Patricia Hollis (ed.), *Pressure from Without*, London: Edward Arnold, 1974, pp. 239–61.

Shipley, Stan, *Club Life and Socialism in Mid-Victorian London*, Oxford: History Workshop Pamphlets 5, 1972.

Sinha, Mrinalini, *Colonial Masculinity: The 'Manly Englishman' and the Effeminate Bengali in the Late Nineteenth Century*, Manchester University Press, 1995.

Sklar, Kathryn Kish, '"Women Who Speak for an Entire Nation": American and British Women at the World Anti-Slavery Convention, London, 1840', in

Jean Fagan Yellin and John C. Van Horne (eds.), *The Abolitionist Sisterhood: Women's Political Culture in Antebellum America*, Ithaca, N.Y.: Cornell University Press, 1994, pp. 301–34.

Smith, F. B., *The Making of the Second Reform Bill*, Cambridge University Press, 1966.

'The "Dependence of Licence upon Faith": Miss Gertrude Himmelfarb on the Second Reform Act', *Journal of British Studies* 7 (1967), 96–9.

Smith, Hilda L., 'Women as Sexton and Electors: King's Bench and Precedents for Women's Citizenship', in Hilda L. Smith (ed.), *Women Writers and the Early Modern British Political Tradition*, Cambridge University Press, 1998, pp. 324–42.

Smith, Paul, *Disraeli: A Brief Life*, Cambridge University Press, 1996.

Sollors, Werner, *Beyond Ethnicity: Consent and Descent in American Culture*, Oxford University Press, 1986.

Solomos, John and Back, Les, *Racism and Society*, Basingstoke: Macmillan, 1996.

Spain, Jonathan, 'Trade Unionists, Gladstonian Liberals and the Labour Law Reforms of 1875', in Biagini and Reid, *Currents of Radicalism*, pp. 109–33.

St John Packe, Michael, *The Life of John Stuart Mill*, Basingstoke: Macmillan, 1954.

Stafford, William, *John Stuart Mill*, Basingstoke: Macmillan, 1998.

Stansell, Christine, 'White Feminists and Black Realities: The Politics of Authenticity', in Toni Morrison (ed.), *Race-ing Justice, Engendering Power: Essays on Anita Hill, Clarence Thomas and the Construction of Social Reality*, New York: Pantheon, 1992, pp. 251–68.

Steele, E. D., 'J. S. Mill and the Irish Question: Reform and the Integrity of the Empire 1865–1870', *Historical Journal* 12 (1970); repr. in Alan O'Day (ed.), *Reactions to Irish Nationalism 1865–1914*, London: Hambledon Press, 1987, pp. 205–36.

Palmerston and Liberalism, Cambridge University Press, 1991.

Stepan, Nancy, *The Idea of Race in Science: Great Britain 1800–1960*, Basingstoke: Macmillan, 1982.

'The Hour of Eugenics': Race, Gender and Nation in Latin America, Ithaca, N.Y.: Cornell University Press, 1991.

Stocking, George, *Victorian Anthropology*, New York: Free Press, 1987.

Stoler, Ann Laura, *Race and the Education of Desire: Foucault's History of Sexuality and the Colonial Order of Things*, Durham, N.C.: Duke University Press, 1995.

Swift, Roger, '"Another Stafford Street Row": Law, Order and the Irish Presence in Mid-Victorian Wolverhampton', in Swift and Gilley, *The Irish in the Victorian City*, pp. 179–206.

Swift, Roger and Gilley, Sheridan (eds.), *The Irish in the Victorian City*, London: Croom Helm, 1985.

Taylor, A. D., '"The Best Way to Get What He Wanted": Ernest Jones and the Boundaries of Liberalism in the Manchester Election of 1868', *Parliamentary History* 16 (1997), 185–204.

Taylor, Barbara, *Eve and the New Jerusalem: Socialism and Feminism in the Nineteenth Century*, London: Virago, 1983.

'Religion, Radicalism, and Fantasy', *History Workshop Journal* 39 (1995), 102–12.

Taylor, Miles, 'The Old Radicalism and the New: David Urquhart and the Politics of Opposition, 1832–1867', in Biagini and Reid, *Currents of Radicalism*, pp. 23–43.

The Decline of British Radicalism 1847–1860, Oxford: Clarendon Press, 1995.

Temperley, Howard, *British Antislavery 1833–1870*, London: Longman, 1972.

White Dreams, Black Africa: The Antislavery Expedition to the River Niger 1841–1842, New Haven and London: Yale University Press, 1991.

Ten, C. L., *Mill on Liberty*, Oxford: Clarendon Press, 1980.

Thane, Pat, 'Women and the Poor Law in Victorian and Edwardian England', *History Workshop Journal* 6 (1978), 29–51.

'Thinking Through Ethnicities', special issue, *Feminist Review* 45 (1993).

Thomas, Joyce, 'Women and Capitalism: Oppression or Emancipation? A Review Article', *Comparative Studies in Society and History* 30 (1988), 534–49.

Thomas, William, *The Philosophic Radicals: Nine Studies in Theory and Practice 1817–1841*, Oxford: Clarendon Press, 1979.

Mill, Oxford University Press, 1985.

Thompson, Dennis, *John Stuart Mill and Representative Government*, Princeton University Press, 1976.

Thompson, Dorothy, 'Women in Nineteenth-Century Radical Politics: A Lost Dimension', in Ann Oakley and Juliet Mitchell (eds.), *The Rights and Wrongs of Women*, Harmondsworth: Penguin, 1976, pp. 112–38.

'Ireland and the Irish in English Radicalism Before 1850', in Epstein and Thompson, *The Chartist Experience*, pp. 120–51.

The Chartists: Popular Politics in the Industrial Revolution, London: Maurice Temple Smith, 1984.

'The Language of Class', *Bulletin of the Society for the Study of Labour History* 52 (1987), 54–6.

'Women, Work and Politics in Nineteenth-Century England: The Problem of Authority', in Rendall, *Equal or Different*, pp. 57–81.

Thompson, E. P., *The Making of the English Working Class* (1963), 3rd edn, London: Gollancz, 1980.

'The Making of a Ruling Class?', *Dissent*, Summer 1993, 377–82.

Tiller, Kate, 'Late Chartism: Halifax, 1847–1858', in Epstein and Thompson, *The Chartist Experience*, pp. 311–44.

Todd, Nigel, *The Militant Democracy: Joseph Cowen and Victorian Radicalism*, Whitley Bay: Bewick Press, 1991.

Tomaselli, Sylvana, 'The Enlightenment Debate on Women', *History Workshop Journal* 20 (1985), 101–25.

Trevelyan, Raleigh, 'Thomas Woolner: Pre-Raphaelite Sculptor. The Beginnings of Success', *Apollo* 107 (1978), 200–5.

Trotter, R. G., 'The Coming of Federation', in J. H. Rose, A. P. Newton and E. A. Benians (eds.), *The Cambridge History of the British Empire*, 9 vols., Cambridge University Press, 1929–59, vol. VI, *Canada* (1930), pp. 438–64.

Tulloch, Gail, *Mill and Sexual Equality*, Boulder: University of Colorado Press, 1989.

Tyrrell, Alex, '"Woman's Mission" and Pressure Group Politics in Britain, 1825–1860', *Bulletin of the John Rylands Library* 63 (1980), 194–230.

Valenze, Deborah, *The First Industrial Woman*, Oxford University Press, 1995.

Vernon, James, *Politics and the People: A Study in English Political Culture c. 1815–1867*, Cambridge University Press, 1993.

'Narrating the Constitution: The Discourse of "the Real" and the Fantasies of Nineteenth-Century Constitutional History', in Vernon, *Re-reading the Constitution*, pp. 204–29.

'Notes Towards an Introduction', in Vernon, *Re-reading the Constitution*, pp. 1–21.

Vernon, James (ed.), *Re-reading the Constitution: New Narratives in the Political History of England's Long Nineteenth Century*, Cambridge University Press, 1996.

Vickery, Amanda, 'Historiographical Review: Golden Age to Separate Spheres? A Review of the Categories and Chronology of English Women's History', *Historical Journal* 36 (1993), 383–414.

Vincent, John, *The Formation of the British Liberal Party 1857–1868* (1966), 2nd edn, Harmondsworth: Penguin, 1972.

Pollbooks: How Victorians Voted, Cambridge University Press, 1968.

von den Steinen, Karl, 'The Discovery of Women in Eighteenth-Century Political Life', in Barbara Kanner (ed.), *The Women of England from Anglo-Saxon Times to the Present*, London: Mansell, 1980, pp. 229–58.

Walkowitz, Judith R., *Prostitution and Victorian Society: Women, Class, and the State*, Cambridge University Press, 1980.

Wallace, Ryland, *Organise! Organise! Organise!: A Study of Reform Agitations in Wales, 1840–1886*, Cardiff: University of Wales Press, 1991.

Walvin, James, *Black and White: The Negro and English Society 1555–1945*, London: Allen Lane, 1973.

Ward, J. T., *Chartism*, London: Batsford, 1973.

Ware, Vron, *Beyond the Pale: White Women, Racism and History*, London: Verso, 1992.

Weeks, Jeffrey, 'Foucault for Historians', *History Workshop Journal* 14 (1982), 106–19.

Weintraub, Jeff, 'The Theory and Politics of the Public/Private Distinction', in Weintraub and Krishan Kumar (eds.), *Public and Private in Theory and Practice*, University of Chicago Press, 1997, pp. 1–42.

Williams, Bill, *The Making of Manchester Jewry, 1740–1875* (1976), repr. Manchester University Press, 1985.

Williams, Catherine S., 'The Public Law and Women's Rights: The Nineteenth-Century Experience', *Cambrian Law Review* 23 (1992), 80–103.

Williams, Gwyn, '18 Brumaire: Karl Marx and Defeat', in Betty Matthews (ed.), *Marx: 100 Years on*, London: Lawrence and Wishart, 1983, pp. 11–37.

Williams, Raymond, *Marxism and Literature*, Oxford University Press, 1977.

Winstanley, M. J., *The Shopkeeper's World 1830–1914*, Manchester University Press, 1983.

Wolffe, John, *God and Greater Britain: Religion and National Life in Britain and Ireland 1843–1945*, London: Routledge, 1994.

Yeo, Eileen Janes, *The Contest for Social Science: Relations and Representations of Gender and Class*, London: Rivers Oram, 1996.

Young, Robert J. C., *Colonial Desire: Hybridity in Theory, Culture and Race*, London: Routledge, 1995.

Yuval-Davis, Nira, *Gender and Nation*, London: Sage, 1997.

Yuval-Davis, Nira and Anthias, Floya (eds.), *Woman–Nation–State*, Basingstoke: Macmillan, 1989.

Zeitlin, Jonathan, 'Engineers and Compositors: A Comparison', in Harrison and Zeitlin, *Divisions of Labour*, pp. 185–250.

Zonana, Joyce, 'The Sultan and the Slave: Feminist Orientalism and the Structure of *Jane Eyre*', *Signs* 18 (1993), 592–617.

UNPUBLISHED PAPERS AND THESES

Bell, A. D., 'The Reform League from Its Origins to the Reform Act of 1867', DPhil. thesis, University of Oxford (1961).

Dingsdale, Ann, '"Generous and Lofty Sympathies": The Kensington Society, the 1866 Women's Suffrage Petition, and the Development of Mid-Victorian Feminism', DPhil. thesis, University of Greenwich (1995).

Dunsmore, Michael, 'The Northern Department of the Reform League: The Working Classes, the Reform League and the Reform Movement in Lancashire and Yorkshire', MA thesis, University of Sheffield (1962).

Euler, Cat, 'Moving Between Worlds: Gender, Politics, Class and Sexuality in the Diaries of Anne Lister of Shibden Hall, 1830–1840', DPhil. thesis, University of York (1995).

Kaplan, Cora, 'White Skin: Ethnology, Nationalism and Feminism in the 1840s', unpublished paper, 1993.

Taylor, Antony David, 'Ernest Jones: His Later Career and the Structure of Manchester Politics 1861–1869', MA thesis, University of Birmingham (1984).

'Modes of Political Expression and Working-Class Radicalism 1848–1874: The London and Manchester Examples', 2 vols., Ph.D thesis, University of Manchester (1992).

Index